Oklahoma author Teddy Bader, M.D. used this book in researching his book: *Wesleyans Help Womens Suffrage*. Amazon 2018

PIETIST AND WESLEYAN STUDIES
Editors: David Bundy and J. Steven O'Malley

This monograph series will publish volumes in two areas of scholarly research: Pietism and Methodism (broadly understood). The focus will be Pietism, its history and development, and the influence of this socio-religious tradition in modern culture, especially within the Wesleyan religious traditions.

Consideration will be given to scholarly works on classical and neo-Pietism, on English and American Methodism, as well as on the social and ecclesiastical institutions shaped by Pietism (e.g., Evangelicals, United Brethren, and the Pietist traditions among the Lutherans, Reformed, and Anabaptists). Works focusing on leaders within the Pietist and Wesleyan traditions will also be included in the series, as well as occasional translations and/or editions of Pietist texts. It is anticipated that the monographs will emphasize theological developments, but with close attention to the interaction of Pietism with other cultural forces and to the sociocultural identity of the Pietist and Wesleyan movements.

1. Gregory S. Clapper, *John Wesley on Religious Affections.* 1989.
2. Peter Erb, *Gottfried Arnold.* 1989.
3. Henry H. Knight III, *The Presence of God in the Christian Life: John Wesley and the Means of Grace.* 1992.
4. Frank D. Macchia, *Spirituality and Social Liberation: The Message of the Blumhardts in the Light of Wuerttemberg Pietism.* 1993.
5. Richard B. Steele, *"Gracious Affection" and "True Virtue" according to Jonathan Edwards and John Wesley.* 1994.
6. Stephen L. Longenecker, *Piety and Tolerance: Pennsylvania German Religion, 1700–1850.* 1994.
7. J. Steven O'Malley, *Early German-American Evangelicalism: Pietist Sources on Discipleship and Sanctification.* 1995.
8. R. David Rightmire, *Salvationist Samurai: Gunpei Yamamuro and the Rise of the Salvation Army in Japan.* 1997.
9. Simon Ross Valentine, *John Bennet and the Origins of Methodism and the Evangelical Revival in England.* 1997.
10. Tore Meistad, *Martin Luther and John Wesley on the Sermon on the Mount.* 1999.
11. Robert C. Monk, *John Wesley: His Puritan Heritage.* 1999.

12. Richard B. Steele, *"Heart Religion" in the Methodist Tradition and Related Movements.* 2001.
13. Diane Leclerc, *Singleness of Heart.* 2001.
14. Charles Yrigoyen, Jr., *The Global Impact of the Wesleyan Traditions and Their Related Movements.* 2002.

The Global Impact of the Wesleyan Traditions and Their Related Movements

Edited by Charles Yrigoyen, Jr.

Pietist and Wesleyan Studies, No. 14

The Scarecrow Press, Inc.
Lanham, Maryland, and London
2002

SCARECROW PRESS, INC.

Published in the United States of America
by Scarecrow Press, Inc.
A Member of the Rowman & Littlefield Publishing Group
4720 Boston Way, Lanham, Maryland 20706
www.scarecrowpress.com

4 Pleydell Gardens, Folkestone
Kent CT20 2DN, England

Copyright © 2002 by Charles Yrigoyen, Jr.

All rights reserved. No part of this publication may be reproduced, stored in a retrieval system, or transmitted in any form or by any means, electronic, mechanical, photocopying, recording, or otherwise, without the prior permission of the publisher.

British Library Cataloguing in Publication Information Available

Library of Congress Cataloging-in-Publication Data

The global impact of the Wesleyan traditions and their related movements / edited by Charles Yrigoyen, Jr.
    p. cm. -- (Pietist and Wesleyan studies ; no. 14)
    Papers presented at a meeting.
    Includes bibliographical references and index.
    ISBN 0-8108-4326-9 (alk. paper)
    1. Evangelistic work—Congresses. 2. Wesley, John, 1703–1791—Congresses. 3. Methodist Church—Doctrines—Congresses. I. Yrigoyen, Charles, 1937– . II. Series.
BV3755 .G56 2002
266'.7—dc21   2002020079

♾™ The paper used in this publication meets the minimum requirements of American National Standard for Information Sciences—Permanence of Paper for Printed Library Materials, ANSI/NISO Z39.48-1992.
Manufactured in the United States of America.

Contents

Editor's Foreward	ix
Preface	xi
Acknowledgments	xiii
Abbreviations	xv
Introduction	xvii

Part I   1

1   *The Global Impact of the Wesleyan Traditions and Their Related Movements*
Donald W. Dayton   3

2   *Pauline Missions: The Wesleyan Holiness Vision*
David Bundy   13

3   *Wesleyan Missiological Theories: The Case of Richard Watson*
Andrew Walls   27

4   *Earthly Food at the Heavenly Banquet: Revitalizing the Historical Wesleyan Love Feast For Evangelism and Discipleship In Global Missions*
Robert Danielson   49

Part II 67

5 *Catholic and Protestant, But Missionary: John Wesley's Explicit and Implicit Ecclesiology and the Methodist Mission in Latin America*
Jose Míguez Bonino 69

6 *The Impact of Wesleyanism on Africa: Toward an Understanding of Divine Grace in a Changing Continent*
David K. Yemba 81

7 *The Doctrine of Holiness and Missions: A Pietistic Foundation of African Evangelical Christianity*
Robert Kipkemoi Lang'at 91

8 *Are They Not Methodist Too? Case Studies of Some African Independent Churches that Call Themselves Methodist*
Joan A. Millard 105

9 *The Evangelical United Brethren Mission in Asia: Two Contrasting Ecumenical Scenarios*
J. Steven O'Malley 119

10 *"Having Received, I Ought to Give": The Impact of Hwa Nan College on Chinese Women*
Laura A. Bartels 131

11 *Alternate Wesleyan Influence: The Impact of 18th Century British Methodism and 19th Century American Revivalism on a Japanese Indigenous Holiness Church*
Kiyoshi Nathanael Kunishige 143

12 *The Impact of John Wesley's Ministry and Theology on the Korean Church: A Model for Church Renewal*
Chongnahm (John) Cho 157

13 *Toward a New Paradigm of Holiness Theology of Mission in Korea: Cosmic Holiness in Divine Ecology*
Hyun Seok (Joseph) Kim 171

Contents

14	*"The Korean Pentecost": A Study of the Great Revival of 1903-1910 in Relationship to Contemporary Worldwide Holiness Revival Movements* Myung Soo Park	185
15	*An Interpretation of the Korean Church in the Wesleyan Perspective* Hong-ki Kim	201
16	*"A Spreading Fire": The Influence of Thomas Collins on the Formation of the Methodist Church of Australia* Daryl H. Lightfoot	217
17	*The Early Impact of Wesleyanism on Continental Europe: The Case of the Germans* Michel Weyer	231
18	*John Fletcher: Paradigm for the Global Impact of Wesleyanism* Timothy M. Salo	245
19	*Wilhelm Nast (1807-1899): Founder of German-speaking Methodism in America and Architect of the Methodist Episcopal Church Mission in Europe* William Harrison Daniel	259

Part III   273

20	*The Impact of Obras de Wesley in the Hispanic World* L. Elbert Wethington	275
21	*The Methodist Archives and Research Centre at the John Rylands University Library of Manchester* Gareth Lloyd	285

Index   293
About the Contributors   299

Editor's Foreward

This collection of essays is based upon the papers presented at the conference on the global impact of Methodism, held at Asbury Theological Seminary from August 14-20, 2000. The conference was sponsored by the World Methodist Historical Society. In a day of increasing interest in the history of the globalization of Christianity, it is appropriate that the concerns of Methodist historiography have been enlarged to include a fresh look at its global outreach. Part I presents essays on theological and theoretical foundations for missions within the Wesleyan context. The contributions to Part II highlight the geographical and gender diversity found within the world Wesleyan mission. They include discussions of autonomous Methodist bodies and independent churches influenced by the Wesleyan spirit, as well as those Pietist traditions that would become constituent parts of United Methodism after 1968—hence the title of the volume, "The Global Impact of the Wesleyan Traditions and Their Related Movements." Part III concludes the volume with a discussion of historiographical sources that is intended to facilitate further research. In a word, the essays contained in this volume reflect the cultural diversity of global Wesleyanism and its larger constituency. In addition, the conversation with Wesleyan and Pietist themes in relation to globalization aptly fits the larger intention of this Series.

Gratitude is extended to Dr. Charles Yrigoyen, General Secretary of the Commission on Archives and History of the United Methodist Church, for his careful work in editing the papers for this volume. His grateful acknowledgment of the work of the principal organizers of the conference at Asbury, found in his introduction to the essays, is shared by the editors of the Pietist and Wesleyan Studies Series.

In a day in which it is widely acknowledged that the centers of vitality and growth in world Methodism lie beyond its North American shores, we are pleased to make available this contribution toward an understanding of that phenomenon. It is hoped that its appearance will be a source of encouragement to further scholarship in the diversity of the people called Methodists and their kin, and to the greater purposes of their renewal for effective witness for Christ in the twenty first century.

J. Steven O'Malley
Co-editor
The Pietist and Wesleyan Studies Series

Preface

Scholars have long acknowledged that the growth and spread of Methodism in England and North America was both rapid and culturally significant. Less frequently studied, or for that matter acknowledged, has been the global spread and cultural impact of Methodism and indigenous Methodist-related bodies in Africa, Asia, South America, Australia, Micronesia, and continental Europe. The World Methodist Historical Society and the Wesleyan Holiness Studies Center of Asbury Theological Seminary, in an attempt to begin to address this inadequately studied phenomenon, sponsored a conference on the campus of Asbury Theological Seminary in August 2000.

International Wesleyan scholar Donald W. Dayton planned the conference principally with the support of Charles Yrigoyen, Jr. and David Bundy. Among the special highlights of the conference were papers by Dayton on the global scope of Wesleyanism, David Bundy and Andrew Walls on Wesleyan Missiological thought, Daryl Lightfoot on Australia Wesleyanism, and John C. Cho and Myung Soo Park on Korean Wesleyanism. Significant papers by David R. Yemba and Robert K. Lang'at explored African Wesleyanism, while Michel Weyer and Steven O'Malley explored German and German-American expressions of global Wesleyanism. The Methodist experience in Latin America was the subject of a significant paper by Jose Míquez Bonino. Other papers focused North America, Samoan, and European expressions of Wesleyanism. Fittingly for a meeting of Wesleyans, worship played a significant role in the conference including the preaching of Asbury Theological Seminary president Maxie Dunnam, Salvation Army officer Kay Rader, United Methodist minister Joy Moore, and United Methodist scholar David Lowes Watson.

One of the highlights of the conference was the attention afforded the collection of historically significant publications and archival material. In a memorable panel discussion of librarians, collectors, and bibliographers from England, Norway, Korea, and the United States explored significant preservation and documentation issues in global Wesleyanism. Among those present were Gareth Lloyd of the Rylands Library, University of Manchester; Myung Soo Park, Korea Evangelical Holiness Church Historical Research Center; Patrick Graham, Emory University; Page Thomas, Southern Methodist University; David Bundy, Christian Theological Seminary; Roger Lloyd, Duke University; and L. Dale Patterson, United Methodist General Commission on Archives and History. In addition to papers from internationally recognized scholars, the conference included a number of papers presented by graduate students on important, but often neglected, dimensions of global Wesleyanism.

D. William Faupel, Director
Wesleyan Holiness Studies Center

William C. Kostlevy, Associate Director
Wesleyan Holiness Studies Center

Acknowledgments

The officers of the World Methodist Historical Society who were gathered for the society's quinquennial meeting in Rio de Janeiro, Brazil, in August 1996 received an invitation from Asbury Theological Seminary in Wilmore, Kentucky, to hold a world conference on the global impact of Wesleyanism at a mutually agreed upon future date. This invitation was gratefully accepted and plans were begun which resulted in the conference being held at Asbury, August 14-20, 2000. Scholars from various nations were invited to present research papers related to the title of this volume, *The Global Impact of the Wesleyan Traditions and Their Related Movements*. All of the papers published here were read at the conference. A few other papers were also presented at the conference, but those authors chose not to submit them for publication.

Appreciation must be expressed to a number of persons for both the conference and this book. Dr. Maxie Dunnam, President of the Asbury Theological Seminary, generously offered not only the use of the Seminary's outstanding facilities, but also made available financial support for the meeting. Dr. D. William Faupel, Director of the Wesleyan Holiness Center at Asbury, and Dr. William Kostlevy, Associate Director of the Wesleyan Holiness Center, handled most of the details of the conference and enthusiastically encouraged the publication of the papers. Additonal sponsorship for the conference was provided by the Wesley and Methodist Studies Centre at Oxford Brookes University, Oxford, England, Dr. Tim Macquiban, Director. Dr. J. Steven O'Malley and Dr. David Bundy, editors of the Pietist and Wesleyan Studies Series were exceptionally helpful in making editorial suggestions. We are grateful for their including this volume in the series.

There are insufficient words to express appreciation to Michelle K. Merkel, Administrative Assistant, General Commission on Archives and History, The United Methodist Church. Without her expert technical skills and attention to detail this book may never have been published. Any remaining problems, of course, are the responsibility of the editor.

Charles Yrigoyen, Jr.
Madison, New Jersey
October 2001

Abbreviations

Works

The Works of John Wesley, begun as "The Oxford Edition of the Works of John Wesley" (Oxford: Clarendon Press, 1975-1983); continued as "The Bicentennial Edition of the Works of John Wesley" (Nashville, Tenn.: Abingdon Press, 1984-).

Works (Jackson)

The Works of John Wesley, ed. Thomas Jackson, 3rd edition, 14 vols. (London: Wesleyan Methodist Book Room; reprinted Grand Rapids, Mich.: Baker, 1979).

Introduction

In his journal entry for 11 June 1739 John Wesley (1703-1791) quoted from a letter he had written earlier to a friend, "I look upon *all the world as my parish*; thus far I mean, that in whatever part of it I am, I judge it meet, right, and my bounden duty, to declare unto all that are willing to hear the glad tidings of salvation. This is the work which I know God has called me to. And sure I am, that his blessing attends it."[1] Wesley's followers have been fond of quoting this passage to justify their commitment to mission work around the world even though their founder, who recognized the importance of missionary work, was somewhat reluctant to encourage his Methodist followers to engage far-flung missionary endeavors.

Wesley was raised in a family which highly regarded missionary work. His grandfather, John Wesley (or Westley), planned to go to the Dutch East Indies as a missionary, but family circumstances did not permit it. Samuel Wesley (1666-1735), John's father, offered to enter missionary service, but his desire, too, was thwarted. John's mother, Susanna, possessed an intense interest in missions and taught her children weekly about the importance of mission work for the spread of the faith. In the Epworth rectory Samuel and Susanna planted positive ideas in John Wesley and his siblings about the importance of spreading the Gospel to other nations and cultures.

It is not surprising that Wesley himself became a missionary when, as a young priest of the Church of England, he ventured to the colony of Georgia in America in 1736. His ministry there among the settlers and Native Americans, however, did not bear the fruit he expected. Furthermore, the collapse of his romance with Sophia Christiana Hopkey, a young parishioner, led to his return to England in 1738. It appeared that his missionary effort was a complete failure.

Upon his return to London, Wesley maintained close friendships among the Moravians which had begun in America and under their tutelage he had a transforming religious experience on 24 May 1738 in a meeting on Aldersgate Street. The following year his friend George Whitefield (1714-1770) persuaded Wesley to take the radical step of proclaiming the Gospel message in the outdoors. In the months and years that followed, his preaching in churches, fields, and wherever else hearers could be gathered, was received eagerly by many who were ready to respond to God's call. Sensing the necessity to provide for the nurture of these changed lives, Wesley organized them into Methodist societies, which later were composed of smaller groups called classes.

As Wesley preached across England, Ireland, Wales, and Scotland his Methodist societies grew. In spite of opposition from ecclesiastical leaders who disliked his evangelical message and strategies, and others who despised his plain speaking about sin and his call for repentance, Methodism became a lively force in British and Irish life. By the time of his death, there were more than 72,000 members in Methodist societies in his British Methodist Conference. His preachers, mostly laypeople, were organized in a "connexion with Mr. Wesley" and met annually "in conference" to discuss doctrine, devise evangelical plans, and assign preachers to the various Methodist meeting places. They were not a church. Methodists were Anglicans who attended their parish churches for worship and to receive the sacraments, but who also attended the weekly gatherings of their societies and classes. They lived by "General Rules" which guided their daily living and which exhorted them to avoid evil of every kind and to do good to all they met.

By 1760 some of Wesley's followers had migrated to America. In 1766 Methodists began to organize in the New World. Among the early leaders were Robert Strawbridge (c.1732-1781) in Maryland, and Philip Embury (1728-c.1773) and Barbara Heck (1734-1804) in New York. As the Methodist movement grew in America, Wesley dispatched missionary lay preachers in 1769, 1771, and 1773 to assist with its organization and nurture. One of these was Francis Asbury (1745-1816), the premier leader of early American Methodism. By 1791, the year of Wesley's death, the American Methodists numbered more than 64,000 members.

Wesley allowed his American followers to form the first Methodist "church" in the world in December 1784 when their preachers met in Baltimore, Maryland. When his attempts failed to have his preachers for America ordained by an Anglican bishop, Wesley ordained two of them himself, Richard Whatcoat (1736-1806) and Thomas Vasey (c.1746-

1826) and dispatched them to America with Thomas Coke (1747-1814) whom Wesley appointed Superintendent of the American work. Their orders were to form a Methodist church, ordain preachers in America for the new body, introduce a book of worship (supplied by Wesley), begin the administration of the sacraments, and make Francis Asbury co-Superintendent with Coke. After Wesley's death British Methodists also organized into a church.

Both American and British Methodism became convinced that their unique understanding and practice of the Christian faith must be shared with people in other lands and cultures. In the first half of the nineteenth century, inspired by the leadership of many women and men who ventured off to other lands with the Gospel message, the Methodist churches formed effective missionary societies to spearhead their efforts. This history has been well studied and documented in a number of places. The essays in this volume provide further evidence.

It is clear from the essays that follow that there is not a single Wesleyan tradition in the world today, but a number of Wesleyan traditions which trace their origins to the movement begun by John Wesley and his brother Charles (1707-1788) in the eighteenth century. As Wesleyanism has developed in different eras, nations, and cultures, variations of it have appeared. Furthermore, there are some movements and churches which originated in and developed from other traditions in addition to that which is identified as "Methodist." For example, the Church of the United Brethren in Christ, founded by Philip William Otterbein (1726-1813) and Martin Boehm (1725-1812), was influenced by Reformed and Anabaptist theology as well as Wesleyanism. Also, the Evangelical Association, founded by Jacob Albright (1759-1808), reflects aspects of Lutheran and radical Pietist influence, alongside Methodism. Recognizing these facts, we title this volume, *The Global Impact of the Wesleyan Traditions and Their Related Movements*.

This volume is divided into three sections. Part I includes four essays which deal with basic missiological and methodological issues. Part II contains fifteen essays which illuminate the impact of the Wesleyan traditions and their related movements on specific areas of the globe: Latin America, Africa, Asia, Australia, and Europe. Part III describes resources for researching and extending the global impact of the traditions, namely, *Las Obras de Wesley*, the Spanish edition of Wesley's published works, and the valuable collection of Wesleyana and Methodistica at the John Rylands University Library of Manchester, England.

At the outset of Part I, Donald Dayton (chapter 1) writes about the important global influence of Wesleyan and Methodist ideas and practices. He reminds us of the variety and complexity of the forms and ecclesiastical institutions which trace their origins to the Wesleyan movement of the eighteenth century. These include not only the traditional Methodist "churches," but movements such as the Oneida community of John Humphrey Noyes and Charles G. Finney's "Oberlin perfectionism." There are also diverse manifestations of the Holiness Movement, Pentecostalism, and a number of indigenous churches which have Wesleyan/Methodist roots. Dayton urges us to consider the global nature of Wesleyanism and the complexity of the Wesleyan traditions in today's world.

David Bundy's essay (chapter 2) speaks of a "Pauline mission" philosophy. He illustrates this approach to the spread of Wesleyanism by describing the ministry of the American missionary William Taylor (1821-1902) whose work was entrepreneurial, transcended national, racial, and gender barriers, and respected Christian converts as equal before God and each other. Taylor's plan aimed at mission work which would become self-supporting, self-governing, and self-propagating. This mission strategy influenced Methodist, Holiness, and Pentecostal mission work.

Andrew Walls (chapter 3) identifies British Methodist Richard Watson (1781-1833) as a key figure in the development of early Methodist, and even broader Protestant, mission philosophy. Watson's ideas about missions took place during the transitional period between Wesley and the earlier years of the Wesleyan Methodist Missionary Society which was formed in 1818. His views were especially important in developing missionary engagement with Africa and were characterized by his hatred of African slavery. Watson advocated the Methodist proclamation of salvation through Christ which leads to practical holiness.

Robert Danielson (chapter 4) writes about the issue of inculturation in missiology with special attention to the role of the sacraments. He points to the highly symbolic nature of food to the world's peoples and raises the question of the relevance of the elements of bread and wine for Africans and Asians in the celebration of the eucharist. While Danielson finds that bread and the fruit of the vine are critical as eucharistic elements for the universal church, he believes that the traditional Methodist love feast may effectively use indigenous food elements. He suggests that employing both the eucharist (with bread and fruit of the vine) and the love feast (employing indigenous food) in this way may provide a means for maintaining the church's universality and providing a viable means of bridging cultural gaps.

Part II opens with an essay (chapter 5) by Jose Miguez Bonino, the Latin American Methodist theologian, which begins with a brief exploration of John Wesley's ecclesiology. Bonino then turns to a consideration of the challenge faced by Methodists and other Protestants in Latin America in their relationships with the Roman Catholic Church and their possible cooperation with each other. He believes that Wesley's approach to evangelization, organization, community, discipline, and social concern may be creatively employed in the circumstances of Latin America as well as other parts of the world.

David K. Yemba (chapter 6) reminds us of the diversity of African life and speaks about external and internal challenges faced by the African peoples. In this context the Wesleyan/Methodist community in Africa has grown rapidly, especially in the last fifty years. The Wesleyan tradition has significantly contributed to the ecumenical movement, not only in Africa, but in the world. The connectional polity of some of the Wesleyan churches has inspired the process of church union.

The focus of Robert Kipkemoi Lang'at (chapter 7) is the Holiness Movement in Africa. He asserts that the Wesleyan doctrine of holiness was critical in the origins of evangelical Christianity in Africa in the nineteenth and twentieth centuries. Wesleyan holiness also influenced mission work which would ordinarily be considered outside the normal Wesleyan fold. He concludes that much more research needs to be done to fully appreciate the impact of holiness teaching on the African peoples.

Joan A. Millard (chapter 8) examines a few African churches which had their origins in Methodism. Those which separated from Methodism did not usually do so for doctrinal reasons. Schisms were caused by authority, governance, and financial issues. Most of the independent churches which have historic Methodist roots would like to participate in a fellowship with other "Methodists," but do not want to surrender their independence. Millard suggests that such an organization might be profitably formed.

Consideration of the Asian context begins with the essay by J. Steven O'Malley (chapter 9). He shows that the Evangelical United Brethren Church (EUB), which united with The Methodist Church in 1968 to form The United Methodist Church, had important mission work in both China and Japan. Predecessor EUB bodies, the Church of the United Brethren in Christ and the Evangelical Church, as well as EUB itself, developed strategies which included the cultivation of indigenous leadership and ecumenical relationships. This plan has made a major contribution to the mission heritage of The United Methodist Church.

Hwa Nan College, a project of the Woman's Foreign Missionary Society of the Methodist Episcopal Church is the subject of the essay by Laura A. Bartels (chapter 10). She describes the origins and development of this Chinese women's school and its objective to evangelize and liberate women. Hwa Nan sought to give women knowledge and skills to improve traditional home life as well as fostering women's economic independence.

The Immanuel General Mission, a Japanese indigenous holiness church, is the focus of Kiyoshi Nathanael Kunishige's essay (chapter 11). Kunishige shows how this denomination, drawing upon Wesleyan and Holiness teaching, has paid significant attention to the theology of John Wesley, especially Christian perfection, though there is still a preference for understanding Wesley in a Pentecostal fashion. The author believes that an emphasis on sanctification will advance Japanese understanding of, and sentiment for, Christianity in their nation.

Chongnahm (John) Cho (chapter 12) turns our attention to Korea. He is convinced that John Wesley's approach to evangelism and social reform has much to teach the Korean Wesleyan/Methodist community. Cho expresses two major concerns. First, the Korean church has lost its evangelical zeal. Second, it needs to reconsider the Wesleyan emphasis on Christian nurture and social action, both essentials in Wesley's ministry.

Hyun Seok (Joseph) Kim (chapter 13) explores the common features of Christian holiness and ecology. He recognizes that the Christian must be concerned not only with a relationship with God and neighbor, but also with nature since God has created the natural world and has placed the human community in the natural world. Kim finds that John Wesley's theology may be helpful in formulating a "cosmic holiness," especially when we consider Wesley's vision of a "new creation."

The Great Revival of 1907 in Korea is the subject of Myung Soo Park (chapter 14). It was the result of other evangelical holiness revivals of the period. Both Wesleyan holiness and Keswick movements, in England and the United States, were influential in its origin and development. Presbyterians and Methodists were important personalities in its leadership. The Great Revival had an immediate and lasting impact on the history of Christianity in Korea.

Another view of Korean church history is offered by Hong-ki Kim (chapter 15). He is concerned to identify the heart of John Wesley's theology as justification and sanctification, with special attention to the latter. Kim divides Korean Wesleyan/Methodist church history into five periods. In his judgment the healthiest eras are those which combine individual and social salvation, personal and social holiness. His essay closes with five concrete suggestions which would strengthen the theology, ministry, and mission of the Korean church.

How can the ministry of a person in one nation, who never left his homeland, influence for generations the lives of many others in another nation for generations? That is the question Daryl H. Lightfoot (chapter 16) seeks to answer. Thomas Collins, who never set foot on Australian soil, deeply touched the lives of many of his parishioners who migrated to New South Wales. Collins, a Methodist preacher who utilized "conversational evangelism," affected the course of Methodism to an extent that remains today in the Uniting Church in Australia.

Michel Weyer (chapter 17) offers an analysis of the early German assessments of Wesley and his Methodist movement. Weyer cites a number of German periodical and book-length judgments on the nature and purpose of Methodism. Some writers were quite severe in their judgments, e.g., G. F. A. Wendeborn and A. H. Niemeyer. Others were sympathetic, such as J. G. Burckhardt's monograph, *Complete History of Methodism in England* (1795). Weyer observes that the impact of Wesleyanism among Germans has been limited, although some of its accents and methods have been adopted by Europe's established churches.

John William Fletcher, one of the outstanding leaders of the early Methodist movement in England, is the subject of the essay by Timothy M. Salo (chapter 18). Fletcher was especially distinguished for his theological writings, saintly life, and effective ministry. His two trips to Switzerland qualify him to be recognized as the first Methodist missionary outside the English-speaking world, the first such missionary to Europe, and, therefore, the first to the "cradle of the Swiss Reformers." Salo contends that Fletcher offers us a paradigm for the global impact of Wesleyanism.

W. Harrison Daniel (chapter 19) writes about Wilhelm Nast, the founder of German-speaking Methodism in North America and the architect of Methodist mission work in Germany. Nast translated into German important writings of John Wesley as well as other significant Methodist documents, edited the Methodist periodical *Der Christliche Apologete*, and was the key figure in German Methodist mission work in the nineteenth century. Much of the Methodist work on the Continent subsequently bore the mark of Nast's German mission work.

Part III considers resources for the theme of this volume. *Las Obras de Wesley* (1996-1998) is the publication project which makes available the major writings of John Wesley in Spanish. L. Elbert Wethington (chapter 20) describes the need for this edition, the challenge of completing it, and the grateful responses of those now using it. He judges that the edition is a valuable theological resource for those of the Wesleyan tradition in Latin America to understand their roots and those who share the tradition with them.

Among the richest repositories of Wesleyan and Methodist primary source materials is the Methodist Archives and Research Centre at the John Rylands University Library of Manchester, England. Gareth Lloyd (chapter 21) offers a description of some of the documentary treasures in this archive and mentions how the collections may be accessed.

Notes

1. *Works*, 19, 67.

Part I

1

The Global Impact of the Wesleyan Traditions and Their Related Movements

Donald W. Dayton

My task is to introduce this conference rather than to present a keynote address. I wish to do this in three steps. In the first place, I wish to indicate some of the history that lies behind this conference. In the second place, I would like to describe the agenda that informed the planning of the conference so that, without imposing a false unity on the papers, I can indicate the theme that holds them together. Finally, as an additional way of introducing the theme I want to give several illustrations of the diversity and complexity of the Wesleyan tradition whose global character we are celebrating.

The planning for this conference began at our last World Methodist Historical Society conference where we pursued the theme of sanctification in a dialogue with the Benedictines held near Rome in the town where the Pope has his summer residence. Some will remember from that meeting that James Udy, our president from Australia, had suffered a severe stroke that prevented him from completing his term of office. I was invited to serve out his term as Interim President. After some dialogue with the Executive Committee, I accepted the assignment which carried with it two responsibilities—to plan the program of the World Methodist Historical Society in Rio de Janeiro and to make preparations for the next world conference of the Society. The suggestion that I serve as Interim President, which came from some of our Scandinavian friends, carried with it an agenda for the theme of this conference.

Our friends from Scandinavia work in a context deeply suffused with the spirit of Pietism and they wished us to explore what they see as a somewhat neglected dimension of the Methodist experience—its pietistic side. I was, of course, sympathetic to this agenda. I immediately thought of Asbury Theological Seminary as an appropriate location for such a conference, not only because of its positioning on that side of Methodism, but also because of the presence there of the Wesleyan/Holiness Studies Center that has already made significant contributions to work in this area. Asbury was happy to host the conference and to provide significant financial support for it.

The agenda of this conference may be described in two images. The first of these is drawn from the field of biblical studies. I studied with Paul Ricoeur at the University of Chicago and then in Buenos Aires at Istituto Superior Evangélico de Estudios Teológicos (ISEDET), perhaps the most prominent Protestant seminary in Latin America. ISEDET is a union seminary housed now in a Methodist building. At this seminary I was surprised to see how Ricoeur's thought was appropriated in that context. In a course about Ricoeur with Beatrix Melano Couch I learned to appreciate a hermeneutical method that she was convinced was crucial for the emergence of liberation theology—one that emphasized the history in front of the text as much as the history behind the text. Or, to appeal to another tradition, more in accord with my training at Yale, one might speak of the *Wirkungsgeschichte* of a text—or the history of influence of a text as a clue to its meaning. Both of these traditions see themselves as a corrective to an historical critical method that places great emphasis on the history of the production of the text as the primary clue to its meaning.

There is a similar issue in the interpretation of Wesleyanism. More often than not we have looked back to the classical traditions of the Christian church for the categories of interpreting Wesleyanism. Is it a form of Protestantism? Should it be interpreted in light of the Eastern traditions of the church? What are the immediate sources of Wesley's thought? And so on. Our dialogue with the Benedictines might be seen as illustrative of this method. This conference looks forward from the rise of Wesleyanism not only to trace the history of its impact, but also to ask if that history provides categories essential for the interpretation of the phenomenon itself.

This is not always easy to do. It cuts across our usual ways of thinking which often reflect a "genetic" bias. We tend to analyze movements in terms of their originating moments and antecedents. But there are also sociological factors at work drawing us in this direction. In my ecumenical experience, I have often noticed that it is easier to undertake ecumenical dialogue that looks back historically and up the social ladder than that which looks forward and perhaps down the social ladder. Wesleyanism has tended to have a theological "inferiority complex" that has pressed it in these directions in an effort to prove its own theological respectability in terms of the classical traditions of the church. The other direction is somewhat threatening. It leads to the Holiness Movement, Pentecostalism, and other such movements that we are sometimes inclined to suppress in the Wesleyan search for wider cultural respectability.

These issues are illustrated in one of my favorite stories about Albert Outler, the great Wesley scholar and ecumenist of the last century. I once heard him speak of an editorial planning meeting at Oxford University Press for a series of texts of the major figures in modern Protestant theology. In a brainstorming session on figures to be included, he suggested John Wesley and was immediately greeted with laughter at the thought that Wesley should be considered a major figure in the emergence of modern *theology*. This so humiliated Outler that he devoted much of the rest of his life to proving that Wesley was a major *theologian*—largely by the historical, genetic method that we have described. Outler, of course, had the last laugh. His volume on Wesley in that series was the only one to go into paperback and remains in print, precisely because the global impact of Wesleyanism produces a number of contexts in which an understanding of Wesley is an essential key to theological identity.

This conference moves in the opposite direction, i.e., forward rather than backward. This is not to deny the significance of the history behind the text, but is more an effort to provide a counterweight to this tradition that has been so influential and productive in Wesleyan and Methodist scholarship. We will come back to this point in our conclusion.

I take as my second image the Mississippi River, hoping that the non-North American participants will forgive the chauvinistic use of this illustration. Those familiar with the geography of the United States will know that the Mississippi River cuts through the middle of the continent, drawing on such great tributaries as the Ohio, Missouri, and other rivers. As it approaches the Gulf of Mexico it overflows its banks to form the Mississippi Delta in which it loses its clear form and works its way into the nooks and crannies of Louisiana. The Wesleyan tradition reveals a similar pattern. It draws on the great tributaries of the classical Christian tradition (Roman Catholicism, Eastern Orthodoxy, Protestantism, Puritanism, Pietism, and other streams), forms a new and powerful tradition that releases great spiritual power, and finally overflows the denominational banks of Methodism.

I first became aware of this image when the librarians at the B. L. Fisher Library at Asbury Seminary attempted to develop a chart that would give them control over the complexity of the Methodist traditions and the various journals and periodicals that they produced. The result was something like the image of the Mississippi Delta in that what began as a relatively simple and coherent stream soon fragmented and moved in a complex pattern of interrelated ebbings and flowings. The point of this image is again to draw our attention to the complexity of the Wesleyan tradition and to suggest that we have much to learn from the exploration of this complexity in search of clues that will help us to understand the tradition. This image emphasizes the history in front of the text rather than the history behind the text.

This conference is also characterized by a global focus. There are two nuances to this global focus, one more literal and the other more metaphorical. The first sense of the word global is its more literal and geographical sense, i.e., that the Wesleyan and Methodist traditions are to be found throughout the world. We need to remind ourselves of that because of our tendency to interpret things in light of our neighborhood or our horizon, forgetting that it looks different and more enriching from a global perspective.

Even from a global perspective, I think it appropriate and somewhat symbolic that we hold this world conference in North America, even though this might appear to be in conflict with a global agenda. Wesleyanism was born in Britain but found its destiny in North America. At the time of the Revolutionary War in this country there were only a handful of Methodists. By the time of the Civil War in the mid-nineteenth century Methodism had grown to be the nation's dominant Protestant body and maintained this position for a century. In fact, some non-Methodists, e.g., Winthrop Hudson, Philip Schaff, and others, referred to the last half of the nineteenth century and the first half of the twentieth century as the "Methodist age in American history." The Methodists were not only the largest denomination numerically. They convinced half of the rest of the Protestants (and some Roman Catholics) to act like Methodists, thus becoming the country's most culturally influential religious tradition.

One of the ironies of American religious historiography is that, in spite of these facts, Methodism has hardly ever, and then only recently, been used as a lens through which to view the larger religious experience. American religion has been classically read through the New England Puritan tradition. One sees this in the work of Sydney Ahlstrom, who when he came to the nineteenth century, had a tendency to speak of the "decadence" or decline of Puritanism into revivalism rather than speaking positively of the influence of Methodism.

Several historians have complained about this odd historiography and there are some signs of a correction. Nathan Hatch has given significant attention to the role of Methodism in his book, *The Democratization of American Christianity*, in his presidential address on this theme before the American Society of Church History, and in a conference at Asbury. Others are following a similar path.

This issue is of wider significance than the interpretation of American religion. The "age of Methodism" on this continent is roughly equivalent to the "great century" of missions. Methodism was a major proponent of the mission impulse. As a result, Methodism has spread around the world. The American role in all of this has led to interesting disputes about whether the British or the American church is the "mother church" of Methodism. The American churches have dominated in Latin American, and in Africa and Asia there is often both a British and an American Methodist tradition (still reflected in Zimbabwe, for example). In some parts of the world (Korea, for example) there were competing Methodist churches representing the North and South after the division over slavery. We see a very complex pattern of diversity even within the major streams of Methodism understood denominationally.

This global impact and complexity has been reflected in the structure of this conference. There is a plenary session devoted to each continent and then parallel sessions in connection with that region of the world. In this manner we have tried to represent the global character of Wesleyanism in the strictly geographical sense by an effort to be inclusive of many national traditions of Wesleyanism produced by its missionary impulse.

There is another, more metaphorical sense, in which we have used the word "global." We need to give attention to a "global" interpretation of Methodism by emphasizing the great variety of Wesleyan traditions that have found their places throughout the world. To make the point in another way, there has been an effort to transcend denominational history to see the great complexity of forms the Wesleyan tradition has taken. I draw attention to at least five streams of Wesleyanism that have informed this conference.

(1) I will give less attention to the first of these, which we have already developed to some extent. This would be the complex set of traditions that we might call (for want of a better term) "main-line Methodism": the British and American churches that dominate the World Methodist Council and the various mission churches from around the world that stand in this tradition. Closely related to these churches in North America would be the black Methodist churches that are a product of the experience of racism and slavery in the United States. These churches are also quite influential and in some cases have their own traditions of missions in Africa and elsewhere.

(2) We sometimes forget that Methodism was originally a "renewal movement" that did not intend to form new denominations. Like the charismatic movement of our time, it had an impact far beyond the denominational lines that have formed since. In fact, Wesleyan influences provide the key for the interpretation of many religious movements of the last two centuries—often in ways that make more traditional Methodists uncomfortable. We sometimes forget that John Humphrey Noyes, the founder of Oneida, was a student of John Wesley and John William Fletcher, though it is sometimes difficult to see how he got from their theologies to the sexual experimentation of his community.

The most important illustration of this dynamic is probably evangelist Charles Grandison Finney and his colleagues who under the influence of Wesley and Fletcher developed the "Oberlin Perfectionism" that dominated the first decades of Oberlin College. The merging of the Reformed and Methodist traditions there unleashed powerful forces of social reform that continue to shape global culture—the struggle against slavery, the rise of feminism and the ministry of women, and similar currents. There are many ways in which the tradition of "modern revivalism" (from Finney through D. L. Moody to Billy Graham—and including the various associated mission movements, both denominational and independent) is a carrier of Wesleyan themes, though in increasingly subdued forms.

Another illustration would be the Seventh-day Adventist Church. It is hard to understand this movement (with its powerful worldwide missions) without reference to Methodism. Early leaders were essentially Methodist evangelists preaching in a camp meeting context a radicalization of Wesley's positive view of the "law" as the ultimate principle of the universe. There is a contemporary debate within Adventism about what Ellen G. White meant when she claimed the movement was raised up to "complete the Reformation." There is a party that understands this as a "Lutheran" agenda (surely wrong), but they are opposed by a "Methodist" party that sees this as a call to extend justification into sanctification (surely the correct reading).

(3) There are also other centers of self-conscious Wesleyan identity, perhaps best illustrated by the Holiness Movement. The Asbury institutions are a product of this movement and something of a hinge between the classical Methodist tradition and various streams of the Holiness Movement—another reason for the venue of this conference. The impact of this tradition is not well understood, but on any given Sunday there may be as many Holiness folks in church as there are United Methodists.

This movement is exceedingly complex and includes some early splits from the Methodist Episcopal Church (the abolitionist Wesleyan Methodists and the related Free Methodist Church), products of the Holiness Movement proper (the Church of the Nazarene and related churches), the Salvation Army, a number of Quaker and Mennonite-like churches swept into the movement, endless lists of campmeetings, various independent institutions (for example, God's Bible School in Cincinnati, Taylor University), and so on. What most of these currents shared was a reaction against the *embourgeoisement* of Methodism and a tendency to identify with the lower classes neglected as Methodism began its social climb. Most of them also carried an "Oberlinite" commitment to the ministry of women.

Most of these currents have become global, like the Salvation Army, or have had great influence through a variety of mission movements, both denominational and independent. The Oriental Mission Society was born in God's Bible School and has produced a church in Japan that suffered martyrdom during World War II and a church in Korea which has become one of the most influential streams of Christianity there before turning to Latin America with the complications of World War II. Similar stories could be told of the World Gospel Mission which has had great impact in Africa, especially Kenya. It is hard to find a part of the world untouched by the Nazarenes and the Christian and Missionary Alliance.

(4) We must also mention Pentecostalism. Though much of Methodism and the Holiness Movement would be anxious to defend themselves against a paternity suit, several have argued that Pentecostalism itself is a product of Methodism (Vinson Synan in *The Holiness-Pentecostal Movement* and myself in *Theological Roots of Pentecostal-*

ism). Synan argues that the first decade of Pentecostalism was universally "holiness," but whatever one makes of that claim, a large part of the Pentecostal Movement remains both "holiness" and "pentecostal," especially the Church of God (Cleveland, Tennessee) and the Pentecostal Holiness Church. This movement is the great phenomenon of the twentieth century and some would suggest that one in four Christians today is a product of one or another branch of this extremely complex movement.

(5) We must also mention the existence of various "indigenous" Wesleyan churches. We find several such churches in Chile, where the Pentecostal churches have a very Wesleyan identity. One of my favorites is the Iglesia Wesleyana, so named to celebrate the work of Wesley among the miners in England and to inspire a similar work in Chile where the founder was a Pentecostal pastor and a member of the junta of the socialist party of Allende. I have visited the Meung Thai church in Thailand produced by the conversion of a young Thai woman under the ministry of an itinerant Korean holiness evangelist who then insisted that her fiancé convert and join her in the founding of this new denomination. I have also visited the Immanuel General Mission in Japan, whose founder claims to be the "John Wesley of Japan." One could go on with such a list. It is important to see in a Wesleyan line several independent figures that are not usually so interpreted. One thinks especially of John Sung, the controversial, but extremely influential, indigenous evangelist in China and southeast Asia, or the international ministry of Sadhu Sundar Singh of India. These are some of the most interesting figures of twentieth-century Christianity.

The point of all this is to argue that we must think of the Wesleyan tradition globally, not only geographically, but also in the complexity and range of Wesleyan traditions in the world today. Underlying this is the conviction that it is only through the exploration of this complexity and diversity that we will really understand Wesley and the Methodist tradition.

Donald Durnbaugh in his book *The Believers' Church* develops a very interesting argument based on a chart that attempts to refine the classical sect/church typology of Ernst Troeltsch and H. Richard Niebuhr. Durnbaugh's analysis results in an equilateral triangle whose points are identified with the Persons of the Trinity and styles of church life that result from an emphasis on one or another Person. The significance of this for us is that he places Pietism and Methodism in the center and suggests that both are constitutionally unstable, inclined to spin apart into fragments. Thus, in a different social location and out from under the control of Wesley, Methodism will develop competing parties and denominations carrying a variety of fragments of original Methodism. For example, we get a liturgical, cathedral style of Methodism, a Christological Protestant version of Methodism, and a pneumatological charismatic reading of the Methodism tradition. The problem is that each of these fragments can sustain a claim to be genuinely Wesleyan, but none of them represents the full Wesley.

I suggest that we understand Wesley and the Methodist tradition only when we bring back together these various fragments. Wesley was both the Anglican priest of liturgical renewal and the street preacher of the Salvation Army or Chilean Pentecostalism. It is this history in the front of the text that can provide essential clues for the interpretation of the dynamic of Wesleyanism and its global impact.

2

Pauline Missions: The Wesleyan Holiness Vision

David Bundy

There are two traditions of the organization of mission within the Methodist, Holiness, and Pentecostal movements. One has to do with "Boards" modeled after the example of the American Board of Commissioners for Foreign Mission (ABCFM). The other is a tradition known in many circles as "Pauline missions" or, as one leader identified it, mission that follows "Pauline mission" methods. The goal of this essay is to trace the theoretical and historical development of the "Pauline mission" tradition of Methodist, Holiness, and Pentecostal missions.

This mission tradition, it is argued, continues traditions of mission central to the Methodist revival of the eighteenth century. According to this paradigm, mission work was generally done on the edge of the established church, whether British Wesleyan Methodist or North American Methodist Episcopal. The story begins with John Wesley (1703-1791) and continues to the Americas as modeled by the missions of Thomas Coke (1747-1814), Francis Asbury (1745-1816), and Lorenzo Dow (1777-1834). Finally, it takes its definitive North American form in the work of William Taylor who served as a mentor for much of Methodist (circa. 1880-1940), Holiness, and early Pentecostal missions. In each case, the acts of mission and the stories of their exploits were more important than what was said about mission. However, for each there was a theoretical base from which mission was done. It was William Taylor who defined "Pauline missions." This mission theory and practice—independent, entrepreneurial, and generally self-directing—was outside the control of the churches. Taylor saw this as the biblical model of the Apostle Paul. Like Paul's churches, modern results of mission were to be self-supporting, self-governing, and self-propagating.

"Pauline missions" method is to be understood apart from and often over against the system of mission boards that developed within the churches in an effort to control funding, missionaries, and the results of mission. The Wesleyan Methodist Missionary Society (British) was founded in 1818 and the Missionary Society of the Methodist Episcopal Church was organized in 1819. Some Holiness denominations would adopt the Methodist Episcopal Church model, while others have sought to follow the tradition of "Pauline missions."

I

Wesleyan/Holiness mission theory and practice began with the model of John Wesley. His own experience of mission in the British colony of Georgia was less than successful. He found many difficulties in the practice of mission, both to the colonists and to Native Americans. Only among the African American slaves, certainly not part of Anglican society, did he experience missionary success.[1] He left Georgia with a sense of personal failure and a crisis of spirituality. Both would be partially resolved by experiences at the Fetter Lane Society and Aldersgate. However, not until he made the decision to move outside the established churches and to preach in the fields to the poor and to the miners did he find his calling and recognizable success in ministry. That decision effectively removed him from the control of the Anglican Church although he never personally withdrew from it. He appointed preachers, just as bishops appointed priests, to nurture converts in Methodist spirituality. What he afforded himself, ministry on the fringes of the church, he was loath to confer on others.[2] Thomas Coke, one of the shapers of Methodist missions, was one of those required to go outside both Anglican and Methodist structures to undertake mission work.

Thomas Coke (1747-1814)[3] was the person who should be credited with the establishment of indigenous missions that were self-governing, self-financing, and self-propagating. His initial experiences were in

Pauline Missions: The Wesleyan Holiness Vision 15

America at the request of Wesley,[4] and in Canada, the Caribbean, Africa, India, and Ceylon (today Sri Lanka) despite the preferences of John Wesley to focus Methodist mission efforts on the British Isles. Coke has been described as "the one-man band" of mission and the inspiration for the eventual establishment of the (British) Wesleyan Methodist Mission Society (1818) is attributed to his efforts and example.[5] It is important to note that the plans laid by Coke were written and circulated widely a full eight years before William Carey, a Baptist, began work on his mission project.[6] Coke raised the majority of the funds for the mission himself, since the Methodist Conference under the leadership of Wesley refused to appropriate funds for the effort. Coke was sometimes forced to resort to begging for funds door-to-door in London in order to support mission projects. He died 3 May 1814 on board ship in the Indian Ocean en route to establish a group of missionaries in Ceylon (Sri Lanka). Like all of his mission activity, this last endeavor was undertaken as an entrepreneurial project outside the structures of the Methodist Church. It was not until after Coke's death that the Wesleyan Methodist Missionary Society was organized (1818).[7] Even then the Society was not integrated into the church. It was a voluntary association of contributors.

In the American context, the version of the Wesleyan itinerancy established by Francis Asbury was responsible for organizing much of Methodism's growth on the changing frontier of the European settlement of North America. It was a flexible and entrepreneurial approach to church governance under the essential control of Asbury. It not only organized the Methodist clergy, but also restricted from entrance to clergy ranks those considered an embarrassment to the church or to powerful figures of the church. One person who was never accepted by the church for ordination was Lorenzo Dow,[8] a persuasive preacher of revival and personal holiness. He was considered by several powerful figures in the church, especially Jesse Lee, too physically weak and unstable to be in the itinerancy as a circuit rider. Furthermore, Dow felt called to the larger American context. He did not want to be restricted to preaching in a few small isolated villages. He had a commitment to ministry among African Americans and was a frequent preacher in Richard Allen's African Methodist Episcopal Church.[9] On the edges of the Methodist Episcopal Church, he traveled more than 250,000 miles in North America and did mission work throughout England and Ireland.[10] Dow became a model for American Wesleyan/Holiness missions. Aspects of that influence characteristic in his ministry are as follows. (1) Dow used American developed means of religious instruction and evangelism, including the camp meeting. (2) He assumed that mission was both to already existing churches to encourage them in their "sanctification" and for the conversion of nonbelievers. (3) He cooperated with and/or built upon already existing structures and worked to enhance those structures rather than create new ones. (4) Dow encouraged the ministry of laity and of women. (5) He endorsed an active bodily response by individuals to an encounter with God as normative. (6) He refused to restrain his mission program at the request of the established churches; the "call of God" took precedence even over Methodist discipline. Dow's missions were "self-supporting" and he appears to have made no effort to control the results of his mission work.[11] Importantly, while he clearly relished his role as transatlantic missionary, there is no evidence that he considered the results of his overseas missions as having any significant difference from the results of his preaching throughout North America. Dow became a significant icon for the Wesleyan/Holiness tradition.

In contrast to the development of the model seen in the ministries and writings of Wesley, Coke, and Dow, was the model of the Methodist Episcopal Missionary Society, founded in 1819 under the leadership of Nathan Bangs (1778-1862). This organization was founded as an official medium for missionary organization to control finances, the activities of missionaries, and the results of mission. Bangs felt that the Methodist Episcopal Church needed the same types of organization found among the Congregationalists (ABCFM) and the Baptists. The language of the founding documents is that of American expansionism and triumphalism. The goals are described in "manifest destiny" and "republican" language. The intentions of the organization were the opposite of those of Wesley, Coke, and Dow. It is profuse in self-congratulation of American Methodists for their growth, and this in turn is understood as a mandate to engage in mission to promote and expand the influence of the American model of the Methodist Episcopal Church. Ironically, there was no room for entrepreneurial activity or trust of either missionaries or converts.[12]

II

William Taylor (1821-1902) is a recurring figure in the narratives relating to the mission activity engaged under the aegis of the Methodist Episcopal Church during the nineteenth century.[13] That story has to do

Pauline Missions: The Wesleyan Holiness Vision 17

with California, Africa especially, India, and Latin America. What happened to Taylor in those contexts is central to this study. He experienced Africa and African culture in ways that rarely happened to Americans during that century. The conclusions to which he came based on that experience transformed his thinking about missions and the role of missionaries. The resultant theory was congruent with that of Wesley, Coke, and Dow.

Taylor began his missionary career in the service of the Methodist Episcopal Church as its second missionary to California (1849-1856). It was the experience of creating and molding a church in San Francisco that marked his understanding of mission. He was given no money by the bishops, Missionary society, or the eastern churches. His converts were organized into congregations, exploited natural resources, established social order out of chaos, and became wealthy enough to support a regular ministerial and educational structure. Thus, as a missionary, he established Methodist Episcopal congregations that were immediately taken into the official structures of the Methodist Episcopal Church as equals to any of the congregations in the older established areas of North America.[14]

In San Francisco, he built a church and temperance hotel. When these burned before they were paid for, he traveled to the eastern United States, Canada, and then Australia, preaching and writing books, hoping to raise monies to pay debts. When American currencies were reduced in value because of the impending US Civil War, he had to look elsewhere to ply his trade as an evangelist. This set him on a global missionary career during which he played crucial roles in the development of Methodism in Australia, Ceylon (Sri Lanka), India, England, the Caribbean, Latin America, and Africa.

When Taylor arrived in South Africa in early 1866, he expected to earn his living by preaching in the British Wesleyan Methodist Church as he had done earlier in Australia. However, the South African English churches were less than impressed with his preaching and he went instead to African villages in the company of a gifted theologian and translator, Charles Pamla. With Pamla he would arrive at a village, ask permission of the chief to preach, preach, organize converts into a congregation, teach the congregation about the Christian faith, establish a convert in charge as pastor, leave a Bible, and then move on to the next village. There was no effort to reformulate African culture. He found that it compared quite well to his own. This trust of Africans and acceptance of African culture caused him to be received enthusiastically by the

Africans. Many were converted.

After six months of evangelism, he commissioned Charles Pamla as his successor and left the continent. On ship, 18 October 1866, off the Cape of Good Hope, Taylor began to reflect on the missiological significance of his experience in South Africa and the theory of "Pauline missions" was born. The concept was not new, he insisted, but rather one "successfully used by St. Paul and his fellow missionaries."[15]

From Africa, Taylor eventually made his way to India and Latin America where he experimented in the use of the method. After his work in India (1870-1875)[16] and in Latin America (1878-1884)[17] brought him into conflict with the Methodist Episcopal Missionary Society, the Methodist Episcopal Church forced him to cease (1882-1884) functioning as a clergyman and missionary. During the initial period of conflict, he went to Latin America where he was instrumental in establishing Methodist Churches in Panama, Peru, Bolivia, Chile, Argentina, and Brazil. Recognizing the need for more "self-supporting" missionaries, he established a sending agency, the "Building and Transit Fund" for helping Wesleyan/Holiness missionaries get to the mission field. From 1884 until his retirement in 1896, he was again in Africa as missionary bishop.[18] Taylor became a model and inspiration for much of Wesleyan/Holiness missions. Conflict between the Mission Board and adherents of the Taylor approach led to missionaries, local clergy, and laypersons becoming Pentecostal after 1906. He served as a theorist for early Pentecostal missions, especially in Europe and Latin America.[19]

Taylor's missiology was worked out in the context of his missionary activity and as a result is a function of his biography. On the basis of that experience he developed a biblical model for his philosophy of mission, i.e., the accounts of the missionary endeavors of Paul. His analysis was as follows:[20]

1. To plant nothing but the pure gospel seed. . . .
2. Paul laid the entire responsibility of Church work and Church government upon his native converts, under the immediate supervision of the Holy Spirit, just as fast as he and his trusted fellow-missionaries could get them well organized, precluding foreign interference. His general administrative bishops were natives of foreign countries in which he had planted the gospel; such men as Timothy and Titus.
3. Paul "endeavored to keep the unity of the Spirit in the bond of peace" with the home Jerusalem Churches by all possibilities short of corrupting his gospel seed, or allowing the home

Pauline Missions: The Wesleyan Holiness Vision 19

Churches to put a yoke of bondage on his neck, or of laying any restrictions on his foreign Churches.
4. ... Hence he went and sent, according to the teaching of the Master, without "purse or scrip," or an extra coat, or pair of shoes above the actual requirements of their health and comfort.
5. In utilizing for the advancement of Christ's kingdom ... all available resources, he uniformly commenced in Jewish communities.
6. To give permanency and continued aggressive force to his organizings ... he remained in each great centre of work long enough not only to effect a complete organization, with administrative elders, but to develop the Christian character of each member. ...

The recurring theme of the national autonomy of Methodist Episcopal churches is seen throughout Taylor's writings after the India experience and the controversy that ensued.[21] His perception was that the Mission Society was seeking to place these new churches in a type of bondage. To a certain extent, the newly formed churches shared or came to share this impression. For example, the debate over control of the Methodist mission in Chile (1884-1906) within the Mission Society and the General Conferences, with no concern taken for the opinions of the Methodist missionaries or laity in Chile, was certainly a factor in the conversion of most of the Methodist Church in Chile to Pentecostalism in 1907.[22] He also inspired generations of Methodist Episcopal missionaries.

Despite Taylor's appreciation for many aspects of the British Empire, he was very sensitive to any transference of colonial ideology into mission policy and ecclesiology. For Taylor, there was no Third World. There was only a frontier that needed the "Gospel," careful stewardship, organization, and ethical exploitation. These he thought could be accomplished most effectively by Christians, but not necessarily North American or European Christians. The missionaries were to become one with their hosts. There was to be no structural difference between missionary and "native." He argued, against the evolutionary theories which equated European culture with the apex of development, that information and intelligence are not the same, and that the children of Africans are no more "heathen" than those of North Americans. Cultural distinctions were relative for Taylor. He ridiculed the missionaries who insisted on North American style food, housing, and customs. Respect for the people "on the frontier" was coupled with a disdain for the kept

minions, as he saw them, of the North American missionary establishment who dared to make decisions for clergy and laity while "10,000 miles from the front."
Taylor's mission theory and practice were key to the evolving Holiness and Pentecostal movements, both to their formulation of domestic mission and foreign mission structures. It would be difficult to overestimate the importance of his role and vision. It gave Pentecostals a model for doing ministry and mission outside the parameters of the state and mission churches of Europe and Latin America.

III

Not only did William Taylor inspire missionaries who worked within the Methodist Episcopal Church, although on the fringes of that church, such as James Thoburn and J.W. Pickett, he also inspired mission efforts among those who chose to withdraw or were forced to withdraw from the Methodist Episcopal and other churches in the United States during the last two decades of the nineteenth century and the first decade of the twentieth century. The nature of these radical Holiness missions can be seen in the examples of the Vanguard Mission in Saint Louis and the Pentecost Bands that related loosely to the Free Methodist Church.

Among those inspired by Taylor's "Pauline Mission" concept were Charles W. Sherman, Bessie Sherman, and Anna Abrams. The Shermans began the Vanguard Mission in St. Louis in 1880. It was a self-supporting mission loosely connected to the Free Methodist Church that did not yet have a mission program. They understood their work as a mission that happened to be in North America. Sherman summarized his understanding of the situation, "No one can deny that Wm. Taylor has in his self-supporting missions eclipsed all that the salary system has ever done. . . . These facts stare the world in the face and speak volumes in favor of apostolic missions and the self-supporting plan."[23]

Sherman, editor of the periodical, *The Vanguard*, served as a communication link as well as a supply and fund-channeling agency for Wesleyan/Holiness "self-supporting" missionaries. He made no effort to control their work and supported them with no strings attached. He and his wife Bessie went to India for four years and cooperated with mission projects already underway, leaving the St. Louis mission and *The Vanguard* under the direction of Bessie's sister Anna Abrams.

Pauline Missions: The Wesleyan Holiness Vision

Abrams was an articulate theologian whose essays were printed and reprinted in many periodicals. Her mission theory depended on William Taylor, but she was also in dialogue with discussions of mission in the mainline churches. She did not differentiate between foreign and home missions or between private and public spirituality and morality. Missionaries were to be "sanctified" and work to reform their world. Mission was to be evangelistic, but was also to strive, within the context of the host culture, to provide Christian literature, care for orphans, and help nationals develop industries to provide a better living standard.[24] The "divine pattern" for Christian living and mission, she argued, "is to manifest faith in God for all things, and to have a life in contrast with men's ideas."[25] Abrams insisted that believers and new converts be organized into house churches according to the models of biblical literature, the Wesleys, the Palmer Tuesday Meetings, and the Vanguard Mission. These churches were to be "strongholds of the saints" like those which, "in times of spiritual decline and apostasy . . . [were] . . . bulwarks and breakwaters of the church." These "always accompany the true work of God" and must not become materialistic as do churches that "run after great things."[26]

The "divine pattern" of "faith missions" asserted Abrams, is to follow the biblical injunction to be self-supporting, to have no care for one's personal needs. She responded to critics, asking, "Was Jesus making a reckless venture when he sent out his disciples without purse or scrip to trust the Lord for all their needs?"[27] The ministry was conceived to "be distinct from all earthly associations and professional callings"[28] and required a "well-cultured mind."[29]

Abrams was an important figure in the development of Wesleyan/Holiness mission theory for nearly four decades, from about 1880 to 1920. The synthesis articulated in her articles had an influence throughout radical holiness movements as they worked to develop patterns for mission. Institutions influenced by her include the Mission Training School of Whittier (later Huntington, Los Angeles, and Azusa, California), Union Bible College and Seminary (Westfield, Indiana), God's Bible School in Cincinnati, and a host of missionary training schools that flourished during the early twentieth century.

Another crucial figure during this period was Vivian Dake.[30] He was a protégé of William Taylor but added elements to Taylor's theory. These additions involved matters of ministry structure and the personal asceticism of missionaries. The innovative feature of ministry structure was to divide the missionaries into "Pentecost Bands" of (normally) four persons who would work to establish local congregations and other ministries, develop local leadership for the ministries, and then move on to another site. These bands originally functioned under the umbrella of the Free Methodist Church. They were active in mission in the North American midwest, Europe, Africa, and India. There was no distinction between home and foreign missions other than the accident of geography. The Christian life was to be one of mission, irrespective of the geography. Each Pentecost Band member was to have experienced "entire sanctification" and be committed to the propagation of the doctrine. They were to live ascetic lives with regard to food, material goods, and sexuality.

Essential to Dake was freedom from ecclesiastical control. Missionaries, following the Pauline pattern, were to be free to follow the guidance of the Holy Spirit. B. T. Roberts, founder of the Free Methodist Church, wrote Dake to encourage his actions: "Organize your Bands . . . be aggressive . . . we must not let the Free Methodist Church become a feeble imitation of the M.E. Church." However, by the mid-1880s the Free Methodist Church began a mission program, insisted on conformity to the regulations of the bureaucracy, and forced the Pentecost Bands to withdraw from the church. Dake died on ship with William Taylor off the coast of Africa.[31] It had been proven that the mission board of a Holiness church could and often did act exactly as the mission board of an older established denomination.

All of these persons acknowledged their debt to Taylor's thought and model. They are examples of an influence that leavened Methodist, Holiness, and Pentecostal missions. All saw themselves in the missional tradition of Wesley and of early American Methodism.

IV

Mission in the Wesleyan/Holiness traditions has been undertaken on the radical edge of the Wesleyan tradition and has continued values and attitudes toward mission expressed by Wesley, Coke, and Francis Asbury, but formulated most definitively by Lorenzo Dow and, especially, William Taylor. It was William Taylor who directly inspired the mission theory of the Shermans, Abrams, Dake, and a host of other Methodist, Holiness, and Pentecostal missionaries of the twentieth century, including those who worked in congruence with his vision of mission such as

James Thoburn, E. A. Seamands, J. Wascom Pickett, and E. Stanley Jones. It was a vision of the experience of sanctification (Christian perfection) providing the basis for mission and spiritual development, of work under the guidance of the Holy Spirit that is entrepreneurial and intense, of a mission that transcends national, racial, and gender barriers, and that respects converts as equal before God and other Christians.

Notes

1. Richard P. Heitzenrater, *Wesley and the People Called Methodists* (Nashville, Tenn.: Abingdon Press, 1995); Richard P. Heitzenrater, *Mirror and Memory: Reflections on Early Methodism* (Nashville, Tenn.: Kingswood Books, 1989).
2. Christian C. Bennett, "John Wesley: Founder of a Missionary Church?" *Proceedings of the Wesley Historical Society*, 50 (1996): 159-70, 229-36.
3. Alexander Gordon, "Coke, Thomas," *Dictionary of National Biography*, 4 (1887), 705; John Vickers, "Coke, Thomas," *Blackwell's Dictionary of Evangelical Biography, 1730-1860*, I, (1996), 238-39; John Vickers, *Thomas Coke: Apostle of Methodism* (Nashville, Tenn.: Abingdon Press, 1969), 355-66.
4. On Coke in America, see Frank Baker, "Dr. Thomas Coke—The First Methodist Bishop," in *From Wesley to Asbury: Studies in Early American Methodism* (Durham, N.C.: Duke University Press, 1976), 142-61.
5. John A. Vickers, "One-Man Band: Thomas Coke and the Origins of Methodist Missions," *Methodist History* 34, no. 3 (April 1996): 135-47; and Vickers, *Thomas Coke: Apostle of Methodism* (Nashville, Tenn.: Abingdon Press, 1969).
6. Thomas Coke, *A Plan of the Society for the Establishment of Missions among the Heathen* (Folio, n.p., 1783) and, Thomas Coke, *Address to the Pious and Benevolent, Proposing an Annual Subscription for the Support of the Missionaries in the Highlands and Islands of Scotland, the Isles of Jersey, Guernsey and Newfoundland, the West Indies, and the Provinces of Nova Scotia and Quebec* (London: n.p., 1786).
7. See Christian C. Bennett, "The Development of the Idea of Mission in British Wesleyan Thought, 1784-1914," (Ph.D. diss., University of Manchester, 1995), 14-55.
8. See Nathan O. Hatch, *The Democratization of American Christianity* (New Haven, Conn.: Yale University Press, 1989). Dow's works were published in a series of editions, together with writings by his wife. One edition is Lorenzo Dow, *The Dealings of God, Man, and the Devil; as Exemplified in the Life, Experience and Travels of Lorenzo Dow, in a Period of Over Half a Century, Together with the Polemic and Miscellaneous Writings, Complete, to which is

added The Vicissitudes of Life by Peggy Dow, with an introduction by John Bowling (New York: Cornish, Lamport and Co., 1852).

9. Dow, I, 110, 130, 148 et passim. He is criticized in a letter from an irate Methodist clergyman as taking the side of Richard Allen in Allen's dispute with Asbury, a charge not refuted by Dow.

10. The best treatment of his transatlantic ministry is Richard Carwardine, *Trans-Atlantic Revivalism: Popular Evangelicalism in Britain and America, 1790-1865* (Westport, Conn.: Greenwood, 1978), 104-7, 134-35, 198-200 et passim.

11. Dow, I, 115-37. See also Carwardine, 104-6 and Hugh Bourne, *History of the Primitive Methodists* from the first American edition in Lorenzo Dow, II, 265-95.

12. On the Missionary Society, see Nathan Bangs, *An Authentic History of the Missions under the Care of the Missionary Society of the Methodist Episcopal Church* (New York: Emory and Waugh, 1832). This essay owes a debt to and argues with Wade Crawford Barclay, et al., *History of Methodist Missions* (New York: Board of Global Ministries of The United Methodist Church, 1956-1973).

13. David Bundy, "Bishop William Taylor and the Methodist Mission Board," parts 1 and 2, *Methodist History* 27, no. 4 (July 1989): 197-210; 28, no. 1 (October 1989): 2-21. See also David Bundy, "William Taylor, 1821-1902: Entrepreneurial Maverick for the Indigenous Church," in *Mission Legacies: Biographical Studies of Leaders of the Modern Missionary Movement*, ed. Gerald Anderson, et al., American Society of Missiology Series, 19 (Maryknoll, N.Y.: Orbis Press, 1994), 461-68; David Bundy, "Swedish Pentecostal Mission Theory and Practice to 1930: Foundational Values in Discussion," *Mission Studies* 14 (1997): 147-74; and David Bundy, "Unintended Consequences: The Methodist Episcopal Missionary Society and the Beginnings of Pentecostalism in Norway and Chile," *Missiology* 27 (1999): 211-29.

14. William Taylor, *Seven Years Street Preaching in San Francisco, California; Embracing Incidents, Triumphant Death Scenes, etc.*, ed. W. P. Strickland (New York: Carton and Porter, 1856), and William Taylor, *California Life Illustrated* (New York: Carlton and Porter, 1858).

15. William Taylor, *Christian Adventures in South Africa* (London: Jackson, Walford, and Hodder; New York: Carlton and Porter, 1867), 509, and David Bundy, "William Taylor in South Africa, 1866," forthcoming.

16. William Taylor, *Four Years Campaign in India* (London: Hodder and Stoughton; New York: Nelson and Phillips; New York: Eaton and Mains, 1875), and Bundy, *Ten Years of Self-Supporting Missions in India* (New York: Phillips and Hunt, 1882).

17. William Taylor, *Our South American Cousins* (New York: Nelson and Hunt, 1878).

18. On the circumstances of his election, see David Bundy, "Bishop William

Taylor and the Methodist Mission Board," *Methodist History* 28, no. 1 (October 1989): 2-21.

19. David Bundy, "Unintended Consequences: The Methodist Episcopal Missionary Society and the Beginnings of Pentecostalism in Norway and Chile," *Missiology* 27 (1999): 211-29.

20. William Taylor, *Pauline Methods of Missionary Work*, (Philadelphia: National Association for the Promotion of Holiness, 1879).

21. William Taylor, *Story of My Life: An Account of what I have Thought and Said and Done in My Minstry of More than Fifty-Three Years in Christian Lands and Among the Heathen: written by myself*, ed. John C. Ridpath (New York: Hunt and Eaton, 1896), 699.

22. J. Tremayne Copplestone, *Twentieth-Century Perspectives: The Methodist Episcopal Church, 1896-1939*, History of Methodist Missions, 4 (New York: Board of Global Ministries, 1973), 589-610, provides a very negative North American analysis of the beginnings of the Pentecostal Movement in Chile. For different interpretations, see J. B. A. Kessler, *A Study of the Older Protestant Missions and Churches in Peru and Chile, With Special Reference to the Problems of Division, Nationalism and Native Ministry* (Goes: Osterbaan en Le Cointre, 1967), Walter J. Hollenweger, "Methodism's Past is Pentecostalism's Present: A Case Study of Cultural Clash in Chile," *Methodist History* 20, (1982): 169-82, and David Bundy, "Unintended Consequences: The Methodist Episcopal Missionary Society and the Beginnings of Pentecostalism in Norway and Chile," *Missiology* 27 (1999): 211-29.

23. Letter of C. W. Sherman to S. B. Shaw published in the *Michigan Holiness Record*, 4, 6 (October 1886): 43.

24. Anna Abrams, "Important Missionary Agencies," *The Vanguard*, 21, 23 (15 Dec. 1901), 4; Anna Abrams, "Industrial Evangelical Mission in India," *The Vanguard*, 29, 15 (14 Aug. 1909), 5; Anna Abrams, "Joanna P. Moore," *The Vanguard*, 29, 10 (29 May 1909), 5-6; Anna Abrams, "Interesting Institutions in India," *The Vanguard*, 29, 17 (30 Sept. 1909), 5; and Anna Abrams, "Village Evangelism," *The Revivalist*, 11, 7 (16 Feb. 1899), 9.

25. Anna Abrams, "Faith Missions," *The Vanguard*, 28, 10 (20 May 1908), 4.

26. Anna Abrams, "Church in Thy House," *The Vanguard*, 21, 18 (13 Aug. 1903), 1.

27. Anna Abrams, "Faith Missions," *The Vanguard*, 28, 10 (20 May 1908), 1.

28. Anna Abrams, "The Missionary Call and Fitness," *The Vanguard*, 23, 16 (15 Sept. 1903), 1.

29. Anna Abrams, "The Missionary Call and Fitness," *The Vanguard*, 23, 16 (15 Sept. 1903), 1.

30. Thomas H. Nelson, *Life and Labors of Rev. Vivian A. Dake. Organizer and Leader of the Pentecost Bands; Embracing an Account of His Travels in*

America, Europe and Africa with Selections from His Sketches, Poems, and Songs (Chicago: T. B. Arnold, 1895), quotation of Roberts on forepage. Nelson makes explicit the relationships with the Vanguard Mission and publishes five letters by Bessie Sherman Ashton.

31. Nelson, 338-46, 413-22.

3

Wesleyan Missiological Theories: The Case of Richard Watson

Andrew Walls

Wesleyanism is about *practical* holiness and about spreading it. There is a long tradition of Wesleyan missionary activity, but no body of Wesleyan missiological theory on a comparable scale. Nor is it easy to extrapolate a body of distinctively Wesleyan missiological theory from the abundance of Wesleyan missionary practice. For one thing, Wesleyan missionary activity was part of a wider movement among evangelical Protestants and it is hard to discern what in its practice is *distinctively* Wesleyan. Protestant missionaries of similar periods often responded to similar situations in similar ways. Those practitioners who stand out among the Wesleyans are often precisely those who do not fit the mold, who are not representative of the general run of Methodist missionaries.

A good example is Thomas Birch Freeman, an Englishman of African descent sent to what is now Ghana by the Wesleyan Methodist Missionary Society in 1838. All his predecessors, and most of his colleagues in that field, died of fever within a year or so of their arrival in Africa. Freeman lived to put the mission on a sure footing and to direct it for nearly twenty years. That is what his mission board wanted him to do. However, Freeman, like Oliver Twist, wanted more. He expanded the mission's activities in every direction, entering into constructive Christian engagement with the powerful independent African rulers of Ashanti, Abeokuta, and Dahomey. As a result he was a pioneer figure not only for the church in Ghana, but in Nigeria and the Benin Republic. With the Yoruba Anglican Samuel Ajayi Crowther, he is the outstanding missionary entrepreneur of precolonial west Africa. But Freeman was frequently in tension with his mission board. After several times hovering on the brink of resignation or dismissal, he and they eventually parted company. The trouble was that he spent too much money and could never be induced to believe that keeping accounts (and what is more solidly Methodistical than keeping accounts?) mattered very much. He did not return to England but lived on in Ghana till 1890, more than thirty years after the breach, marrying a local Christian convert (their descendants are there to this day) and eventually reentering the Methodist ministry there.[1]

A different approach to Methodist missiology might be from the point of view of distinctively Methodist doctrines about conversion and sanctification. From Wesley's time Methodists accepted a distinctive paradigm of the normal Christian experience of both, what Wesley called "the experience of real Christians." They could not even open their hymnbooks (that "little handbook of experimental and practical divinity," as Wesley called it) without seeing that paradigm laid out in the way the hymns were arranged. Could the paradigm be transferred to the mission field? The answer was not always clear-cut.

Some of the early Methodist missionary encounters did result in popular movements towards the Christian faith. In Fiji, Tonga, and New Zealand, whole communities abandoned the traditional cult, destroyed its symbols, forsook long-standing practices that missionaries had preached against, and willingly took on a new lifestyle which included Christian worship and study of the Bible. But such community movements did not always follow the paradigm laid out in *Hymns for the Use of the People called Methodists.*[2]

In particular, there was not much evidence in these early movements of mourning for sin. Sometimes there was a subsequent movement where this deep sense of sin became manifest, but this happened to church people, not "the heathen." Such movements could be seen as revivals and missionaries thus had a vocabulary that enabled them to interpret them in traditional Methodist terms. It remained the case that the preaching of the Gospel, even when there was an evident response, did not always produce on the mission field the pattern of conversion that had been characteristic of Methodist preaching in the lands where Methodism arose.

This was not the experience of Methodists only. Calvinistic

evangelicals, and early Protestant missionaries who were overwhelmingly evangelical in origin, had exactly the same difficulty as Wesleyans. They saw signs which they could only interpret as a work of God (people were evidently "turning from idols to serve the living God"), but they did not have the marks which experienced pastors had long recognized as signs of true conversion. The reason probably lies in the nature of historic evangelicalism. Evangelicalism, whether Wesleyan or Calvinistic, arose in Christendom as a protest movement against nominal Christianity. It emerged in societies which claimed the Christian name, but neither understood the Gospel nor observed the practice it called for. Evangelicals, in fact, took Christendom for granted—a Christian civil society, an official profession. They were concerned for "real," over against "nominal" or formal Christianity.

In Fiji and Tonga, as in Samoa and Tahiti where the Calvinistic evangelicals of the London Missionary Society operated, there was no preexisting Christian civil society, no Christendom, no "nominal" Christianity to be confronted with the "real" thing. People were not convicted of failure to meet standards they had never professed or heard about. Many factors might lead them to the momentous decision to break with ancestral custom and with an ancestral cult and make a commitment to the Christian way of life, but these factors lay in the local situation and in accumulated local experience. Evangelical conversion as experienced in the West assumed Christendom. People were not converted from another religious system nor even ordinarily from unbelief, but from "nominal" to "real" Christianity. Where there was no Christendom, conversion followed a different itinerary. People in the non-Western world responded to the Gospel preached by missionaries from Britain and America, but not always to those missionaries' *experience* of the Gospel.[3]

There is one part of the world where distinctively Methodist attributes did determine the development of the mission, but in a manner accidentally, and with an outcome best described as ambiguous. In the Cape of Good Hope, as in the Pacific, Calvinistic missionaries of the London Missionary Society (LMS) preceded the arrival of Wesleyan missionaries. The immediate concern of the LMS missionaries being with the indigenous people, their relations with the European settler community, which identified itself as Christian, soon became tense.[4] The settlers' complaint was that missionaries were siding with "the heathen" over against "Christian people." Methodist mission origins in the Cape lie in a display of entrepreneurial evangelistic flair so often characteristic of Methodism. The first Wesleyan missionary seized the opportunity to assume pastoral responsibility for the first organized group of settlers from England, who came in 1820. These settlers, of humble background, landless, but industrious and enterprising, represented the very constituency which so often responded to Methodist preaching in England. They did so again in South Africa. Their interests were in direct competition with those of the Xhosa of the Cape frontier. The Wesleyan mission had been established in the first place to reach the Xhosa. From its earliest days the Cape mission found itself torn between its original aim of reaching Africans and the secondary task of responsibility for Europeans that it had acquired by acting according to characteristically Methodist standards. The story, however, is more about pragmatic compromise than missiological theory.[5]

Yet another approach to the topic might be through a group of Methodists who enriched missiological theory by helping to lay the foundations of a Christian scholarship that took seriously the investigation of the religious traditions of other faiths and of Christianity in the non-Christian world. Notable among them is Edwin W. Smith, son of a Primitive Methodist missionary in South Africa, himself a serving missionary in Zambia until ill-health forced him to Europe, where, without ever holding an academic position, he produced the pioneer academic studies of African religion and foreshadowed much later studies of the nature and importance of African Christianity.[6] A generation later, a serving missionary, Geoffrey Parrinder, began those studies of the religions of Africa which helped to give a generation of African Christian scholars the confidence to explore the structures of Africa's old religions that underlay its new religion.[7] W. E. Soothill, a missionary who became professor of Chinese at Oxford, showed the Christian relevance of the Chinese classics and saw the hand of God in the oldest religion of China.[8] The modest, retiring C. P. Groves became the Eusebius of Africa by writing four volumes on *The Planting of Christianity in Africa* which trace the story of Africa in Christianity from biblical times to 1954.[9] For most people, including the entire church history academy, this was the first indication that African Christianity had such a substantial history. Groves' colleague in the Selly Oak Colleges, J. Windrow Sweetman, produced a vast but uncompleted work on *Islam and Christian Theology*[10] which still provides one of the fullest comparative investigations of historic Christian thinking and Islamic thinking about God, informed by the sense that in all these centuries Muslims have not yet heard the Gospel in a way which can profit them.

These missionary scholars—the list could be much enlarged—belonging to and working within the Wesleyan tradition in missions, prepared the way for the liberation of western Christian scholarship from its Babylonian captivity. It is not obvious, however, that it was specifically Methodist influences that took them in this direction. One might perhaps make a case for a genuinely Methodist theology of mission in Eli Stanley Jones,[11] American interpreter between India and the Christian West; but like Freeman, Jones is an exceptional, not a representative figure.

All these routes to a Wesleyan missiological theory are thus possible, but difficult. For brevity's sake we take yet another way and center this study on an archetypally Methodist figure who was at the heart of official Wesleyanism for most of his life and who, though not a missionary, thought, spoke, and wrote much about missions and influenced their course within the Methodist connexion. He is surely a fair representative of the thinking of at least British Methodists of the generation after the death of John Wesley. That generation represents the period in which the Anglo-American Protestant missionary movement established itself and achieved stability.

I

Richard Watson was born in 1781 and died in 1833.[12] Like so many representative Methodists of the time, he came from an artisan background. His father was a saddler and he himself had served an apprenticeship as a joiner. Though he spent some time at a grammar school he was largely self-taught, but immensely well-read, an impressive preacher in a classical mold, and enough concerned with the analysis of current events to serve for a brief interval as a newspaper editor. These considerations make him a specially suitable choice for our purposes.

First, Watson was a genuine theologian, probably the first systematic theologian of Wesleyanism. His *Theological Institutes*, first published in three volumes in 1823,[13] was the textbook for the training of candidates for the Methodist ministry in England until well past the middle of the nineteenth century. Second, he was closely involved with Wesleyan missions. He was a leading figure in the creation of the "Methodist Missionary Society for the Leeds District," which led to the formation of the connexion-wide Wesleyan Methodist Missionary Society.[14] His sermon at the Society's inauguration in 1813 was printed and circulated with the fifty-page report that formed the prospectus of the Society.[15] This placed the overseas work of the Conference on a new and surer footing. Watson was one of the secretaries of the Society from 1816 until 1826, when he became President of the Conference. He returned to Society duties for awhile after his presidential year. He is, in fact, probably the most significant figure in the development of Methodist missions after Thomas Coke, whose missionary advocacy has been thoroughly described by John Vickers.[16]

Watson is very much a figure of the Methodist establishment, conservative by instinct and temperament, concerned to preserve Wesley's legacy in churchmanship as well as theology, anxious to maintain civil as well as ecclesial order. Jabez Bunting, also a keen supporter of the Missionary Society, was a personal friend and the *Institutes* are dedicated to him. By Watson's time, it was clear that the Methodist connexion was no longer, and could not be, a society within the Church of England. Watson did not see it as a free church either and acknowledged that in principle he was in favor of an established church.[17] He made free use of the Anglican liturgy, accompanying this with extempore prayer. He challenged those Methodists who criticized the use of the Anglican liturgy on the grounds of its familiarity and predictability to apply the same reasoning to hymnody and produce extempore hymns.[18] Politically, his instincts were equally conservative, though Stuart Piggin has sufficiently exploded the thesis of Bernard Semmel and others that the creation of the Missionary Society in which Watson was so prominent was a device agreed with government to channel the energies of Wesleyan enthusiasts into harmless activity overseas and away from potential troublemaking at home.[19] It is clear that the people who were concerned about missions overseas were, very largely, the people who were most concerned about the expansion of mission at home. This was certainly true of Richard Watson.

Watson is thus a good representative of Wesleyan missionary thinking in that formative period when Wesley had left the scene and the influence of Coke, who had long been the personal embodiment of the overseas missionary cause, was coming to an end. He was at the heart of the new institutional framework for missions being created within Methodism. Watson is also a viable source for theological investigation, for quantities of his sermons and sketches of sermons, as well as the *Institutes* and other published writings, are available. These include sermons preached for the Missionary Society and on other occasions related to missions. We also have specimens of his regular pulpit ministry.

Richard Watson's missiological concerns were not anchored in specific missionary proof texts, but arose from the biblical witness as a whole. There is no published sermon of his on the so-called Great Commission of Matthew 28:19, and his *Exposition of the Gospels of St Matthew, and St Mark* does not explicitly mention overseas missions in relation to this passage.[20] What he did there was to link verse 19 firmly with verse 18 ("All power is given unto me in heaven and in earth"), so that the command to teach all nations is rooted in "Christ's universal and unlimited dominion." His famous sermon at the inauguration of the Missionary Society expounded a passage he often used, Ezekiel's vision of the dry bones.[21] Some of his texts are surprising. The sermon, "Excitements to Missionary Effort," is based on the first six verses of Ecclesiastes 11.[22] This long passage is not a mere epigraph to the sermon. The preacher came back to it time and again, inculcating the missionary relevance of each of the six aphorisms it contains. If this is a very extended text for a sermon he made do with a very short one, even for a rather long sermon. A discourse for the Missionary Society on, "The Religious Instruction of the Slaves in the West India Colonies Advocated and Defended," has the simple text: "Honor all men."[23] He preached on "The Mission Field Admeasured," from as complex a passage as II Corinthians 10:13-16.[24] There he used the words, "But we will not boast of things unmeasured . . . having hope that when your faith is increased, we shall be enlarged by you . . . to preach the Gospel in the regions beyond you," as the basis of an argument. According to this, the general field that is measured out for preachers of the Gospel is the world. Particular parts of this general field are often marked out for "immediate and zealous cultivation" and the missionary spirit exemplified in Paul looks beyond these well-worked areas to areas unworked. Just as Paul hoped that Corinthian Christians would enable him to reach the regions beyond, so British Christians must enable the spread of the Gospel in the regions beyond them.

This "admeasurement" of the mission field (i.e., the world) illustrates the close connection in Watson's mind between overseas missions and the regular preaching of the Gospel carried out by Methodist preachers in England and elsewhere. His concern was not overseas missions in themselves. It was the widest possible proclamation of the Gospel. There was no hard and fast line between spreading the Gospel at home and doing so abroad. The confidence in what the Gospel can do abroad was supported by what it had already done at home.

Watson often adverted to Britain's pagan past, with its isolation and savagery, dwelling fondly on the sacrificial knives of the Druids.[25] Britain had no innate superiority over the heathen world.

The leading aspects of the Gospel as he himself preached it are those one would expect from a Methodist of his period. They are indicated in the titles of published sermons: "Christ Sealed by the Father,"[26] "The Fountain for Sin Opened,"[27] "The Results of Messiah's Death,"[28] "The Crucifixion,"[29] and "Glorying in the Cross."[30] When he preached on, "God would have all men to be saved," a text often used by promoters of overseas missions, he concluded with a direct appeal to those in the congregation who had hitherto resisted the will of God.[31]

II

Certain elements of Watson's theology are particularly noticeable in carrying his thought about missions. The first of these is *his strong and pervasive eschatology*, his sense of the coming consummation of the Kingdom of God and the visible establishment of Christ's rule. Typical sermon themes are, "The Destruction of Idolatry,"[32] "The Enemies of Christ Vanquished,"[33] and "The Coming of the King to Zion."[34] A sermon on the phrase in the Lord's Prayer, "Thy Kingdom Come," held before the listeners, "the splendour of the latter day glory beginning already to flame," and ended with a picture of missionaries going out to their laborious and frequently discouraging task.[35] The context in which Watson presented the missionary task was that of the coming victory of Christ to which events are already visibly moving. He had evidence that the consummation was on its way. The clearest sign of "latter day glory" was the impact, which was there for all to see, of missionary witness on the African peoples of the Cape of Good Hope, west Africa, and the West Indies.[36] Watson's eschatology is firmly historicist and traditional. He saw the fulfillment of Matthew 24:14, which proclaims that the end will follow the preaching of the Gospel throughout the world, in the evangelization of the Roman Empire in apostolic times and the fall of Jerusalem in AD 70.[37] He found the idea of a personal rule of Christ on earth from Jerusalem incongruous: "[T]he Kingdom of Christ is not to be displaced by any dispensation differing in its principle." This spiritual Kingdom was already immovably established.[38]

The second element in Watson's staple theology which undergirds his thinking and concern about missions is a traditionally Methodist one, *the universality of the Gospel appeal*, based on the universality of the Atonement. This is frequently applied to missions. The fact that God has made the whole human race "of one blood" (Acts 17:26) is linked with the fact that Christ tasted death for everyone (Hebrews 2:9).

> Behold the foundation of the fraternity of our race, howsoever coloured and however scattered. . . . There is not, then, a man on earth who has not a Father in heaven, and to whom Christ is not an Advocate and Patron; nay more, because of the assumption of our common humanity to whom he [that is, Christ] is not a Brother.[39]

The immediate reference in the passage above is to slaves in the West Indies. It is they, in particular, who had "a Father in heaven" and it is they to whom Christ is a brother. As has already been mentioned, the text for the sermon is, "Honor all men," (I Peter 2:17). In other words, Christians should honor the slaves on the plantations because they are human and, therefore, children of the heavenly Father and brothers of Christ, people for whom Christ suffered. Watson went further, analyzing the nature of the honor owed to slaves. Honor was more than formal courtesy. It involved estimation at the true value. The sermon gives two indications of the value of the Caribbean slaves which required such honor. One would come naturally to a Methodist preacher used to asserting the universality of the Gospel, i.e., the Redeemer's sufferings for them that indicate the true value of the slaves. The second indicator is their human potential—religiously, intellectually, morally—as revealed in their response to the Gospel. This indicator relates to another element in Watson's theology, the transformation of society by the preaching of the Gospel, a theme to which we must return.

A third feature of Watson's thinking which is regularly applied to missions is *the Christian duty of benevolence*. Time and again Watson cited this as a prime factor in missionary motivation. Selfishness is the degradation of human nature and part of its misery. When the Gospel is accepted it creates benevolence as the fruit of the humility and gratitude to God. "The first collection that was ever made for the poor was made in a Gospel church."[40] Furthermore,

> [W]hen we perceive his love in the ruin from which it has saved us; when we reflect on all it has purchased; and when we connect it with our souls, and God, and eternity; then we come under the influence of all the motives we can wish to feel, in order to produce true benevo-

lence, and to constrain us to act for our fellow creatures, till all the wants of all the men on earth are met. And this same principle shall keep men in a happy, unbroken society in the kingdom of God forever.[41]

This passage occurs in the preliminary argument of the sermon entitled, "Excitements to Missionary Effort," and the particular expressions of benevolence that Watson had in mind here relate to missionary work. He went on to adduce motives for missionary benevolence. These are related to hope, to fitness, and to human mortality.

[H]ow soon may all our sympathy for our fellow creatures be in vain! If those who are now within our reach, if those who are now in darkness, be not benefitted by an application of the means God has given us in his providence, "a great gulf" will soon be fixed, over which no pity, no exertion, can step. How important it is to do the work of the day in the day! ... We are dying, and the world is dying around us![42]

Christian benevolence is called for because of moral bankruptcy. "The great reason of Missionary efforts is the moral destitution of the world."[43] That moral bankruptcy is revealed in human religion apart from Christ. Watson believed that his generation had knowledge of the heathen that the intellectuals of an earlier time, misled by idealized pictures of noble savages or the wonders of classical India, did not have. The actual religion of the heathen had no God, no hope of immortality, no moral dynamic. It was full of superstition, immorality, and, above all, fear.[44] It is this aspect of fear, the lack of security in dealing with the spirit world, that comes uppermost when Watson expanded on this theme. Perhaps it is the obverse of the Methodist doctrine of assurance, the blissful knowledge of acceptance with God.

In the section of the *Theological Institutes* which deals with paganism it is clear that Watson had been reading the writings of the East India Company chaplain Claudius Buchanan whose descriptions of popular religion in Bengal reached a wide audience.[45] For good measure Watson added citations from Latin and Greek authors about classical pagan practices. He mentioned some Hindu schools and the atheistical tendency of some of them. In general, Watson saw non-Christian religion as an undifferentiated paganism which did not require complex classification.[46] Despite this dark depiction, however, he had no difficulty in recognizing that there are wholesome elements in non-Christian religion.

Nor do these create any theological problem for him. They represented the survival, to a greater extent in some communities, a lesser in others, of the patriarchal religion, the period before the Law was given to Israel. It should not be called natural religion because it, "was given by oral revelation to the Patriarchs and . . . was preserved by tradition," though soon mingled with human folly, vain philosophy, and vulgar superstition.[47]

The worst case of all was the religious condition of the slaves in the West Indies whose former religion had been broken up, leaving them with only disconnected practices with no coherent meaning. Thus, they have lost the spring both of hope and of fear. Since they had lost their system of belief, they had lost the intellectual stimulus that exploration of beliefs might give: "I am not sure, this life only being considered, whether the Negro would not be a gainer in intellect and quickened feeling by the introduction of some of the milder forms of Paganism itself."[48] Watson's understanding of non-Christian religion (all, of course, from literary sources) was thus more complex than appears at first sight.

The final strand of what one might call Watson's mission theology to be noted here is his insistence that *the reception of the Gospel transforms society*. It is a theme that recurs continually, often in the context of the moral destitution of society without the Gospel. He frequently adverted to institutions—legislative and educational—that are necessary, but limited in effectiveness. Indeed, his political conservatism arose from the low expectations he had of human benefit from political activity. The true spring of reformation is the Gospel, through its power to break down the isolating selfishness of humanity, release general benevolence, and create brotherhood.[49] This had been proven throughout history, in the Roman Empire, in barbarian Britain, and in the results of modern missionary activity. Watson saw a striking contemporary example of just such a transformation in the changes taking place in Caribbean society as a result of Christian preaching there. There had been an intellectual, a moral, and a social transformation. There were at least 10,000 pupils in Methodist schools alone and they compared favorably with English pupils at the same age in motivation and intelligence. Despite repeated hysterical claims that Christian teaching would inflame passions and create uncontrollable situations, the Christian slaves were quiet, sober, and industrious, gaining worldly respect and influence as a result. As a worshiping community the slaves were exemplary. The element of fear and hopelessness in the face of trouble, sickness, and death had been greatly reduced. Marriage, once almost unknown, and still not recognized in civil law, was widespread and stable family life developed. Even the white population was improving as a result. There were now pious planters who encouraged Christian ministry on their estates and supported mission work, though there were others who hated it. The free colored (i.e., mixed race) population shared in the social transformation and its women were particularly active in the work of the church, providing teachers and other agents and running the benevolent societies. A Christian civil society was growing up among an oppressed and utterly demoralized people and the transformation was having an effect upon the oppressors.[50]

III

The sermon from which much of the above detail is taken was preached in 1824.[51] Watson's ministry fell largely in the period between the outlawing of the British Slave Trade in 1807 and the abolition of slavery in the British dominions, achieved in 1833, the year of his death. The Caribbean plantations which presented to his view such a remarkable transformation of society were still being worked by slave labor, and planter resistance to what they saw as insufferable interference in their civil and property rights was unabated. So was their hatred of abolitionist propaganda and their association of it with the evangelical and, thus, the missionary constituency. Watson, a representative of that constituency, was pleading for the "religious instruction" of the African population of the Caribbean and declared it to be a prime aim of the Wesleyan Society. Such an aim could only be carried out with the cooperation, or at the very least, the acquiescence, of slave owners. Hence, Watson devoted much argument to showing that planters had nothing to fear from the pious, orderly, industrious, sober-living, family-oriented, literate community that the unfettered preaching of the Gospel would produce. Many slave owners thought they knew better and could produce evidence on their side of the case.

Caribbean slavery created a dilemma for early Protestant missions. On the one hand, there was a strong antipathy to slavery among evangelicals generally in which British Methodists shared. Wesley himself, unlike Whitefield, had declared against it. Watson was unequivocal on this subject. Slavery, he declared, "is a blot which cannot remain among the glories of Messiah's reign."[52] Poverty was a necessary evil, perhaps a corrective one, while slavery was an unnecessary and punitive evil. Treating human beings as property demoralized both slave and slave owners and was wholly incompatible within the Golden Rule. All Christian history since Roman times indicated that Christianity undermined slavery. Watson not only preached against slavery. Despite his general political conservatism, he campaigned publicly against it. Like Jabez Bunting he was an active member of the Anti-Slavery Society. On the other hand, Protestant missions were deeply involved in the Caribbean. Methodists were working there before the Missionary Society came into being.[53] The planters had the power to restrict, inhibit, or harass missionary activists and frequently exercised it. Mission policy, therefore, sought to distinguish the preaching of the Gospel from "political activities," and to insist that missionaries had nothing to do with the latter. At the same time they affirmed the political implications of their understanding of the Gospel. Thus, Watson could combine his unequivocal denunciations of slavery with a reasoned statement that planters had nothing to fear from missions. Christianity (he meant, of course, "real," Christianity, "inward religion," urged by the missionaries as distinct from the nominal variety widely practiced in white society) created orderly, sober, industrious, and responsible communities. In forty years of Methodist work in the Caribbean, not a single Methodist had been convicted of violent or subversive behavior.[54] He would have found more difficulty making such a case for Baptists. This argument was directed to slave owners to persuade them to allow their slaves access to the Gospel. Yet he maintained that Christianity undermined slavery and that slavery could not coexist with Christ's rule. Even as an *ad hominem* argument it may seem naive, but within the sermon a certain set of political expectations appear that place it in context. One is that slavery will certainly be abolished in the foreseeable future. This would make it sensible for the planters to adjust to the inevitable while they still had some freedom of action. In the light of this the colonial governments in the British West Indies had a responsibility to prepare the African communities for their new role and thus reduce the risks of a violent transition.[55] No doubt he expected the removal of slavery to come in stages. The growth of a Christian community would be the best preservative of order amid change. But political matters, he insisted, were no part of the Missionary Society's business. Their business was to preach the Gospel and build up the Christian community, the political effect of which would tend to produce a cultured, educated self-sufficient people.

IV

Beyond the *ad hominem* arguments, beyond slavery itself, there is a wider aspect of Watson's vision of the emerging church of the Caribbean. For Watson and his contemporaries, Afro-America was still part of Africa, an African population transported to the new world. Africa was the focus of much of the early Protestant missionary effort. Watson's days in the Mission House saw the opening of a mission in Sierra Leone (which was itself based on a preexisting church of African Methodists who had come from the American colonies arriving in Sierra Leone in 1792),[56] in Gambia,[57] and in the Cape of Good Hope. But of all Methodist missions, the oldest, the most encouraging, those with most visible fruit, were those in the islands of the Caribbean.

Watson saw the Caribbean churches as the first fruits of Africa's redemption.

> In those crowded congregations, in those spacious edifices, Ethiopia already "stretches out her hands unto God." . . . And the prophetic promise is dawning upon parent Africa also. Hottentots, Caffres, Boschuanas, Namaquas, Corannas, Griquas, in the south, Bulloms, Foulahs and Mandingos in the west, some of all your tribes are already in the fold and hear and love the voice of the great Shepherd. We hail you as our brethren![58]

These are the front ranks of vast millions of the peoples of Africa who would one day be joining in praise to the long-concealed but faithful God of Africa.[59]

Thus, even in the 1820s, Watson had a vision of a Christian Africa and saw the first signs of it in Afro-America. The vision was worked out in some detail with an interpretation of Africa's past glories and present miseries. Watson insisted strongly on a glorious past for Africa, using materials from both biblical and secular learning.

Watson identified the Africans of the past with the peoples known to the Hebrews as Cush, Mizraim, and Put.[60] He would have nothing to do with the interpretations which derived the Africans from Ham and thus subject to the curse of Genesis 9.25-27, often used to justify African slavery. With the possible exception of those inhabitants of North Africa of Punic origin, Africans were not the children of Ham/Canaan. Even if they were, Watson observed, that curse is abrogated in Christ, in whom all nations are blessed.[61]

The achievements of ancient Africa were mighty. Africans produced the great Nilotic civilizations, made Egypt fertile, and gave the world its first writing system. Africa produced heroes, bishops, and martyrs for the early church and in more recent times generals, physicians, mathematicians, and merchants. Why then, do we not see the same arts of civilization in Africa today? The answer is not in lack of capacity, but in the loss of cultivation through the movements of populations. It is noteworthy that Watson spoke of Ashanti and Dahomey as "semi-civilized" states. Many contemporaries reserved that term for India and China, and saw Africa as living in unrelieved barbarism.[62]

At the present time, Watson continued, Africans were "the most unfortunate of the family of men." They had been uniquely harshly treated as the history of slavery demonstrated. They were also consistently traduced and insulted. White savages sneeringly devalued their humanity for the sake of protecting profit. Pseudoscientists claimed to be able to demonstrate from skull measurements that they were a lower race.[63] Perverted exegesis burdened them with the curse of Ham. Yet through all this, despite all the ill usage they had suffered from others, Africans had been remarkably patient and unaggressive. They had not employed their overwhelming superiority in numbers against their oppressors in the Caribbean.

Watson's picture of Africa is a triptych: a magnificent past; a brutalized, miserable present; and a rapturous glimpse of a future in the Kingdom of God. He believed he could already see the dawn of that future, most clearly in the Caribbean which was at once the shame of Christendom and earnest of Africa's redemption. The psalmist's vision of Ethiopia "stretching out her hands to God" was endlessly echoed through the nineteenth century by missionaries and the friends of mission, and above all by Christian Africans. It was clearly articulated early in the century as part of a comprehensive and coherent view of the continent, by Richard Watson, one of the quiet molders of Wesleyan missions, who in the days of brutal slavery found, "Honor all men," to be the fitting text from which to proclaim African dignity.

V

Mission is a learning experience. Methodists, like other missionaries, began the task of world evangelization by doing the things they had always done in the ways they had always done them. Gradually, they realized that the realms they were entering were not charted on any intellectual or religious maps in their possession. Faith required them to go forward, but it would not be enough to clothe old things in the old ways. They must find new ones. It is in such experiences of present frustration, wrestling with the conviction of future certainty, that missiology develops.

Watson represents an early stage of the modern Protestant missionary movement and a very early stage of its engagement with Africa. He was long enough at the Mission House desk to realize that the missionary task, far from one of triumph, was regularly laborious and frequently discouraging. But, while fully recognizing the frustration, he retained the conviction of final certainty with its basis in the Scriptures, and its evidences, modest but unmistakable, in the mission field.

It is easy to point to the areas for which Watson, a particularly well-read, thoughtful Methodist of his day, has no intellectual or religious maps. The issue of what we now call culture, and see at the heart of many missiological concerns, was not on the horizon in Watson's day. For him, the clearest indicator of the Christian future of Africa was the evident capacity of Africans to absorb western "civilization." A later generation was to discover the important Christian significance of the indigenous cultures of Africa, but Watson campaigned against powerful commercial interests working for the degradation of Africans. The evidence of African abilities to absorb western culture served well in that campaign. Watson's reasoning was simple: those abilities derive from the common humanity of Africans and Europeans. He went on to assert that full humanity must be within the sphere of Christ's redemption. Full humanity implies the possibility of full salvation.

The culture issue had to wait on the language issue. It is remarkable how little Watson talked about language and translation.[64] In the Caribbean, where he saw the brightest beams of dawn, the language in use was English (sometimes in modified form). Even in west Africa only modest progress of the study of African languages had been made during his lifetime. One of its pioneers died a little before he did. Hannah Kilham designed Africa's first vernacular literary program. Though a practicing Quaker, she had deep Methodist roots.[65] Only after long wrestling with language could missionaries, let alone missionary secretaries, discover that language was but the outer skin of the complex network of consciousness we now call culture.

Watson's political theology was constrained, as political theologies usually are, by an estimation of contemporary realities. He was a leading figure in the Connexion at a time of national emergency when critics of Methodism claimed Methodists as disturbers of civil order when it was manifest that they had breached ecclesiastical order with which civil order was linked in the minds of many. He also concurrently denounced slavery as the enemy of Christianity and sought to convince slave owners that they had nothing to fear from the spread of Christianity. Perhaps he never fully reckoned with the principalities and powers. We may think his view of the relations of Gospel Christianity to social progress both naive and inconsistent, but his insistence on the intellectual, social, and economic concomitants of Gospel preaching is a pointer to what in our own is often called holistic mission. He never lost sight of the central affirmations of a Methodist preacher which must surely underlie any missiology that claims to be Methodist: the message of salvation through Christ is universal in its application and salvation involves practical holiness.

Notes

1. On Freeman see Allen Birtwhitstle, *Thomas Birch Freeman, West African Pioneer* (London: Cargate Press, 1955); Paul Ellingworth, *Thomas Birch Freeman* (Peterborough, England: Foundry Press, 1996); and F. L. Bartels, *The Roots of Ghana Methodism* (Cambridge, England: Cambridge University Press, 1965). Freeman's *Journals of Various Visits to the Kingdom's of Ashanti, Aku, and Dahomi in Western Africa*, 2nd ed 1844 was reissued with an introduction by Harrison M. Wright, (London: Cass, 1968).

2. See, e.g. Thomas Williams, *Fiji and the Fijians; and Missionary Labours among the Cannibals, Extended, with Notices of Recent Events by John Calvert*, ed. George Stringer Rowe (London: Hodder and Stoughton, 1870). (The earlier editions separated these two volumes.) See also *Diaries and Correspondence of David Cargill, 1832-1843*, edited with an introduction and annotations by Albert J Schütz (Canberra, Australia: Australian National University Press, 1977).

3. Cf. Andrew F. Walls "The Evangelical Revival, the Missionary Movement and Africa," *Evangelicalism: Comparative Studies of Popular Protestantism in North America, the British Isles, and Beyond*, ed. M. A. Noll, D. W. Bebbington and G. A. Rawlyk (New York: Oxford University Press), 310-30; see also Andrew F. Walls, *The Missionary Movement in Christian History* (Maryknoll, N.Y.: Orbis, 1996), 79-101.

4. Cf. Ido H. Enklaar, *Life and Work of Dr. J. Th. Van der Kemp 1747-1811* (Rotterdam and Cape Town: Balkema, 1988) and Andrew Ross, *John Philip*

(1775-1851): Missions, Race, and Politics in South Africa (Aberdeen: Aberdeen University Press, 1986).

5. William Shaw, the first missionary, gives his account in *The Story of My Mission in South-Eastern Africa, Comprising some Account of the European Colonists, with Extended Notices of the Kaffir and other Native Tribes* (London: Adams, 1860), and W. D. Hammond-Tooke, ed., *The Journal of William Shaw* (Cape Town: Balkema, 1972). See also Richard Elphick and Rodney Davenport, eds., *Christianity in South Africa: A Political, Social and Cultural History* (Berkeley: University of California Press, 1997), and Norman Etherington, *Preachers, Peasants and Politicians in Southeast Africa 1835-80* (London: Royal Historical Society, 1978).

6. Smith's output was prodigious. There is a study by Malcolm J. McVeigh, *God in Africa: Conceptions of God in African Traditional Religion and Christianity* (Cape Cod, Mass.: Stark, 1974).

7. On Parrinder, see Ursula King, ed., *Turning Points in Religious Studies: Essays in Honour of Geoffrey Parrinder* (Edinburgh: T and T Clark, 1990); Martin Forward, *A Bag of Needments: Geoffrey Parrinder and the Study of Religion* (Bern, N.Y.: P. Lang, 1998); and Andrew F. Walls, "A Bag of Needments for the Road: Geoffrey Parrinder and the Study of Religion in Britain," *Religion* 10 no. 2 (1980): 141-50.

8. Cf. William Edward Soothill, *The Hall of Light: A Study of Early Chinese Kingship* (London: Lutterworth Press, 1951).

9. C. P. Groves, *The Planting of Christianity in Africa* (London, Lutterworth Press, 1948-1958). See *Biographical Dictionary of Christian Missions*, ed. Gerald H Anderson, (New York: Macmillan, 1998), 265.

10. J. Windrow Sweetman, *Islam and Christian Theology*, 5 vols. (London, Lutterworth Press, 1945-1967).

11. Among appraisals of E. Stanley Jones, see R. W. Taylor, *The Contribution of E. Stanley Jones* (Madras: Christian Literature Society for Christian Institute for the Study of Religion and Society, 1973).

12. The fullest biography of Watson remains the earliest, Thomas Jackson, *Memoirs of the Life and Writings of the Rev. Richard Watson, Late Secretary to the Wesleyan Missionary Society* (London: John Mason, 1834). This became Volume 1 of the Collected Works. *The Works of the Rev. Richard Watson* were published as a twelve-volume set by John Mason, the Connexional Book Steward, between 1834 and 1837, though the series does not include some of his best known works. Except where otherwise stated, this edition has been used for citations here.

13. Reprinted in four volumes, vols. IX-XII of the Collected Works; references in this article are to this edition.

14. See George G. Findlay and W. W. Holdsworth, *History of the Wesleyan Methodist Missionary Society* vol. 1 (London: Epworth Press, 1921-1924), 45ff.

15. *A report of the principal speeches delivered at the formation of the*

Methodist Missionary Society, for the Leeds District. To which is added a speech delivered by the Rev Richard Watson . . . (1813).

16. John A. Vickers, *Thomas Coke, Apostle of Methodism* (London: Epworth Press, 1969); and *Thomas Coke and World Methodism* (Bognor Regis, England: World Methodist Historical Society British Section, 1976).

17. Watson, *Works*, II, 119. Cf. Watson, *Works*, VIII, 121-32.

18. Watson, *Works*, XII, 74.

19. Stuart Piggin, "Halévy Revisited: The Origins of the Wesleyan Methodist Missionary Society: An Examination of Semmel's Thesis," *Journal of Imperial and Commonwealth History* 9 no. 1 (1980): 17-37.

20. Richard Watson, *Exposition of the Gospels of St. Matthew and St. Mark, with Notes on Some Other Parts of Sacred Scripture* (London: John Mason 1833), 319-20.

21. "Ezekiel's Vision of the Dry Bones." Preached in Albion Street Chapel, Leeds, at the formation of the Methodist Missionary Society for the Leeds District, 6 October 1813. This is the first sermon in the *Collected Works* (Watson, *Works*, vol. II, 1-19).

22. Watson, *Works*, II, 352-70.

23. Watson, *Works*, II, 88-130.

24. Watson, *Works*, III, 455-70.

25. Eg., Watson, *Works*, II, 17, 356.

26. Watson, *Works*, III, 306-18.

27. Watson, *Works*, III, 375-78.

28. Watson, *Works*, III, 385-91.

29. Watson, *Works*, III, 392-400.

30. Watson, *Works*, III, 55-66.

31. Watson, *Works*, III, 419.

32. Watson, *Works*, II, 478-95.

33. Watson, *Works*, II, 302-16.

34. Watson, *Works*, III, 163-81.

35. Watson, *Works*, III, 189-206.

36. Cf., Watson, *Works*, II, 125f.

37. Watson, *Works*, III, 233-39.

38. Watson, *Works*, III, 405.

39. Watson, *Works*, II, 89.

40. Watson, *Works*, II, 354.

41. Watson, *Works*, II, 355.

42. Watson, *Works*, II, 361.

43. Watson, *Works*, II, 478.

44. See *Institutes* part 1, chapters 6-8, "State of religious knowledge among the heathen; "State of morals among the heathen"; and "The religions of the heathen." Watson, *Works*, IX, 60-96. See also Watson, *Works*, IV, 213, part of a sermon on "The Remedy for the World's Misery": "In proportion as the

knowledge of these principles which are embodied in our Revelation have faded away from the human mind, nations have become, in every sense, more disordered and miserable. . . . China alone affects to be an exception. But we begin to know that country better than formerly. The fables of infidel writers respecting it begin to be detected; and as we know, by dint of being driven to examine the subject, how to appreciate the character of the 'virtuous Hindoos'; so will the virtuous Chinese ere long be stripped of their assumed excellencies."

45. On Buchanan, see Allan K. Davidson, *Evangelicals and Attitudes to India 1786-1813: Missionary Publicity and Claudius Buchanan* (Abingdon, England: Sutton Courtenay Press, 1990).

46. In Watson, *Works*, VIII, 4, however, he views Islam, like Romanism, as a corrupt form of Christianity. This is a review in the *Wesleyan Methodist Magazine* of William Lawrence Brown, *A Comparative View of Christianity and of the Other Forms of Religion* . . . See Watson, *Works*, VIII, 3-17 and *Institutes* part 1, chapter 5, "The origin of these truths which are found in the writings and religious systems of the heathen" (Watson, *Works*, IX, 33-59).

47. Cf. Watson, *Works*, IV, 212: "The progenitors of all nations lived in the patriarchal times, and they knew much of the truth of God. This was not lost all at once; but as it was lost, political society became more miserable."

48. Watson, *Works*, II, 112. Elsewhere he raises the question whether the "worst forms of Christianity" are more corrupting of society than complete paganism. He concludes, however, that while "Popery perfected by Jesuitism" is more subversive of morality than Islam or any known form of heathenism, it has been counteracted in practical Catholic countries by vital Christianity. "The truth, therefore, which has always existed in Popish countries, has maintained some moral control," and shed more charity, mercy and purity among the unsophisticated peasantry than pagan or Muslim countries know. Watson, *Works*, VIII, 5f.

49. Watson, *Works*, II, 106ff. Cf. Watson, *Works*, II, 10: "When Christianity is introduced, civilization follows of course. . . . Religion is the most efficient instrument of civilization."

50. Watson, *Works*, II, 108-17, 121-23.

51. Watson, *Works*, II, 88-130.

52. For Watson as anti-slavery campaigner, see Jackson, *Memoirs* (Watson, *Works*, I, 398, 400, 527, 533).

53. See, e.g. Findlay and Holdsworth, *History* vol. II; and more recently, John Saillant, "Antignan Methodism and Antislavery Activity: Anne and Elizabeth Hart in the Eighteenth Century Black Atlantic," *Church History* 69 no.1 (2000): 86-115.

54. Watson, *Works*, II, 111.

55. Watson, *Works*, II 117ff. Watson's earlier battles on this issue can be seen in *A Defence of the Wesleyan Methodist Missions in the West Indies* published in 1817 in reply to literary attacks. Republished in Watson, *Works*, VI, 421-533.

56. On this church, and its relations with the WMMS, see Andrew F. Walls, "A Christian Experiment: The Early Sierra Leone Colony" in *The Mission of the Church and the Propagation of the Faith* ed. G. J. Cuming (London: Cambridge University Press, 1970), 107-30.

57. The nearest approach to a history of Methodism in the Gambia is Barbara Prickett, *Island Base: A History of the Methodist Church in the Gambia, 1821-1969*. ([Gambia]: Methodist Church, 197?).

58. Watson, *Works*, II, 126.

59. Watson, *Works*, II, 126.

60. Watson, *Works*, II, 94.

61. Watson, *Works*, II, 95ff.

62. On Africa's glories, see Watson, *Works*, II, 92-95.

63. On the "petty philosophy" which sees Africans as a "missing link" between apes and humans, and its theological implications for "the covenant of grace, and that fraternity which the Scriptures have extended to the whole race of Adam." See Watson, *Works*, II, 90, 94.

64. Cf. Watson, *Works*, II, 10: "[T]here are but few, very few, perhaps none, of the Heathen so completely savage as not to be able to comprehend the main doctrines and duties of Christianity, when once their language is understood by their teachers." As is usual at this period he sees language as essentially an obstacle, and the main obstacle, to be overcome, and assumes that once it is overcome, missionaries will be able to proceed as they would at home. Cf. *Works*, II, 366: "[W]hile we are waiting for [profound scholars and excellent linguists] God is raising up linguists on the spot; and while we are considering and scheming, the word of God gets translated into the language of the land; and words spoken from the hearts of men who know little of worldly science are spoken to the heart; and Christian churches . . . arise."

65. She was the widow (though her married life was very short) of Alexander Kilham, founder of the Methodist New Connexion. See Sarah Biller, *Memoir of Hannah Kilham* (London: Darton, 1837) and Mora Dickson, *The Powerful Bond* (London: Dobson, 1980).

4

Earthly Food at the Heavenly Banquet: Revitalizing the Historical Wesleyan Love Feast For Evangelism and Discipleship In Global Missions

Robert Danielson

Food is not just our primary source of life and energy, it is also material culture imbued with symbolic meaning which plays a powerful role in building community, clarifying identity, and establishing the boundaries of a society. Religious community, identity, and society are not immune from the prominent presence of food. The Buddhist prohibition on eating meat, the Muslim and Jewish dietary laws, the Hindu reverence for the cow, and even modern New Age vegan movements, all serve as ways to categorize people and identify individual levels of belief and obedience. A religious community which abstains from eating pork can identify itself as a "good" Jewish or Muslim community, but within this group are subgroups where the degree of dietary strictness may define one's personal level of piety in relation to one's community.

Christianity launched a religious dietary revolution with its eventual abandonment of the traditional Jewish dietary laws and sacrificial system. However, the Christian community, individual piety, and the understanding of a Christian religious society did not escape from the symbolic power of food. Rather, for the Christian faith, one meal, primarily symbolized by bread and wine, became the focal point of the faith in symbolism and ritual. Over time, the forms and symbolic power of the eucharistic meal have become solidified and rigid, encompassing the Mediterranean forms from which these symbols evolved. As long as Christianity remained geographically European or Mediterranean, these forms conveyed meanings somewhat parallel to those meanings given by Jesus and interpreted by the early church fathers. Unfortunately, these meanings did not remain as constant as the forms during the geographical spread of Christian mission. The forms of bread and "the fruit of the vine" had become so solidified in church tradition and Christian belief that little room for change existed.

The Eucharist, like other aspects of the Christian faith, has become part of the tug-of-war which exists in missions between the local indigenous nature of the church and the global universal nature of the Body of Christ. Nowhere has this been more evident than in Africa and Asia, especially among Christians from highly sacramental traditions. This paper hopes to examine the love feast in the history of Wesleyan missions and to understand how a revival of this uniquely prominent tradition can play a key role in bridging this tension and increasing Methodist mission effectiveness in a more contextual manner.

I

The Moravians revived the love feast at Herrnhut in 1727 and were responsible for influencing John Wesley, who attended his first love feast in Savannah on Monday, August 8, 1737. While the Moravian love feast may have begun as a full meal, over time it became "a symbolic meal of a sweet roll or cookie and coffee or chocolate."[1] The River Brethren and Dunkard traditions, which also developed from the Moravians, kept the love feast as a simple full communal meal, usually of soup, sandwiches, and fruit. At the end of December 1738, John Wesley recorded the first Methodist love feast of the Fetter Lane society in his journal. This powerful experience, which lasted beyond 3:00 AM, involved a symbolic sharing of water and bread. The focal point of the love feast within the Wesleyan tradition was on the sharing of individual experience through personal testimonies. The food elements were not a rigidly essential part of the early Methodist love feast. So, the meal was mostly symbolic and peripheral. Baker noted, "The physical ingredients of the meal among the Moravians at first were bread and wine, though the wine was later replaced by tea in order to make the Agape quite distinct from the Eucharist. Similarly in the Methodist usage the beverage has usually been water (and occasionally tea), shared from a two-handled mug passed round from hand to hand. The food has varied from bread or biscuit to semi-sweet buns."[2]

Unlike Mediterranean Europe, wine was not a staple drink in Britain or other northern European nations where Christianity spread. The selection of alternative drinks by German Moravians and British Methodists, as a replacement for wine, demonstrated a minor contextualization in the Christian ritual meal. This additional religious meal opened the door for some level of flexibility given cultural or geographic limitations. Thus, middle or lower class Methodists could reinforce their religious identity and piety with the more culturally meaningful water, rather than wine. This was not without precedent, however. Andrew MacGowan has pointed out that the historic Christian ritual meal was much more diverse then previously thought.[3] Accounts or suggestions exist in which elements such as water, milk, honey, cheese, oil, salt, vegetables, and fish may have been used in the early church. The primary requirement in the early church, according to MacGowan, appears to be a radical opposition to possible links to the Roman sacrificial rites, so that all red meat and for many groups even wine was prohibited.

Theologically, Methodists separated the sacramental Lord's Supper from the nonsacramental love feast. However, this boundary has always been rather vague and ill-defined. I would argue that for the common person of faith no such line existed. Rather, the love feast became more of a contextualized Eucharist which created and strengthened the religious community of early Methodists and helped to clarify one's individual level of piety through the act of participation in the love feast. This assertion is supported by the close guarding of the love feast from non-Methodists. Communion may have been "open" to other denominations in Methodist history, but the love feast was strictly private and limited to Methodists in good standing and very serious seekers.[4] Especially on the frontiers of the United States and in the regular quarterly meetings of the Methodists, participation in the love feast proclaimed one's identity and membership in the Methodist community. In the early days of Methodism, many believers had to rely on sympathetic Church of England ministers for the celebration of the Lord's Supper. However, more often than not, these people were excluded from the sacrament. Baker recognized the early Methodist need for a substitute sacrament, which was often located within the love feast. He wrote:

> When Methodists were repelled from the Lord's Table, or when their isolated position made communion extremely difficult, the love-feast could almost become a substitute for Holy Communion. This process was forwarded by the fact that there was no ecclesiastical obstacle to

prevent laymen like Wesley's Assistants from conducting love-feasts, though they were long prevented from administering Holy Communion.[5]

As Methodists entered the mission field they took the uniquely Methodist practice of the love feast with them. By 1830, references to the love feast could be found in accounts from the Caribbean,[6] Sierra Leone,[7] India,[8] and South Africa.[9] Easter weekend in 1835 saw the introduction of the love feast into Ghana.[10] By 1840, references could be found in Liberia,[11] New Zealand, Fiji, and other Polynesian islands.[12] On 9 October 1858 the first Methodist love feast was held in Fuzhou, China. The first Japanese love feast was celebrated on 2 October 1875 in Tokyo.[13] Guanajuato, Mexico held their first love feast 19 June 1877.[14] By 1900, numerous references existed in journals and memoirs from almost every corner of the globe, adding Swaziland, Nigeria, and the Gold Coast to areas where the love feast was already being practiced. Most of the accounts make no mention of the elements used in the meal. The traditional elements of water and bread were probably the rule. However, some interesting exceptions do come to light. The account of a love feast in Bombay, India on 1 April 1872 recorded:

> We did not introduce the custom of taking a little bread and water at the love feast. . . . I could not claim Scriptural authority for introducing a ceremony so closely resembling the sacred feast ordained by the Master, so I administered the sacrament of the Lord's Supper at the love-feast instead. The time may come when we may bring food to our fellowship-meetings, to supply the need of the multitude of poor persecuted saints, and revive the real "agape," or ancient love-feast, instead of a commemorative ceremony of it . . . but in these days of ritualistic ceremonies, and in this country of heathenish feasts, having the opportunity of breaking new ground, we just quietly leave this ceremony out.[15]

In the example from Fuzhou, China, one of the missionaries wrote:

> The furnishings of the [love] feast were somewhat peculiar. Wishing to train our converts to self-reliance in such matters, we instructed the brethren to provide the symbols of brotherly love for the feast. They were unanimously of the opinion that tea should take the place of cold water, and as bread, such as foreigners use it, is not used here by the Chinese they proposed a small kind of cake as a substitute for it. We approved of the arrangement, and accordingly the stewards served the meeting with cakes and tea instead of bread and water.[16]

It is interesting to note that there are few other references to an Indian love feast. Speculation leads us to believe that neglecting the love feast in India may have less to do with "heathenish feasts" and more to do with the strict caste structure and strongly held taboos regarding eating with other castes and from common plates. It is also important to note that the Chinese contextualized love feast was not a one-time event. Another account recorded a love feast in Kucheng, China in 1877, almost twenty years later, where the elements consisted of "sweet cake and tea."[17]

Few references exist to the elements of the love feast in mission for two main reasons. First, the food was less a focal point than the testimonies given by believers at the feast. This is why the Indian example is still referred to as a love feast. Accounts from Africa and the Caribbean seem to indicate that the testimonies at love feasts were very lively and inspiring. It is often in this context that references to the love feast even appear in mission sources. Secondly, with the exception of the previously mentioned accounts in China and India, the love feast appears to have remained unchanged in the mission context. Bread and water were used in Ghana, and probably in almost every other case noted. Thus, there is no need for more comment on the ritual by the participants. For example, an account from Argentina in 1861 even noted the traditional use of admission tickets for love feasts, as do other accounts.[18]

As can be seen in the early examples from Methodist mission history in China especially, both inculturated love feasts and the traditional sacrament of Communion existed side by side at the quarterly meetings. Historically, the love feast often preceded Communion, and it also appears that it was more flexible in the food items selected to symbolically represent the feast. Therefore, even if I am correct in arguing that the love feast was itself a contextualized form of Communion, there is solid historical support that both the love feast and the Eucharist can exist simultaneously. If fact, they should not be separated because part of the function of the love feast is to point to Holy Communion

II

If the love feast is indeed closely tied to the practice of the Lord's Supper, then it is important to examine how Christian mission has dealt with the food elements in the sacrament as well. The initial question of what elements could or should be used for Holy Communion must have caused a great deal of concern in areas where Western bread and grape wine or juice were unavailable or even unknown. In China, when Methodist missionary Samuel Pollard was asked by a sick missionary colleague to serve Communion, he recorded his response, "A couple of Chinese cups, a small pot of tea, and a Chinese biscuit were all we needed. These I brought up the ladder on a small Chinese cardboard tray of a bright red colour. We never use wine for our sacrament, but nearly always plain weak Chinese tea."[19] This problem was not limited to Methodists alone. Kessler recorded the content of several letters received from Presbyterians in China. He wrote that on the mission outstations, "the missionaries might bring makeshift communion provisions from Jiangyin-raisins to be stewed into wine and soda crackers to be broken up for bread."[20]

As these brief and extremely rare insights into Protestant eucharistic practices demonstrate, there was no commonly accepted norm for what elements were acceptable. When the elements are not mentioned, it is probably safe to consider that Western bread and wine or grape juice was utilized if possible. However, it is equally probable that some random common element was chosen, such as Pollard's tea and biscuit. Many may also have tried to find closely related substitutes, such as the Presbyterian use of stewed raisins and soda crackers, neither of which is common to the Chinese diet. This is likewise true of the Methodist love feast in mission. Only the rare exception of the Methodists in Foochow, China, seems to extend to an inculturation of the love feast, but when the same description goes on to mention the Lord's Supper served later that same day, no comment is given on the eucharistic elements. No serious theological reflection, except perhaps on the part of the Chinese converts at the love feast (which was hardly a feast by Chinese standards), appears to have taken place. As we face the increasing globalization and multicultural nature of the church, this minor issue is appearing more frequently in the works of two-thirds of the world's theologians. Inculturation is a growing issue of concern in missiology, and sooner or later we must deal with this issue at the sacramental level in world mission.

Model One (below) may help to demonstrate the traditional understanding of the Eucharist in a mission context. Note that the traditional model is outward through the traditional Jewish form, heavily interpreted by Western theologians. As such, the historical Mediterranean forms of bread and wine are viewed as sacrosanct and unchangeable, as if revelation included the forms of food used at the Last Supper as well as their symbolic meanings. The Eucharist is seen as originating with God and spreading unidirectionally. The Roman Catholic view of transubstantiation added to this traditional view making any change in the physical substance almost impossible. While some change in interpretation of the symbolic meaning behind the forms of bread and wine has occurred, the forms have remained relatively static. The

Earthly Food at the Heavenly Banquet

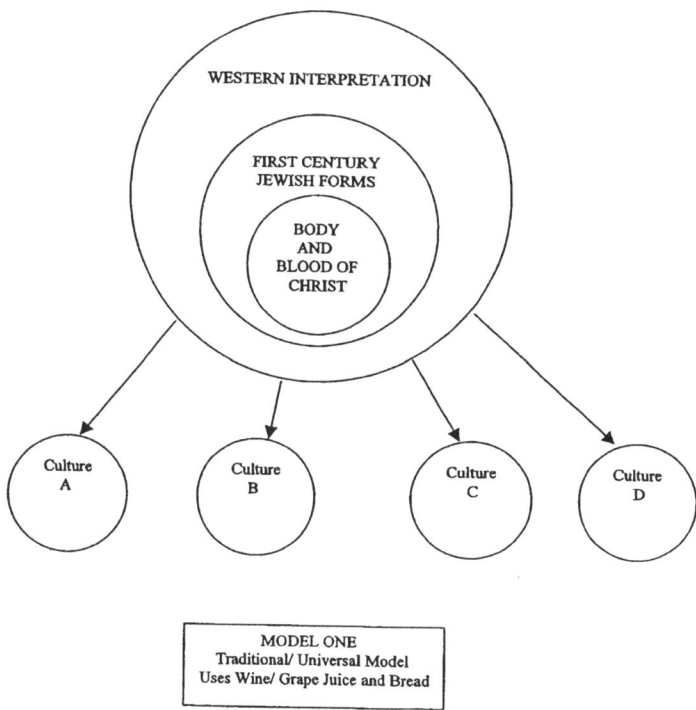

symbolic meanings of the Jewish Passover feast have shifted to the sacrificial meanings of the Eucharist and even more recently to the memorial meal of Holy Communion, but the forms of bread and wine have seldom changed. Unfortunately, missions have often neglected to realize that food is highly symbolic and thus the introduction of foreign substances such as bread and grape wine in Africa and Asia send mixed and confusing symbolic messages. Often the Eucharist becomes something magical or incomprehensible and the original message of the sacrament goes unheard or is ignored. As Japanese theologian Masao Takenaka put it:

> [Westerners] tend to consider wheat, or bread, as the symbol of daily food everywhere. But to many Asian people bread is a foreign product. It comes from abroad. We Japanese had never seen this kind of food until the Portuguese missionaries and traders brought it to our country about the middle of the sixteenth century. In fact, we still use the Portuguese term for bread, pan, in Japanese. The most popular indigenous food has been,

and still is, rice. We like rice.[21]

III

Recent studies by cultural anthropologists[22] and social psychologists[23] have pointed out the power of food and food symbols in creating community and identity. Beyond its nutritional importance, food is highly symbolic culturally, especially to agriculturally based and hunter-gatherer based economies, where the food supply may be more uncertain. Most missionaries emerged from complex economic societies where food was readily available. In such societies, food symbolism and meaning is primarily personal, at best a minor regional occurrence, at worst totally irrelevant. Missionaries entered cultures where food is of primary importance and is vital to the culture as well as the life of the people. For the missionaries, the elements of bread and wine or grape juice had only minor traditional significance, but for many indigenous Christians, this new food was foreign or even magical.[24] Food does carry powerful meaning, but most missionaries did not recognize this. If missionaries attempted any inculturation of the eucharistic species it was usually accidental, with more thought being given to the form than to the symbolism behind the chosen elements. However, with the growth of ideas such as indigenization, inculturation, and contextualization in mission, the traditional model was bound to be challenged.

In the early 1970s the Catholic bishops of Chad and Cameroon took a bold theological step in replacing the wheat bread and grape-wine of the Eucharist with the local staples of millet bread and millet beer in Chad, and cassava and palm wine in Cameroon. Bishop Dupont of Chad was subsequently removed from his office and these contextual experiments were ended.[25] In Asia, Filipino Catholic theologian, Anscar J. Chupungco wrote:

> Time and again the question of using native food and beverage for the Eucharist has been raised in regions where wheat and grapes are not grown and importation has become difficult. The use of wine becomes even more problematic in Buddhist countries where devout Buddhists take offense at the public drinking of alcoholic beverages. Religious culture has branded wine a thing of vice and the Christian cup of salvation has become a cup of malice.[26]

Rome responded aggressively to such ideas by declaring that the elements must consist of only wheat flour and water and pure grape wine.[27] Further clarification by Cardinal Joseph Ratzinger, the Prefect of Vatican Congregation for the Doctrine of the Faith, dated 19 June 1995, suggests that bread must contain wheat gluten and wine must contain wine alcohol, and thus, those who may be allergic to wheat gluten or who suffer from alcoholism may not be admitted to holy orders.[28] However, this has not stopped the theological debate on this issue.

African theologian A. Mampila notes, "Whatever material element is used it signifies not only itself, but refers to the labor through which Christians cooperate in building the present world. Africans too would like to bring an offering to signify their intention to be united with Christ's sacrifice, to offer him the world that is theirs, to express their participation in the Eucharist."[29] Various arguments have been made for and against the inculturation of the communion elements. Key to this problem involves the view of wheat bread as "white man's bread" and its resulting connotations of colonialism and an ecclesiastical elitism expressed from the church in Europe and North America.

While this issue has been discussed among some African scholars, it is of great importance to the practice of Christianity worldwide. The World Council of Churches issued a text in 1986 titled, "Baptism, Eucharist, and Ministry." Over several years, various national churches and church leaders responded to the text and the responses are very interesting. The Melanesian Council of Churches responded positively, pointing out the cultural significance of coconut milk and sweet potato as well as traditional ceremonies such as the Fijian kava ceremony which may provide useful parallels to Communion.[30] The Theology Committee of the National Council of Churches in Korea also responded in a positive manner with the use of rice cakes and rice wine, also suggesting veneration of the ancestors may take place in an indigenized "koinonia feast."[31]

Earlier efforts at inculturation had been tried in Asia. One foreign missionary in Hong Kong wrote to me,

> I readily recall my earliest years as a HK Methodist missionary (1966). We were anxious to move towards a "Chinese" version of the Eucharist, or at least a HK version. We thought the answer was with tea and mantous (a steamed roll). We did this in a number of local churches (once for Worldwide Communion Sunday) and gradually learned most of "this" was coming from the outside. We also quickly realized we were talking about "form" and not substance/meaning.[32]

The problem with this type of inculturation is that outsiders were attempting to maintain a Western form and simply replace the elements with close parallels, rather then actually theologize about the cultural meaning of the food symbols. In 1984, Chinese theologian C.S. Song took a more symbolic and indigenous approach to the same issue. Celebrating with a bowl of rice, he wrote, "That Communion reminded us more strongly than ever before of the fact that rice is life. Rice is not merely the material substance we eat. Rice is life-substance. It is life-power. It embodies the sum-total of Asian humanity."[33] Choosing "Green Bamboo Leaf" wine for the sacrament, Song says,

> Just as rice, bamboos are rich in meaning for the life of Asian people. Asia is blessed with an abundance of bamboos. Asia without bamboos is less than Asia. Bamboos give Asia its beauty, poetry, vitality and tenacity.... They can also become a parable of resistance to the repressive powers that infringe upon people's conscience and trample down their humanity . . . it dawned on us that the bamboos, swaying, bending and cracking in a storm but springing back to life in good time, pointed to the body broken and the blood shed on the cross. It also pointed to the new life that was to rise from the tomb after three days.[34]

Song's experiment does not seem to have caught on in Asia, in part because Asian cultures are highly traditional and look for an historical validation for such efforts.

This indigenizing concept has been put into practice on the African continent in many ways. Most noticeable are the indigenous churches which have proliferated in many areas of Africa. Perhaps the most carefully thought out Communion was conducted by the Kimbanguist Church of Zaire on 6 April 1971, fifty years after they were founded. This was not an accidental afterthought. Serious debate about the elements had been under way for years prior 1971. Finally, the elements chosen were a bread made from potatoes, maize, and bananas and a drink made from honey and water, each element a cultural or biblical symbol with indigenous meaning.[35]

David Power, in his book *The Eucharistic Mystery*, writes, "One necessary preliminary to the association of Eucharist with cultural models would be to allow the people to bring their own lives and life struggle to the table in the food and drink that their earth and their hands provide. In this way, they would be blessed in Christ's memory in their own lives and commune with his body and blood in the transformation of the symbols of their own existence and life-world."[36] This concern is one of the strongest arguments posed by African writers on this subject. Can Christ only be present in foods of a Mediterranean or European origin? Can Christ be African or Asian? While the theology of the Incarnation clearly claims the universal relevance of Christ for every culture, limiting the eucharistic species to wheat bread and grape wine clearly runs contrary to our theology and sends mixed and confusing symbolic messages tinged with the sin of

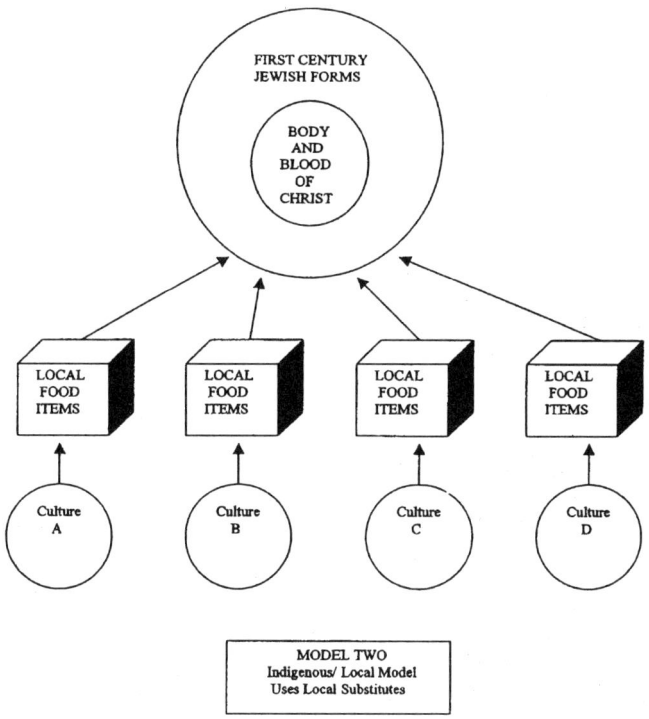

MODEL TWO
Indigenous/ Local Model
Uses Local Substitutes

colonialism, racism, and ethnocentrism. As can be seen, the question of the Incarnation is not the only difficulty. Other deeply disturbing questions of the equality of people, the value of indigenous staple foods (and thus the value of the people themselves) in the eyes of God, and the value of people's common everyday existence is at stake. In a world where colonialism has been cast off, where multiculturalism and equality are fast becoming normative, the symbols of the church have failed to keep pace.

Model Two (above) demonstrates the inculturation model for the Eucharist. Like the traditional model it is also unidirectional. However, this time the direction is reversed. In this view of the Eucharist, the sacrament originates with human beings, who bring their gifts and their very lives to God who in turn sanctifies them for the use of the church. Thus, the forms of bread and grape wine become an insult, arguing that only food typical of the Mediterranean world is suitable, or even acceptable for God's use. If God does not accept our food as a symbol of the Word incarnate, can God possibly accept us as a people? The implications of such a question are obvious and these types of questions seriously undermine the traditional model of the Eucharist in world mission. However, the incarnational model is also not without its critics.

Portuguese Catholic missionary Jose Antunes da Silva has stood opposed to such attempts at inculturating the eucharistic species.[37] Of his numerous arguments, one especially stands out. He argues persuasively that the use of culturally diverse elements will lead to difficulties in conveying the unity of the Body of Christ. Likewise, in his book, *Towards a Theology of Inculturation*, Aylward Shorter writes, "Bread and wine, as the common food and drink of first-century Palestinians, have cultural connotations. If they are to be replaced in cultures where such forms of food and drink are unknown by less unfamiliar and more available materials, it can be asked how far one can go before symbolism and reality are invalidated and the link with the historical Christ severed."[38] There is not enough time to debate all of the historical and scriptural arguments raised both for and against inculturation. Suffice it to say, the strongest argument lies with the tension between the local and global nature of the Body of Christ. Does inculturation undermine the universal nature of the church?

Random selection of food elements for the eucharistic species often fails to take into consideration the previously existing meanings which these foods carry. Instead the focus is on something like bread and wine in form, most likely which can be broken and shared quickly in a large gathering. Perhaps it is time for meaning to take precedence over form in this arena of the church. But here we run into de Silva's troubling arguments about the universality of the church. Rev. Ewing Carroll, the Hong Kong missionary quoted earlier, responded to Song's indigenous Eucharist this way,

> I'm not at all certain Green Bamboo Leaf wine and rice are the best representatives of an Asian contextualization. For instance, Northern Chinese, whose diets appear more attuned to wheat than rice, might take issue with you. Southern Asia certainly has tons of rice, but recall how many Indians eat *chapatis* (or something akin). While I'm far past my earliest Florida Methodist roots when it comes to "the unfermented juice of the grape," there would be those who would push for non-alcoholic tea. But then, which kind of tea?[39]

The difficulty with any type of inculturation at the indigenous church level, is that the universal nature of the church is endangered. Local forms of the Eucharist highlight diversity within the Body of Christ, but cross-cultural worship could become more difficult. It is also possible that greater divisions and infighting will occur among Christians of different ethnic or national origins. Rice and green bamboo leaf wine or tea may highlight the meanings of the Eucharist for some, but it constantly runs the danger of distancing the Asian church from the church in other parts of the world.

What alternatives can be found to answer this dilemma? So far, the first two models seem to be seriously flawed. The incarnational message of Jesus Christ is lost in the traditional model of the Eucharist in missions. Random selection of eucharistic elements usually tried to maintain traditional Western forms, but lost the essential meaning of the biblical sacrament, by ignoring the relevance of local food symbols. While indigenous theologians and religious leaders seem to have surpassed the obstacles of the traditional model, capturing the meaningful symbolic use of food to make Christ a reality within a different culture, they are in danger of losing the universality of Christ. The church is one body, the Body of Christ, but how can all of these issues be brought into one central sacrament?

IV

So, how does the historical Methodist love feast help answer these tensions between the global and local aspects of the Body of Christ? Some might argue it is an outdated and defunct ritual, which may be interesting in an academic way, but has no real relevance. However, I would like to propose the Methodist love feast as a valuable tool for bridging the gap between the traditional and inculturation models of the Eucharist in mission. Methodism and the Brethren traditions alone offer a dualistic model, which might meet both needs. Traditionally at quarterly meetings, both Lord's Supper and love feast were held, one element pointing to the vertical relationship between God and humanity and the other emphasizing the vertical dimension of human community. This model offers a strong historical tradition, which could overcome the suspicions of highly traditional cultures like the Chinese who shy away from modern interpretations of Holy Communion. Yet this model allows for creative and meaningful contextualization to occur, which may solve many of the issues raised by African and Asian indigenous theologians.

The Eucharist, in Model Three (below), comes both from God and from the offerings of the people. The love feast becomes an incarnational form of Communion, while the traditional elements remain as a constant reminder of the universality and historical origins of the Body of Christ in the world. The theology of both the traditional and indigenous models are reinforced and upheld by this model. Symbolically, the connection of the Eucharist with the real meal in any culture, will open bridges for discipling and evangelizing through the Eucharist. When we ask relevant questions about why cassava is important to some Africans or what

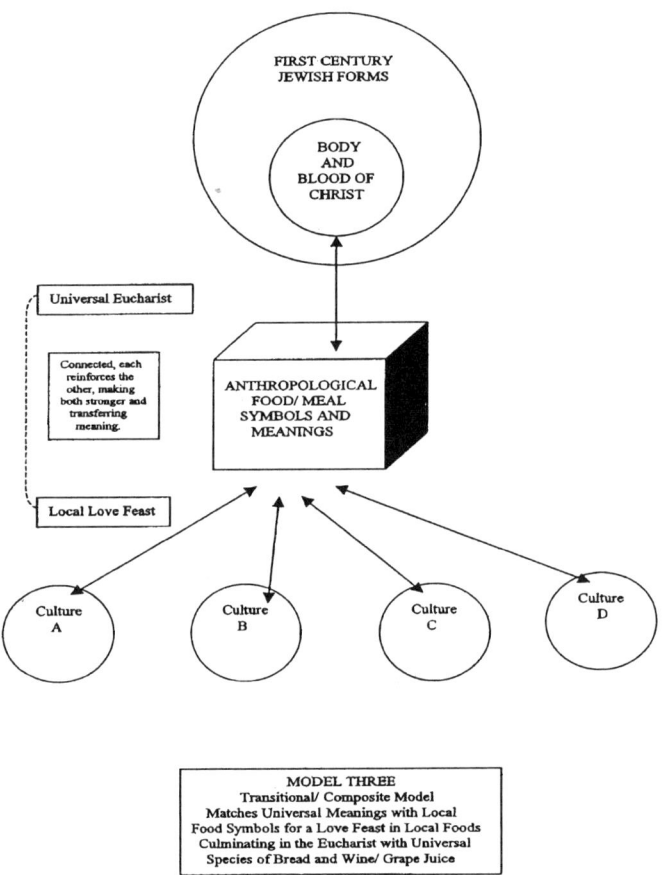

symbolic importance rice holds in Japan, we are creating avenues for local Christians to understand the meanings Christ intended when breaking the bread, rather then perpetuating a form with no meaning at all. Such food questions are the heartbeat of evangelism and discipleship. What would it mean for Christ to announce, "I am the rice of life," to a Chinese person, or "I am the sweet potato of life," to an indigenous native of the South Pacific?

Some question the use of the sacrament for evangelism and discipling depending on various denominational theologies. However, Methodist theology stands firmly behind this idea. From the foundation of Methodism, the Lord's Supper has been viewed as both a confirming and converting ordinance. This opens the possibility for utilizing the Eucharist for both discipling and evangelism. Currently little or nothing is being done in developing methods of reaching seekers through the powerful symbolism of food, nor are modern congregations being taught about basic theological truths through these same powerful symbols. Food teaches at an experiential level. I have seen flavors, tastes, and smells transport people to different times and places as they relate food to their personal memories and experiences. I have also seen healing, reconciliation, and restoration occur over the table. It is almost impossible to share food with an enemy, yet sharing food often creates incredibly close-knit communities.

Yet the local church is not an isolated unit. We must never allow a passion for inculturation to divide and split the Body of Christ. For this reason, the universal elements of bread and fruit of the vine remain essential. What better way to visualize the universal church than to perceive it as a common family at the same table. Our Wesleyan heritage has provided us with the tools necessary to have our cake and eat it too! We have both a universal Eucharist and a contextualized love feast, as well as a theology of open communion which welcomes serious seekers as well as long-time believers to the feast. It is time for the table to become a teaching tool rather than a passive decoration, a tool which makes Christ relevant to all of our brothers and sisters who are drawn to the table, a tool which teaches the Incarnation powerfully and symbolically, yet which also draws the global body of Christ together at a common meal.

V

In conclusion, the love feast is not only a historically valid expression of the Christian ritual meal, it is also theologically supported by the Methodist tradition, but it is in need of reform if it is to function effectively in global missions today. It can be a major key to solving the local and global tensions surrounding the Eucharist, but it must become more open to inculturation and it must become part of regular eucharistic practice, not an occasional addition. The flaw of the traditional model, which denied the Incarnation of Christ through the locally available foods, is now overcome through a culturally diverse and contextually flexible love feast, where Christ can be meaningfully incarnate in the communal meal. The problem of trying randomly to select eucharistic elements but maintain the form of the Lord's Supper, is solved by consciously choosing food elements which are culturally relevant and spiritually symbolic for the love feast, and allowing total contextualization for the love feast while maintaining a universal form for the Eucharist. The indigenous model, which leans toward ignoring the universal nature of Christ, is corrected by maintaining a universal type of Eucharist and eucharistic species for the Lord's Supper. Thus, Jesus is both incarnate in every culture and universally relevant through a dual type of sacrament. This dualistic sacrament is steeped in historic church tradition and also carries a great deal of potential for evangelizing, discipling, and healing divisions. Both the intimate and ultimate natures of God are held in tension and communicated symbolically through the powerful language of food and food customs.

Perhaps the vision of the prophet Isaiah best summarizes the goal of both love feast and Eucharist in mission,

> In Jerusalem, the Lord Almighty will spread a wonderful feast for everyone around the world. It will be a delicious feast of good food, with clear, well-aged wine and choice beef. In that day he will remove the cloud of gloom, the shadow of death that hangs over the earth. He will swallow up death forever! The Sovereign Lord will wipe away all tears. He will remove forever all insults and mockery against his land and people. The Lord has spoken! (Isaiah 25:6-8, New Living Translation).

May our meals become a powerful appetizer for this banquet!

Notes

1. Jonathan R. Stayer, "An Interpretation of Some Ritual and Food Elements of the Brethren Love Feast," *Brethren Life and Thought* 30, no.4 (1985): 200.

2. Frank Baker, *Methodism and the Love Feast* (New York: Macmillan Co., 1957), 15.

3. Andrew MacGowan, *Ascetic Eucharists: Food and Drink in Early Christian Meals* (Oxford: Clarendon Press, 1999).

4. Lester Ruth, *A Little Heaven Below: Worship at Early Methodist Quarterly Meetings* (Nashville, Tenn.: Kingswood Books, 2000).

5. Baker, 66.

6. Isaac Whitehouse, "Jamaca,—Extract from the Journal of Mr. Isaac Whitehouse," *Missionary Notices* (November 1826), 168. See also "St. Christopher's —Extracts of a letter from Mr. Cox, dated Oct. 12, 1825," *Missionary Notices* (July 1826), 107.

7. "Montserrat,—Extracts from a Letter and Journal of Mr. Wood," *Missionary Notices* (May 1828), 460.

8. "Trincomalee,—Extract of a Letter from Mr. Percival, dated Dec. 26th, 1827, including Extracts from his Journal," *Missionary Notices* (November 1828), 545.

9. B. Shaw, "Khamies Berg,—Extracts from the Journal of Mr. B. Shaw," *Missionary Notices* (May 1826), 69. See also "Extracts from the Journal of Mr. Davis, dated Graham's Town, (continued),"*Missionary Notices* (April 1828), 438-39.

10. F. L. Bartels, *The Roots of Ghana Methodism* (Cambridge: Cambridge University Press, 1965), 16.

11. J. M. Reid, *Missions and Missionary Society of the Methodist Episcopal Church* (New York: Phillips and Hunt, 1879) 1:184.

12. John Waterhouse, "Extract of a Letter from the Rev. John Waterhouse, dated Mangungu, May 19th, 1840," *Wesleyan Missionary Notices* (December 1840), New Series 1 (24): 397-98. See also John Waterhouse, "The Rev. John Waterhouse's Second Journal," *Wesleyan Missionary Notices* (February 1844), New Series 2 (62): 461, 473-74.

13. J. M. Reid, *Missions and Missionary Society of the Methodist Episcopal Church* (New York: Hunt and Eaton, 1896), 3:426.

14. Reid, 3:373.

15. William Taylor, *Four Years' Campaign in India* (New York: Philips and Hunt, 1875), 178-79.

16. R. S. Maclay, "China," *Missionary Advocate* 14, no. 12 (1859): 89.

17. J. M. Reid, 2:10.

18. Reid, 1:272.

19. Samuel Pollard, *Tight Corners in China*, 3rd ed. (London: Henry Tooks Publishing, n.d.), 81-82.

20. Lawrence D. Kessler, *The Jiangyin Mission Station: An American Missionary Community in China 1895-1951* (Chapel Hill: University of North Carolina Press, 1996), 107.

21. Masao Takenaka, *God Is Rice* (Geneva: World Council of Churches, The Risk Book Series, 1986), 16-17.

22. Most notably the early work of Claude Levi-Strauss in the volumes *of The Introduction to a Science of Mythology*, *From Honey to Ashes* (New York: Harper and Row, 1973), *The Raw and the Cooked* (New York: Harper and Row, 1975), and *The Origin of Table Manners* (New York: Harper and Row, 1978). This has been followed by the work of Mary Douglas, including "Deciphering a Meal," *Daedalus* (1972), 101:61-81, "Food as a system of communication" from *In The Active Voice* (London: Routledge & Kegan Paul, 1982), 82-124, and *Food in the Social Order: Studies of Food and Festivals in Three American Communities* (New York: Russell Sage Foundation, 1984). Additional work has included Gillian Feeley-Harnik's *The Lord's Table: The Meaning of Food in Early Judaism and Christianity* (Washington, D.C.: Smithsonian Institution Press, 1994), as well as Margaret Visser's *Much Depends on Dinner* (Toronto: Harper Perennial, 1986) and *The Rituals of Dinner* (Toronto: Harper Perennial, 1992). A more recent work is by Daniel Sack, *Whitebread Protestants: Food and Religion in American Culture* (New York: St. Martin's Press, 2000).

23. Cf. Paul Rozin, "Social and Moral Aspects of Food and Eating," in *The Legacy of Solomon Asch: Essays in Cognition and Social Psychology*, ed. Irvin Rock, (Hillsdale, N.J.: Lawrence Erlbaum Associates, 1990); L. Miller, A. Fiske and

P. Rozin, "The Social Meaning of Sharing Food in the United States," *European Journal of Social Psychology* 28 (1998): 423-36; and Judith Friedlander, Paul Rozin, and Raymond Sokolov, "Everyday Life: Ordinary Pleasures, Rituals and Taboos," *Social Research*, 1999, 66 (1).

24. Darrell Whiteman, *Melanesians and Missionaries* (Pasadena, Calif.: William Carey Library, 1983).

25. Elochukwu E. Uzukwu, "Food and Drink in Africa, and the Christian Eucharist," *AFER (African Ecclesial Review)* 22, no. 6 (1980): 370; Aylward Shorter, *Toward a Theology of Inculturation* (Maryknoll, N.Y.: Orbis Books, 1988), 65; and Joseph G. Donders, "We Should Take a More Catholic View of the Eucharist," *U.S. Catholic* 61, no. 2 (February 1996): 29.

26. Anscar J. Chupungco, *Cultural Adaptation of the Liturgy* (Ramsey, N.J.: Paulist Press, 1982), 71.

27. Sacred Congregation for the Sacraments and Divine Worship document, *Inaestimabile Donum: Instruction Concerning Worship of the Eucharistic Mystery* 1980: A8.

28. Donders, 28-29.

29. A. Mampila, "Eucharist without bread and wine?" *Theology Digest* 34, no. 2 (1987): 133.

30. Max Thurian, ed., *Churches Respond to BEM: Official Response to the "Baptism, Eucharist and Ministry" Text* (Geneva: World Council of Churches, 1988) volume five, Faith and Order Paper no. 143: 182.

31. Thurian, volume six, Faith and Order Paper no. 144: 137.

32. Rev. Ewing W. Carroll Jr., 14 April 1999, personal correspondence.

33. Choan-Seng Song, "A Bowl of Rice with Green Bamboo Leaf Wine: An Account of the Theological Seminar-Workshop I," *The East Asia Journal of Theology* 2, no. 2 (1984): 181.

34. Song, 181-82.

35. Max Thurian and Geoffrey Wainwright, *Baptism and Eucharist: Ecumenical Convergence in Celebration* (Geneva: World Council of Churches, 1983), Faith and Order Paper no. 117, 231-34.

36. David Power, *The Eucharistic Mystery* (New York: Crossroad Publishing, 1992), 341.

37. Jose Antunes da Silva, "Bread and Wine for the Eucharist: Are They Negotiable?" *AFER (African Ecclesial Review)* 34, no. 5 (1992): 258-71.

38. Shorter, 65.

39. Carroll, personal correspondence with the author, 14 April 1999.

Part II

5

Catholic and Protestant, But Missionary: John Wesley's Explicit and Implicit Ecclesiology and the Methodist Mission in Latin America

Jose Míguez Bonino

My interest in Wesley's ecclesiology was not primarily awakened by academic reasons but rather by what one could call contextual or experiential concerns. I had always seen Wesley's theology as determined by the doctrine of sanctification. I still think this is the key, whatever other subjects may have demanded his attention. But two issues led me to look at his ecclesiology. The first, around the 1950s and 1960s, had to do with our (Protestant, Methodist) relation to the Roman Catholic Church. As all Latin American *evangélicos* I grew up in a permanent, frequently aggressive and even violent, theological, missionary, ethical, political confrontation with Catholicism.[1]

In the late 1950s some of the echoes of the biblical and theological renewal in European Catholicism began to arrive in Latin America. As the new decade opened under the leadership of John XXIII the ecumenical movement, to which Methodism was committed, was unavoidably involved in dialogue with the Roman Catholic Church. I was personally included in the World Methodist Council's observers at the Vatican II Council.[2] Could Wesley's understanding of the church help us, not so much in terms of his own view of Catholicism but in his ecclesiology, to face this new situation? On a more internal level, later in the 1970s, my church, the Argentine Evangelical Church (IEMA), was confronted with internal conflicts which threatened to end in a schism. That did not happen, but it led me to look back to earlier conflicts and to ask the question as to whether there was something in Wesleyan ecclesiology which prevented the kind of schisms that other evangelical churches were suffering. Naturally, my concerns in both cases did lead me to look at certain aspects of what I will call the explicit and implicit ecclesiology of Wesley. I will try to: (1) sketch what I understand by this implicit and explicit Wesleyan view of the church; (2) relate it to our relation to the Roman Catholic Church; and (3) address the problem of internal conflict in the church. This will be only a sort of outline which would require much more study to complete.

I

A study of ecclesiological issues in the time of Wesley can only be understood in relation to the challenges posed by the spirit of modernity and the social and economic changes that would, in the eighteenth and nineteenth centuries, shake all the established churches of Europe. A new model of the church was also emerging in the United States which the Wesleyan awakening, possibly unaware, helped to produce. The Church of England, in the nation where the Industrial Revolution began, was especially affected.

Writing in 1778 to Mary Bishop, daughter of a Quaker leader who was trying to think through her relation to the Church of England, Wesley strongly asserted his fidelity to his church: "God surely has raised us up for the Church, chiefly that a little leaven may leaven the whole lump."[3] He retained this view until the very end. In 1763 he strongly reminded his Methodist preachers that they had an obligation of "going to the Church," and that all the faithful should "constantly go to the Church and receive the sacraments in all occasions," to be "warned against all scorn of the prayers of the Church." Furthermore, they should be careful "not to call [the] Church our Society" or to call our preachers "ministers."[4] He faithfully quoted the definition of the church in the Thirty-nine Articles (see Article XIII). When he finally came to terms with a new Methodist "church" in the United States, he offered her a synthetic version of the Articles on the church, sacraments, and ministry. There is no point in quoting the hundreds of times where Wesley strictly followed the definition of the church, worship, and the sacraments that he found in the Church of England.

There are, however, two important directions in Wesley's implicit and explicit ecclesiology which are worth noting. The first has to do with a tendency to underline certain aspects of the understanding of the church. In *An Earnest Appeal to Men of Reason and Religion,*[5] he explained the three requisites included in the Anglican definition of the church: "a living faith, without which . . . there can be no Church at all," "preaching, and consequently hearing, the pure Word of God, else that faith would languish," and "the sacraments—the ordinary means whereby God increases faith."[6] In his sermon, "Of the Church,"[7] he followed the same line of explanation: "faith . . . a sure trust and confidence in God." The quotations could be multiplied, almost *ad infinitum*. There is clearly a dominating emphasis on the *"fides qua creditur,"* faith as living trust, and a certain hesitance to apply too strictly a doctrinal test. Commenting on the sentence, "the pure Word of God," he was reminded of churches and confessions—he mentioned specifically the Roman Catholic Church—whose preaching and administration of the sacraments he could hardly recognize as "pure" or "duly" done, but which he "would not dare to exclude from the Church Catholic." In a "Letter to various ministers" written in 1764,[8] he drew a distinction between "essential doctrines," those which constitute the message that must be proclaimed to the world (original sin, justification by faith, and sanctification of the heart and life) and "opinions," "expressions," or "external order," the function of which is nourishment (including things for which he fought as in the opposition between Arminianism and double predestination). In these areas, he said, diversity of doctrine can be admitted because it does not harm the basic thing: the common witness of the Gospel before the world and common worship in the larger congregation. Nobody has a right to separate from the church on doctrinal grounds unless, on the basic points, "sinful terms of communion" were imposed—which to him arose for the Reformers of the sixteenth century.

On the basis of these emphases on living faith and the apparent minimizing of the doctrinal and sacramental interpretation, it would be easy to classify Wesley's ecclesiology as pietistic and subjectivist, basically the "sect type" in Troeltsch's terms. Other features would strengthen this interpretation. In the already quoted sermon, "Of the Church," Wesley wrote: "The Church is called holy because it is holy, because each of her members is holy, even though in different degrees." Nevertheless, it is not possible so easily to catalogue Wesley's ecclesiology as subjectivist. Side-by-side with these traits must be placed the numerous attitudes and statements that underline an objective understanding of the church. In the first place, he does not exclude from the church those Christians who he himself calls "nominal" or those who have only "the form" but not the "power" of faith.⁹ Summarizing, while there is no doubt that Wesley wanted to define the church by the maximum rather than by the minimum—justification and sanctification—he was not willing to restrict the membership only to those who are conscious of these gifts. The church continued to be for him an open place where the grace of God objectively present in the ministry, and above all in the sacramental ministry, is made accessible to men and women in order to lead them to the full maturity of sanctification which is the purpose of redemption.

We must pose here the debated question of Wesley's separation from the Church of England insofar as it sheds light on our problem. Wesley was very explicit in his insistence on not separating from the Anglican church. This was the decision reached at the first preacher's Conference in 1744. A separation would contradict the very purpose for which the Methodist societies existed, namely "to awaken our brethren."¹⁰ A series of measures were taken in order to avert the possibility of separation and to tie more firmly the Methodists to the Church of England, e.g., the insistence that preachers and people would attend the church, that Methodist meeting places would not be called "meeting houses," or the Methodist societies called "churches." Other similar measures were enjoined as late as the Conference in 1763.

All through these statements and resolutions runs, nevertheless, a conditional mood. "We will not separate from the Church . . . unless we are expelled from it." We shall do everything possible to avoid separation, "but we cannot with a good conscience neglect the present opportunity of saving souls while we live." It would be contradictory of the very purpose of the Methodists to leave the Church, but "if we must separate from it or be silent, *actum est*! We have no time to trifle."¹¹ There was a price which he was not ready to pay, even for the sake of unity, "I know that God has committed to us a dispensation of the Gospel: yea, my own salvation depends upon preaching it. If then I could not remain in the Church without omitting this, without desisting from preaching the Gospel, I should be under necessity of separating from it or losing my own soul."¹²

It was the consciousness of urgency and constriction that made it impossible for him to renounce lay preachers and that impelled him to break ecclesiastical canon law forbidding him to preach or minister in a territory in which he had no jurisdiction, which led him finally to the debated and momentous decision of consecrating a "superintendent" for America.

We reach here the end of this summary of Wesley's ecclesiology. We could summarize our brief and incomplete search by saying as follows. (1) Wesley shaped his doctrine of the church on the basis of the classic Protestant and Anglican definition in terms of faith, preaching the Word, and administering the sacraments. (2) These elements are, nevertheless, in tension in Wesley's conception. On the one hand, a living faith, a conscious faith, attested by the Spirit and active in love, is underlined as the requisite for belonging to the church. Thus, a strong pietistic element is introduced. But on the other hand, in Catholic fashion, a larger membership related to baptism and the Eucharist is recognized and a similar tension is introduced in relation to the question of doctrine. (3) The question of "order," which we have not discussed, enters in a subordinate way in his definition of the Church. He accepted the ministerial structure of the Church of England as the most convenient, scriptural, and reasonable, but not the only possible or essential structure. However, when strict obedience to church order threatened mission he believed he had received from God, he did not hesitate to break with order. The point at which he faced this decision was not the question of doctrine but that of mission. We find, therefore, a classical Protestant ecclesiology, with pietistic and Catholic elements, placed entirely in the context of an evangelizing passion.

A very decisive historical phenomenon took place here. In a situation in which "authority" was the most debated and underlined ecclesiological feature, Wesley called the Church to enter the modern world as a missionary force, proclaiming the freedom and the power of the Gospel. The church was not ready to answer to this call and separation was precipitated. But, beyond this historical circumstance, he introduced a tension within the scope of his ecclesiological vision. Perhaps without fully realizing it, he placed all these elements—the purity of order, sacramental practice, and above all ecclesiastical order (we could say "canon law"), at the service of an evangelizing proclamation. Such an act introduces a tension in classical Protestant and Catholic ecclesiology, which is conceived in terms of the inner life and order of the church rather than in her outgoing mission. Probably, Wesley did not perceive the seriousness of the problem. Conservative and Tory that he was, he thought that his whole movement could fit in the framework of the traditional conception of things. This tension has plagued and blessed Methodism ever since.

II

At the crest of the missionary wave in the nineteenth century, Wesley's claim carried imperialist overtones. In fact, as Bernard Semmel has shown,[13] the Methodist shift of emphasis from social concern to overseas mission, is far from free of such tendencies. It is impossible not to hear it in as prominent a Methodist leader as Richard Watson's "enthusiasm." Christianity in England, Watson said, is prepared for "her great assault upon the Heathen world . . . now darkened and corrupted by the grossest Idolatry." For that purpose God's providence was awakening missionary zeal in a nation with a powerful navy and overseas colonies. He continued, ". . . [this] coincidence, between our duties and our opportunities, our wishes and our means, cannot be overlooked. . . . It is the finger of God pointing out our way." British ships were carried by "[God's] winds to every clime." They bore "not only our *merchandise*, but our *Missionaries*; not only our *bales*, but our *blessings*. . . ."[14]

For Wesley, however, it meant that the claim of the new poor crowding at the edge of the cities all over the country to receive the liberating word of the Gospel could not be denied or subordinated to ecclesiastical jurisdictions. He would respect all the laws and institutions of his church, but not at the price of resigning the mandate of the Lord to carry the good news to the whole creation.

This ambiguity is present in Christian missions in Latin America. By the mid-1850s the Methodist, and other mainline Protestant churches, were present in several Latin American countries. The absolute prohibition of any non-Roman Catholic religious expression which had been in force since conquest and colonization began to break under the liberal governments which wanted to introduce the new countries to the modern world.[15] But the international missionary movement which found its first institutional expression in the 1910 Edinburgh World Missionary Conference considered Latin America to be outside its jurisdiction. It was already a Christian territory. Therefore, it could not be represented at the Conference. Other religio-political considerations played a role in this decision, but it was clear that it could not be sustained for a long time. Churches which were present in Latin America were already in dialogue and finally a Congress was held in Panama in 1916.[16] In all this process, British and North American Methodist churches had a leading role. The long and careful discussions of the relation of these mission churches to the Roman Catholic Church would deserve a much more precise study. Although aware of the somber aspects of the role of the Roman Catholic Church in the conquest and early evangelization of the continent and of the negative

Catholic and Protestant, But Missionary

aspects of the popular religion it had created, the Conference never denied the Christian significance of the Roman Catholic Church, nor claimed to replace it. The claim to have a legitimate place in the Christian mission to Latin America turns around two foci. First, evangelization is still incomplete. There are large sectors of the Latin American population which have not been actively incorporated into the Christian faith and practice. These would be the "nominal Christians" whom Wesley addressed. In this sense, Protestant missions could play a similar role to the Wesleyan societies. Naturally, if such relation turned out to be impossible in Britain, it was totally unthinkable from the start in Latin America. Second are the social conditions of the people—poverty, lack of education, the condition of children, health needs, etc. Here, Panama dared to hope for cooperation. The following quotation shows the dominant attitude:

> A religious approach to Latin America by evangelical forces, just to the degree of cogency of its justification, is likely to find cooperation with our Roman Catholic brethren difficult, for every approach on our part is likely to be met by churchly conservatism and exclusivism, and not infrequently by aggressive opposition. Nothing should be imposed upon these peoples, but they should be given an intelligent opportunity to exercise freedom of choice in the form of religious faith. To withhold from them the fullest knowledge of evangelical principles would be to deny them their rights.
>   On the other hand, the religious and social needs to be dealt with are so widespread, so complex and so deep seated that the evangelical forces must have the help, not only of each other but of all those individuals and groups . . . who recognize these needs and are ready to take any step . . . towards cooperation. . . . Moreover, among the laity of the Roman Catholic Church there is a growing element which regard the evangelicals with no animosity and would even welcome a participation in the struggle for the betterment of social, civil and religious conditions of all who name the name of Christ.[17]

Although these statements are ecumenical, it is clear that the Wesleyan dialectic is at work here. Nothing can come between the religious need of the people and the freedom to evangelize, to invite them to faith and a new life. This was, now in modern terms, defined by the principle of freedom of religion. On the other hand, over against the blank rejection of Catholicism as heretical and perverse, which has been rampant in Latin American evangelicalism, there is a recognition, critical, to be sure, of its legitimacy, and an invitation to dialogue and cooperation. For spiritual, social, cultural, and political reasons which would be interesting to analyze, what was a utopian dream in 1916 has become a difficult, but real possibility and even reality in our time. The Methodist ambiguity which was frequently interpreted, not without some reason, as lack of courage and conviction, opens new possibilities in the quest for responses to the social and religious needs of our people.

III

"Our party breaks but does not bend." This was the motto of a political party. It also applies to a number of churches. In Latin America, but certainly not only there, the multiplication of churches continues by division over social, doctrinal, liturgical, and organizational differences, or simply because of power struggles. The Methodist churches, as I indicated at the beginning, have not been strangers to these conflicts. In the majority of the cases this has not led to division. I was struck by this fact in our own church in Argentina. The crisis to which I referred at the beginning had to do with an educational institution which some church-elected members of its Executive Committee felt that it was, in its institutional leadership and in its social and political choices, in contradiction with the spirit and the policies of the Argentine Methodist Church. This is one of a number of critical situations in this church since its birth in the 1850s. One of them seems to me to be particularly interesting. It took place between 1954 and 1960. In the city of Córdoba, in the interior of the country, the membership of the Methodist Church had a strong congregationalist and fundamentalist component, related to Southern Baptist and Plymouth Brethren influence, which collided with a more liturgical, sacramental tendency of a significant part of the ministry. Two other components complicated the picture. One was theological: the fundamentalism of some of the membership over against the more classical Protestant theology of the ministry with a strong Barthian component. The other involved a conservative political attitude of the former over against a "socialist" inclination of the pastors and the younger generation. What began in Córdoba extended to other parts of the country and became a generalized conflict that threatened to divide the church.

What seems to me of particular interest in this case was the way in which the church through its Annual Conference met the conflict. It created a twelve-member committee (nothing new about that) to receive and analyze information in order to prepare a report and make proposals to the next annual session. The committee was formed by laypersons and ministers, coming from the different lines but not directly involved in the conflict. The conclusion to which they arrived tried to be conciliatory, but by interpreting the propositions of the critical Córdoba group the report neutralized destructive potentiality. The committee expressed appreciation for the concern of the group for piety and evangelism, that is, the evangelical dimension. However, it interpreted it in the framework of an organic ecclesiology and a pluralistic theology in which the Anglican, Reformed, and Lutheran strands of the sixteenth century tradition are vindicated and the evangelical revival of the eighteenth century was incorporated into that tradition. While it welcomed plurality, it built upon the "connectionality" of Methodism and invited an open discussion within the limits of the institutional channels. What is particularly interesting and profoundly Wesleyan in this report is that the committee is not simply trying to appease a conflict by appealing to goodwill and tolerance, but places the conflict within its total history and defines an ecclesiological framework which is able to relate dialectically the two sides of the dilemma, precisely finding the particularity of the Methodist ecclesiology in its possibility of keeping alive that dialectical element. It defines a Methodist identity. The Methodist Church is neither a fundamentalist or a purely congregationalist church nor is it a Catholic Church in the sense of the hierarchical structure of that ecclesiology. It is an historical church, tied to the Reformation and to the Wesleyan movement. It is also a modern church which recognizes freedom and progress in the methods of theological and biblical interpretation.

I will conclude by suggesting some themes which could be profitably explored and discussed:

1. The apparent or real contradiction that we find in Wesley's ecclesiology is the result of an historical shift that was taking place in Europe from the state church which was dominant and the voluntary model of the free church which would become the dominant model in the modern age. Although the change has taken different forms and in some ways is still in motion, the process of globalization has made it the only possible alternative.
2. Wesley's resistance to abandon central aspects of the traditional churches of the Reformation in terms of the *fides quae*— objective doctrine and sacraments, liturgy and connectional structure—expresses a necessary tension which should be understood and faced dialectically rather than unilaterally avoiding it.
3. In his insistence on recognizing the validity of and in engaging a critical and positive debate and a possible cooperation with other churches, including the Roman Catholic, Wesley antici-

pated an ecumenical model which has been significant, at least for our Latin American (and other Third World churches).

It is precisely these qualities that have given Latin American Methodism the possibility of playing a major role in the construction of ecumenical relations, i.e., common action in theological and social issues, and working, on the one hand, with the so-called historical churches of the Reformation and, on the other, with the evangelical and holiness churches of Anglo-Saxon origin which experienced or were born in the revivals of the nineteenth century. There is, of course, a price and a risk in this dialectical position. At times, Methodism appears as ambiguous, uncertain, or simply confused. This is not totally an appearance. The risk is there and we cannot claim that it has always been avoided.

It has also been claimed that this "mediating role" weakens the fervor and commitment which characterized the Wesleyan movement and produces a lukewarm attitude in which the church loses a passion for evangelization. The question is whether competitiveness or a sense of exclusiveness are the main or even healthy dynamics for evangelization. An evangelization which is not born from compassion and love is not likely to build a healthy church.

In the complex and pluralistic conditions in which our churches have to serve today, the dialectical way in which Wesley related evangelization and an ecumenical openness, classical Protestantism and evangelical piety, a structured connectional organization and a warm and personalized community, a personal ethical discipline and a committed social concern, remains a heritage and a challenge which we must creatively translate to the social, cultural, and religious conditions of our own world.

Notes

1. A brief background on the question of conflicts on issues of religious freedom in J. Míguez Bonino, "Religious Freedom—Argentina," *Religious Freedom and Evangelization in Latin America*, ed. Paul Sigmund (Maryknoll, N.Y., Orbis Press, 1999), 187-203.
2. Cf. J. Míguez Bonino, editorial in "La Aurora," in *Concilio Abierto*, (Buenos Aires, 1967).
3. From John Telford, ed., *The Letters of the Reverend John Wesley*, 8 vols. (London: Epworth Press, 1931), henceforth *Letters*, VI, 326-27.
4. *Works* (Jackson).
5. *Works* (Jackson), VIII, 3-45.
6. In italics are the sentences which are added as explanation to the Article in the XXXIX Articles of the Church of England.

7. Sermons in the Bicentennial Edition, *Works*.
8. *Letters*, IV, 236f.
9. *Works* (Jackson) VII, 152; II, 362; *Letters*, III, 128.
10. *Works* (Jackson), VIII, 280.
11. *Works* (Jackson), VIII, 281.
12. *Works*(Jackson), VI, 408.
13. Bernard Semmel, *The Methodist Revolution* (New York: Basic Books, 1973).
14. Semmel, 162-63.
15. Cf. note 1 above. A fuller discussion of the issue in J. Míguez Bonino, *Faces of Latin American Protestantism* (Grand Rapids, Mich.: W. B. Eerdmans, 1997), ch. 1.
16. *Christian Work in Latin America: The Panama Congress Report* (New York: Committee on Cooperation in Latin America, CCLA, The Missionary Education Movement 1917).
17. *Christian Work in Latin America*, 14.

6

The Impact of Wesleyanism on Africa: Toward an Understanding of Divine Grace in a Changing Continent

David K. Yemba

I still remember a conversation that I had in Strasbourg, France with a French woman more than twenty years ago. She knew that I was from Africa, from the Congo, known as Zaire at the time the conversation took place. She was enthusiastic to talk to somebody from Africa because she had a member of her family who was living in Senegal for professional reasons. As the conversation developed, I began to have the impression that she thought that Senegal was geographically close to Zaire. She was surprised when I told her that although the two countries were francophone, there were eleven different countries between Senegal and Zaire.

One would like to think that this is an isolated example. It is not the case. When people talk about Africa from outside the continent, one sometimes has the impression that Africa is seen as a single country. Moreover, while geographically Africa is sometimes considered as one country from outside, culturally it is also sometimes considered as a single ethnic group from inside. Very often native Africans themselves give the impression that a culture or a tradition of one ethnic group in a given African country applies to any other African ethnic group. These impressions, geographical and cultural, are far from reality.

Therefore, my intention is not to present in this paper the complex history of the mission of the church in Africa. It would be too ambitious. Rather, the intention of this paper is to give a survey of what I consider, from a theological point of view, as the important impact of the Wesleyan/Methodist tradition on the evangelization of Africa. A continent of over fifty nations, Africa offers a diversity of peoples, races, cultures, languages, histories, political systems, and natural resources. Desmond Tutu likes to describe the peoples of one African country, the Republic of South Africa, as a beautiful rainbow.

The history of this continent is complex to describe, be it in politics, economics, and culture, or religion. It is particularly complex when one considers what has been going on during the second half of the twentieth century. One is tempted to assess the impact of the Wesleyan tradition in just one country or one region used as a sample. Yet in doing so, one would run the risk of being too partial. On the other hand, if one talks about the whole continent in a paper, one risks being too general, too superficial, which is as high a risk as that of being partial. In any case, the main reason to talk about the impact of Wesleyanism on the whole continent is a matter of theological emphasis. The Wesleyan/ Methodist tradition, as a Christian tradition, has its specific emphasis in the way the Gospel of Jesus Christ ought to be proclaimed. In the heart of this proclamation and Christian experience is divine grace for humankind.

In contemporary Africa, the proclamation of the Gospel with a particular emphasis on divine grace has a double importance. The interpretation of grace as prevenient, justifying, and sanctifying according to the Wesleyan/Methodist tradition, is not only a contribution to and with *oikumene*, but is also a challenge for the life of the churches which claim to belong to this tradition. Before reflecting on divine grace, the essence of Wesleyanism, and its significant impact on evangelization, we begin by offering a brief historical background of Africa and its changing context.

I

In Africa, Wesleyanism is known as one of the missionary endeavors of the historical Christian traditions. This missionary enterprise was introduced into all regions of the continent together with other historical Christian traditions such as the Anglican, Baptist, Lutheran, Reformed, Presbyterian, and Roman Catholic. The presence of Wesleyanism on the continent of Africa is noted as early as the end of the eighteenth century. Its first roots are found in west Africa, in Sierra Leone more precisely, among the group of freed slaves who went from the American colonies to that part of the continent as early as 1792. The members of this group organized themselves into a church. After a few years of ministerial experience, they felt the need to develop the work further. They made an appeal to Dr. Thomas Coke in Britain. As a result, the first Wesleyan Methodist missionary was sent to Sierra Leone in 1811. In the meantime, the British garrison introduced Methodism to South Africa in 1806.

Since then the Gospel has been spread by the Wesleyan/Methodist tradition in the five regions of the continent: the north, the south, the east, the west, and the center. In addition to Sierra Leone and South Africa, one will find the active presence of Wesleyanism today in the following African countries: Liberia since 1822; Ghana, 1835; Benin, 1843; Kenya, 1862; Angola, 1885; Central Africa, 1888; Ivory Coast and Mozambique, 1890; Zimbabwe, 1891; Nigeria, 1893; Algeria/Tunisia, 1908; Democratic Republic of Congo and Zambia, 1914; and Burundi, 1935.[1]

The modern evangelization of Africa, however, should not be seen as the beginning of an encounter between this continent and the peoples of the Bible. There is a long history of this encounter, a history with ups and downs, heroes and victims. One thing should be noted: never have the people of Israel been closer to any other neighboring people than they were to the people of northern Africa. I once indicated this historical relationship in these terms:

> It would be incorrect to assume that the history of the church in Africa began with the modern missionary movement of the West. Biblical and historical witnesses indicate that relations between the people of Israel and the peoples of Northern Africa date back to Abrahamic times. Though situated geographically between Babylon and Egypt, Israel was never drawn as much towards Babylon as towards Egypt in its history. African relations with Mediterranean civilizations date prior to the Christian era. Contrary to the widespread belief of the nineteenth century, Africa has not been historically an isolated continent.[2]

As to the mission of the church in Africa, this is mainly characterized by three stages of evangelization, each of which was accompanied by a strange challenging phenomenon. The three stages, from the early church history to nineteenth-century missionary movements, can be summarized as follows:

The first stage relates to the implantation of the church in antiquity. In the second century after Christ, the church of Northern Africa made an original and remarkable contribution to the development of the Western Church, most notably in its theology. The Latin language, which forged and mediated theological expression in the West, benefitted as well from such Africans as Tertullian; Cyprian, bishop of Carthage; and St. Augustine, bishop of Hippo. Despite the remarkable and rapid growth of the North African Church, despite its solid organization and spirituality—accompanied by schisms and divisions—the patristic Church in Africa north of the Sahara could not, unfortunately, withstand the assaults of Islam. . . .

Secondly, we may note the contact between the gospel and tropical Africa. At the end of the Middle Ages in Europe, the Roman Catholic Church began to show an interest in missionary activity south of the Sahara. The churches which issued forth from the sixteenth century Reformation showed the same interest. But this evangelization of tropical Africa was more or less sporadic in character, and was followed by the tragic period of slavery. Truthfully, this period of missionary activity has left no lasting impact.

Thirdly, one must deal with the modern evangelization of the African continent. Sub-Saharan Africa received the gospel for a second time via missionaries from Europe and the New World. . . . Educational and health institutions as well as assistance and development efforts were established and continue to be established on the African continent in addition to the ministry of evangelism. Nevertheless, in spite of such success, one need not be surprised that also at this time the mission of the church in Africa was accompanied with another sad feature. This time it was the colonial phenomenon. . . .[3]

One might think that the historical assaults of Islam, the commerce in slaves, and colonialism would have completely stopped the development of Christianity in Africa. On the contrary, however, the evangelization which was picked up by the Africans themselves has had a lasting impact. To understand the impact of Wesleyanism within this global view of mission and evangelism in Africa, it is important to describe briefly the changing situation of the continent.

II

Anyone who is familiar with what is written about Africa today, about its politics, economy, and religion, but mostly about its people, becomes familiar with dramatic changes which are taking place on the continent. Although these changes are due to internal as well as external factors, the external factors are more predominant. These include technological development, interconnection of economies, new power alignments, and the like. They affect the life of African peoples the most, both positively and negatively, because of historical ties with the external world, especially the western world.

We live in a changing world. Some people believe that the real global revolution of the contemporary epoch is still to come. What we experience now is just the beginning. Already, however, African nations are going through an experience of economic and social division as the gap widens between the northern and the southern hemispheres. We are witnesses to multiple causes for human suffering, among them the unjust distribution of resources, the proliferation of weapons, increasing numbers of political and economic refugees, the epidemic of violence against the more vulnerable, the resurgence of racist discrimination and practices, the spread of the AIDS pandemic, constant transfer of wealth from poor to rich countries, and flagrant violations of human rights.

These observed changes are also influenced by internal factors. In Africa, we not only witness the emergence of new nations, but also the disintegration of nations already in existence. Some African leaders, instead of investing the money in their countries to serve their people, prefer to export national wealth to other rich, developed nations. The economic and social divide is growing not only between the northern and the southern hemispheres, but also within the countries and among the groups of nations. Much can be said and written about political and economic imbalances as contexts in which the Gospel is proclaimed in Africa. However, for the purpose and scope of this paper, we say more about the changes in religious life.

Anyone who studies African cultures and religions notes that in this continent individual and collective human existence, as well as fundamental institutions which support such existence, are perceived as part of a religious universe. Without a clear awareness of this cultural reality, one could not understand the importance accorded to the meaning or sense of life in African societies, especially when it comes to the initiation of young people, sense of equilibrium or harmony of life, togetherness within the family and clan, social solidarity, relations between human beings, and their physical and social environments.

In African cultures and religions, God is not a strange divinity. God is the Creator, known by specific names according to the culture and language of each ethnic group. In my *Otetela* mother-tongue for instance, we call God, among other names, *Unyashungu*. Linguistic analysis shows that in this name there are three words, namely, *Wunya* (the sun), *she* (father of), and *ulungu* (the sky or the created heavens). Originally, the whole name was probably *Wunya she ulungu*, but the phrase-name was shortened to become *Unyashungu*. The sky and the nature are perceived as the works of the "Sun" which is understood to be older than the sky. Human beings are not only above nature, but are part of nature as a creation of God. Spirituality is understood and experienced in the context of relationship among living human beings, the ancestors, and the Creator on the one hand, and among living human beings, complex systems of social relationships, and nature on the other. The changes which are taking place in African societies have significant influence on the traditional sense of the religious universe as change occurs from African traditional religions to Christianity.

Second, for Christians, what were formally called mission fields are today changing into established churches. This description gives an idea of the context in which evangelization is taking place in Africa. Statistics from individual denominations, world communions, and the ecumenical movement as a whole, indicate that the Christian church is growing in Africa. As far as the Wesleyan tradition is concerned, in four decades of mission work, for instance, the membership of this Christian tradition in Africa went from 1,000,740 in 1956 to 5,054,140 in 1997. "Membership," in a more inclusive sense includes persons in the sphere of the church's influence (community). This increased in the same period from 1,948,850 to 14,628,990.[4] From these membership statistics one can assess the influence of Wesleyan institutions in the areas of education, health care, and other areas where the impact of the Gospel is significant and ongoing.

III

The term Wesleyanism, and synonymously Methodism, refers to the movement that John Wesley (1703-1791) started in England. The term is also used to describe the theology of the founder as well as theologies and practices of various churches and Christian groups associated with Wesley's theology and practice of Christian ministry. Today, many churches around the world belong to Wesleyan tradition, including those related to Methodism, the Holiness Movement, Pentecostalism, and some united churches. Wesley's theology is essentially revivalist, combining the proclamation of the Good News, the experience of God's grace, and reflection on the history of salvation that God once for all offered to humankind in Jesus Christ. In the "Doctrinal Standards and Our Theological Task" part of the United Methodist *Book of Discipline,* the section which deals with "Doctrinal Heritage" describes the essence of the Wesleyan message in the following words:

> Although Wesley shared with many other Christians a belief in grace, justification, assurance, and sanctification, he combined them in a powerful manner to create distinctive emphases for living the full Christian life. The Evangelical United Brethren tradition, particularly as experienced by Phillip William Otterbein from a reformed background, gave similar distinctive emphases.
>
> Grace pervades our understanding of Christian faith and life. By grace we mean the undeserved, unmerited, and loving action of God in human existence through the ever-present Holy Spirit. While the grace of God is undivided, it precedes salvation as "prevenient grace," continues in "justifying grace," and is brought to fruition in "sanctifying grace."[5]

This quotation reflects the way the United Methodist Church, as one of the churches of the Wesleyan tradition, understands the distinctive emphases of the Wesleyan message. Individual theologians and other churches of the Wesleyan tradition have expressed these emphases in various ways. At the top of the list, however, one finds grace as the starting point of the order of salvation. John Wesley himself wrote in his sermon, "On Working Out Our Own Salvation":

> Salvation begins with what is usually termed (and very properly) preventive grace; including the first wish to please God, the first dawn of light concerning his will, and the first slight transient conviction of having sinned against him. All these imply some tendency toward life, some degree of salvation, the beginning of a deliverance from a blind, unfeeling heart, quite insensible of God and the things of God. Salvation is carried on by convincing grace, usually in Scripture termed repentance, which brings a larger measure of self-knowledge, and a further deliverance from the heart of stone. Afterwards we experience, the proper Christian salvation; whereby, "through grace," we are "saved by faith," consisting of these two grand branches, justification and sanctification.[6]

These emphases are the result of a way of doing ministry and theology usually known by the term, "the Wesleyan Quadrilateral," which includes scripture, tradition, reason, and experience. A theological debate continues within Wesleyanism as to how these sources of theological reflection relate to each other, including how the "Quadrilateral" is viewed in the works of John Wesley himself.[7]

In any case, the four sources constitute, it is generally believed, the basis on which the core of Christian faith is not only elaborated, but also illuminated. John Cobb has pointed out the essence of Wesleyanism (he used the term Methodism) in his analysis of John Wesley's thought in these terms:

> To follow Wesley's standard doctrines in our preaching is not primarily a matter of dealing with his most controversial and problematic teachings. It is primarily a matter of presenting the essentials of Christian faith as he did, calling always for the love of God and neighbor, and evaluating all doctrines in terms of their relation to this.[8]

IV

There has often been severe criticism of the evangelization of Africa, especially the theology or ideology which accompanied this evangelization. The Roman Catholic approach to the mission enterprise was often accused of partnership with the colonizers who went to Africa in the spirit of conquest. The Protestant approaches, on the other hand, were criticized, in spite of their efforts to translate the Bible into African local languages, for lack of sensitivity to local cultures. In both cases the target was theology which was conveyed by the mission work. Alphonse Ngindu Mushete, a Roman Catholic theologian, among many others, has expressed this concern in the conclusion of his overview of African theology in these words:

> In concluding this overview of African theology, it should be noted that for a long time Westerners have not noticed that there is not one world that exists, but worlds; there is not one history, but histories; not one culture, but cultures; not one theology, but theologies. The fact is that every people, every human community, conceives and organizes its historical existence not according to a universal, immutable model, but according to its own particular situation in space and time. A perception of the world and its values always depends on the locus from

which that perception comes into being. Since persons live in different spaces, they experience and theorize their human relationships, their culture, and their religion differently.[9]

The Wesleyan tradition has something to say about the way its theology was conveyed in Africa. I think of its contribution to the ecumenical movement and to the creation of such vehicles as united schools, national councils of churches, and Bible societies. The connectional system of some Wesleyan churches has been an inspiration to the search for the unity of the church as *koinonia*, especially in the process of church union. In his beautiful book already mentioned, Theodore Runyon has pointed out the important place that ecumenism occupied in Wesley's thought and life.[10] Any assessment on the impact of Wesleyanism should take into consideration the challenge of ecumenism and the pluralistic societies in which the Gospel is proclaimed today.

Wesley presented the Gospel, interpreting divine grace, in such a way that this message continues to have impact to change lives for the better, inspiring people to lead lives toward perfection. This interpretation goes from creation to redemption, not in terms of platonic or neoplatonic dualism, but in terms of understanding both polarities of creation and redemption as grounded in God's grace. It is in that context that Wesley espoused his theology through sermons, his theological cosmology as well as his theological anthropology. His theological anthropology includes the understanding of the human being created in the *imago Dei*, in a state of perfection and guiltlessness, yet fallen in original sin. In other words, this anthropology goes from the state of human perfection to the state of imperfection due to the fall. The originality of this interpretation finds its expression in the triple meaning of the concept of grace as prevenient, justifying, and sanctifying. God is always present in the created world. But at the same time, Wesleyan theological anthropology does not exclude human responsibility.

How was the doctrine of God's grace introduced in Africa and how was it received? Any attempt to describe the impact of Wesleyanism in Africa without serious research which answers this question would not do justice either to Wesley's theology or to African culture and religion. The reflection I have made on this topic may serve as an eye-opener to a larger research field which may include, in the light of our common understanding of God's grace, both the review of missionary work in Africa and the ways Christian faith has been received by Africans. Such assessment would contribute to a new understanding of divine grace as well as the better practice of Christian ministry in a continent from where, according to the prophet Zephaniah, the Lord will receive offerings from his African worshipers, "Then will I purify the lips of the peoples, that all of them may call on the name of the Lord and serve him shoulder to shoulder. From beyond the rivers of Cush [the upper Nile region, Ethiopia] my worshipers, my scattered people, will bring me offerings.[11]

Notes

1. *Handbook of the World Methodist Council* (Lake Junaluska, N.C.: Biltmore Press, 1997).
2. David K. Yemba, "The Experience of the Holy Spirit in Today's African Context," *Andover Newton Review* 2, no. 1 (1991): 25.
3. Yemba, 25-26.
4. Ivan Lee Holt and Elmer T. Clark, *The World Methodist Movement* (Nashville, Tenn.: The Upper Room, 1956), 145-47; *Handbook of the World Methodist Council*, 243-46.
5. *The Book of Discipline of The United Methodist Church, 1996* (Nashville, Tenn.: United Methodist Publishing House, 1996), 43.
6. Quoted by Colin W. Williams, *John Wesley's Theology Today: A Study of Wesleyan Tradition in the Light of Current Theological Dialogue* (Nashville, Tenn.: Abingdon Press, 1960), 40. See also Theodore Runyon, *The New Creation: John Wesley's Theology Today* (Nashville, Tenn.: Abingdon Press, 1998), 31.
7. For this debate see W. Stephen Gunter, et al., *Wesley and the Quadrilateral: Renewing the Conversation* (Nashville, Tenn.: Abingdon Press, 1997).
8. John B. Cobb, Jr., *Grace and Responsibility: A Wesleyan Theology for Today* (Nashville, Tenn.: Abingdon Press, 1995), 141.
9. J. A. Ngindu Mushete, "An Overview of African Theology," in *Paths of African Theology*, ed. Rosino Gibellino (New York: Orbis Books, 1994), 24.
10. Mushete, 207-21.
11. Zephaniah 3:9-10 (New International Version, 1984).

7

The Doctrine of Holiness and Missions: A Pietistic Foundation of African Evangelical Christianity

Robert Kipkemoi Lang'at

The doctrine of holiness has played a crucial role in shaping the nature of Christianity in Africa. The task of explicating this phenomenon has not been fully explored. Hence, no historical account of Christianity in Africa thus far fully explains what role holiness played in the spiritual and theological formation of the missionaries who went to Africa. Furthermore, how they perceived this doctrine in view of missions and their specific objectives as they ministered in Africa await full analysis. Additionally, there is the challenge of studying the process of cross-cultural establishment of a holiness constituency in Africa. What holiness meant to Africans living within cultural and linguistic contexts different from those of the western missionaries needs investigation. More importantly, how the national leadership has continued the vision of propagating the heritage once delivered is yet to be understood. The purpose of this paper is to give a brief historical overview of the doctrine of holiness as it relates to African missions with a view of stimulating further research and discussion along the same lines.

I

Whether Africans had a concept of holiness prior to the advent of western missionary Christianity is a contested issue. Thus, part of the process of understanding how Africans appropriated the doctrine involves a thorough study of the traditional African view of sanctification. It requires a study of the African understanding of soteriology as mediated through cleansing rituals. Postulating the absence of the idea of holiness in Islamic and Bantu literature before the advent of European missionaries, P. J. L. Frankl and Yahya Ali Omar have noted that, "the available evidence suggests that in the mid-nineteenth century at the second coming of European-Christians to the East African coast, there was no lexical equivalent for [the term] holy or its near synonym in the spoken language of the Swahili people."[1] Though the absence of a lexical equivalent neither invalidates the necessity of holiness nor suggests that Africans could not process holiness through their thought patterns, it does suggest that there is a sense in which the total implication of holiness theology is novel to African spirituality.

John S. Mbiti, in his study of African philosophy and religions, argues that there is no direct reference to the holiness of God in Africa and that though the "concept of holiness" is present in ritual and moral matters, and linguistically in many African languages, the word "holiness" or "holy" in its theological usage does not seem to exist.[2] Of course, much depends on what Mbiti meant by the difference between "concept" and "theological usage." If Mbiti's assertions are correct, they raise questions on how far the African languages and rituals prepared them for the reception of biblical holiness. They also lead one to wonder how the missionaries succeeded using these inadequate media, if they did at all, as they were often more critical of the "profanity" that prevailed in African religious practices. More research is required to ascertain whether the African concept of holiness had an ontological transformative nature, where one would be thought to be like a god, or the concept was merely ceremonial providing positional cleansing.

II

In the 1783 sermon, "The General Spread of the Gospel," John Wesley saw the rise of Methodism in England as a providential leaven to spread scriptural holiness throughout the world. Wesley foresaw a time when the "leaven of pure and undefiled religion . . . of inward and outward holiness would spread to the remotest parts not only of Europe but of Asia, Africa, and America."[3] In *The Larger Minutes* of British Methodism, the founder of Methodism formulated the movement's purpose as, "to reform the Nation, particularly the Church; and to spread scriptural holiness over the land." In a further reformulation and expansion over the frontiers, early American Methodists understood their purpose as, "to reform the Continent and to spread scriptural holiness over these lands." Russell E. Richey has correctly noted that the Americans substituted "continent" for Wesley's "the Nation, particularly the Church" and they also made the singular "land" plural.[4] Perhaps a story that has not been fully told is that of an even wider reformulation during the late nineteenth century that witnessed the emergence of agencies and saw their purpose as "spreading scriptural holiness to the ends of the earth."[5] This effectively completed Wesley's original vision. The transformation moved from "Nation" to "Continent" to the "World" and from "land" to "lands" to "foreign lands."

Many American mission agencies understood the world as their "last frontier." But this understanding was encapsulated in a "specialized" holiness world vision. Therefore, by the beginning of the twentieth century holiness was no longer a mere incentive or justification for world evangelization, but an organizational strategy, the very ground and object of missions.

The National Association for the Promotion of Holiness, organized early in 1867, thought the time had come "for the holiness people, to use their holiness money, through holiness channels, to support holiness missionaries, who will do holiness work in the foreign fields."[6] This perception had profound consequences with regard to the role of the doctrine of holiness in world evangelization.[7] Certain events, however, were prelude to this larger organizational endeavor for the course of holiness overseas. Most of these efforts were individual and, though respected, were often deemed by the holiness people as "unorganized."

Amanda Berry Smith and William Taylor are two individuals mentioned in the history of the National Holiness Missionary Society (NHMS)[8] as being among the holiness people that could not be confined to one country because of their "holiness world vision."[9] Though the two came at the time of ecclesiological and missiological tensions in mainline Methodism, they did not belong to the tradition of "the come-outer," but were in the group that sought to use camp meetings, literature, foreign missions, and other means to promote the doctrine of entire sanctification. When William Taylor organized revivals in South Africa in 1866, before the Keswick Conventions started (1875), he introduced Andrew Murray of the Dutch Reformed Church to the doctrine of sanctification.[10] Murray turned out to be a prolific writer on holiness and closely allied himself to

Keswick Conventions in South Africa in the latter part of his life.[11] Murray's holiness legacy is difficult to ascertain. Though perhaps an unusual candidate for holiness promotion, his theological contributions do not seem to have made a significant impact for interracial equality or against the growing seeds of apartheid in the Dutch Reformed Church (DRC).

On the other hand, Amanda B. Smith helped William Taylor in Africa "turn the Methodist mission there into a holiness crusade."[12] Taylor produced a mix of Methodist doctrines, self-supporting missions strategy, and holiness theology.[13] Holiness had not been the central theme of the Liberian revival and its impact had waned by the time Smith arrived in 1882.[14] In Clay-Ashland, Liberia, she wrote that, "for a long time there has been a good deal of interest manifested among a number of Christians on the subject of personal holiness."[15] In a language reminiscent of that used in America, she stated that she had begun a "meeting once a month, for the promotion of holiness."[16] Out of these arose an association called "Clay-Ashland Holiness Association."[17] A holiness camp meeting was held at Cape Palmas, Liberia in 1886. It brought together Christians from Presbyterian, Baptist, Congregational, and Methodist churches.[18] This testifies to the fact that the Wesleyan doctrine of sanctification influenced Reformed theology within contexts beyond North America. In this case a revivalist ecumenicity emerged in west Africa as a result of Taylor/Smith holiness revivals. At the advent of the twentieth century William Taylor and Amanda B. Smith retired from active missionary service. The duo represent a generation of maverick holiness missionaries that operated with a loose attachment to their denominations.[19]

III

It is in the rise of what has been generally referred to as "faith missions" and distinctively holiness missions where the doctrine of holiness became an important force in missions. Peniel Mission stood as a transitional influence for a number of missionaries who went to Africa under the faith principle. The role of Peniel in world missions has not been fully appreciated. It was the culmination of holiness revivals gaining momentum on the American western frontiers. Manie Payne and Theodore Pollock Ferguson were behind the inception of Peniel Mission in 1886. Pollock, a Presbyterian, was introduced to the experience of sanctification in Wesleyan terms during a holiness meeting under Lucius B. Fuller at Oberlin College.[20] Ferguson eventually was sanctified at Santa Barbara,

California, in 1880 under Harden Wallace and Henry Ashcraft.[21] He attended and participated in several Methodist camp meetings across the United States.[22] There is no doubt that one of those who inspired Ferguson was Bishop William Taylor whom he heard and "bought all his books" at the Round Lake Camp Meeting, New York, in 1882.[23]

Peniel Mission and the World Gospel Mission merged in 1957.[24] Before this event became a reality, Peniel Mission played a vital role in the "pre-history" of the World Gospel Mission (WGM) and other "faith missions." A missionary couple, Burnette and Gerald Fish, mentioned in their book the three "full-circles" in relation to the development of WGM in Kenya.[25] These "full circles" point to the way the Africa Inland Church (1895) and the Kenya Yearly Meeting of Friends (1902) were related to the Africa Gospel Church (1932). What needs to be emphasized even more is the fact that the three denominations trace their theological history to the influence of holiness revivals, particularly through Peniel Mission, on their missionaries.

It is important to know that most if not all of faith missions were born out of holiness revivals. Albert B. Simpson, a Presbyterian and founder of Christian and Missionary Alliance Church, associated with Peniel Mission during the 1890s, was instrumental in the training, ordination, and commissioning of Peter Cameroon Scott for African missions in the 1890s. Available sources do not indicate how early Scott and Simpson met. However, Scott, a Presbyterian from Scotland, trained at New York Missionary Training College (now Nyack College), first went to Africa under the aegis of the International Missionary Alliance in 1890. Due to health reasons he resigned. Scott definitely went through some type of sanctifying experience.

In 1895, Peter C. Scott returned to Africa with a team that included Willis R. Hotchkiss, a Quaker Wesleyan/holiness evangelist, to start the work of the Africa Inland Mission.[26] Andrew M. Andersen, who became a key leader in the Africa Inland Mission (AIM) in Kenya was sanctified in 1903 at Peniel Mission. Andersen attended Cleveland Bible College where he met Hotchkiss and decided to join him in Kenya in 1907 at the Africa Inland Mission. When the WGM, whose forerunner was Peniel Mission, was searching for a field in Kenya in the late 1920s, Andersen in "gratitude for his conversion through Peniel Missions, a holiness work," assisted in the early years of the mission in Kenya.[27]

The work of Friends Africa Industrial Mission (FAIM) in Kenya is part of the larger influence of the doctrine of holiness in missions. Willis R. Hotchkiss who had earlier resigned from the AIM, took Arthur Chilson and Edgar Hole to start this mission in 1901. It is fascinating to note that enroute to Africa the trio paid a courtesy call on Bishop William Taylor while in London. Taylor, who had become "a patron saint" for holiness missionaries, prayed for them and used his knowledge of Africa to direct them to work near Lake Victoria.[28] Thus, the Quaker "Inward Look" continued to be replaced by "World Vision" as a result of the Methodist connection. Thomas D. Hamm summarizes the extent of American Methodism's impact on Quakerism by writing:

> Late in the summer of 1875 a Methodist Minister decided to indulge his professional curiosity by attending the annual gathering of Yearly Meeting of Friends in Richmond. Unlike his military brother fourteen years earlier, the Methodist minister felt completely at home. The devotional meeting opened with the singing of a familiar hymn. Then the presiding preacher called for testimonies . . . then an altar call was issued, and soon seekers after conversion and sanctification crowded around several mourners' benches.[29]

This period has been depicted not only as a time of the Wesleyanization of Quakerism but also of the American religious landscape and the larger world. Douglas and Dorothy Steere at the Friends World Committee in 1954 noted that it was not until 1868 that the Friends Foreign Missions Association was formed:

> [a] clear sign that the Society of Friends was far from being a leader in the cause of missions. Had it not been for the strong influence of the Wesleyan Evangelical Movement upon Society both in England and America, arousing it to witness to Christ who spoke to its condition and setting a powerful example to it in the wave of missionary enthusiasm that swept the church in the nineteenth century, there is little to indicate that English Quakers would have ventured on these undertakings.[30]

Ann Marie Bak Rasmussen has noted that "international revivalism was dominated by Holiness Methodism" that stressed sanctification as a second definite experience after conversion.[31] She also correctly recognizes that, "the evangelical influence which led to the great revival among Friends also aroused in them an interest in foreign mission work."[32]

IV

There are two kinds of distinctively Wesleyan/Holiness missions that began to take root in Africa during the "institutional" phase of the revivals: denominational and interdenominational. James R. Bishop, the Executive Director of the World Gospel Mission in the 1960s wrote that "though keen missionary interest existed and scattered support was given to various missionaries and missionary projects through the National [Holiness Association] prior to June 1910 . . . the leaders of the National [Holiness Association] were not satisfied with the haphazard expression of the organization's missionary zeal."[33] A number of their missionaries who were involved with mainline Methodism and other missions did not find what the holiness people called, "an unhindered field for the aggressive pushing of holiness."[34] Those missionaries operating independently had no system of accountability. Many who had gone out had not been examined on doctrinal matters such as speaking in tongues and "third blessing" holiness. There was also concern about preaching a general advancement of grace rather than the type of holiness that supporters at home wanted communicated to the uttermost parts of the earth.[35] Even the concept of faith missions was taught insufficiently to advance holiness in foreign land. A clear example is in the situation surrounding the circumstances leading to the founding of the National Holiness Missionary Society, where Woodford Taylor and Cecil Troxel, the first two missionaries, broke from the Chihli Mission because of what was perceived as unclear Wesleyan interpretation of scripture and lack of unity in policy. They wanted "unity in doctrine and experience of holiness" which was not available in faith missions.[36]

Clara Ford was the first missionary sent under the auspices of the National Holiness Missionary Society to Africa. She marks a connection between the inauguration of the NHMS and the beginning of holiness work among the Kipsigis people of Kenya. Ford arrived in Africa in 1929. She represents the wider acceptance that a number of holiness mission agencies had for women in ministry. The East Africa Holiness Association was organized with Ford as secretary and for months she edited and published a holiness magazine, the only interdenominational religious magazine published in east Africa in the 1930s.[37] The magazine was called *Matangazo Ya Injili*, Swahili for "Gospel Herald." This publication had a circulation of 1,300 throughout east Africa by 1935.[38] It appears the efforts to develop an interdenominational outreach with an objective of spreading scriptural holiness prominently occupied the minds of the early WGM, Quaker, and AIM missionaries. Virgil Kirkpatrick said of one of their meetings, "please pray that this beginning will develop into a great annual holiness convention."[39]

V

To some holiness mission agencies, the matter of understanding the teaching and possessing the experience of entire cleansing as a second definite "work of grace" was imperative. It was important on the field and no one was to be sent without the experience.[40] What was demanded of the missionaries also became their mandate for reaching Africa. Some of the missionaries said, "we go then looking to [God], determined by His grace to pierce Africa's darkness with the pure light of 'Holiness unto the Lord': trusting that its glow may constantly radiate from our own lives until those [to] whom we minister will catch and carry over, even until the utmost part."[41] There is a sense in which Africa's "darkness" was in itself a justification for the "deeper" cleansing power. The African adherents were expected to break away from traditional ceremonies, superstitious past, witchcraft, and polygamy, as well as embrace a lifestyle of abstinence from alcohol, tobacco, dancing (including traditional dancing), and sexual promiscuity.

The missionaries sought to ensure that national pastors attained and shared the experience of holiness. One of the missionaries wrote, "our hope for speedy ministry does not lie in our personal ministry among the masses but in a sanctified native ministry."[42] Therefore, efforts were made to pass on the theological heritage to a group of native evangelists. A missionary, Faye Kirkpatrick, anticipated that, "the greatest missionary accomplishment in these latter days shall be through the sanctified native church."[43] Orville Leonard reported that, "much of the real missionary work away from the main station is carried on by native ministers."[44] Early Africa Gospel Church pastors were not only required to be sanctified, but it was part of their monthly report to register those who sought sanctification experiences.[45] The most rapid and direct way to spread the good news was when the natives attained the holiness experience. They would effectively articulate and make a strong argument for Christianity among their people. It was also seen as the best way of ensuring the permanence of evangelistic results. Robert K. Smith hoped the church would become, "a permanent structure, definitely converted, wholly sanctified, constantly spirit-led and filled with joy awaiting His coming."[46]

VI

A review of available literature on influences from the holiness movement

The Doctrine of Holiness and Missions

in Africa reveals that the missionaries had to grapple with the appropriateness of the doctrine of sanctification in African Christianity. Early Methodist missionaries and preachers gave "much attention to Christian Perfection [and] personal journals and letters witness to their having been very conscious of this teaching as part of Methodist heritage. The ministers were regularly asked, during synods and conferences, if they continued to preach the doctrine."[47] However, Kwesi Dickson also notes that in Africa, "the edge of this teaching has been blunted by the fact that the church has tried to separate its members from life as they know it from the particularity of their circumstances" and, therefore, in his judgment this doctrine has not constituted a potential for change in Africa.[48] Kwesi's theological analysis borders on a rejection of holiness as irrelevant for Africa. This position is difficult to sustain in the light of the history of revivalism and its potential for social change. It is not easy to understand why a doctrine based on perfectionist love for God and humanity, supported by a strong connectional system and whose prime exponent, John Wesley, had vehemently fought the enslavement of the African race would not have a potential for change in Africa.[49]

It has been argued that despite most of the leaders of the church in Kenya being influenced for forty years by the East African Revival,[50] much of Kenyan Christianity is full of bitter divisions, nominal beliefs, tribalism, and differences of personalities and customs. John Martin stated that in Rwanda eight of ten people claim to be Christian and yet the country was penetrated by ethnic purification. He blamed the massacres on the shortcomings of the East African Revival and missionary legacies which lacked social engagement, put limited stress on human rights, failed to give systematic instructions, retreated to "apolitical" pietism, substituted testimonies for biblical instruction, and emphasized private morality over structural evil or corporate sin.[51] This study attacks holiness revivalism at the core of its strength. It calls for a re-investigation of the doctrine of holiness in the light of the African situation because, as indicated earlier, these findings are also based on a superficial understanding of holiness.

Perhaps the most curious of all the statements on holiness in Africa is that made by Klaus Fiedler, a researcher on faith missions. Fiedler sees holiness as a revival phenomenon that suited the, "people who had long been converted and yearned for deeper Christian life" in the missionary's homeland. For him such a situation did not exist in the mission field where the missionary had to establish the church first. This process of establishing the church, according to Fiedler, was "done not by means of preaching holiness, but by preaching conversion." Therefore, Fiedler concludes, missionaries "did not try to build holiness structures they were used to, such as conferences, camp meetings, and fellowship groups, . . . did not translate holiness literature into African languages, nor did they write their own holiness literature in those languages." To him the slow process of conversion left little energy and time for preaching holiness.[52] Though he does not want to conclude that holiness did not take root in Africa, he sees little success achieved even by missions like the World Gospel Mission (before the 1954 National Holiness Missionary Society) which defined their primary mission based on the doctrine of entire sanctification.[53]

Fiedler's work is perhaps the most definitive study of holiness in Africa. His faith missions lens and limited holiness corpus from which the research is drawn led him to miss crucial theological developments in the doctrine of sanctification as understood within missionary circles. His interpretation separates holiness from the soteriology of the African missionaries. Though his purpose was to describe the theology of faith missions in the African context, he eventually skipped major cultural issues assuming that this had been done by others. Our study suggests that missionaries did seek to communicate the doctrine of holiness. Ann Marie Bak Rasmussen concurred that the gospel that the FAIM missionaries brought to Kenya was a revival gospel which meant that the Africans could find forgiveness for their sins and also had the opportunity to experience sanctification as in America.[54] The structures similar to those in America including conferences, camp meetings, and fellowships were also available to the African people for the purpose of leading them to sanctification.[55] This challenges Fiedler's assumptions. In summary, there are a number of historical, theological, cultural, sociological, and missiological hurdles that are crucial for interpreting the development of the doctrine of holiness in Africa.

VII

The doctrine of holiness played a major role in the inception of evangelical Christianity in Africa. This role included spiritual and theological foundations of missions that would be considered outside the Wesleyan family. It also became, in the nineteenth century, the rallying point for most of the evangelical missions. This teaching and experience was embodied in the lives and practices of missionaries. It defined their objectives in reaching Africa with the Gospel. The missionaries perceived that the message of holiness was understood and received in Africa as the essence of the deepest relationship with Christ. They relied on this for the permanency of their results. They also saw holy living as an alternative to what they thought as "heathen" traditional practices of the African people. Though documentation is wanting, it is clear at this point that pietistic Christianity when understood properly was spiritually edifying for African Christians, but when misapplied it became counter-productive. This research is based almost entirely on secondary materials published in the West. More work needs to be done using all the possible research apparatus to ascertain the historical, theological, as well as contextual underpinnings of the experience of sanctification in Africa.

Notes

1. P. J. L. Frank and Yahya Ali Omar, "The Idea of the 'Holy' in Swahili," *Journal of Religion in Africa*, XXIX (1999): 1.
2. John S. Mbiti, *Concepts of God in Africa* (London: SPCK, 1970), 41-42.
3. John Wesley, "The General Spread of the Gospel, *Works* (Jackson), VI, 277-88.
4. Russell E. Richey, *Early American Methodism* (Bloomington: Indiana University Press, 1991), 36.
5. Burnish Bushong, *Reaching the Unreached Now: A Short History of the World Gospel Mission* (Marion, Ind.: World Gospel Mission, 1995), 7.
6. C. W. Ruth, "Some Reasons for the New Missionary Society," *Christian Witness and Advocate of Bible Holiness*, 1 September 1910: 9.
7. The interrelationship between holiness and world missions is a subject that has not been fully explored. This paper is limited to the African context.
8. This was the official missionary society inaugurated in 1910 by the Methodists aligned to the National Camp Meeting Association for the Promotion of Holiness. It is currently the World Gospel Mission. When it first started, the missionaries were sent to China. Kenya is at present the largest field of this Wesleyan mission organization.
9. W. W. Cary, *Story of the National Holiness Missionary Society: The Whole Gospel for the Whole World* (Chicago: National Holiness Missionary Society, 1940), 293.
10. William Taylor, *The Flaming Torch in the Darkest of Africa* (New York: Eaton, 1898), 365.
11. Andrew Murray, in a clear divergence from his Reformed theological heritage, wrote over two hundred books, most of them on the subject of holiness and the Holy Spirit. See the reprints by Bethany House Publishers which include Andrew Murray, *The Believer's Full Blessing of Pentecost* (Minneapolis, Minn.: Bethany House, 1984) and *Revival* (Minneapolis, Minn.: Bethany House Publishers, 1990).
12. Timothy L. Smith, *Called Unto Holiness: The Story of the Nazarenes* (Kansas City, Mo.: Nazarene Publishing House, 1962), 41.
13. See *Report of Bishop Taylor's Self-Supporting Missions*, 1 July 1884-24 March 1888, 24, 26. Bishop Taylor's committee listed holiness and self-

supporting policy as part of the covenants to be subscribed to by the missionary candidates in addition to the Methodist Episcopal Church's questions on going on to perfection. Taylor included being entirely consecrated to God and cleansed from all sin as qualifications for the missionaries. In addition they were to indicate abstinence from the use of liquor, tobacco, and other narcotics.

14. Adrienne M. Israel, *Amanda Berry Smith: From Washerwoman to Evangelist* (Lanham, Md.: Scarecrow Press, 1998), 76.

15. Amanda Berry Smith, *An Autobiography: The Story of the Lord's Dealings with Mrs. Amanda Smith, the Colored Evangelist* (New York: Oxford University Press, 1988), 380.

16. Amanda Berry Smith, 381.

17. Amanda Berry Smith, 381.

18. Amanda Berry Smith, 472-73.

19. Nathan O. Hatch, *The Democratization of American Christianity* (New Haven, Conn.: Yale University Press, 1989), 214.

20. Manie Payne Ferguson, *T. P. Ferguson: the Love Slave of Jesus Christ and His People and Founder of Peniel Missions* (Los Angeles: n.p., n.d.), 21. The title of the book is suggestive of the two Wesleyan motifs: love for God and humanity. This also motivated the Salvation Army missiological approach and was used by other Wesleyan bodies to justify the connection between holiness and missions. See editorial in *The Christian Witness and Advocate of Bible Holiness*, 12 January 1911: 8. "Jesus forever settled the question of holiness and foreign missions [when he affirmed the lawyer's respond that] thou shall love the Lord thy God with all thy heart and with all thy soul and with all thy strength and with all thy mind, and thy neighbor as thyself."

21. Ferguson, 23.

22. Ashcraft has been identified as representing the more radical "come-outism" movement within the Methodist Episcopal Church and that part of the move to establish Peniel Mission was meant to be a middle ground between staying in the denominations and forming new ones, a move that provided the holiness people a "third way" that would lead to formation of independent missions and consequently gave "the Holiness Movement institutional form without conflicting with the Churches." See Carl Bangs, *Phineas F. Bresee: His Life in Methodism, the Holiness Movement and the Church of the Nazarene* (Kansas City, Mo.: Beacon Hill, 1995), 185.

23. Ferguson, 101-2.

24. Laura Trachsel, *Kindled Fires in Africa* (Marion, Ind.: World Gospel Mission, 1960), 109-11.

25. Burnette C. Fish and Gerald W. Fish, *The Place of Songs: A History of the World Gospel Mission and the Africa Gospel Mission in Kenya* (Kericho, Kenya: World Gospel Mission, 1989), 527.

26. Kenneth Richardson, *Garden of Miracles: The Story of the Africa Inland Mission* (London: Africa Inland Mission, 1976), 20-36.

27. Fish, 527.

28. Edna H. Chilson, *Ambassador of the King* (Wichita, Kans.: Esther Chilson Choate and Rachel E. Chilson, 1943), 14.

29. Thomas D. Hamm, *The Transformation of American Quakerism* (Bloomington: Indiana University Press, 1988), 74.
30. Douglas and Dorothy Steere, *Friends Work in Africa* (London: Friends World Committee, 1954), 6-7.
31. Ann Marie Bak Rasmussen, *The Quaker Movement in Africa* (London: British Academic Press, 1995), 16.
32. Rasmussen, 19.
33. James R. Bishop, "The Birth of the National Holiness Missionary Society," unpublished manuscript, Delbert Rose Collection, Asbury Theological Seminary, Wilmore, Kentucky.
34. Iva Durham Vennard, "Is the National Association for the Promotion of Holiness Justifiable in Organizing a Department of Foreign Missions," *The Christian Witness and Advocate of Bible Holiness*, 31: 23, 15 June 1911.
35. The NHMS was in part a reaction to Keswick holiness espoused by most of the "Faith Missions," see C. B. Ward, *Christian Witness and Advocate of Bible Holiness*, 26 September 1907, 9.
36. Mrs. Cecil Troxel and John J. Trachsel, *Cecil Troxel: The Man and the Work* (Chicago: National Holiness Missionary Society, 1948), 88.
37. Cary, 342.
38. Cary, 342.
39. Virgil Kirkpatrick, "Meetings," *Call to Prayer*, August 1935, 13.
40. Bushong, 13.
41. Virgil Kirkpatrick, "Why We Go to Africa," *Call to Prayer*, July 1932, 9.
42. Fish, 268.
43. Faye Kirkpatrick, "God is Still on the Throne," *Call to Prayer*, December 1935, 8.
44. Orville E. Leonard, *Pioneering* (sl: privately printed, n.d.), 18.
45. Leonard, *Pioneering*, 20.
46. Robert K. Smith, "Building Christian Character in Africa," *Call to Prayer*, June 1935, 9.
47. Theodore Runyon ed., *Sanctification & Liberation* (Nashville, Tenn.: Abingdon, 1981), 198.
48. Runyon,198.
49. See Wesley's letter to William Wilberforce urging him to fight slavery: *Works* (Jackson) XIII, 153.
50. The East African Revival was strongly influenced by the American holiness revivalism and most of the early revivalists were from the Free Methodist Church, the Friends Africa Industrial Mission, the National Holiness Missionary Society and the Africa Inland Mission. Unfortunately history has presented this movement as mainly Anglican-Keswick revivalism. See J. E. Church, *Quest for the Highest: An Autobiographical Account of the East African Revival* (Exeter: Paternoster Press, 1981).
51. John Martin, "Revivalism and Ethnic Conflict," *Transformation: An International Dialogue on Mission and Ethics*, April/June 1995, 1-2.
52. Klaus Fiedler, *The Story of Faith Missions: From Hudson Taylor to*

Present Day Africa (Oxford: Regnum Books, 1994) 247.
   53. Fiedler, 248
   54. Rasmussen, 43-44.
   55. Rasmussen, 59-60.

8

Are They Not Methodist Too? Case Studies of Some African Independent Churches that Call Themselves Methodist

Joan A. Millard

Methodists have long been wary of the possibility of breakaways or schisms in the church. This is hardly surprising considering that so many early Methodists were first Anglicans. In this paper we will look at schisms that have involved Methodists, each one unique in itself, but each the end result of a process during which dissatisfaction with mainstream Methodist tradition led to irreconcilable differences resulting in a new group being formed. We will see that although the members of the new churches were no longer members of the Wesleyan Methodist Church, they nevertheless considered themselves Methodist.

Although John Wesley (1703-1791) never left the Anglican Church, the process that would lead to the formation of Methodist churches started during his lifetime. Did it perhaps begin when Wesley called the first Conference in 1744 without reference to the Anglican hierarchy? Or, perhaps it was forty years later in 1784 when Wesley, then "eighty-one years of age, constituted by deed 100 of his preachers [to be] the legal conference which was to be the supreme legislative body in the Methodist Church. In this document he established for Methodism through all time a definite and separate existence as a Church."[1]

Wesley feared that after his death some of his preachers would feel excluded and leave the Methodists. Jackson quoted a letter written by Wesley to be read at the first Conference after his death. In it he pleaded with the preachers, "never to avail yourselves of the 'Deed of Declaration' to assume any superiority over your brethren, but to let all things go on, among those itinerants who choose to remain together, exactly in the same manner as when I was with you."[2] While the early Methodist preachers heeded his words, by the end of the nineteenth century they were no longer remembered by Methodist preachers in the colonies. Accusations of differences in the treatment of white and black preachers were among the reasons put forward for the formation of the Ethiopian Church in South Africa.

In spite of Wesley's desire for unity there were schisms in early Methodism. The earliest was probably the New Connexion, formed in 1797. Other independent groups of Methodists followed. The Primitive Methodists formed a separate movement in about 1800. They were expelled from the Wesleyan Methodists in 1810 for issuing preacher's licenses without the sanction of the itinerant preachers or the quarterly meeting. The Primitive Methodist Church was formally constituted in 1811 and was reunited with the Wesleyan Methodists in 1932. In South Africa there were Primitive Methodist missions at Stone Street in Johannesburg and at Jamestown, near Aliwal North in the eastern Cape.

I

In September 1784 Wesley wrote a letter "To Dr. Coke, Mr. Asbury, and our brethren in North America." He wrote, "The case is widely different between England and North America. Here there are Bishops who have legal jurisdiction. In America there are none, neither many parish ministers. So for some hundreds of miles together, there is none either to baptize, or administer the Lord's Supper."[3] Was Wesley implying that context influenced the manner of ministry? He continued, "I have accordingly appointed Dr. Coke and Mr. Francis Asbury to be joint Superintendents over our brethren in North America."[4]

On 1 September 1785 Wesley wrote in his *Journal* from Bristol, "Being now clear in my own mind, I took a step which I had long weighed in my mind, and appointed Mr. Whatcoat and Mr. Vasey to go and serve the desolate sheep in America."[5] This was done without any recorded reference to Anglican authorities. Wesley was not a bishop entitled to ordain ministers in the Anglican Church, even if he felt entitled to ordain according to New Testament teaching. For what denomination was he ordaining them? At this stage there was no Methodist church yet there were men ordained to serve the Methodists. This can be seen as another step in the process towards an independent denomination. Asbury served as one of the first superintendents, or bishops, of the American Methodist Episcopal Church from his ordination in 1784 until his death in 1816.

American Methodism came into a frontier situation and appealed to ordinary people because the circuit riders (itinerant preachers) preached a theology that was relevant to their everyday lives. Methodism evolved a hierarchy from the bottom up consisting of local class meetings with class leaders, itinerant preachers for circuits, districts, and annual conferences. In South Africa, Methodism also had to work in a frontier situation. The difference, however, was that in South Africa what became by far the majority of Methodist Church members came from the indigenous population and not from overseas as settlers or slaves. In America, too, there were splinter groups of Methodists. The only group to which we will refer here is the African Methodist Episcopal Church (AMEC) because it has direct links with the African Independent Church movement.

The AMEC grew out of the pain and struggle for freedom of African slaves in America during the eighteenth century. In spite of the difficulties they faced, slaves met together for worship and during the Second Great Awakening large numbers were converted. One of the young slaves was Richard Allen (1760-1831) who became the founder of the AMEC. Allen was a member of St. George's Methodist Episcopal Church, Philadelphia. In 1791 white members of St. George's became alarmed at the growing numbers of black worshipers and voted that black members should be moved to the back rows of the gallery. Allen and others left the building and started to collect money to build a church of their own. Racial tension increased between black and white Methodists and in 1816 black congregations from Delaware, New Jersey, and Pennsylvania united and formed the African Methodist Episcopal Church with Allen as the first bishop. The same year the first General Conference of the AMEC adopted Methodist teaching as their official doctrine. The motto of the AMEC became, "God our Father, Christ our Redeemer, Man our brother."[6] Eighty years later, in 1896, the Ethiopian Church invited the AMEC to start working in South Africa. By that time the AMEC already had numerous churches in America, an interest in mission in Africa

(Sierra Leone), and a university, Wilberforce, at which men and women who would become important members of the African Independent Church movement in South Africa were educated. None of the independents appears to have given doctrine as the reason for leaving the Methodist Church. All subscribed to Wesley's teaching and scriptural holiness continued to be preached in most of the new churches. Indeed the Holiness Movement of the nineteenth century had its roots in American Methodism and Wesley's teaching on Christian perfection. Was it doctrine that led people to leave the mainstream Methodists and form their own churches? Why did they feel they could no longer remain within the Methodist connection? Every split was the result of the culmination of a series of events. We have seen how Methodism itself was formed in this way. We will see this as we examine the South African Independent Churches that call themselves Methodist.

II

The first Methodists in South Africa were British soldiers belonging to the occupying force. In 1806 the British took over the Cape from the Dutch due to hostilities in Europe. The first Methodist was George Middlemiss (72nd Regiment).[7] He was joined by Sergeant John Kendrick (21st Light Dragoons), a recognized local preacher, who formed a small Methodist Society made up of soldiers.[8] They requested that a minister be sent to the Cape. In 1816 Barnabas Shaw became the first permanent Methodist minister. At his mission station, Lilyfountain, Shaw trained the first indigenous candidate for the Methodist ministry, Jacob Links, whose name was recorded as an "assistant missionary" in 1822.[9] He was martyred in 1825 while on a missionary journey in the northern Cape with Methodist preacher William Threlfall and Johannes Jager, a convert.

William Shaw opened the way for Methodist missions in the eastern Cape. As the number of missionaries grew, the work spread further inland. In the Transvaal pioneer work was done by Africans who left home to seek work in the Cape or Natal where they joined the Methodist Church. When they returned home they started small societies and when the missionary Owen Watkins arrived he found that there were already people there who called themselves Methodists.

Towards the end of the nineteenth century the so-called "Ethiopian" movement came to the fore in South Africa. Ethiopia had long been a symbol for black aspirations of freedom from white domination. In the Revised Standard Version of the Bible, Psalm 68:31 reads, "Let Ethiopia hasten to stretch out her hands to God." This became the motto of the Ethiopian movement, but it had been used many times previously. The so-called African or Ethiopian churches, founded between 1880 and 1920, saw continuity in Ethiopian Christianity and formed churches that were run for Africans by Africans, but differed only in detail from the mission churches whence they had originated.

Many South Africans, both black and white, saw these churches as a threat. There was a fear of rising African nationalism among whites. Mission work had produced a new African middle class, educated at mission schools and able to hold responsible positions. However, positions with any kind of status were seldom open to African applicants and the church was the only place where they could expect recognition. The top hierarchy of all the churches in South Africa was white, usually expatriate, so there was little opportunity of promotion for African ministers.

From 1903 to 1905, and again in 1925, the South African Native Affairs Department ordered Commissions to look into the existence and influence of the African Independent Churches. Many of the AIC leaders gave evidence before the Commissions and left accounts of the origins and membership of their churches. In 1926, shortly after the publication of the Report of the 1925 Commission, a Methodist minister, Allen Lea, published a book titled, *The Native Separatist Churches in South Africa* in which he described the causes of schism as he understood them. He saw Ethiopianism as "anti-white" and said that the main causes were the:

1. Desire for independence in church matters
2. "Color bar" among white missionaries (racism)
3. Discipline of black clergy
4. Example of Europeans
5. Personal ambition
6. Desire for a tribal church (recognition of African culture)
7. Desire to administer church property and money.[10]

Methodist doctrine was another predisposing factor that made black clergymen feel confident that they would be able to run their own affairs. Setiloane believes that Methodist doctrine gave people assurance of their own self-worth, even if they did not feel appreciated by the missionaries.[11] He holds that the doctrines of regeneration and Christian perfection brought Christianity closer to how indigenous people experienced God and divine activity. This perhaps explains why so many of the Independent Churches claimed to follow Methodist doctrine.

III

Although not the first in southern Africa, the first breakaway to take place from a Methodist Church in South Africa was that of Nehemiah Tile (d.1891). His reasons for leaving varied from lack of understanding by, and a personality clash with, the District Superintendent, desire for recognition of the importance of African culture, and a desire to unite the tribe to which he belonged. Tile left the ministry in 1882 after a disagreement with the District Superintendent at the time, Theophilus Chubb. At the time Tile was still a probationer minister. The immediate cause of Chubb's anger was Tile's donation of an ox to the circumcision feast of Dalindeybo, the son of the Chief.[12] This was in accordance with African culture, but Chubb had little sympathy with any African customs he considered pagan. Tile was called to appear before a minor Synod and when he refused to leave Thembuland he was asked to resign from the ministry.

In 1884 Tile founded the Thembu National Church at Qokolweni near Umtata. He had great respect for the British Crown, made the Chief the head of the new church, and followed Anglican tradition. When Chief Ngangeliswe died soon after the church was formed, Dalindeybo succeeded him. Tile died in 1891 and Dalindeybo again joined the Methodist Church in 1895. Slowly, Tile's church changed and today there are still members of the church he founded in the eastern Cape who call themselves the "Ethiopian Church," the "African Native Mission Church," and the "Ethiopian Catholic Church of South Africa." They claim Tile as their founder.

IV

The Ethiopian Church was established in 1892 and that year is usually taken to mark the beginning of the Ethiopian Movement in South Africa. The founder, Mangena Mokone (1851-1931), was born in Sekhukuniland, Transvaal. After his father was killed in the Swazi War of 1863 Mokone and a friend fled to Durban where they found work. Mokone went to night school and learned to read. He also attended the Aliwal Street Methodist Chapel where he was converted. He attended Edendale College, Pietermaritzburg, and became a local preacher. In 1880 he was selected by the Methodist Synod of Natal to become a probationer minister. Two years later he was sent to work in Pretoria.[13] Mokone next went to the newly established gold-mining town of Johannesburg where he made friends who would later join the Ethiopian Church. During these years District Meetings or Synods were segregated. At the so-called "Native Meetings" the work of evangelists and "native assistant missionaries" (probationers) was discussed and tuition given to those on trial. At this time there were only two ordained black ministers, Mangena Mokone and Daniel Msimang, from Swaziland. The meetings were separated so as to allow white ministers to return to their circuits. However, black ministers did not agree with this policy and understood that the meetings were segregated and that there appeared to be discrimination between black and white preachers.

Mokone not only rejected the separate District Meetings, he also felt that some of the evangelists were treated unfairly, especially Samuel Mathabathe, the pioneer of Methodism in Sekhukuniland, who had never been ordained.[14] In African culture age and status go hand in hand. Mokone resigned from the Wesleyan Methodist Church in 1892, "to serve God in my own way."[15] He gave a number of reasons for resigning, among them lack of understanding by white ministers, no family allowances for black ministers, and poor wages.

In November 1892 the founding service of the Ethiopian Church took place in a private home. Mokone took as his rallying call Psalm 68:31, "Ethiopia shall soon stretch out her hands to God." He then traveled to the eastern Cape to gain support for the new movement where he met James Dwane (1848-1915). Dwane was a fellow Methodist minister who was also unhappy with his treatment by the church authorities. Dwayne was a graduate of Healdtown where he had spent some time living in the home of the missionary minister Robert Lamplough.[16] He decided to offer for the ministry and after being recognized as a local preacher, returned to Healdtown to study theology.[17] Three years later, his studies completed, he joined Lamplough as assistant minister at Annshaw Mission[18] near Middeldrift in the eastern Cape. He was ordained in 1881. His potential was soon recognized and he was made a member of the committee to enlarge the Xhosa hymnbook. In 1890 he became one of the examiners for African probationer ministers.

In 1892 Dwane went to Britain to raise money to build a college in the Seplan circuit near Queenstown where he worked. He sent home glowing reports that were printed in the *South African Methodist*. For example, in September 1892 he preached at Armagh Methodist Church where, "he gave a most touching and beautiful account of mission work among the Kaffirs, in which he had been engaged for over twenty years."[19] However, when he returned home the Methodist authorities decided that the money would best be used in the general mission fund. Disappointed, Dwane decided that he could no longer remain a member of the Wesleyan Methodist Church. Thus, when he met Mokone in 1893 he was ready to join the Ethiopian Church.

In 1895 the leaders of the Ethiopian Church discussed amalgamating with the AMEC in America. Mokone's niece, Charlotte Manye[20] was a student at Wilberforce University and wrote glowing accounts of the ministry of the AMEC. She emphasized that the leadership of the autonomous denomination was black. Mokone and the others decided to investigate the possibility of amalgamation. Dwane was sent to America where he was re-obligated (or ordained) and returned to South Africa to re-obligate the ministers of the Ethiopian Church, most of whom had been members of mission churches.

In March 1898 Bishop Henry M. Turner of the AMEC in America visited South Africa. He ordained a number of new ministers and, when he returned home, left Dwane in charge. Dwane became unhappy with the AMEC and in 1899 approached the Anglican Archbishop, West-Jones, in Cape Town to ask if he and his followers could join the Anglicans as an independent Order of Ethiopia. This was agreed and in 1900 a "Compact" was signed. At the Anglican Synod held at Durban in 1999, the Order of Ethiopia decided to become the autonomous Ethiopian Episcopal Church and discussion is currently taking place as to the future relationship between the Order and the Anglicans. Mokone remained in the AMEC and became an elder in the church[21] serving until his death in October 1931. The AMEC in South Africa celebrates "Mokone Day" in his memory.

One of the problems of amalgamation was that the AMEC sent American bishops to lead the South African branch of the church. The first South African bishop was Francis Gow, elected in 1956. There is a new movement within the AMEC, called the AMEC of South Africa, whose members are looking to be less bound by their links to America.

V

The Independent Methodist Church grew out of the Methodist Church in Swaziland. Joel Msimang, the founder, was the son of the pioneer missionary of the Swazi church, Daniel Msimang (d.1903).[22] The Methodist Church in Swaziland was established at the invitation of King Sobuza I who had a dream that white men would come and bring a book. He wanted education for his people, so he sent envoys to the missionaries at Thaba 'Nchu asking them to send a teacher. It was only in 1844 that the Superintendent of the District, William Shaw, under whose guidance the territory fell, sent James Allison and Richard Giddy to Swaziland to assess the situation.

When Allison later returned the old King had died and the new King, Mswati, was asserting his authority among the people. Allison did not understand Swazi customs and did not greet the King nor listen when he was told to keep out of the hostilities. As a result, he and the converts at the mission at Mahamba were forced to flee to Natal. They settled at Indaleni and later at Edendale and Driefontein. Among those who accompanied Allison was a young man named Nhlanhla Daniel Msimang. He had grown up near the Methodist mission at Imperani.[23] While still a young shepherd boy he had a vision that white men would come in peace and help them become prosperous. A few months later Allison arrived and the missionaries were welcomed. Visions and dreams are often seen as signs that the dreamer will become a great leader. Msimang was destined to become a leader in the Methodist Church of Southern Africa.

In 1880 when John Kilner of the Wesleyan Methodist Missionary Society visited South Africa he reported on the indigenous ministry and noted that Africans were doing the, "greater part of the vernacular work on their respective stations, preaching, teaching, visiting, etc. . . . The Lord had blessed their work abundantly . . . and they had the spirit and bearing of gentlemen."[24] He complained that so few African preachers were ordained and wondered why this was so. A number of African preachers were called to become probationer ministers, among them Daniel Msimang and Mangena Mokone.

In 1877 Msimang was one of the leaders who initiated Nzondolelo, a missionary outreach to the people of Zululand by the Methodists at Edendale and Driefontein. The move came from the local people and was not started by the missionaries who heard about it when presented with the money collected for the mission. Through the Nzondolelo movement money was collected to reopen the church in Swaziland.[25] In 1883 Msimang moved to Swaziland to serve the Mahamba mission. He visited the King and everything was done in accordance with Swazi culture. The Swazi mission had its difficulties, but was very successful. Msimang was ordained and although he was under the white circuit superintendent, he was too far removed from the rest of the circuit to find this irksome. In 1885 the Reverend Underwood was sent to Mahamba, but remained there only for a year. Otherwise, Daniel Msimang was in charge and was later joined by his son Joel. Joel had been challenged to become a minister by Owen Watkins. As a probationer he was sent to help his father who was old and unwell. When his father died, Joel expected to remain in Swaziland, but the Methodist Synod decided to send him to Mozambique. Robert Mashaba, the minister in Mozambique had been unfairly accused of treachery by the Portuguese authorities and could no longer work there.[26] Joel was afraid that his children, accustomed to the healthy climate in Swaziland, would catch tropical diseases. His eldest son was finishing his schooling and would later go to London to become a lawyer. Msimang knew what Mozambique was like because his father had visited the country in 1891[27] for the Reverend Watkins.[28] However, Msimang left the Methodist Church not just for personal reasons. The Ethiopian movement had been growing and he knew Mokone. In 1885 Underwood had tried to impose the British style of worship on the people. He wrote, "my intention is to make a circuit as near as possible to the English model and put on the plan large kraals in the neighbourhood."[29] When Underwood left, it was easier to be more African and less British in their style of worship. Msimang left the Methodist Church in 1904 and in accordance with a request from some of the old Mahamba congregation founded the Independent Methodist Church in 1906. These "Methodists" use the Methodist hymnbook and keep Methodist traditions. They have an annual conference. Their manner of worship is the same as any Methodist African congregation in South Africa.

VI

The "Donkey Church" is a twentieth-century independent church. It received its name because of the role played by a donkey when the church was first established.[30] The bitterness caused by the schism remains in the memory of the older members of both the Albert Street Methodist Church, Johannesburg, and the Methodist Church in Africa. The events that led to the formation of the church began in 1929 when the Synod of the Transvaal and Swaziland District decided to raise the price of the quarterly class meeting tickets from two shillings to two shillings and sixpence. During the Great Depression the African population of Johannesburg felt the repercussions of the falling economy. The subject of the class money remained on the agenda of quarterly meetings and synods without agreement being reached.

Distrust grew and at the Easter Day service in 1933 it reached a climax. The police were called to protect the white ministers. From that time there was talk of breaking away from the Methodist Church. When their pleas were turned down by the Conference of 1933 a meeting was called to start their own church. On 28 May 1933 the launch of the new church was celebrated with a procession through Sophiatown led by a donkey, the sign of humility. The Reverend Malakia Ramashu, the leader of the new church, was a senior and highly respected minister who had held several offices in the Methodist Church. This schism was caused by the economic climate of the time and lack of understanding by the authorities. Visitors from the Methodist Church in Africa are welcomed in Methodist services today.

VII

To what extent can the members of African Independent Churches that have left the Methodist Church be considered Methodists? Starting with the earliest days of Methodism we see that Methodists have been prone to schism. This does not appear to have been for doctrinal reasons. Wesley's teaching, based as it is on Scripture, has never been disputed and is accepted, albeit with African interpretation, by these churches. The causes of schism appear to be more mundane.

Starting with the New Connexion we see a yearning for more training for local preachers and recognition of the abilities of the laity. Lack of recognition was also a contributory cause of schism in many of the African Independent Churches. We see this when Mangena Mokone objected to separate District Meetings as he felt that the opinions of black preachers were being overlooked. Another cause was money, often combined with lack of understanding by the Methodist authorities. Examples of this are Dwane's defection from the Methodist Church and later from the AMEC when neither would help build the educational center he felt was needed. Money also caused bitterness in the Methodist Church of Africa. Services among African Methodists in South Africa are often more liturgical than in the so-called white churches. The singing is African-style and many of the hymns are written in the African languages and are not just translations of the hymns in the Methodist hymnbook. The same Xhosa or Sotho hymnbook used in Methodist worship is used by the Independent Methodists and other churches of Methodist origin.

Could we all belong to the same Methodism? There are many groups started by people who were once Methodists. None of these would wish to be governed by the Methodist authorities, yet most of them would like to be welcomed in a Methodist fellowship. Is it not time that there was some umbrella organization where all that call themselves "Methodist" can feel at home? The time has come to recognize the African Independent Churches as the fastest growing and largest group of Christians in Africa. Many of them call themselves Methodist. Are they not Methodists too?

Notes

1. J. Whiteside, *History of the Wesleyan Methodist Church of South Africa* (London: Paternoster, 1905), 16.

2. T. Jackson, *The Centenary of Wesleyan Methodism: A Brief Sketch* (London: John Mason, 1839), 223.

3. Jackson, 152.

4. Jackson, 152.

5. Elisabeth Jay, ed., *The Journal of John Wesley: A Selection* (Oxford: Oxford University Press, 1987).

6. J. R. Coan, *The Expansion of Missions of the African Methodist Episcopal Church in South Africa 1896-1909* (Ph.D. diss., Connecticut, 1961), 20.

7. *Methodist Magazine*, 1908, in *The Journal of the Methodist Historical Society of South Africa*, no. 1 (October 1952): 3.

8. Whiteside, 35.

9. W. Shaw, *Memorials in South Africa* (Cape Town: A. A. Balkema, 1970), 133.

10. A. Lea, *The Native Separatist Churches in South Africa* (Cape Town:

Juta and Co., 1926), 20, 48.
11. G. Setiloane, "The Contribution of the Methodist Church to the African Indigenous Church Movement" in G. C. Oosthuizen, ed., *Religion Alive Studies in the New Movements and Indigenous Churches in Southern Africa* (Johannesburg: Hodder and Stoughton, 1986), 191.
12. C. Saunders, "Tile and the Thembu Church: Politics and Independency on the Cape Eastern Frontier in the Late Nineteenth Century" in *Journal of African History* 11 no. 4 (1970): 555.
13. Joan A. Millard, *Malihambe Let the Word Spread* (Pretoria: Unisa Press, 1999), 48.
14. *Minutes of the Synod of the Transvaal and Swaziland District*, 1895.
15. *Minutes of the Synod of the Transvaal and Swaziland District*, 1892.
16. Millard, 20.
17. Healdtown trained teachers as well as preparing men for the ministry.
18. Annshaw Mission was named after the wife of the Reverend William Shaw, pioneer missionary, in the eastern Cape.
19. *S A Methodist*, 10 September 1892. The word "Kaffir" was the name given to indigenous South Africans by the European settlers. The use of the word is illegal today.
20. Charlotte Manye Maxeke (c1872-1939) was the first black South African woman to graduate with a B Sc. She was a founder of the Bantu Women's League, the forerunner of the African National Congress Women's League and is still considered a role model.
21. *Minutes of the Cape Conference* of the AMEC held on 20-21 December 1901.
22. Obituary in the British *Minutes of Conference* 1904.
23. Today this is in the Ficksburg area of the Free State.
24. J. Kilner, *Report* (London: Wesleyan Methodist Missionary Society, 1881).
25. Nzondolelo means to desire earnestly. Daniel Msimang told the missionaries, "We heard the cries of those who want to be saved. . . . We felt we ought to send people to them . . . ." Whiteside, 402.
26. For awhile Mashaba was imprisoned on Cape Verde but was released at the insistence of the Methodist authorities on condition that he did not return to Mozambique.
27. *Notices of the Wesleyan Methodist Missionary Society*, 1891.
28. Letter from Watkins to the WMMS dated 1890 explaining that due to an outbreak of smallpox he could not visit Mozambique but that Msimang would do so the following year.
29. *Notices of the Wesleyan Methodist Missionary Society*, 1896.
30. The church was known for its dramatic enactments. On one occasion while dramatizing Christ's triumphant entry into Jerusalem, a temperamental bucking donkey threw its rider to the ground. This church was also known as the Bantu Methodist Church.

9

The Evangelical United Brethren Mission in Asia: Two Contrasting Ecumenical Scenarios

J. Steven O'Malley

The mission work of the Evangelical United Brethren (EUB), and their predecessor bodies, the Church of the United Brethren in Christ (UB) and the Evangelical Church (EC) were characterized overall by distinctive patterns of structure and strategy which were emphatically ecumenical in nature. This article will explore those patterns as found in two different Asian cultures, with a view of discovering how these ecumenical experiments in overseas missions were impacted in diverse ways by political conditions in those fields. The fields to be examined are China and Japan.

Since we are concerned with an aspect of missions that developed within a non-Methodist tradition which was only later organically joined with that tradition in 1968, an introduction to their distinctive missional perspectives will be included. EUB origins are traced to German-American revival leaders of the late eighteenth century, who were German Reformed, Mennonite, and Lutheran in affiliation. They stood in fraternal but not in organic relationship with early American Methodist leaders. Initially influenced by German Pietism, especially its Reformed and Radical Pietist expressions, William Otterbein and Martin Boehm (for the UB) became the chief catalysts for disseminating the revival movement, earlier represented by George Whitefield, into the German population of

Pennsylvania, Maryland, and the Shenandoah Valley of Virginia. The Evangelicals, based in the itinerant evangelism of a Lutheran-born layman, Jacob Albright, showed greater affinities with Methodist polity and doctrine, although Methodist influences were recast in the vocabulary of Pietism. Unlike "church" and "plain" Dutch (colloquial for "Deutsch"), they became known as the "bush meeting Dutch," due to their preference for outdoor "big meetings" (*grosse Versammlungen*) which sought to introduce their frontier adherents to an intense experience of new birth in Christ.

The Pietist heritage of the EUB is seen not only in the centrality of the new birth, but also in a forward-looking view of salvation history, in which traditional European churches would be superceded by new end-time configurations of Kingdom life among the reborn. These manifestations of that life would herald the return of Christ as the final Lord of history. In accordance with that outlook, the UB also diverged more significantly than did the Evangelicals from Methodist missional structures. This was a reflection of their formation as an "unpartisan brotherhood" in Christ (1800) among German Americans of conflicting ecclesiastical backgrounds (primarily German Reformed and Mennonite). In their bush meetings, they identified themselves as pilgrims "on the journey home" as they sang, "*Wir sind auf der Reise heim.*"[1] Their Kingdom goal gave definition to their deeds and the communities they were instituting were to them precursors of a transformed humanity that God was preparing. In Otterbein's words, their hope was "a more glorious state of the church than ever has been."[2] Whether at home or overseas, UB were never really at home with a self-sufficient denominational outlook. They were mandated by their founders to embark upon an ongoing search for other "sisters and brethren in Christ." Furthermore, the visible form which that "brotherhood" would assume was not mandated by an a priori design of polity. It would be configured in accordance with the Kingdom-manifesting leadership of the Holy Spirit and in ways that were appropriate to the cultural identity of those peoples who were being served. Given the largely rural and ethnically provincial outlook of the mid-Atlantic and midwestern home base which undergirded that enterprise,[3] EUB achievements in overseas ecumenical missions may be considered noteworthy, if not astonishing.

How, then, did this ecumenical mission strategy play out in the Asian fields of China and Japan? In each case, it did so in ways that caused strains in that strategy, thereby requiring major adjustments of expectations for each field.

I

A plausible case can be made that an indigenous and eventually united Protestant witness was established in China in the late nineteenth and early twentieth centuries to a considerable degree through the initiative of the UB mission in South China. Although, after three decades of service, this entity would be attacked and dismantled by the Maoist regime that gained political control after the Second World War, its legacy remains a testimony to the UB/EUB ecumenical approach to world missions.

The UB entered China in 1889 under the auspices of their Woman's Missionary Association (WMA), who made early initiatives in overseas mission fields for their denomination.[4] This was the year following the prejudicial "Exclusion Act" of the United States Congress, which prohibited Chinese immigration to the United States, thus adversely affecting Sino-American relations. The British Governor of Hong Kong had stated that "business interests" were paramount to "religious" and merely "humanitarian sentiments" in relating to the Chinese culture.

Into this volatile atmosphere, the WMA voted to send a party of four. It was led by George and Ellen Sickafoose who had operated a UB school for Chinese immigrants in Portland, Oregon. It included a Chinese-American, Moy Ling, and a remarkable woman, Austia Patterson, who remained on the field the longest and became the first superintendent of the mission. She was soon joined by a physician, Sarah Halverson. Together they made forays into the new areas where no Christians and no Caucasians had ever been seen.[5] They chose to live in the community they served rather than in a mission compound. Numerous institutions followed, including medical and educational facilities. The facilities survived the anti-western Boxer Rebellion (1900) unscathed. This may reflect the fact that their work was among that minority of western missions that was not closely associated with political powers then attempting to open China to world trade. A mission conference was started in 1908, shortly before the founding of the Republic of China (1910).[6]

While these women provided the early focus on indigenous ministries, which also laid a basis for a self-governing and strongly evangelistic Chinese church, the key UB ecumenical leadership on this field was provided by Charles and Kathryn Shoop. They exerted decisive influence in the founding of the Church of Christ in China (CCC) between 1926 and 1928. During that time, UB work was transferred to the Kwangtung Synod of the CCC in south China. It was the first response on an overseas field to the 1925 UB General Conference decision to "establish victorious native churches as quickly as possible."[7] The Shoops served 46 years in this field, surviving two world wars, internment under Japanese occupation, and the Maoist revolution of 1949. It was the rise of nationalist sentiment in the 1920s that alerted them to the need to transfer the mission fully into Chinese hands. Its institutions included two hospitals, several secondary schools, and a theological seminary (Miller Seminary), as well as numerous local churches. Plans for a united church had been discussed by Presbyterians and Congregationalists, but, according to Latourette, the initiative was taken by the UB mission, which "promptly approved the plan in its entirety, and the other cooperating missions sanctioned it with reservations."[8] This became the model for the ecumenical work of the CCC throughout China.

The Shoops are to be credited with facilitating this decision lauded by Latourette. Charles Shoop's "profound respect for my Chinese brothers" led him to value indigenous leadership. His goal was to recruit only missionaries who would "have faith in the Chinese." He was the personal mentor to Peter Wong, who became the foremost interpreter of Chinese work to EUB in America and who later served as Superintendent of the Hong Kong Synod of the CCC. Shoop's nonpaternalistic attitude reflected the UB pattern of seeking authentic unity in Christ among persons of diverse backgrounds expecting God to do a new thing as old patterns submit to the movement of salvation history.

While the UB were toiling in south China, Evangelicals began their work in the Hunan Province of central China in 1898. Evangelicals entered China as two separate groups, following a traumatic division that occurred in 1891-1894. They adopted a strong declaration on world missions in its Articles of Faith.[9] C. Newton Dubs, MD, who was appointed United Evangelical Church (UEC) Missionary Superintendent, arrived in Changsha, the capital of Hunan, in 1900. He was assisted by language training and cultural orientation provided on location by Griffith Johns, head of the London Missionary Society. Within the first 20 years, numerous mission stations, two hospitals, and a secondary school (Albright Academy) were opened. A theological school was opened in cooperation with Presbyterians, Wesleyan Methodists, and the Reformed Church (USA). Following in close succession, the EA began its work in adjacent west Hunan in 1900, carried out in consultation with J. Hudson Taylor of the China Inland Mission.

By 1926, the reunited Evangelical Church had a mission force of 60 with 220 Chinese pastors, a momentum that would be reversed by the waves of civil conflict that racked Hunan between 1923 and 1928. The weak Manchu dynasty was overthrown by a heady brew of Bolshevik and anti-western nationalist sentiment. Order was restored at last with the triumph of Chiang Kai Shek and a more moderate Nationalist Party, but the number of missionaries had been reduced from 60 to 8 and mission properties were ravaged. This led the Evangelicals to launch an indigenous China Conference in 1937. However, that year also brought the Japanese invasion of China, followed by civil strife between Nationalists and Bolsheviks, which brought the China Conference to a state of prostration. After the EUB union in 1946, the Hunan work, like the earlier work of the UB in south China, was transferred completely to the CCC. It contributed 100 churches and preaching stations to the united church.[10] The strenuous efforts to reconstruct the war-shattered institutions of the China fields in the postwar era were only to be overcome by the Maoist victory in 1949, resulting in the arrest or flight of all EUB leaders in China and the transfer of all assets into the hands of the indigenous synods of Hunan and Kwangtung. Calvin Reber of the south China mission observed that the Chinese pastors, under pressure to denounce the missionaries, did all they could to maintain their loyalty and friendship, and maintain the time-honored UB tradition of "unpartisan spiritual fellowship in Christ."[11] Only a vestige of the extensive EUB China mission would continue until 1968, based in Hong Kong.

II

While Evangelicals selected Germany as their first and primary overseas mission field (1850), the first of their numerous secondary fields was Japan. The call to establish a mission there was heard in 1853. As distinct from the mission to the German *"Vaterland,"* this was called the "heathen mission" (*heidnische Mission*). This was before an ecumenical, indigenous approach to world missions had been manifested among Evangelicals. In this field, that approach would be introduced only under imperial governmental pressure in the twentieth century.

The Evangelical mission was launched in 1875 when General Conference endorsed a resolution to send a team to Yokohama. This was an international team consisting of an American teacher, Rachel Hudson, an American physician, Frederick Krecker, and a Swiss preacher, Karl Halmhuber.[12] Their work established the Evangelical mission in Japan as among the early Protestant missions operating there.

A breakthrough in their efforts occurred when an aristocratic youth of the Samurai class was converted under Krecker's ministry. Soon a Bible training school was started in Tokyo. In 1880, Krecker and Jacob Hartzler published their translation of what continued through the mid-twentieth century as the only complete version of the Old Testament in the Japanese language.[13] Krecker's ministry to typhoid victims in Tokyo led to his premature death. His legacy of sacrificial service reportedly turned numerous Japanese hearts to the foreigner's religion. In 1886 one of the largest Protestant church edifices was built in Tokyo, bearing the name, the "Krecker Memorial Evangelical Church."

Soon a plethora of other projects were launched, including a boat ministry among urban dwellers living on canal boats, an English school, a deaf-oral school, and a theological school in Tokyo.[14] One of the seminary students was Gumpei Yamamuro, the first leader of the Salvation Army in Japan.[15] In the earlier years these mission institutions were fervent champions of the Evangelicals' prized emphasis on entire sanctification, which then served as the *raison d'être* for maintaining their identity in overseas missions.

Hudson's appeal for support led to the first denomination-wide organization of the Woman's Missionary Society (1884). Although the novelty of women in mission leadership was not initially accepted by the patriarchal leadership of the denomination's Mission Board, the women's success in raising awareness and funding for missions throughout the brotherhood soon won them the respect of the Board. With their decisive assistance, a Japan Conference was organized in 1891, the same year as the traumatic division that occurred in the North American mother church.[16] By 1918, 47 kindergartens had been established by the conference, and an Evangelical, Lois Kramer, was serving as President of the Japanese Kindergarten Union. By 1927, all district superintendents in the conference were Japanese. Superintendent Paul S. Mayer served as President of the Japan Christian Council in 1929, which then represented all Protestant missions in Japan.

By comparison, the UB work in Japan manifested a concern for an indigenous church that would be led by Japanese pastors from its beginnings. That mission began in 1895 by sending Japanese nationals who had trained in America to the Osaka area. Their first encounter with Japanese culture indicates how that enlightened strategy was not flawlessly executed.[17] Japan Superintendent Arthur T. Howard, later the Asian missionary bishop for the UB, developed a long-term strategy for this mission, which resulted in the formation of a Japan UB conference in 1902 composed exclusively of indigenous ministers. This, in turn, led to UB cooperation with Congregationalists in operating Doshisha University where a UB missionary, A. B. Shively, served in the chair of religious education. One of his colleagues, missionary J. Edgar Knipp, pioneered union mission work among Buddhists in the Kyoto area. The outstanding indigenous Japanese UB preacher was Takejira Ishigura, pastor of First UB Church, Kyoto. The growth of the Evangelical and UB missions would continue until the political disruptions of 1940.

The Evangelicals and the UB participated in every pan-Japanese Christian movement from those sponsored by the Evangelical Alliance in 1901 to Kagawa's extended "Kingdom of God movement" in the 1930s.[18] However, all of these efforts were overshadowed by the events of April 1940, when the Japanese Diet passed the so-called "Religious Organization Control Act." By this decree, Christianity gained status as one of three recognized religions, alongside Buddhism and Shintoism. It further resulted in the formation of the Church of Christ in Japan (the *Kyodan*) in August, 1940, with a single executive head and a common creed. This comprehensive Protestant church represented twenty denominations then operating in Japan. It represented a self-governing and self-supporting entity that grew by 1941 to include 42 denominations. Moreover, the Kyodan was not solely the creation of government policy. It can also be characterized, at least in part, as the inspired action of Protestant leaders who were responding to new pressures from Japanese society. Although Christianity was now on a par with the traditional religions in Japan, this Act was also a signal that the prevailing American denominational consciousness could not long endure.

In actuality, Christian activity in Japan would experience severe restrictions during the Second World War. Japanese pastors were often enlisted for manual labor while their wives continued to lead services. While there was official recognition of the Kyodan, there was a sharp rise of nativist sentiment during the war, with many Japanese viewing Christianity as a "foreign faith" from "enemy nations." Under those conditions, the number of Protestant missionaries in Japan was reduced from about 100 to 39, half of whom were German or Finnish. The fifteen American missionaries who remained were interned. The American denomination with the largest number of interned missionaries (three) was the Evangelical Church.[19] One of those interned, Laura Mauk, had a considerable following in Japanese society. In a volume chronicling her service, there appears a lengthy list of prominent Japanese pastors, scientists, journalists, businessmen, and educational leaders, all of whom were alumni of her Bible classes and who called themselves her "spiritual sons."[20] After the War, Mauk became an honored figure in EUB mission circles in North America.

Rising like a phoenix from the war's devastation, this governmentally-imposed ecclesiastical structure, the Kyodan, would continue to function with renewed energy in the postwar years. It would remain the vehicle through which the newly-formed EUB Church would continue to work through 1968.

The first postwar report from this field surveyed an occupied, devastated land filled with human tragedy and despair.[21] In late 1945, the Foreign Missions Conference of North America, which represented the American denominations participating in the Kyodan, received an urgent request from Japan for missionaries to return. One of the two named by General MacArthur to lead the way in launching rehabilitation of the Protestant churches was Superintendent Paul S. Mayer of the Evangelical (soon to be EUB) mission. Although MacArthur rescinded the Japanese legislation that had created the Kyodan, 85% of Japanese Protestants remained within it. Eight American denominations, including the EUB, joined in an Interboard Committee, based in New York, to direct efforts in church development. By 1949, the Committee had overseen the reconstruction of 200 churches and four theological seminaries, two of which had EUB roots.

As the decade of the 1960s approached, membership in the Kyodan increased to 172,000, with 130,000 students enrolled in its schools.[22] However, the Christian community was still less than one percent of the total Japanese population. In all, this field remained a prime instance of the EUB effort to immerse its own mission aims and strategies into the needs of indigenous and eventually ecumenical expression of the church with all the difficulties involved in such a venture. For this reason, it represented an advance in the vision that they were called to be a "homeward journeying folk," now beckoning even former enemies to join in their procession.

III

The China and Japan missions of the UB/EC/EUB developed into indigenous churches at later stages of their development, the former by the initiative of the cooperating missions and the latter by the impetus of government decree.[23] This policy, based on the 1925 UB General Conference declaration, came to its full expression in the thinking of the World Missions Division of the Board of Missions during the EUB era. Evidence of this outlook is found in: (1) the freedom to structure overseas relationships that was given to the Board; (2) its authority to consecrate and assign missionaries overseas independent of episcopal appointment; and (3) the mandate to transfer titles to overseas properties and funds to indigenous churches on those fields.[24] This freedom was to enable the

The Evangelical United Brethren Mission in Asia 127

Board to discern where consensus was building on a given field. It could then move to establish structures which would address the needs of that field in ways that did not replicate annual conference patterns prescribed for North America.

The end result of these structural aspects was not the development of a "world EUBism," but rather a more comprehensive realization of a unified Christian witness whose intent was to "uplift Christ and His coming Kingdom" as the Lord of the nations. The retired head of World Missions stated in 1987 that the EUB Church has, "through the years voluntarily surrendered its denominational sovereignty . . . for the sake of united church programs in every overseas area of its missionary operations where a united church organization has been formed."[25]

In the Asian field, only in Japan did both EUB and Methodists share a commitment to united churches, thanks to the Kyodan. Here is where the patterns diverge. In John Schaefer's words, "the majority of the Methodist overseas' conferences are part of Central Conferences organically related to the Methodist Church in the United States," while most overseas fields related to the EUB were "autonomous, united churches."[26]

However, caution should be exercised in referring to these as autonomous church bodies. They also received missionaries, regular budget subsidies, and much capital fund assistance from the home mission agency. Each was also entitled to send a fraternal representative to the EUB General Conference. They also related to a variety of other mission boards which cooperated through an interboard committee. The result is what Schaefer called a "network of connections with other sending boards."[27]

When EUB were called to be missionaries overseas, they were called to "win converts to Christ, baptize believers and establish Christ's church." However, given the very different cultural environment being faced, that church did not prove to be the EUB Church. The Asian fields offer us different scenarios whereby EUB went about the task of "exalting Christ and leaving their denominational loyalties on the North American shores."[28] This policy did not proceed without lapses. However, where it succeeded, it was marked by the following commitments: (1) to develop a fully indigenous church in each place of service as rapidly as possible; (2) to guarantee its complete independence from jurisdictions of the denomination over its affairs; (3) to encourage it to seek union with other Christian bodies within its national boundaries under a common allegiance to Jesus Christ; and (4) to encourage it to develop its own confessional and liturgical expressions and evangelistic strategies appropriate to its needs in its environment and with faithfulness to the "Church Universal through the ages," that will "best serve the interests of the Kingdom in that place."[29]

With these policies the EUB sought ways to continue their "journey homeward" pilgrimage by seeking new manifestations of Kingdom life that they believed were emerging within the cultures of the younger churches of Asia. EUB sought to demonstrate that they had a higher commitment to "unpartisan" unity in Christ than to replicating an American denominational pattern on a global scale. The political and cultural challenges encountered on those fields ultimately served to deepen and mature, rather than to discourage, their commitment to Kingdom-oriented, ecumenical missions. It was possibly their finest contribution to United Methodism.[30]

Notes

1. From "200th Anniversary Pilgrimage, 1767-1967, Commemorating the Historic Meeting of Philip William Otterbein and Martin Boehm, the Human Founders of the former United Brethren in Christ Church" (1967).

2. Arthur C. Core, *Philip William Otterbein; Pastor, Ecumenist* (Dayton, Ohio: EUB Board of Publication, 1968), 102; see also, J. Steven O'Malley, *Pilgrimage of Faith; the Legacy of the Otterbeins* (Metuchen, N.J.: Scarecrow Press, 1973), Part III.

3. In 1906, UB were cited as the most rural of all major American denominations, with over 92 percent of their churches in rural areas. See H. Richard Niebuhr, *The Social Sources of Denominationalism* (Hamden, Conn.: Shoe String Press, 1954), 183. The EUB constituency worldwide in 1947 exceeded 1,000,000 (including members, friends, and children enrolled in Christian training; the North American membership was 727,000).

4. The WMA was organized in 1875 with the strong encouragement of the male-led UB Missionary Society. The WMA had previously provided support for the UB mission to Sierra Leone (founded in 1853) and they worked with the freedmen in the American south in the Reconstruction era following the Civil War.

5. Report of Lydia Patterson *The Evangel* (March 1897), 41.

6. A. W. Drury, *History of the Church of the United Brethren in Christ* (Dayton, Ohio: Otterbein Press, 1925), 605.

7. *Report of Proceedings and Debates; The Twenty-Ninth General Conference* (Dayton, Ohio: 1925), 486.

8. Kenneth Scott Latourette, *History of Christian Missions in China* (New York: Macmillan, 1929), 803.

9. The original body founded by Albright, the Evangelical Association, experienced division over language, doctrinal, polity, and personality issues in 1891-1894, resulting in the continuation of that body alongside the United

Evangelical Church. Their reunion in 1922 produced The Evangelical Church of North America. For the UEC Mission Statement, see Harold P. Scanlon, "The Origin of the Articles of Faith of the United Evangelical Church," *Methodist History* (July, 1980): 235.

10. The CCC then represented 175,000 members in 21 synods with the fastest-growing synod being the UB-led Kwangtung Synod. Carl Heinmiller, "The Gospel in Asia," (unpublished report from June 7, 1950, in the United Methodist Archives, Madison, N.J.), 22.

11. The testimony of Dr. Calvin H. Reber, Jr., a former UB/EUB missionary in the South China field, in his unpublished personal papers, shared with the author.

12. Paul Eller, *History of Evangelical Missions* (Harrisburg, Pa.: Evangelical Press, 1942), 204. Halmhuber's records disclose the way in which candidates for baptism were examined. See Paul Mayer, "The Beginning of our Work in Japan," *Telescope Messenger* (July 1, 1950), 10.

13. Eller, 204.

14. Founded in 1893 as the Missionary Seminary of the Evangelical Association in Tokyo, it was united with a Methodist seminary, Aoyama Gakuin, in 1914. Eller, 206.

15. See R. David Rightmire, *Salvationist Samurai; Gunpai Yamamuro and the Rise of the Salvation Army in Japan* (Lanham, Md.: Scarecrow Press, 1997), 6, and Eller, 217.

16. See note 9 above.

17. Dr. Javan Corl, a former UB missionary to Japan reported the case of a Japanese-American who professed conversion in Japan and came to America to be educated at UB Lebanon Valley College. He was then recruited by the Mission Society and ordained to "return and preach to [his] fellow countrymen" in 1895. He reportedly committed an undisclosed cultural "indiscretion," described only as a "moral failure," that so alienated his Japanese hosts that he was forced to withdraw from Japan. *The Religious Telescope* (3 July 1895) and author's interview with Dr. Javan Corl, 27 July 2000.

18. Eller, 225.

19. One was a Methodist. Paul S. Mayer, "Short History of the Evangelical United Brethren Church in Japan," (1951?, unpublished manuscript in the United Methodist Archives, Madison, N.J.), n.p.

20. In 1945, Mauk wrote from her cell, "my love for Japan was so great that I chose to die if necessary with the Japanese people rather than to flee safely." When the camp officers received word that Japan had surrendered, it was reported that all Americans would be shot. Mauk records a vision of Jesus in her cell, beckoning her to maintain confidence in Him, and her fear disappeared. Laura J. Mauk, *Bridge Over Eden* (published by the Koishakawa-Hakusan Church and Miss Mauk's Monday Meeting, 1986), 11f.

21. Statistics from former Evangelical and UB missions reported 24 of 84 congregations destroyed and seven of 72 pastors killed. There remained 75 kindergarten and Bible teachers still serving. *EUB Mission Yearbook* (1948), 85, and *EUB Mission Yearbook* (1949), 65.

22. Vernon L. Farnham and W.O. Williams, "The Kyodan," (unpublished report from 1958), n.p.

23. By comparison the UB/EUB mission to the Philippines, launched by the WMA, was ecumenical from the beginning and resulted in the formation of a strongly indigenous United Church of Christ in the Philippines (1948) that was parallel to the formation of the republic of the Philippines (1947). A fuller account would include this field as well.

24. The Board of Bishops would supervise mission work abroad only where overseas annual conferences existed, which was only in Europe and Sierra Leone, West Africa.

25. Unpublished letter from former Executive Secretary of the Division of World Mission, Dr. Carl Heinmiller, 28 September 1987, provided by Dr. Calvin Reber from his personal papers. Other places where ecumenical, indigenous missions were established included the Philippines, Puerto Rico, the Dominican Republic, Ecuador, Brazil, and northern Nigeria.

26. John F. Schaefer, "The Relationship of the Evangelical United Brethren Church with Churches Overseas," *The Seminary Review* (January 1966): 17.

27. This paragraph paraphrases information provided in Schaefer, 18.

28. Schaefer, 20.

29. "Actions of the Board of Missions of the Evangelical United Brethren and Methodist Churches" (in joint deliberation), 1968 (unpublished text from personal papers of Dr. Calvin Reber, used with permission), 2.

30. A more extensive treatment of EUB mission fields is found in the author's *On the Journey Home: The Central Role of Missions in the Evangelical United Brethren Church* (New York: General Board of Global Ministries, 2001).

10

"Having Received, I Ought to Give": The Impact of Hwa Nan College on Chinese Women

Laura A. Bartels

This paper grew out of an interest in a set of missionary scrapbooks from China contained in the United Methodist Archives collection, Madison, New Jersey. I was particularly interested in the photographs of Methodist schools and hospitals and I wondered about the impact these western institutions had on the Chinese. I decided to find out more about one of those institutions, Hwa Nan College for Women, which opened in Foochow, China in 1917. Adrian Bennett has suggested that western-style educational institutions for women laid the foundation for progressive reform movements in twentieth-century China.[1] I will test Bennett's thesis by evaluating the social service activities of Hwa Nan College in order to determine how progressive they were.

In one sense the creation of Hwa Nan was a form of progressivism. The Woman's Foreign Missionary Society of the Methodist Episcopal Church (WFMS) established women's colleges because they saw them as an important tool in the evangelization and liberation of women. According to Dana Robert, nineteenth-century American missionary women frequently engaged in activities which combined evangelism with social advocacy. While at the time there were questions raised about the propriety of mixing religious and secular activities, Robert affirms it as a "holistic" approach to mission work.[2] American women's evangelization efforts were motivated by the belief that non-Christian faiths marginalized women. Because of this belief, American women sought to convert their foreign sisters in order to introduce them to a God who equally valued women and men.

Beside faith conversions, American missionary women also wanted societal conversions. They wanted to change practices in foreign cultures which they thought subjugated women. Through educational missions they sought to "raise up" foreign women to the same status they believed Christian women enjoyed in western cultures. In China this meant WFMS missionaries not only taught in schools but also took stands against such practices as foot-binding, female infanticide, slavery, and concubinage.[3] By tackling controversial issues such as these, American women optimistically believed they were "working toward the reign of God."[4]

Robert states that a "kingdom-orientation" was another common feature of nineteenth-century American women's missiologies.[5] An example of this kingdom-orientation can be found in a report given by the first president of the college, Lydia A. Trimble:

> [w]e keep ever before us, the main idea, the training of Christian leaders. We cannot forget for a moment that we are but one link in the chain which binds us all together, from the smallest dayschool up through intermediate and high school to the college. And united we will help to usher in the Kingdom of God in southern China.[6]

Granted, this sounds overconfident. However, considering the success they were having at reaching women, bringing them out of their homes, educating them, and putting a stop to the traditions of foot-binding and arranged marriages, it is understandable that the missionaries felt their ministry was gaining momentum and would soon claim all of China.

China's vast size meant that many Kingdom builders would have to be trained. That was Hwa Nan's purpose. This college would train the female leadership necessary for the advance of the church. The school's motto, "Having Received, I Ought to Give," captured the ideal of service the school tried to instill in its students. This service ideal was written into the Constitution of the college:

> Article II. Purpose and Character—The Purpose of Hwa Nan College shall be to give to young women of China under Christian auspices a literary, scientific and professional higher education and, in particular, to develop the highest type of character expressed in self-sacrifice and service.[7]

The students were to receive the best western education available. In return it was expected that they would use that training to serve in the church's mission and ministry. There is no concept here of higher education as a path to self-advancement or self-fulfillment. Hwa Nan saw its role as an educator of those who would unselfishly use the gift of education to serve others.

The missionaries' statements about the school repeatedly emphasized the necessity of service. For example, the first Dean of the college, Ethel Wallace, wrote, "Ever the strongest emphasis was laid, by word and deed, on the fact that the privilege of a higher education brings an inescapable call to serve. This feeling of responsibility for one's less-favored fellows was woven like a golden thread into the spiritual fabric of the institution."[8] For the missionaries the school's motto was more than a slogan printed on the school's letterhead. It was the reason for the school's existence. The church needed workers in order to accomplish its goals and Hwa Nan would see to it that these workers were ready and willing to serve. It should be noted that this ideal was not unique to Hwa Nan. Gael Norma Graham states that the ideal of service was a commonly held belief among missionary women in China and that it was "constantly set before their female students."[9]

The service ideal permeated the publications of Hwa Nan. The earliest example appears in a 1920 booklet from the school. An article by the Reverend W. S. Bissonette described the 1911 sod-breaking ceremony for the school in which about a dozen students from the Hwa Nan junior college took part. As workmen broke the sod, the school girls hauled the dirt away with "dangs" and baskets which they carried across their shoulders. Bissonette described these bamboo poles and baskets as "symbols of service and suffering" because of their association with the peasant class in Chinese society.[10] Bissonette saw the ceremony as an act of solidarity between two different classes, "It was fitting that these girls, privileged through the gospel of service, to enter a higher realm of usefulness, should help to bear the yoke of their toiling brothers and so set the seal of their common humanity upon the natal spirit of the new institution."[11] This observation highlights some recurring themes in Hwa Nan's historiography. The first noticeably repeated theme is the idea that the reception of the gospel is a privilege and has placed a responsibility for service on Hwa Nan students. The second is the belief that the students have a particular responsibility to minister to the poor.

The earliest example of students' work among the poor is the Sunday School program they ran for children in the villages near Hwa Nan. Many of the publications and reports from the 1920s highlight the hundreds of children reached by this student-led ministry.[12] As a part of the program the young women taught the children to sing songs, tell stories, play games, as well as instructing them in personal hygiene.[13]

Graham believes that school administrators' encouragement of this kind of extracurricular activity can be traced to three factors: the influence of the Social Gospel, the desire to create "school spirit," and the student nationalist movement. Graham states that in the early twentieth century missionaries who had been influenced by the Social Gospel began to arrive in China. She defines the Social Gospel as a theology "which emphasized social rather than individual salvation."[14] This is an oversimplification. As Janet Fishburn points out the "Social Gospel men" idealized the Victorian view of the family with its traditional gender roles. Because of this, their vision of social progress was limited to those things which "kept the Victorian family ideal intact."[15]

If Fishburn is correct, the Social Gospel would have promoted different activist roles for men and women. The social service projects carried out by men would be unlike those carried out by women given the different spheres they occupied in society. The ideal woman was identified with the domestic sphere and her projects would have reflected the type of work she did as a wife and mother. This has implications for the type of projects to which missionaries influenced by the Social Gospel might gravitate. Graham's analysis of the influence of this theology on missionaries would be improved by a discussion of its ideological roots.

Beside theological influences, Graham believes school administrators had other reasons for promoting social service. For example, she points out that college students came from different parts of China. In order to prevent the student body from splintering into provincial cliques, the administrators tried to unite students through shared labor.[16] In this way bonds of friendship were formed as students worked side by side in the community.

Furthermore, Graham thinks such service projects helped to put students' patriotic zeal to good use. Many Chinese students during this period took to the streets to express their dissatisfaction with the government. The missionaries tried to teach their students that the best way for them to help their country was through positive actions, such as starting schools for the poor, not through negative means, such as skipping class to march in the streets.[17]

However, Hwa Nan does not seem to fit the pattern Graham describes. The reports from the school do not mention any social service projects other than the Sunday Schools. While the Sunday School may have created a sense of community among the students, the only reference we can find to school spirit was in connection with the singing of school songs and the creation of school cheers.[18]

Finally, in 1927, when a group of students from other schools showed up at Hwa Nan and demanded the young women join their protest march they were rebuffed by the Hwa Nan students without the school administrators having to interfere.[19] There is no indication in the Hwa Nan reports that administrators felt the need to redirect students' patriotic fervor. Dean Wallace had nothing but praise for the mature way students expressed their patriotism during that period.[20]

Because of the student nationalist movement of the 1920s, many colleges felt it would be prudent to turn over the leadership of their schools to Chinese nationals. Lucy C. Wang took over as Hwa Nan's president in 1928. She had been one of the first students to attend Hwa Nan, and as the following quote makes clear, she was committed to Hwa Nan's ideal of Christian service:

> Having been born and having lived among the echoes of "lack of ability among the fair sex is considered a virtue" and "Boys first" in everything, on all occasions, the questions came to me! "What can a woman do?" "What does a woman amount to?" Throughout my childhood days, I realized that a Chinese woman found it impossible to live life happily. As a child, I often rebelled against the fact that I was not born a boy. When I grew older, I did at a great cost many things which a girl would not have done at that time. More than once my heart was "heavy-laden." Inequality of treatment of boys and girls made life even bitter for me at times.
>
> Hwa Nan College was the open door for me. I owe to Hwa Nan what I have and am. It was during my student days at Hwa Nan that I heard Christ call "Come unto me all ye that are heavy-laden and I will give you rest." "I am the Way, the Truth, and the Life." It was within these halls of learning and within these walls of love that I found the way of life which is Jesus Christ. Since then life has become brighter and full of promise and adventure instead of despair and darkness. I began to realize that it was my responsibility as well as my opportunity to help the mass of Chinese women to seek for a more abundant life.[21]

Just as WFMS missionaries had hoped, Wang experienced the Gospel as a liberating message which offered her a more meaningful life in comparison to the Chinese Confucian culture. Furthermore, Wang expressed the missionary women's ideal of service when she stated that she felt a responsibility to help other women find fulfillment and meaning in life. Dr. Wang satisfied her desire to help other women by serving as Hwa Nan's president from 1928 to 1952. In that role she guided the school through all the times of war and hardship that beset China during those twenty-four years.

President Wang managed to keep the school open throughout the duration of World War II although the school did have to move to Nanping before the Japanese invaded Foochow. It was during this period of tension between Japan and China that Hwa Nan's community programs began to expand. The Sunday School program was no longer the only project mentioned in reports and publications. Stories appeared about the student-run Social Center which offered services to the poor such as dispensing bean milk to children and teaching sewing classes.[22]

In 1938 all the colleges in China were ordered to begin some type of social outreach program. Wang described Hwa Nan's program in a letter to Mrs. Frank E. Baker:

> Several members of the Hwa Nan Staff got their heads together over this order and really became quite enthusiastic over planning for it, but their enthusiasm was soon clouded by the fact that we had *no* funds for such a scheme and that it could not be inaugurated without money. We canvassed every possibility, but there seemed no way out, and we were quite distressed and wondered just how we could comply with this order—and we especially wanted to because it seemed so in line with the work of Hwa Nan and the church. Just then, at what seemed like our zero hour, came word from you that we were to have the Junior Thank Offering for 1938. I wonder if you can begin to imagine what that meant to us? It was like turning on an arc-light in a candle-lit room! And then came the further word saying that Miss Margaret Seeck would join us soon for the purpose of organizing Child Welfare Work.—Just the thing that Madame Chiang had urged on the women of China!!—and so all the wonder grew! Our planning here had been rather directed toward teen-age girls and women and now God was supplying the way to round out the whole program through your interests in Child Welfare. How little we realized that He was working it all out, but how grateful I am that we can all be links in the chain of His forging.[23]

It is telling that this government order was met with anticipation rather than dread. The school's schedule and budget were already stretched to the limit, but the administration was eager to do more to serve others. They saw this service as a way to live out their calling and be faithful to God.

Jessie Lutz stated that the enthusiasm for service projects died down during WWII, and that while social service was emphasized in reports to American donors, she believed that, "such activities never became a major function of the colleges."[24] Lutz offered no corroborating evidence to support her assertion which is very different from the impression created by Hwa Nan publications. If Lutz is right then the reports and brochures coming from the school during this period are misleading, even fraudulent. However, Lutz's generalization does not apply to Hwa Nan. The pictures and reports coming out of Hwa Nan are a genuine reflection of the level of commitment the school invested in social service.

This assertion is based on two pieces of evidence. One is the crude hut Hwa Nan built to serve as their social service department after the school was forced to move to Nanping during World War II. It certainly would have been understandable if school administrators had decided to drop their social service programs during this time. The war put a great strain on resources, food, and finances. The fiscally responsible thing to do would have been to eliminate extracurricular activities and focus the budget on the basics. Yet, this was not the course taken by Hwa Nan administrators. Instead they carried out a full range of programs, first from their little hut and later from a larger facility. The type of programs undertaken during these war years included clubs for mothers and working women, a night school, a child welfare project, extension courses, and, of course, Sunday Schools.[25]

The second thing which leads us to believe these programs were carried out is a scholarship established at the school by a Nanping businessman in recognition of the students' unselfish service during the war.[26] Such recognition from outside the missionary and church community leads us to trust that Hwa Nan's publications did not overstate the amount of social service they carried out just to impress the American Board of Directors.

Hwa Nan students' commitment to community service seems to have been genuine. As Lydia Trimble made clear in a 1936 article, "Dreams Come True," Hwa Nan alumnae were expected to live by this ideal of service even after they left school:

> But we saw even greater visions than anything material, of the service "our girls" would render to their own folks, and so our motto—"Having received, I ought to give." We saw them go out thoroughly equipped in mind, body, and soul, as teachers from kindergarten up through college. We saw them as evangelists, nurses, and doctors. Dearest, perhaps, of all to a woman's heart, we saw them gracing hundreds of Christian homes, they the very heart and center of these homes. And these dreams have come true to a satisfying extent.... Are we fully satisfied? By no means. We have only a good start. There are large areas of life still untouched, many of which will be spoken of by others. I shall mention but one, our alumnae—I mean those in homes, not employed. Is it true, I wonder, that some have settled down in smug complacency, and are just

enjoying the good things of life with their families? We can think of scores of ways in which the alumnae of Hwa Nan, with graduates from other Christian schools, might be making a tremendous contribution to their communities,—namely, forming mothers' clubs, with all their possibilities, organizing neighborhood Sunday Schools, being leaders in the Mass Educational Movement and the New Life Movement.[27]

This quotation is an excellent summary of missionaries' aspirations for their "girls." These young women were supposed to graduate and go on to work in Christian schools and hospitals. If they were not employed, then they were at least to be active in Christian women's organizations in their communities. Trimble was clearly unhappy with reports that some alumnae aspired to be nothing more than housewives. Instead of staying home, she felt these women should be volunteering to help with social programs run by neighborhood churches.

The WFMS missionaries of Trimble's generation saw their work as "organized motherhood" and the type of projects mentioned by Trimble in the above quotation reflects this notion.[28] In her book, *Grace Sufficient*, Jean Miller Schmidt lifts up Frances E. Willard as a popular spokesperson for this vision of women's role in society. Schmidt quotes from Willard's book, *How to Win: A Book for Girls*:

> If I were asked the mission of the ideal woman, I would reply: *It is to make the whole world homelike*. . . . A true woman carries home with her everywhere. . . . But 'home's not merely four square walls.'. . . Woman will make homelike every place she enters, and she will enter every place on this round earth.[29]

It is easy to see how the activities Trimble wanted "her girls" involved in and the projects Hwa Nan initiated coincide with Willard's goal of making the world homelike. These projects all reflect a traditional view of women's work. They focused on women and children. They were concerned with families and the home. They did not challenge women to take their place in politics or business. Rather, they helped women become more effective mothers and housewives.

According to Graham, Methodists were not the only missionaries directing their students toward "gender specific" activities. She cited Presbyterian guidelines which suggested that male students minister to boys and men while female students ministered to women and children. She compared the list of activities for boys and girls and found that while boys were supposed to go on prison visitations, girls were assigned hospital visitations; boys worked with "boat boys" and girls with "boat girls"; boys were to preach and girls were to cook, sew, teach mothers' courses and serve as assistant nurses.[30]

Another scholar makes the same observation. In her essay, "Chinese Women and Protestant Christianity at the Turn of the Twentieth Century," Kwok Pui-Lan observes that a Victorian attitude towards women's domestic role in society was prevalent among all Protestant missionaries in China. Like Schmidt, she points out the influence of Frances E. Willard's views on women missionaries.[31] Those views encouraged women to act outside the home to help reform society, but Kwok sees these actions as "the extension of women's housekeeping roles into the public realm."[32]

In the 1950s there is evidence that Hwa Nan administrators realized they would have to expand their concept of what constituted an appropriate service program for women, not because they wanted to expand women's roles in society, but because they wanted to please the Communist government. After the Communist takeover of China President Wang wrote:

> I do hope the U[nited] B[oard] has passed our budget for our folk school. . . . The present government is putting much emphasis on education for the under privileged. Our project has a wonderful appeal and will be meeting one of the most urgent needs of our people and at the same time strengthen our position for existing.[33]

Dr. Wang clearly felt the school's future was in jeopardy and because of this she tried to build a case for the importance of the school's work. In the 17 April 1950 "President's Letter" she reported that the Folk School was offering weaving classes, and according to Delia Davin, the Communists were looking for just this sort of project.[34] They were more interested in projects which taught women a vocational skill than in projects which taught them housekeeping skills.

As mentioned at the beginning of this paper, Adrian Bennett believes western missionary schools laid a foundation for progressive reform movements in China. One must carefully define the meaning of "progressive." Bennett insinuates that the example set by female missionaries was a contributing factor in students' later involvement in radical Communist activities.[35] However, the picture painted by Hwa Nan documents does not fit such a generalization. The students may have been progressive in their attitudes towards women's abilities and place in society, but they were not radical. Their service projects reflect WFMS attitudes towards women's work rather than Communist beliefs in the priority of production.

Students at other Christian mission schools did take up the Communist cause but not students at Hwa Nan. In Dr. Wang's last President's Report she wrote:

> For a while I was very apprehensive and discouraged fearing that the student difficulties which had assailed other Christian institutions would inevitably come to us at Hwa Nan. But I firmly believe that a veritable act of God saved us that ordeal and I am deeply grateful. Fortunately college girls are more mature and less easily swayed and our fine large Christian group again helped us save the situation.[36]

Hwa Nan students were not radicals, but the school was trying to adapt its work in order to meet the expectations of the Communist Party. Unfortunately, Hwa Nan did not get a chance to expand its social service projects. In 1952, the Communists closed Hwa Nan and created the Foochow National University by combining the resources of Hwa Nan with Fukien College, Fukien Christian University, and the Provincial Agricultural College. The former Hwa Nan campus became the College of Science for the newly formed university.[37]

In thinking about the impact this Methodist college had on its Chinese students, one's thoughts keep returning to Hwa Nan's Home Economics Practice House. It symbolized the WFMS goal of "organized motherhood." In a 1947 publication one faculty member described the Practice House's purpose, "Our emphasis is placed on improving the traditional home, and home life, developing children to be worthy citizens and Christians, and fostering the spirit of economic independence of women."[38]

This quotation reflects the WFMS's desire to both evangelize and liberate. In keeping with these American goals, the Practice House was designed to help women establish Christian homes, improve their standard of living, and enable them to take their rightful place in the community. The missionaries brought a message of equality to their students and they taught them that women could make important contributions to society.

Having received, they ought to give. However, the forms these contributions took were very specific. They reflected American missionary women's traditional understanding of the type of work appropriate for women. Judging from the information contained in the United Methodist Archives, the goal of making the world homelike by establishing Christian homes and extending the values of that home into the broader society was a message Hwa Nan students took to heart and lived by long after their college days were over.

Notes

1. Adrian A. Bennett, "Doing More Than They Intended," in *Women in New Worlds*, ed. Rosemary Skinner Keller, Louise L. Queen, Hilah F. Thomas, vol. 2 (Nashville, Tenn.: Abingdon Press, 1982), 267.
2. Dana Robert, *American Women in Mission: A Social History of Their Thought and Practice* (Macon, Ga.: Mercer University Press, 1996), 188.
3. Robert, 170.
4. Robert, 410. Robert mentions that holiness piety inspired the WFMS's social advocacy (144). None of the other WFMS histories draw a connection between the Society and the Holiness Movement, although a chapter in Frances Baker's history does report on the camp meetings at which WFMS leaders spoke (64-72). Robert's unique observation deserves further research particularly with regard to how missionaries communicated their experience of holiness to foreign women and how such a message shaped piety and social advocacy in the mission field. Unfortunately this section of Robert's work only deals with American women and their piety.
5. Robert, 134.
6. L. Ethel Wallace, *Hwa Nan College* (New York: United Board for Christian Colleges in China, 1956), 8.
7. "Constitution of Hwa Nan College as revised by Board of Directors and adopted July 2, 1927 and as revised by Board of Trustees: May, 1928; Oct. 1930; May, 1931; Final revision—June 1941," (Typed Document) 1, Article II, United Methodist Archives, Madison, N.J.
8. Wallace, 19.
9. Gael Norma Graham, "Gender, Culture, and Christianity: American Protestant Mission Schools in China, 1880-1930" (Ph.D. diss., University of Michigan, 1990), 279.
10. W. S. Bissonette, "Sod Breaking," *Brief Book of the Woman's College of South China: Woman's Foreign Missionary Society* (n.p., Methodist Episcopal Church, 1920), 7. United Methodist Archives, Madison, N.J.
11. Bissonette, "Sod Breaking," 7.
12. *Woman's Work: Foochow Conference*, (Shanghai: Methodist Publishing House, 1920, 22; 1921, 16; 1922, 11), (Foochow City: Steward, Peet Memorial Press, 1923), 10; and (Nantal, Foochow: Bing Ung Press, 1924, 19; 1928, 16, 17).
13. Wallace, 20.
14. Graham, 316.
15. Janet Fishburn, *The Fatherhood of God and the Victorian Family* (Philadelphia: Fortress Press, 1981), 124, 125.
16. Fishburn, 343, 344.
17. Fishburn, 346.
18. Jane Hunter, *The Gospel of Gentility: American Women Missionaries in Turn-of-the-Century China* (New Haven, Conn.: Yale University Press, 1984), 244.
19. Ida Belle Lewis, "Hwa Nan College," *Woman's Work: Foochow Conference* (Nantal, Foochow: Bing Ung Press, 1927), 19.

20. Wallace, 27, 34, 36, 37.

21. Lucy C. Wang, "My Call," *The China Christian Advocate* 23 (October 1936): 5.

22. "Hwa Nan College," pamphlet, n.d., United Methodist Archives, Madison, N.J.

23. Lucy C. Wang, to Mrs. Frank E. Baker, TLS, 3 March 1939, 2, United Methodist Archives, Madison, N.J.

24. Jessie G. Lutz, *China and the Christian Colleges, 1850-1950* (Ithaca, N.Y.: Cornell University Press, 1971), 297.

25. "Hwa Nan, October 1946," pamphlet, United Methodist Archives, Madison, N.J.

26. Wallace, *Hwa Nan College*, 111.

27. Lydia A. Trimble, "Dreams Come True," *China Christian Advocate* 23 (October 1936): 4.

28. Mary Isham, *Valorous Ventures* (Boston: WFMS Publication Office, 1936), 61.

29. Frances Willard, *How to Win: A Book for Girls*, quoted in Jean Miller Schmidt, *Grace Sufficient: A History of Women in American Methodism, 1760-1939* (Nashville, Tenn.: Abingdon Press, 1999), 151.

30. Graham, 349.

31. Given Dana Robert's thesis that the Holiness Movement was influential in the WFMS, researching whether or not Phoebe Palmer was also a role model for WFMS missionaries is worth examination.

32. Kwok Pui-Lan, "Chinese Women and Protestant Christianity at the Turn of the Twentieth Century," in *Christianity in China*, ed. Daniel H. Bays (Stanford, Calif.: Stanford University Press, 1996), 204.

33. Lucy C. Wang, to Miss Louise Robinson, TLS, 15 September 1949, United Methodist Archives, Madison, N.J.

34. Lucy C. Wang, "President's Letter," TLS, 17 April 1950. Cf. Delia Davin, "Women in the Liberated Areas," in *Women in China: Studies in Social Change and Feminism*, ed. Marilyn B. Young (Ann Arbor: Center for Chinese Studies, University of Michigan, 1973), 76-79.

35. Bennett, 267.

36. Lucy C. Wang, "President's Letter," TLS, 25 September 1950, 1, United Methodist Archives, Madison, N.J.

37. Wallace, 126.

38. "Hwa Nan College Bulletin," [1939], pamphlet, United Methodist Archives, Madison, N.J.

11

Alternate Wesleyan Influence: The Impact of 18th Century British Methodism and 19th Century American Revivalism on a Japanese Indigenous Holiness Church

Kiyoshi Nathanael Kunishige

About one hundred thirty years have passed since the first Protestant church was established in Japan. In this relatively short period a sectarian Japanese Methodist preacher started the Japanese Holiness Movement with the help of American Holiness Movement missionaries.

Throughout the history of the Japanese Holiness Movement there have been both success and schism, struggles against other Japanese religions, and even systematic persecution by the government during the Second World War. The movement has been much influenced by the American Holiness Movement, yet some Japanese ministers decided to return to the very roots of Holiness Movement, John Wesley's early British Methodism. They established their own denomination without missionaries' involvement, the Immanuel Sogo Dendodan (Immanuel General Mission, hereafter IGM), founded by Tsugio David Tsutada. Although IGM started their church with a handful of Japanese people, they are now the second largest Holiness denomination in Japan, and the average Sunday worship service attendance is the largest among the evangelical churches in Japan.

This paper is a study of this indigenous church and its effort to interpret the American Holiness Movement and British Methodism. The founders of IGM were aware of some doctrinal differences between the American Holiness Movement and Wesley's Methodism, and tried to reformulate the Japanese Holiness Movement according to Wesley's theology. We will examine how this indigenous church viewed both John Wesley and the American Holiness Movement and how they utilized them in Japan. Before analyzing IGM doctrinal synthesis, we will summarize the Japanese religious situation and the history of Christianity in Japan. The history of the Japanese Holiness Movement will be offered in detail because IGM was established as a critique of the Japanese Holiness Movement. In this study of the IGM we will introduce what concerned this group, and as a consequence, what they wanted to achieve. The following section will examine their accomplishment. Finally, the future prospects of IGM will be offered.

I

Japan is a unique country in terms of its religious situation. According to Japanese government data, the number of followers claimed by different religions are: Shintoism, 109 million; Buddhism, 96 million; and Christianity, 1,460,000.[1] The sum of these figures is nearly twice Japan's population (126 million), a situation without parallel in other countries. In fact, most people believe both Buddhism and Shinto. Shinto is a pantheistic natural indigenous religion and the Japanese people gradually accepted Buddhism in the form of a Japanese religious concept since the coming of Buddhism in the fifth century.

Japanese Christian history started in 1549 with the arrival of a Jesuit missionary, Francis Xavier. Since then, many Roman Catholic missionaries came to Japan and their mission work was somewhat successful. At first, Japanese people accepted Christianity and many people from farmers to rulers, and even some Buddhist monks, became Christian. Meanwhile, the feudal government eventually decided to break off relations with foreign countries, prohibiting foreign travel and entering into an era of isolation in order to secure internal stability and national security. It resulted in the rejection of Christianity. Missionaries were expelled and persecuted. So were Japanese Christians. Shinto and Buddhism were regarded as the national religions and Christianity was strongly prohibited. From the seventeenth to the eighteenth century, no Christian church existed in Japan except among some hidden Christians.

In the modern era Japan opened the door to foreign countries and

Catholic, Orthodox, and Protestant missionaries reached Japan. The feudal government turned over its power to the Japanese Emperor in 1867 and the new government attempted to modernize Japan. The new government held Shinto as the national religion and persecuted both Buddhism and Christianity in their initial era, yet eventually extended religious freedom. Since then, Catholic, Protestant, and Eastern Orthodox missionaries have established churches in Japan.

The Japanese Holiness Movement started with a charismatic Japanese preacher, Juji Nakada (1870-1939). He was ordained as a Japanese Methodist preacher in 1894. He came to the United States and studied at Moody Bible Institute in 1897. Influenced by R. A. Torrey and A. M. Hills, Nakada experienced a so-called baptism of the Holy Spirit at the Institute. He returned to Japan in 1898 and began to publish the first Japanese Holiness magazine, *Honoonoshita* ("Tongues of Fire"). His doctrinal emphasis on a baptism of the Holy Spirit caused theological conflict with the Japanese Methodist church and he left that church in 1900. Nakada sought to have his own Holiness-oriented church, and occasionally the Kaufmans, whom Nakada had met at Moody Bible Institute, came to Tokyo to start a Holiness church in Japan. Eventually Nakada and the Kaufmans decided to work together and established a Holiness church in Kanda, Tokyo in 1903. In the daytime the facility was used as Seisho Gakuin (Tokyo Bible Institute) and the new Holiness church held a revival every night. They planted six churches around Tokyo the next year and organized their churches as a Japanese Holiness denomination, named Toyo Senkyo Kai (Oriental Mission Society, hereafter OMS) in 1917. Later they changed the name to Nihon Holiness Kyokai (Holiness Church in Japan). Eventually, the OMS became an international Holiness missionary society founded in order to evangelize Asia under Kaufman's leadership and Nihon Holiness Kyokai began to indigenize itself under Bishop Nakada.

Though Nihon Holiness Kyokai was led by Japanese ministers, they received theological and financial support from OMS, which was modeled on American Holiness revivalism. Their main doctrinal emphasis was baptism of the Holy Spirit and the Fourfold Gospel.

According to their records, the Holiness Church experienced rapid growth through two revivals (in 1919 and 1930),[2] and suffered a schism because of a radical eschatology. While the 1919 revival centered on world mission, the 1930 revival focused on eschatology. The Holiness Church's radical premillennialism produced enthusiastic followers and Nakada came to advocate a radical eschatology. Nakada had great interest in dispensational premillennialism and he longed to experience the Second

Coming of Jesus Christ. Nakada eventually concluded that one ought to pray for the restoration of the Jews because the initial stage of the Second Coming is, according to scripture, the restoration of the Jews. He believed that Japanese people bear a special vocation to restore the Jews and that prayer for the Jews was the mandatory mission for Japanese Holiness Christians. Furthermore, he came to relate his eschatological restoration to nationalism and stated that Japanese racial hegemony should come prior to individual salvation.[3] Nakada demanded that his Tokyo Bible Institute teach this doctrine, but some faculty members refused to do it. They insisted that prayer for the Jews is not necessary for a Christian; Jesus Christ is the only necessary way to be a Christian. The debate became so bitter that the Bible Institute teachers insisted that Nakada was too radical to be their bishop. They attempted to open a general conference in a proper manner to elect another bishop, but Nakada fired the teachers before the conference. Bitter fights broke out on several occasions,[4] and both sides entered a lawsuit against each other in a secular court in order to decide rightful leadership of the church. Eventually they reconciled, then divided in 1936. Nakada's side named its church Kiyome Kyokai (Holiness Church), and the faculty members' church called themselves Nippon Sei Kyokai (Japan Holiness Church). Three years later Nakada died.

During the Second World War, Japanese Protestant churches united together to survive pressure from the government and established Nihon Kirisuto Kyodan (United Church of Christ in Japan). Both Holiness churches belonged to the new church. The government's systematic persecution took place against those ex-Holiness churches because of their doctrine of premillennialism.[5] It was a warning to the other churches regarding the authority of the Japanese Emperor. Arrested Holiness preachers were condemned, church properties were destroyed, and some died in prison. After the war, freedom of religious belief was secured and many ex-Holiness Church members left the United Church of Christ in Japan to establish Holiness churches. Nakada's group named their church Kirisuto Kyodaidan (Brethren of Christ) in 1947 and the group of faculty members established their own Nihon Holiness Kyodan (Japan Holiness Church) in 1948. Others formulated other Holiness churches. In the 1980s, the Japan Holiness Association was organized under the leadership of a Keswick preacher, Koji Honda, and these Holiness churches began to overcome the past bitter division and hold annual conventions regularly. In addition to Kirisuto Kyodaidan and Nihon Holiness Kyodan, there are five denominations originating from Nakada and the OMS tradition.

II

IGM was begun by Japanese preachers immediately following the Second World War. The key figure was Tsugio David Tsutada (1906-71). He was born in a wealthy Christian family and educated in England. He was converted in London during his study abroad and became a minister of the Nihon Holiness Kyokai in 1930. In the division of the Holiness Church, he took the side of the faculty and belonged to Nippon Sei Kyokai. During the war he was arrested by the government because of his emphasis on the authority of Jesus Christ in relation to premillennialism. In solitary confinement in prison he recognized the weakness of the enthusiastic Holiness Movement and decided to establish his own Holiness Church which emphasized both John Wesley's teachings on instantaneous and gradual sanctification.

After the war Tsutada left Nihon Kirisuto Kyodan and in 1946 he began to organize his own denomination, Immanuel General Mission. The IGM created not only a domestic evangelism department but also a preschool, medical, and agricultural[6] departments because it was Tsutada's vision to have a comprehensive evangelical mission. The main denominational emphases were Sei (holiness) and Sen (mission). As the key words signify, their mission statement was characterized by holiness evangelicalism.

It is not easy to define IGM. Is it an indigenous church or not? It is true that the church was established by Japanese ministers' leadership. No missionary was involved in the process and IGM has maintained theological freedom to formulate its own doctrinal standards. From the beginning of IGM, four things have been emphasized: Jikyu (self-support), Jiritsu (self-control), Jiiku (self-education), and Jiten (self-propagation). Several missionaries worked for a short time in the denominational school, yet this work was limited due to the language barrier.

The IGM occasionally received financial support from The Wesleyan Methodist Church and other churches in North America.[7] In 1952 the Immanuel Wesleyan Fellowship was organized to have close relationship with the Wesleyan Methodist Church and the World Gospel Mission joined it later. Up to the present time, several missionaries from both the Wesleyan Church and the World Gospel Mission have worked with IGM. Tsutada especially enjoyed a personal friendship with Roy Nicholson who was the Bishop of the Wesleyan Methodist Church. While Nihon Holiness Kyodan maintained the relationship with OMS, IGM has continued a close relationship with the Wesleyan Church and the World Gospel Mission.

Whether a church is "indigenous" depends upon one's definition of the term. If the term rejects any type of missionary involvement, IGM is not an indigenous church.[8] If the term, however, means indigenous people's independent leadership, IGM is an indigenous church. I submit that IGM is an indigenous church in terms of its self-understanding within its historical context. When IGM began to have a relationship with the Wesleyan Methodist Church, Tsutada explained the reason in the official monthly publication. He stated that the relationship was a mutual partnership on the ground of close doctrinal agreement with the Wesleyan Methodist Church and that it was important to have international fellowship to be a part of church catholic. He stated that indigenosity should not be confused with isolation, which denies the one, holy, catholic, and apostolic church. Tsutada's church received financial support from North American churches, but not on a regular basis. Denominational doctrinal standards were formulated by Japanese ministers. Political decisions were determined by Japanese ministers. Missionaries were invited to the IGM's Annual Conference as observers. In fact, when one Wesleyan Church missionary questioned IGM's strong emphasis on John Wesley's Methodism, the IGM continued to hold a study of Wesley as a central part of their theological identity.

IGM published its doctrinal statement in their *Book of Discipline* where its theological position is clearly stated. There are mainly two theological pillars: eighteenth-century British Methodism and nineteenth-century American revivalism.

American revivalism was extremely popular among IGM clergy and laity. In its infancy IGM emphasized the Fourfold Gospel and the baptism of the Holy Spirit. The so-called "altar theology" was strongly proclaimed and the doctrine of entire sanctification was characterized in Pentecostal language. IGM's denominational Bible school adopted Scofield's *Study Bible* and R. A. Torrey's *What The Bible Teaches* as its main textbooks. Finney's *Revival Lectures* was also a very influential source. IGM translated these and other books by A. M. Hills, Daniel Steele, S. A. Keen, H. Jessop, and books by selected Nazarene and Wesleyan theologians. In this respect, IGM was significantly influenced by the American Holiness Movement.

IGM has paid great attention to Wesley. Typically, the Japanese Holiness Movement did not regard Wesley's theology as the official doctrinal standard. This emphasis on Wesley sometimes perplexed other Japanese Holiness preachers and even some North American Holiness Movement missionaries. IGM's seminary curriculum required each student to study Methodism. This curriculum covers John Wesley's life and theology, and the history of Methodism. For ordination, IGM required an applicant to read all eight volumes of the *Journal of John Wesley*, edited by Curnock, and to write a paper on it. Wesley's sermons have been translated into Japanese on a regular basis. While most Holiness preachers spoke of the baptism of the Holy Spirit in their revival meetings, Tsutada introduced Wesley's sermons in his church revival meetings.[9] Eventually, characteristic terms of American revivalism, such as the Four-fold Gospel and the baptism of the Holy Spirit became less important for IGM. Today, IGM seldom mentions latter and the former is not referred to at all.

The reason why IGM put much emphasis on John Wesley's British Methodism was due to their bitter experience of the schism in The Nihon Holiness Church in 1933. Nakada was a well respected church leader, yet he eventually adopted a radical eschatology which resulted in schism. An ugly fight broke out on a Sunday morning at a church among those who were supposed to be entirely sanctified. They could not be reconciled within the Nihon Holiness Church. The result was a lawsuit. Observing this chaotic situation, Tsutada concluded that the lack of doctrinal emphasis on the gradual process of maturity was one of the main reasons for the trouble. He found many insights in John Wesley's writings to help solve the problem of the Japanese Holiness Movement. He was particularly interested in Wesley's warnings against enthusiasm, Wesley's emphasis on the means of grace, and his stress on gradual growth. Tsutada was convinced that these Wesleyan emphases were useful in fixing a radicalized Holiness revivalism in Japan.

Thus, Tsutada and his colleagues came to understand that John Wesley's British Methodism ought to be their doctrinal standard. With the help of American Holiness missionaries, the Holiness Movement started in Japan with IGM recognizing in its initial period that a return to John Wesley and early Methodism was the remedy to fix the problems in the Japanese Holiness Movement.

IGM was disappointed with the Japanese Holiness Movement to a certain degree and found that John Wesley's theology helped them address this problem. Interestingly, no missionary influenced their theological conviction to return to John Wesley. In other words, the return to John Wesley was a purely indigenous decision by Japanese ministers. In appearance, IGM would not be an indigenous church in view of their emphasis upon a westerner, John Wesley. However, it was their decision as an indigenous church to seek to rectify the missionary related Holiness Movement in Japan.

According to its *Book of Discipline*, the IGM relates John Wesley's theology to their own revivalistic tradition. However, there are exceptions to this. IGM now has some features of a revivalistic Holiness church, yet it also holds other theological elements which are not compatible with

Wesley. This section will illustrate this difference, indicating what has not been altered in IGM's original revivalism tradition.

One significant change is IGM's use of such traditional holiness terms as baptism of the Holy Spirit or the Holy Spirit's "fire." Instead of "baptism of the Holy Spirit," IGM now prefers "Christian Perfection" because of Wesley's writings.[10] IGM no longer considers the Fourfold Gospel as its theological identity.[11] Rather, it regards Wesley's Methodism as its doctrinal standpoint. In this sense they differentiate themselves from the original American Holiness movement in Japan.

IGM ministers have not, however, fully accepted Wesley's theology. Most of them still prefer the Holy Spirit's instantaneous work of "fulfillment" to the "gradual growth" in sanctification.[12] They preach that the way to receive entire sanctification is not only by faith but also by consecration and they tend to view the Holy Spirit not as a personal being but as a functional agent which cleanses the heart and provides power for evangelical activity. When these ministers talk about justification, the Holy Spirit is virtually absent in their teaching and preaching. In turn, when they speak about sanctification, Christ is absent. It is a sort of dispensational tritheistic soteriology.

Wesley would disagree with these theological issues. For Wesley, the Holy Spirit was a personal being who illumines sin, justice, and judgment, thereby showing Christ. Wesley related the grace of Christian perfection with maturity of love rather than power to serve in church ministry. He consistently held to the scriptural phrase, "by grace, through faith" instead of "by grace, through faith and consecration" to describe sanctification. After all, his soteriology was characterized by a trinitarian formula. The Triune God was always present in his discussion of both justification and sanctification.

The first reason for this doctrinal distance from Wesley was the Holiness preachers' difficulty in interpreting Wesley's works. Though all eight volumes of Curnock's *The Journal of John Wesley*, Wesley's *Standard Sermons*, and several other sermons are available in Japanese,[13] there were not many useful secondary resources for Wesleyan study for many years.[14] Furthermore, IGM did not have an expert teacher on Wesley for a long time. They read Wesley's writings, but they did not understand them very well.

Second, IGM ministers' doctrinal preference is still for Pentecostal sanctification rather than Wesley's therapeutic sanctification. Though the leaders of IGM have encouraged ministers to learn Wesley and his writings, most ministers still prefer the Pentecostal sanctification motif. They seldom mention the restoration of the *imago Dei*.[15] For most IGM preachers sanctification is an instantaneous event to cleanse the heart entirely, thereby providing power for evangelism. Japan is one of the toughest mission fields in the world, and many churches face financial difficulty due to small memberships. Church growth is, therefore, the biggest concern for many preachers.[16] In this serious situation these churches long to have sanctified Christians who are able to help the growth of their congregations.

Another reason is the influence of fundamentalism's emphasis on a penal substitution theory in terms of the work of Christ. In the early period of IGM, their pastors held a close relationship with fundamentalist churches due to their antiliberal interests and they adopted a doctrine of inerrancy and infallibility regarding the nature of scripture. In this process they were influenced by a fundamentalist emphasis on the substitutionary theory of Christ's atonement. As a result they understand that the death of Christ was strictly substitutionary for the forgiveness of sin, thereby losing the link between Christ and sanctification in their doctrinal thought. The stress on the Holy Spirit in Pentecostal sanctification also helped radicalize the absence of Christology in their doctrine of sanctification. As a result, IGM pastors came to have a sort of dispensational tritheistic soteriology: God the Father created the world and promised salvation; Christ the Son did his work in his crucifixion for human forgiveness; and the Holy Spirit now comes to us to cleanse and provide the power for Christian life. Accordingly, these pastors have difficulty seeing sanctification in relation to Christ.

At present, it is hard to conclude how much IGM have achieved in terms of visible success in overcoming their bitter failure to be fed from Wesley's theology in the past, yet they are still putting forth an effort. The lack of accessibility of Wesley's theology for Japanese people due to the language barrier is gradually being solved.

For instance, the Wesley and Methodism Society of Japan[17] was organized to introduce Wesley and his Methodism to Japan in 1999. This society drew members from both the Japanese Holiness and the Japanese Methodist traditions. The society influences the younger generation to study Wesley and Methodism more seriously. In this sense, IGM's initial vision, to adopt Wesley's theology to fix their problems, has just begun. The emphasis on Wesleyan studies had been done by denominational leaders without useful resources, but now people have more accessible Japanese language Wesleyan theological resources written by Japanese theologians. IGM ministers have known that their theological identity is supposed to rest on Wesley, yet most of them actually do not understand Wesley's theology. Now they have begun to correct this deficiency.

Finally, it is important to mention the role of the Japanese Holiness Movement in terms of indigenization of the Christian religion in Japan. In the light of Japanese indigenous religious interests, it is expected that the Japanese Holiness Movement will play a considerable role in the future of Christianity in Japan.

Traditionally, the Japanese people's main religious concern has been cleansing (*misogi* and *harai*; both terms mean purification) from impurity. This interest has been so strong that even Buddhism shifted its emphasis toward it for the sake of indigenization and enjoyed marvelous success in Japan.

Originally, Buddhism started in India and reached Japan in the sixth century via China and Korea. Though the governmental authority accepted Buddhism as their principal religion, it took more than six centuries to become a popular religion in Japan. In this indigenization process they formulated so-called Japanese Buddhism which is different from its original form in India.

One significant characteristic of Japanese Buddhism is the emphasis on *bussho* (buddhisattva). Its meaning is probably "the nature of Buddha." This term signifies that every person has the nature of Buddha. Most Buddhist monks in Japan today teach that our hearts are spoiled by *bonno* (defiled worldly desire) and prevent us from seeing the truth, though we have *bussho*. If one becomes free from evil desire, the nature of Buddha fully appears in oneself. According to Japanese Buddhism, the goal is to cultivate each one's own *bussho* by discipline. This teaching is called *nyoraizo shiso* (theory of Buddha's existence in oneself). This theory was formulated in the third or fourth century in India, yet it was never a main teaching of Buddhism in India and Tibetan Buddhism rejected it as a heretical teaching because the existence of certain truth or deity in an earthly visible being is fundamentally incompatible with original Buddhism. Some Buddhist scholars still debate the legitimacy of the theory in Buddhism and reject it as a heretical teaching. Nonetheless, it has been one of the main teachings of Japanese Buddhism.

It has been pointed out that such a unique emphasis in Japanese Buddhism was caused by Japanese animist belief. Before the coming of Buddhism, Japanese people embraced animism and observed deities in the mountains, rivers, rocks, grasses, and so on. They were afraid of being defiled by evil gods and asked good gods to cleanse and protect them from disasters. In other words, they held a pantheistic worldview and cleansing for a stable life was the main concern for the Japanese people. When Buddhism came to Japan and was indigenized slowly, Japanese Buddhism employed indigenous animism with the help of *nyoraizo shiso* (the theory of Buddha's existence in oneself). These teachers taught the state of enlightenment as a holy state. They encouraged people to practice Buddhist disciplines for the sake of receiving purification which enabled them to see the truth. Put into Christian theological terms, they taught that one's heart is corrupted by the nature of sin and sinful acts, yet certain religious practices sanctify the heart and allow one to see the truth. A perfectly sanctified and enlightened heart will see the truth without any darkness. This type of doctrine is heretical to some "original" Buddhists, but Japanese Buddhists have held it and it has enjoyed popularity in Japan.

As this illustration shows, the Japanese people favor a religious cleanness/uncleanness motif in relation to the cultivation of one's religious discipline.[18] A foreign religion such as Buddhism gained popularity with the help of a rather heretical Buddhist teaching of sanctification. For this reason, the Holiness Movement is probably the most appropriate approach to Japan because of the prior emphasis on sanctification.

This is probably one of the reasons why the Japanese Holiness Movement enjoyed success in comparison to other traditions of Christianity in Japan. In spite of a relatively shorter history, a smaller number of missionaries, and a weaker relationship to the government, Japanese Methodist and Holiness churches enjoyed a more rapid growth than Calvinism, Lutheranism, and Catholicism in Japan. It is difficult to count the exact number,[19] but it is commonly said that Christians in the Wesleyan-Arminian tradition represent one-third of the total Christian population in Japan. It has been pointed out that some revivals in the movement contributed to its success, but the religious affinity to Japanese religious mentality also played an important role. Subsequently, it is our conviction that Methodism and the Holiness Movement will continue to have a significant role in the indigenization of the Christian religion in Japan because of its therapeutic soteriology.

III

The Japanese indigenous Holiness Movement started after the Second World War. The nineteenth-century American Holiness Movement had been imported to Japan before the war, but it faced problems because of radical enthusiasts. Some Japanese ministers recognized the need to fix the problem and they were convinced that the return to John Wesley and early British Methodism was the most useful remedy for the radicalized Japanese Holiness Movement. The decision was made by indigenous people on behalf of their church though their theological interests rested on a westerner, John Wesley.

These Holiness preachers have not fully achieved their initial goal due to the lack of resources to learn Wesley, yet they continue to learn how

Wesley and other Christian traditions understand sanctification. It is our conviction that their effort will bear some fruit not only in the globalization of Wesleyanism but also of Christianity itself. As the western Christian tradition enjoyed considerable clarity in soteriology with the help of the Latin court system, or the Eastern Orthodox Christian tradition found help in elaborating Christianity with Greek philosophy, the Japanese people may also embrace the Christian religion through their affinity for sanctification.

Notes

1. Bunkacho (Agency for Cultural Affairs, Japanese Government), 1991.

2. According to their records in 1927, the number of the churches was 165, the membership was 6,374, and the ordained ministers were 206. After the 1930 revival, the number of churches was 439, the membership was 19,523, and the ordained ministers were 428. These figures represent about ten percent of the whole Japanese Protestant church.

3. Nakada viewed Japan as the prophet in Asia who liberates other Asian countries from Western imperialism. In fact, many Japanese churches justified wars against other countries and colonization of Korea and Taiwan in the name of Daitoakyoeiken (Greater Asia Codevelopment), which was originally advocated by the Japanese government. It affirmed liberation of Asian countries from the western nations' imperialism, but it actually attempted to keep other Asian countries under the Japanese government control. Ironically enough, the concept of indigenosity here served to overwhelm the neighboring countries. In the history of the world, many invasions took place in the name of liberation, and this was one of such cases.

4. One of the ugliest conflicts happened at Kanda church (Tokyo). Both sides' preachers appeared on a Sunday morning, each insisting on the right to preach at the church. Their quarrels eventually became actual fights at Kanda in downtown Tokyo at a neighboring publishing housing area. Police intervened in the fight and nationwide newspapers reported the incident.

5. The problem of Premillennialism was actually a question on the authority of the Japanese government. In those days according to state constitution, the Japanese emperor was supposed to be a deity. The prosecutor questioned: "If Jesus Christ comes back and judges all sinners according to your preaching, will our Japanese emperor be judged as a sinner?"

6. It was a sort of social gospel aspect of the church. In the post-WWII era, Japan faced starvation, so food supply was needed for the sick, widows, and orphans. In response to this the IGM organized an agricultural department and attempted to supply foods to the weak. Likewise, they intended to provide enough education to children who were in hard circumstances.

7. For example, when the IGM built their denominational school, Bible Training College in 1950, they received about $6,888 from North American

churches, which was roughly 80 percent of the whole budget.

8. M. R. Mullins, for example, employs this criterion in his study about indigenous movements in Japan. Mark R. Mullins, *Christianity Made in Japan: A Study of Indigenous Movements* (Honolulu: University of Hawaii Press, 1998), 8f. This criterion, however, is too radical to use in indigenous study. For example, so-called Japanese Buddhism was formulated with the help of Chinese and Korean Buddhism. If we take Mullins' criterion, then there exists no Japanese Buddhism. Many religious scholars however acknowledge distinctive characters of Japanese Buddhism in comparison with Indian, Chinese, and Korean Buddhism. Behind Mullins' idea, there exists a premise: as long as a missionary is involved, he must be in control. Often this is true, but not always.

9. As a preacher reads a scriptural passage then begins to preach, Tsutada read Wesley's sermon and explained its doctrinal character during his revival meetings in his church. Tsutada's practice lasted for a while, and these lectures were edited and published.

10. In the initial period of Japanese Holiness Movement, IGM usually used "Baptism of the Holy Spirit," and they seldom used "Christian Perfection."

11. Many other Japanese holiness churches still emphasize the Fourfold Gospel as their denominational identity.

12. For example, IGM recently published a book about sanctification and human nature. Among nineteen writers (all are Japanese), only two quoted Wesley.

13. Sermons have been translated by various translators. So-called "Standard Sermons" are all translated, and some other sermons published from the *Bicentennial Edition of the Works of John Wesley* (Nashville, Tenn.: Abingdon Press) are also available in Japanese from IGM Publishing House. Curnock's all eight volumes of the *Journal* were translated by Yamaguchi, and are now available from IGM Publishing House.

14. Most Japanese ministers do not have access to English written resources due to the language barrier. Among many Wesley study books, only two are translated into Japanese, Harald Lindstrom's *Wesley and Sanctification* and Lycurgus M. Starkey, Jr.'s *The Work of the Holy Spirit*.

15. I interviewed several IGM ministers and laypeople in terms of the therapeutic motif of sanctification. And all of them said that they have never heard of therapeutic sanctification unto the image of God. They have heard that sanctification is an event based upon Pentecostal experience—fulfillment of the Holy Spirit and power for evangelicalism.

16. IGM do not guarantee minimum payment to their preachers. Furthermore IGM preachers' wives should serve full-time ministry, and they are forbidden to have part-time work outside of their church. Consequently their payment is given only from their church. As a result they are very serious in expanding the membership of their church. It is a matter of life or death to have a certain number of members in their church. In this situation, the Pentecostal success is a very real goal for them.

17. http://member.nifty.ne.jp/WMSJ

18. Recently a radical religious cult Ohmu Shinri Kyo attacked subways in

Tokyo. Even though Japanese people know that they are a now notorious religious sect, still their membership is increasing. One of the reasons is, as it has been commonly suggested, their doctrine: to cultivate one's mysterious potential power by cleansing, enabling one to reach new being. Not only this sect but also other growing cults adopt the same soteriological concern. In the Christian field, some Japanese charismatic churches employ this approach, and they also enjoy tremendous success in terms of membership.

19. Nihon Kirisuto Kyodan (United Church of Christ in Japan) is the largest Protestant denomination in Japan. It includes Presbyterians, Congregationals, Baptists, Lutherans, Methodists, and EUB. It is therefore difficult to ascertain the precise number of adherents to each tradition in Japan.

12

The Impact of John Wesley's Ministry and Theology on the Korean Church: A Model for Church Renewal

Chongnahm (John) Cho

As an Asian, I wish I could speak about the Wesleyan impact on the Asian continent. I find it very difficult to talk about that in a responsible way because Asia is a large and diverse continent. Therefore, I have chosen to narrow the scope to the Korean church. However, what I say may apply in some degree to Christian churches on other continents because in Korea there are many different denominations, from the Presbyterian to the Assemblies of God church, and from theologically conservative to liberal.

I

Officially, Protestant missions began in Korea in 1884 with Methodist and Presbyterian missionaries from the United States of America. In 1907, the Oriental Missionary Society came to Korea with a holiness message, and the Salvation Army in 1908. Other denominations, including Lutherans and Baptists, are also working in Korea.

In South Korea there are over 11.3 million Protestant Christians with 40,000 churches. There are 270 theological colleges and seminaries, six of which have more than 2,000 students each. Recently, the Korean church has been challenged to the work of overseas missions. In the 1930s the Korean church began sending a few missionaries to China. After the Lausanne Congress (1974), the number of oversea missionaries greatly increased. By 1998, the number of Korean missionaries had increased to more than 5,000 from 127 mission agencies.[1] God has greatly blessed the Korean church. For example, we continue to be strong in our prayer life, dedication to church work, and mission.

Nevertheless, a few church leaders recently began to show a sincere concern for the future of the Korean church and to pray for its renewal. In recent years certain problems have emerged that cause our concern. Even though the Korean church has grown rapidly, we notice that the number of nominal Christians is growing. There has been much Pentecostal revival in the Korean church and much talk about the work of the Holy Spirit. However, this emphasis is more on power and miracles than on the life of holiness. The Korean church has also received external criticism. It is often challenged to show what it has done for a society that is so corrupt, even though the church has greatly grown in numbers.

The church has recently been led to emphasize social responsibility in its mission. Some churches have become radically involved in sociopolitical activities. In reaction, some conservative churches have been very critical, insisting the mission of the church is evangelism in words, not social action. This debate has created a polarization between evangelism and social responsibility in the mission of the church, thereby confusing many Christians.

Such situations and concern demand the renewal of the church. Church growth without renewal can foster corruption. At this point, the ministry and theology of John Wesley may be taken as a relevant model for the renewal of the Korean church. The purpose of this paper is to show some of the distinctive characteristics of Wesley's ministry and theology and to examine how these could impact the Korean church and bring about renewal.

II

Wesley devoted his life to preaching the saving Gospel of Jesus Christ. The theme of his preaching was scriptural salvation. "Wesley's normal procedure in evangelistic preaching was to establish the sinfulness of his hearers and, on this basis, offer them the grace of God."[2] Therefore, Wesley first preached repentance from sin.[3] He then lifted up Christ's atoning work to save sinners. Wesley wrote, "Wheresoever, therefore, the gospel of Christ is preached, this 'His kingdom is nigh at hand.' . . .

'Repent ye, and believe the gospel.' This is the way; walk ye in it. And, first, 'repent';... This is the first repentance, previous to faith...."[4]

He also challenged nominal Christians to repent of their sins. Wesley preached, "'Verily, verily, I say unto you, ye' also 'must be born again.' ... Lean no more on the staff of that broken reed, that ye *were* born again in baptism.... notwithstanding this, ye are now children of the devil. Therefore, ye must be born again."[5]

Here Wesley differed from Calvinism, which holds the doctrine of double predestination. According to Calvin, "faith must flow from regeneration" and "Faith always precedes repentance."[6] Following its view of God's eternal decrees, Calvinism teaches that regeneration is accomplished by God's irresistible grace apart from human repentance. If this doctrine were true, would it not allow room for carelessness on the part of humans on "working out their own salvation"?

The Korean church needs to revive such evangelistic preaching, because without true evangelistic proclamation there can be no genuine renewal of the church. It would be tragic if one believes "the forgiveness of sins without repentance."

It appears that not much repentance has been preached in Korean church pulpits in recent years. In many pulpits the sermons of secular blessings of believers replaced the preaching of repentance. Today the Korean church appears to spend more time and energy in institutional maintenance and nurturing her congregations through education than evangelistic ministry for conversion.

The lack of an evangelistic message in the pulpit may be a main reason for the decline of church membership in recent years. In recent years the rate of Korean church growth has been decreasing. One statistic shows that in the 1960s, the Korean church maintained 41.2 percent growth, in the 1970s a 12.5 percent growth, in the 1980s a 4.4 percent growth, and in the 1990s the growth rate dropped to 3 percent.[7]

How should we cope with this growing problem? Here we are led to mention a part of Wesley's theology that supports Wesley's evangelism. For Wesley, to preach the whole counsel of God as it is revealed in the Bible, "there must be a clear association of God's sovereignty and man's responsibility."[8] Wesley firmly believed that people are sinners and unable to save themselves. He believed that when Adam disobeyed God he fell from the original state in which God created him. He was separated from God, in union with whom his spiritual life consisted.[9] Thus, Wesley affirmed original sin.[10]

At this point, Wesley came to "the very edge of Calvinism," but he differed from Calvinism "within a hair's breadth" in how God's grace operates.[11] For Wesley, alongside his view of fallen man as totally corrupt and guilty of Adam's sin, he laid out his view of fallen man as seen in the state of grace. Wesley presupposed that humankind is already in a state of grace, namely, under the operation of prevenient grace. Wesley saw fallen man as living, not under a covenant of works, but under a covenant of grace. The grace of God whence comes our salvation is "free in all and free for all."[12] Wesley believed that "by preventing grace the guilt of original sin is cancelled,"[13] and ". . . there is a measure of free-will supernaturally restored to every man . . . ."[14]

It seems important therefore for us to observe, as Robert E. Cushman pointed out, that Wesley made no sharp separation between nature and grace in his description of fallen man, because man's whole existence is enveloped by the wooing activity of God. Nevertheless, the distinction between nature and grace in fallen man is not dissolved.[15] This approach is a characteristic of Wesley's theology.

Therefore, Wesley was able to maintain human responsibility in soteriology, without falling into Pelagianism. At the same time, Wesley did not fall into the difficulty which marks Calvinism. The working relationship between God's grace and human response in Wesley is also distinguished from the synergism of Semi-Pelagianism. For Wesley, "First, God worketh in you; therefore, you *can* work: otherwise it would be impossible."[16] Moreover, it was this methodology and position that made Wesley safeguard the doctrine of the fallen man from the teaching of "stillness," found in some Moravians, on the one hand, and from the teaching of "good works" of the Roman Catholic Church, on the other.

Wesley's approach is insightful for the theology of evangelism and missions for the Korean church. His position would insist, on the one hand, upon the universal need of salvation by God's grace because of his assertion of the depth and universality of human sin, and on the other hand, upon his emphasis on the possibility and hope of salvation for all men, because of his assertion of the free grace of God in all and for all. Thus, in Wesley, the hope of salvation for all men is emphasized and yet the responsibility of man and the church's mission is equally stressed.

III

Another distinctive aspect of Wesley's ministry is holiness. Wesley strongly believed that the regenerate must grow in faith, and in the course of growth there is a stage that he terms entire sanctification. For this, Wesley preached the repentance of believers. Wesley said, "In this sense, we are to repent, after we are justified. And till we do so, we can go no farther. For, till we are sensible of our disease, it admits of no cure. But, supposing we do thus repent, then are we called to believe the Gospel."[17]

Today, as in the days of Wesley in England, some Calvinistic preachers in Korea emphasize faith alone and the imputation of righteousness so that Christians may tend to fall into antinomianism. In this case, Christians tend to neglect holiness while residing in the comfort zone of belief that they are elected for salvation. If believers seek only power without holiness, they often become arrogant and authoritarian in their attitude.

At this point, Wesley's preaching of the repentance of believers brings a challenge and impact to the Korean church. John Wesley explained salvation in a twofold way: justification and sanctification, deliverance from guilt and cleansing from depravity. It was Wesley who put more emphasis on sanctification.

Christendom as a whole believes that God is holy. Therefore, persons must ultimately be holy.[18] Without pursuing holiness no one will see the Lord.[19] This is a grand doctrine that all Christendom maintains. The question is how and when holiness will be realized in our lives. In this holiness doctrine Wesley's theology has its distinctive character.

According to Wesley, we are cleansed from depravity partially by regeneration and we are cleansed completely from inward sin by entire sanctification, although we are to be delivered from all infirmities and limitations by glorification. Reformed theologians think that one cannot be free from sin while living on earth. But Wesley did not stop with pessimistic despair. He moved on to victory and hope because he believed "the glad tidings of great salvation, which God hath prepared for all people."[20]

How can we come to entire sanctification? Wesley showed that it is through repentance and faith. He departed from William Law, his former teacher, who taught a voluntary approach to the doctrine. Entire sanctification is not something to be achieved by moral endeavor or man's willful behavior. Wesley also criticized the Moravian way of quietism. Sanctification is not something to be reached by passivity toward the means of grace. Wesley insisted that it is what God does in us. We receive it by repentance and faith. Repentance is necessary in order to have faith.[21]

As to the effect of entire sanctification, Wesley explained that we are both cleansed for purity and we are empowered to love. This interpretation of Wesley troubles Reformed theologians in Korea. They emphasize only the empowering of the Holy Spirit, but they do not mention anything about cleansing the heart from sin.

Nevertheless, the Bible speaks of "purifying the heart" in relation to Pentecost (Acts 15:8-9). Therefore, Wesley explained that, negatively speaking, "It is love excluding sin;" positively speaking, it is "love filling the heart, taking up the whole capacity of the soul."[22] He said it is the "Pure love reigning alone in the heart and life,—this is the whole of scriptural perfection."[23] Wesley called it Christian perfection. Many people have and continue to abuse the doctrine. For, "they include as many ingredients as they please, not according to Scripture, but their own imagination, in their idea of one that is perfect."[24] For Wesley, Christian perfection is not perfection in an absolute sense. Rather, it is relative perfection. By perfection, Wesley meant not more or less than what the Bible says, so it is scriptural perfection and Christian perfection.[25] It is not freedom or perfection from error, mistakes, or ignorance. According to Wesley, Christian perfection does not mean freedom from the possibility of being tempted. It doesn't mean perfection from infirmities, nor freedom from falling out of grace.

We must not overlook that Wesley taught the need for the repentance of the perfect. He spoke of different kinds of sins. He once divided sins into two categories. First, there is voluntary transgression of the known law of God, which is a sin properly so called.[26] But there is another kind of sin—"an involuntary transgression of a divine law, known or unknown."[27] This is transgression of the perfect law of God without knowing, which he apprehends "to be naturally consequent on the ignorance and mistakes inseparable from mortality."[28] Therefore, "It follows, that the most perfect have continual need of the merits of Christ, . . . and may say for themselves, as well as for their brethren, 'Forgive us our trespasses.'"[29] "The best of men still need Christ in His priestly office, to atone for their omissions, their shortcomings, . . . their mistakes in judgment and practice, and their defects of various kinds."[30]

We must admit this fact as a reality. It is like eyeglasses. I can clean my eyeglasses, make them really clean, but as I walk in the dust, they get dusty again. So, even the perfect Christian, as he lives, is involuntarily sinning in a sense. Therefore, even the entirely sanctified still need repentance.

At this point, one might think that Wesley was pessimistic, like Luther who holds the doctrine of "simul justus et peccator." It is similar, but different. Wesley's dynamic approach sees the one who is standing in relationship with God. We dare not think that Jesus Christ's death on the cross ended his involvement with us. He is still interceding for us at the throne of God.[31] Wesley sees the Christian, although entirely sanctified, as involuntarily sinning, yet subject to the continual working of Jesus

Christ. Here, Wesley showed the interplay between sinning and cleansing. Humans stand at the juxtaposition of these two works. On one hand, one sins without knowledge. So, repentance is needed. On the other hand, one is under the cleansing work of the Holy Spirit in faith. Therefore, Wesley believed that holiness can be maintained through moment-by-moment trust in Christ as prophet, king, and priest. This is echoed in his words, "Every moment, Lord, I *want* the merit of Thy death; but, likewise, in the full assurance of faith, Every moment, Lord, I *have* the merit of Thy death!"[32]

This is the lifestyle of the perfect. Like our eyes, we are in a state of purity; we remain pure although the dust comes, because tears from the eyelid flow down whenever dust enters. If the work of grace is greater than the contamination of sin, there is upward progress. Surely, "where sin abounds, grace abounds much more."[33] Therefore, more than anyone else's, Wesley's theology is a theology of grace that sees the work of grace dynamically here and now.

I am sure that the dynamics of Wesley's theology should exert a great impact upon the Korean church. For, in the Korean church we often see that some of the Calvinists tend to take a refuge in the comfort zone of their belief in election. They do not preach the repentance of believers. On the other hand, Wesley's theology brings a great challenge to holiness groups because some holiness people are not serious about involuntary transgression of the perfect law of God unknown to them. They often think presumptuously as though they no longer need to pray the Lord's Prayer—"Forgive us our trespasses."[34]

IV

We have noticed that the whole of scriptural perfection that Wesley preached is pure love reigning alone in the heart and life.[35] Therefore, the holiness Wesley preached naturally motivated a social ministry. He required his Methodists to be active in the world, first of all, preaching the Gospel, performing acts of charity, attending to the economically disadvantaged, and transforming urban blight through industry, frugality, and education. By the nature of love, personal holiness extends to its largest possible limits a Christian society.[36] Apart from this outreaching love, holiness has no content.[37] Wesley once said, "The gospel of Christ knows of no religion, but social; no holiness but social holiness. . . . And in truth, whomsoever loveth his brethren, not in word only, but as Christ has loveth him, cannot but be 'zealous of good works.'"[38]

Therefore, from their beginnings, Methodists have carried on social work such as helping the poor and visiting prisons. They spoke against political corruption and bribery in elections. Wesley did not hesitate to speak out against prison conditions, debtor laws, usury, intemperance, child labor, industrial exploitation, and slavery. Thus, the ministry of Wesley was holistic. Edwards testifies that such ministries of Wesley produced a great effect upon the English Society, affecting the whole realm of life in the eighteenth century.[39]

At this point, we should observe that there was no room allowed in Wesley's theology for a polarization between evangelism and social responsibility. In Wesley, evangelism in word and deed sprang from his message of sanctification—love for the neighbor.

We are aware that the church has been faced with two extreme emphases with regard to its mission. One view concentrated on verbally proclaiming the Word and saving individual souls. In the second view, the emphasis shifted from preaching the Word to social action.[40] This polarization of emphasis in mission has confused many people. We faced this problem in the Korean church. At this point, it is worthwhile to pay attention to Wesley's theology which delivers us from such confusion.

There is another feature in Wesley's ministry which we must not overlook. In his ministry there was a powerful work of the Holy Spirit, including the inner witness of the Holy Spirit in believers, and external signs and miracles accompanied the Spirit's work.

It is well known that Wesley experienced the heart-warming experience by which he received the full witness of the Holy Spirit. As Starkey says, such experience of the Spirit gave Wesley dynamic power in his Christian life and ministry.[41] It is not uncommon among many Spirit-filled Christians in Korea to testify to the full witness of the Holy Spirit, although their churches do not believe this doctrine. Surely, it is the "great evangelical truth that has been recovered" by Wesleyanism and gives dynamic in Christian life.

It is also to be noticed that in Wesley's ministry, extraordinary manifestations of the work of Holy Spirit accompanied the revival, such as divine healings and casting out demons. These miracles made his preaching powerful. He personally experienced God's miraculous healing when he was sick.[42] Wesley also saw that God healed many sick people in his meetings when he and other Christians prayed for them.[43] Wesley's journal also reveals that other extraordinary works of the Spirit were manifested, such as casting out demons[44] and other outward signs, which so often accompanied the inward work of the Spirit.[45] Sometimes miracles occurred before more than two thousand witnesses.[46]

Concerning these strange works he was questioned and criticized by many who denied that God now engages in these works. The Church of England did not believe the direct witness of the Holy Spirit or miracles of the Spirit.[47] Wesley wrote a long letter to defend his position.[48] He believed that such extraordinary operations of the Holy Spirit are never wholly withheld where the gospel is preached with power and where people are alive to God.[49] He admitted that for more than two or three centuries miracles did not appear because the love of almost all Christians, so called, was weak. "Christians were turned heathens again, and had only a dead form of faith left."[50] Thus, Wesley rejected the skepticism which denied miracles. However, Wesley never missed the opportunity to emphasize that the most important thing is that miracles must come from God. Therefore, Wesley emphasized that appearances must be tested by the Scripture.[51] Wesley warned against the danger of enthusiasm because he sensed that sometimes the work of the Devil appears in very similar ways as the Holy Spirit works.[52]

At the same time, Wesley rejected the presumption which demands miracles and triumphalism, and which shrinks from the weakness in which God's power is made perfect. Here once again we observe that Wesley strongly maintained the primacy of evangelism to save souls and lead people to holiness. There can be no greater miracle than that the believer is set free from the bondage of Satan and sin, fear and futility, darkness and death. Wesley charged his workers:

> You have nothing to do but to save souls. . . . It is not your business to preach so many times, and to take care of this or that society; but to save as many souls as you can; to bring as many sinners as you possibly can to repentance, and with all your power to build them up in that holiness without which they cannot see the Lord.[53]

In the Korean church there is a certain group that is skeptical about signs, divine healing, and casting out demons, which accompany evangelism. On the other hand, there is also a group that presumptuously demands extraordinary gifts of the Holy Spirit as a sign of being filled with the Spirit. Here Wesley's view concerning the operation of the Holy Spirit offers a valid lesson and challenge.

V

Another characteristic of Wesley's ministry is that he discipled the Methodist converts. In order to provide thorough pastoral care and nurture, he divided each society into classes with about twelve people in each class.[54] Wesley also divided dedicated groups into smaller companies called bands.[55] Wesley also formed a small group called the "select society" which was composed of core leaders of Methodism. They were selected leaders of Methodism.[56] Through such strict and well-organized discipline, Wesley produced many able leaders and mobilized them for ministry. Surely, it was Wesley who took seriously the "Reformation principle—the priesthood of all believers" and put it into practice.

This example has a great impact and challenge for the Korean church. In many local churches in Korea pastors still monopolize ministries rather than encouraging the laity to use their gifts and train disciples to make disciples. We ought to realize that the domination of the laity by the clergy robs both laity and clergy of their God-intended roles, causes clergy breakdowns, and weakens the church.

VI

Wesley believed that the church must be filled with the Holy Spirit. He thought this was the character of Christianity from the beginning. They were born again and had assurance of their salvation. They loved God and neighbors, not only in words but also in deeds. Truly, they were Spirit-filled Christians.[57] However, Wesley acknowledged that the church had fallen. He wrote:

> [t]he whole essence of true religion was struck in the fourth century by Constantine the Great, when he called himself a Christian, and poured in a flood of riches, honours, and power, upon the Christians; more especially upon the Clergy. [W]hen the fear of persecution was removed, and wealth and honour attended the Christian profession, the Christians did not gradually sink, but rushed headlong into all manner of vices.[58]

Despite the fact that the church in history was corrupted, Wesley believed that the church was still holy because Christ, the head of it, is holy, and all its ordinances were designed to promote holiness. Every church member is holy, "though in different degrees."[59] This is the objective or given holiness of the church. However, Wesley claimed that for the church to be truly holy, objective holiness, in terms of the given presence of Christ in the Word and sacraments, must lead to subjective holiness, which is a living response in believers.

How is this possible? "His answer seems to lie in his use of the Pietist concept of *ecclesiolae in ecclesia*, small voluntary groups of believers living under the Word and seeking by a life of discipline to be a leaven of holiness within the great congregation of the baptized."[60]

As we have observed above, his emphasis was on renewing people and the church by the ministry of preaching and discipline based on sound theology. Wesley's movement appears to be a charismatic approach toward church renewal that contrasts with the view whose emphasis is on objective holiness of the church, namely an institutional approach. However, Wesley tried to hold in tension these two apparently contradictory views.[61] Wesley believed these two emphases to be essential to the being and the mission of the church. He believed that God's design in raising up the people called Methodists was, "Not to form any new sect; but to reform the nation, particularly the Church; and to spread Scriptural holiness over the land."[62]

In his view, the church grows by renewing itself like a great tree that survives and grows. The tree, partially deadened, is still alive and continues its growth by sending forth new shoots. The renewal movement represents "new life," a sprouting forth of new growth. Wesley believed that Methodism, consisting of *ecclesiolae in ecclesia*, could be the means of church renewal by spreading scriptural holiness throughout the land.

In Korea, we have seen so often in many local churches that the rising sprouts of renewal movements among congregations have been quenched because of the grudging recognition of them by the church. This failure resulted in schisms. The church authorities were like the Anglican Church in Wesley's day. On the other hand, we hope that charismatic groups raised up by God will understand their role as ecclesiolae. At this point, the most important thing is that the "Wesleyan church" must be alive as a leaven of holiness and as *ecclesiolae in ecclesia*. Here, we hear the concern Wesley expressed in his later years.

> I am not afraid that the people called Methodists should ever cease to exist. . . . But I am afraid, lest they should only exist as a dead sect, having the form of religion without the power. And this undoubtedly will be the case, unless they hold fast both the doctrine, spirit, and discipline with which they first set out.[63]

Let Methodism be the remnant God has reserved for today!

Notes

1. These statistics were supplied by the Korea Research Institute for Missions

in Seoul.
2. Robert John Hillman, "Grace in the Preaching of Calvin and Wesley," (Ph.D. diss., Fuller Theological Seminary, 1978), 63.
3. *The Standard Sermons of John Wesley*, ed. Edward H. Sugden (London: Epworth Press, 1921), hereafter *Standard Sermons*, I: 155-56.
4. *Standard Sermons*, I: 155.
5. *Standard Sermons*, I: 296.
6. John Calvin, *Institutes of the Christian Religion*, 3:3:1, quoted by Ronald S. Wallace, *Calvin's Doctrine of the Christian Life* (Edinburgh: Oliver and Boyd, 1959), 96.
7. Cf. "Monthly Pastorate (in Korean)," July 1996.
8. *Works* (Jackson), X: 456.
9. *Standard Sermons*, II: 229, I, 117.
10. *Works* (Jackson), IX: 420.
11. *Works* (Jackson), VIII: 284-85.
12. *Works* (Jackson), VII: 373.
13. *Works* (Jackson), IX: 303; *The Letters of the Reverend John Wesley*, 8 vols., ed. John Telford, (London: Epworth Press, 1931), hereafter *Letters*, VI, 240; *Works* (Jackson), VIII: 277.
14. *Works* (Jackson), X: 229-30. Also see *Works* (Jackson), X: 392.
15. Robert Cushman, "Salvation for All: Wesley and Calvinism," in *Methodism*, ed. W. K. Anderson (Nashville, Tenn.: Methodist Publishing House, 1947), 110.
16. *Works* (Jackson), VI: 511. L. Starkey calls it "evangelical synergism." Starkey, *The Work of the Holy Spirit* (Nashville, Tenn.: Abingdon Press, 1962), 116.
17. *Standard Sermons*, I: 391.
18. Lev.11:44-45, 19:2, 20:7, I Pet.1:16.
19. Heb.12: 14, I Thess 4:3.
20. *Standard Sermons*, II: 391.
21. *Standard Sermons*, II: 452.
22. *Standard Sermons*, II: 448.
23. Wesley summarized Scriptural perfection in three words. "It is purity of intention, and if you look at it from another angle, it is to have the mind of Jesus Christ, that means, cleansing from all evil. Then finally, if you look at it from anther angle, it is perfect love." Wesley preferred to use the term "pure love." *Works* (Jackson), XI: 401.
24. *Works* (Jackson), XI: 401.
25. *Standard Sermons*, II: 152-56; *Works* (Jackson), XI: 397.
26. *Works* (Jackson), XI: 396.
27. *Works* (Jackson), XI: 396.
28. *Works* (Jackson), XI: 396.
29. *Works* (Jackson), XI: 305.
30. *Works* (Jackson), XI: 396.
31. Rom 8:34, Heb.7:25; 9:24.
32. *Standard Sermons*, II: 393.

The Impact of John Wesley's Ministry and Theology   169

33. Romans 5:20.
34. But Wesley did believe that this is the prayer of "the most perfect" for themselves as well as for their brethren. *Works* (Jackson), XI: 395.
35. *Works* (Jackson), XI: 397.
36. *Works* (Jackson), V: 45.
37. L. O. Hynson, *To Reform the Nation* (Grand Rapids, Mich.: Francis Asbury Press, 1984), 100.
38. *Works* (Jackson), XIV: 321.
39. For the details of his and Methodist social works, see Maldwyn Edwards, *John Wesley and the Eighteenth Century: A Study of His Social and Political Influence* (London: Epworth Press, 1955). See also Manfred Marquardt, *John Wesley's Social Ethics: Praxis and Principles*, trans. John E. Steely and W. Stephen Gunter (Nashville, Tenn.: Abingdon Press, 1992).
40. Arthur Johnston, *The Battle for World Evangelism* (Wheaton, Ill.: Tyndale House Publishers, 1978), 37-38, 41, 59-62, 229-37, 274-87.
41. Starkey, 16.
42. *Works* (Jackson), I: 310.
43. See Wesley's Journal entries for 26 May 1740, 27 March 1757, 10 Jan. 1736, and 5 May 1757. *Works* (Jackson), II: 402. See also Wesley's Journal for 10 Jan. 1736, 26 May 1740, 31 March 1742. 27 March 1757.
44. See Journal for 23 Oct. 1739, 21 May 1740, and 23 May 1740.
45. See Journal for 9 May 1739, 1 Jan. 1739, 20 May 1739, 21 May 1739, 15 June 1739, 7 July 1739, 23 Dec. 1744, and 25 Dec. 1744.
46. *Works* (Jackson), I: 196.
47. Maximin Piette, *John Wesley in the Evolution of Protestantism*, trans. J. B. Howard (New York: Sheed and Ward, 1938), 12; Luke Tyerman, *Life and Times of John Wesley*, vol. I (London: Hodder and Stoughton, 1880), 246, 456.
48. *Letters*, iv: 344-45; and *Works* (Jackson), IX:119-20.
49. Wesley's comment on I Thess. 1:5, in his *Explanatory Notes Upon the New Testament*.
50. *Works* (Jackson), vii, 26-27; cf. *Letters*, iv, 374.
51. *Letters*, II, 117.
52. Cf. Journal entries for 11 Jan. 1741 and 12 Jan. 1741.
53. *Works* (Jackson), VIII: 310.
54. *Works* (Jackson), I: 357, 364; see also VIII: 253.
55. *Works* (Jackson), VIII: 258.
56. *Works*, (Jackson), VIII: 260, 261.
57. *Standard Sermons*, I, 92-94.
58. *Works* (Jackson), VI: 261-62.
59. *Works* (Jackson), VI: 400.
60. Colin W. Williams, *John Wesley's Theology Today* (New York: Abingdon Press, 1960), 149.
61. Howard Snyder, *The Radical Wesley and Patterns of Church Renewal* (Downers Grove, Ill.: Intervarsity Press, 1980), 150.
62. *Works* (Jackson), VIII: 299.
63. *Works* (Jackson), XIII: 258.

13

Toward a New Paradigm of Holiness Theology of Mission in Korea: Cosmic Holiness in Divine Ecology

Hyun Seok (Joseph) Kim

Charles Van Engen, a leading missiologist, complains about the ignorance of asking the deeper question in the study of missiology, which is a question of mission theology. He says:

> Regardless of the theological tradition, missiology concerned itself with a host of activist issues and agendas like the role of the church (its clergy, structures, and members) in the mission enterprise, relevant economic and sociopolitical action, liberation, evangelism, church growth, relief and development, Bible translation, theological education, mission-church partnership, church-to-church sharing of resources, dialogue with people of other faiths, and the relation of faith and culture. Unfortunately, in the midst of such busy global activism, the deeper questions of mission theology were too seldom asked. [1]

The Korean Holiness Church (hereafter, the Korean Church) needs to ask the more fundamental question of mission theology for the sake of the Kingdom of God. As David Bosch points out, "our theological reflection on mission is a more serious matter than merely one of making a choice between the optimism of an earlier period and the pessimism of today. While theology concerns itself with reflection on the nature of the gospel, the theology of mission concerns the relationship between God and the world in the light of the gospel."[2]

The message of Wesleyan holiness has had a great impact on the history of the Korean Church. Since the Oriental Missionary Society launched its mission in Korea in 1907, many people have met Jesus Christ through the holiness message and the Korean Church has grown remarkably in the last few decades. But what about today? A few years ago, Keith Drury claimed that the holiness movement as a movement is dead. Unfortunately, echoing his gloomy view, many would agree that the message of Wesleyan holiness does not have the great impact that it had in earlier days upon the Korean people and society. Why? Today, the Korean Church hardly tries to create a relevant paradigm for the message of holiness to meet contemporary contextual needs in Korea. The meaning of Christian holiness has too often been interpreted in terms of personal piety, overlooking the broader dimension of the message. It is a crucial time for the Korean Church to prepare a new paradigm to recover the broad nature of biblical holiness and to develop a holiness theology of mission for witnessing the "holiness gospel" and expanding God's holy and cosmic reign in the land of Korea.

I

According to Theo Sundermeier's categorization, since Warneck's definition of mission as "planting the church of Christ among non-Christians," there have been four paradigms (or models) in mission theology: the conversion and church-planting model; the salvation history model; the history of the promise model; and the communication model.[3]

The most recent paradigm in mission is the communication mode in which mission is the communication of Christian faith. Here the difference between the sender, (originally God) and receiver (originally humanity) of the message is crucial. Yet as God, through the *kenosis* of the Son, established communication with humanity, so today's mission-senders must involve themselves in the limitations of space and the culture of others. Thus, mission is more than translating the Word of God into another language. Christian mission means the effort of contextualization or indigenization of the Gospel in the given context. Anthropological study of culture and its implication for mission provide helpful insights for this model.[4]

However, Christian mission is also more than the communication of the Gospel. It should also be theological and missiological engagement in current local and global issues in particular context. Therefore, there must be a new paradigm of mission theology for today's missiological agenda in Korea. Emphasizing the role of theory in mission studies, Wilbert R. Shenk gives a working definition of mission studies: "mission studies are concerned with the mission of God as it encounters the world in time and space" and "such studies concentrate on the interface between mission and world as a matter of critical reflection." According to Shenk, the function of mission studies is "to describe, analyze, and interpret this process in its many dimensions." He says, "To do this effectively a theoretical framework must be developed."[5] This study seeks such a theoretical paradigm in developing a holiness theology of mission.

David Bosch in his book, *Transforming Mission*, examining the paradigm theory of Thomas Kuhn, speaks about paradigm shifts in both theology and missiology. We need a new paradigm for Christian mission since we live in a world fundamentally different from that of the nineteenth century. The new situation challenges us to an appropriate response. The contemporary world challenges us to practice "transformational hermeneutics," a theological response which transforms us first before we involve ourselves in mission to the world.

II

Reflection on the purpose and methods of Christian mission has always paid attention to social environment, including political, religious, linguistic, economic, and other cultural elements, in which mission activity has sought to accomplish its tasks. Their interrelationships and relative importance can be closely correlated to distinct approaches to mission philosophy, efforts, and goals. Such an understanding builds upon at least some social and cultural elements in specific contexts in the construction of an appropriate contextual approach to mission. Recently, according to Hadsell, "such sensitivity to the human social environment has led toward a growing sensitivity to the natural environment, the wider context and the larger realm of God's creation, in which human life is embedded and without which human life cannot be sustained."[6] Therefore, an ecological paradigm becomes more and more relevant to current agendas of Christian mission.

Wesley saw holiness as the renewal of the "nature of God" in our soul through the renewal of divine-human relationship. This prompts a new Wesleyan understanding of holiness as the recovery of divine life in the human being by restoring the image of God. Thus, we may define Christian holiness as the Christian's ongoing participation in the life of the living God, throughout the continuous relationship with God (through the renewal of God's image) by the sanctifying power of the Holy Spirit. As Runyon states, holiness is "partnership with and participation in the divine Spirit as transcendent resources."[7] Here our focus is on the divine-human partnership (or relationship) with the living God. When we understand holiness in this way, it opens our understanding of the message in an ecological sense.

By ecology, I mean the study of how the earth works; in other words, the house rules of our home. As we know, the word "ecology" is from the Greek *oikos* (house or home) so ecology is the study of organisms in their home. In addition, according to Moltmann, the word "ecology" can mean "the doctrine of the house" in the theological sense.[8] Ecology, therefore, deals with the issue of all living things in this cosmos and shows that all living creatures are dynamically interrelated. Hence, what we need for a new discussion about holiness is an ecological understanding. As Howard Snyder says, "ecological thinking reminds us that everything is related to everything else, and it emphasizes the need to trace and comprehend these interrelationships."[9]

The Wesleyan view of holiness is relational (both to God and to the world) and dynamic (in its growing nature), based on the recovery of divine life as God's image in human nature. This leads us to an ecological view of holiness which focuses on a living and dynamic divine-human interconnectedness and interrelationship in the Christian life. Christian holiness as the recovery, or renewal, of the image of God means the recovery of the nature of life, as a true human being, to have a proper relationship with the Creator.

We see here some common features between Christian holiness and ecology. First, both are "life (or bio)-centered" approaches. While the former focuses on the life of the living God, the latter focuses on all living things in the earth. Second, both deal with the dynamic interrelationships. Whereas the one concerns one's relationship to God (the Creator), the other concerns one's relations with nature (the creature). Third, both ask about the responsibility of human being. Christian holiness requires our faithful responsibility to God's grace, while ecology asks for our ethical responsibility to God's creation.

Another essential of the Wesleyan understanding of Christian holiness is the wholeness, or health, of humanity. Under the influence of the Eastern (Greek) Fathers, which typically emphasized more the therapeutic concern for healing our sin-diseased nature, Wesley's understanding of sin and Christian life is also therapeutic. Thus, Wesley wrote, "By salvation I mean, . . . a restoration of the soul to its primitive health, its original purity; a recovery of the divine nature."[10] Furthermore, his doctrine of holiness is large enough to offer healing for the whole earth and of the cosmos. It is contained in the redemptive offering of Jesus Christ and in the pledge of the Holy Spirit. In the divine economy of salvation, the Father's will, before all creation, predetermined that whosoever will may enter into the fullness of God.[11] Consequently, we can say that Christian holiness is the living dynamic toward the healing and restoration of wholeness of every living creature in God's creation. The ecological idea of holiness that focuses on life extends our mission to the whole world as well as to the earth itself.

The ecological view of Christian holiness, which can be characterized as both renewal of the divine life of the Christian and the Christian's interrelationship with God, is very relevant to the Asian context, particularly the Korean. There are two reasons for this. First, with a long history, since the establishment of the nation of Korea, the Korean people have sought a vision of the meaning of the fullness of life. Life itself as "being" has been the core value in the Korean culture. For Asian people, including Koreans, the core of the vision of this life is the conviction that "being" is far more important than "having." In Korean culture, the human being functions as catalyst in forming one holistic reality through the unity of heaven, earth, and humanity. Thus, the oriental vision of life can be the unity of one's being with the Ultimate and of the individual with the cosmos. Yet this is not in the anthropocentric sense. While western humanism sees the human being as the supreme, standard, and master of all creatures, eastern thought treats the human being as one who lives in harmony with the whole cosmos. One's spirit embraces the whole of things in the universe in their organic interrelationship.[12] Consequently, for the Korean people, life is oneness and, at the same time, wholeness.

Second, the Korean worldview is primarily a worldview of interconnection and togetherness. The Korean people hardly know the concept of "I" (*Na*) that emphasizes an autonomous individual, but rather they have the word "we" (*Oori*) referring to one's interrelation with the other, nature, and cosmos. Jung Young Lee, a prominent Korean-American theologian, says:

> In Asia, and particularly in Korea, "I" and "we" or *Oori* are synonymous. For example, my parents are our parents, my home is our home, my dog is our dog, and my children are our children. "I am" is "pluralistic," even though it is not the combination of I with others. It is pluralistic because of it is relational.[13]

This means our relationships are more important than who we are. In east Asia, for example, the kind of connections we have is often more important than what kind of qualifications we possess if we look for a job. Even in doing business, people spend more time establishing relationships than in consummating transactions. They act and think relationally because the basic principle that governs all things is relational. In other words, Korea has a communal culture focusing on the "togetherness" of all. Thus, Kyung Jae Kim points out that the Korean people have a spirituality of community which sees life as living together.[14]

III

One of the major characteristics of the postmodern worldview might be a search for the wholeness of life and the relational meaning of life. According to Wilbert Shenk, we are moving beyond the mechanical worldview that defined the modern paradigm and are entering a new period marked by a search for wholeness and connectedness.[15] This means that the new postmodern age requires us to have a new paradigm of a holistic dynamic. Ecology, the study of the relationships between living things and their environment, has recently come to be acknowledged as related to dealing with our management of God's creation. Mostly, therefore, Christian ecology or ecological theology as an approach to mission has recently been developed with the increasing concern about our natural environment. What then would be a relevant paradigm in affirming the holiness message in the Korean context today? Here we might propose what could be called "a divine ecological paradigm" as an alternative approach by which to read Wesley's holiness theme in light of his creation theology. The new paradigm embraces three dynamics of the holiness message for Christian mission today.

First, Wesley's lifelong fascination with the natural world and his works on the natural science lead us to his view on God's creation and divine economy.[16] Through Wesley's understanding of creation before the fall, his thoughts about nature in his time, and his cosmic vision of the new creation as the consummation of all things, we can find some helpful insights for our discussion on divine ecology.

The most distinctive description on the perfect condition of the earth before the fall is his sermon, "God's Approbation of His Works" (1782). In this sermon Wesley stated "'And God saw that' every one of these 'was good,' was perfect in its kind. The earth was good: the whole surface of it was beautiful in high degree." He then continued:

> Every part was exactly suited to the others, and conductive to the good of the whole. There was "a golden chain" (to use the expression of Plato) "let down from the throne of God"—an exactly connected series of beings, from the highest to the lowest: from dead earth, through fossils, vegetables, animals, to man, created in the image of God, and designed to know, to love, and enjoy his Creator to all eternity.[17]

This shows that the popular idea about the natural world was the so-called "Great Chain of Being" in Wesley's day. This idea insists on the interrelatedness of all things, providing a principle of coherence and a sense of meaning and purpose as well. However, Wesley's view is "less static than the traditional view because of his dynamically personal understanding of God and his strong emphasis on the image of God in men and women, making them 'capable of God' (i.e., with the capacity for deep, transforming communion with God)."[18] Nevertheless, it is a hierarchical idea rather than organic.

Although Wesley's view of the created order remains in the idea of hierarchy, his sermon, "On Divine Providence," stresses God as Preserver for his creatures. He wrote, "He knows all the animals in this lower world, whether beasts, birds, fishes, reptiles, or insects. He knows all the qualities and powers he hath given them, from the highest to the lowest. . . . He sees all their sufferings, with every circumstance of them."[19] In addition, Wesley gave a key passage for our further discussion on divine ecology by saying:

> As certain as it is that he created all things, and that he still sustains all that he has created, so certain it is that he is present at all times, in all places; . . . Perhaps what the ancient philosophers speak of the soul in regard to its residence in the body, that is *tota in toto, et tota in qualibet parte*, might in some sense be spoken of the omnipresent Spirit in regard to the universe—that he is not only "all in the whole, but all in every part."[20]

Wesley asserted a concept of God's presence and providence that is strikingly modern in its sound, similar to the ecological idea, but he has put the emphasis on divine sovereignty. Wesley acknowledged that God knows every connection and relation in His world. Furthermore, Wesley's vision of the new creation in the future notably gives us a clearer picture of divine economy in an eschatological sense. In his sermon, "The New Creation," Wesley underscored his favorite theological theme of God's universal restoration of all creation. In an introductory comment on that sermon, Albert Outler noted:

> The aged Wesley returned again and again to his vision of cosmic redemption: the restoration of all creation including the entire human family, as the final, full benefit of God's unbounded love. . . . Wesley begins by taking the implied future tense seriously, showing that he is talking about 'the universal restoration which is to succeed the universal destruction.' Surprisingly, the bulk of the sermon describes how the qualities (though not the nature) of air, fire, water, and earth (the four Greek elements) will be new.[21]

In this sermon, Wesley described the beauty of the new creation in divine economy. He stated:

> We shall no more regret the loss of the terrestrial paradise, . . . For all the earth shall then be a more beautiful paradise than Adam ever saw. Such will be the state of the new earth with regard to the meaner, the inanimate parts of it. . . . The whole animated creation, whatever has life, from leviathan to the smallest mite, was thereby "made subject" to such "vanity" as the inanimate creatures could not be.[22]

Second, even though ecological thinking is not really a new approach to look at things, the twenty-first century will be an age of ecology in which people seek a new meaning of life through a dynamic interconnectedness and interrelationship with the others, society, and even with the nature. Here we need to develop a Christian "divine ecology" for mission theology while avoiding the danger of a pantheistic understanding of the reality and the universe in oriental thought and religion. By divine ecology, we refer to one complex system of how God continues to relate to and is involved in creation. It should be biblically solid and sound enough for dealing with the "pantheistic" and even "panentheistic" tendencies of oriental religion and the Korean worldview, and for affirming an evangelical trinitarian doctrine of God. In divine ecology we seek a clear distinction between the Creator and the creation, proposing all living creatures are interrelated under God's reign over creation. God created the cosmos so that in this sense God is distinct from the created order. Yet the scripture teaches that God continues to be involved with the whole creation and is working to bring its full redemption through the salvific work of Jesus Christ and the restoring power of the Holy Spirit.

All theological discussion on holiness has to be rooted in the Holy Trinity itself, since the holiness of the Triune God reflects the trinitarian understanding of Christian holiness. We need to begin with the profound conviction that the Triune God is the only source of our knowledge and spirituality. He alone reveals our nature and destiny. The holy God is both transcendent and immanent. Trinitarian thinking about God's holiness expresses God's passionate engagement with creation for its salvation. Within the "divine ecology" all living things under God's creation are interconnected with each other to maintain and sustain the created world (Col. 1:15-20; cf. Heb. 1:1-4). However, the central point of divine ecology is summed up in II Corinthians by the Apostle Paul, "Therefore, if anyone is in Christ, there is a new creation: the old has gone, the new has come! All this is from God, who reconciled us to himself through Christ and gave us the ministry of reconciliation: that God was reconciling Christ the world to himself in Christ" (II Cor. 17-19). The basis of this reconciliation is the creating, renewing, and recreating work of the Holy Trinity. According to Snyder, "Every human relationship is a reflection of God's internal communion, and our harmony with nature reflects the harmony of God's being." He continues:

> Here is an awesome basis for ecological peace and for just human community, whether in marriage and family, in neighborhood and nation, or globally. When we are in harmony with God through Jesus Christ by the Spirit, we are potentially in harmony with every other human and in tune with the cosmos. [23]

In the Wesleyan understanding of divine ecology, human beings are created in the image of God as the "divine life" to have a holy relationship with God. However, human beings lost the divine life because of their disconnection with, and alienation from, God through the fall. Under the grace of God, through his death on the cross, Jesus came to give us the fullness of his life in order to renew the image of God (John 10:10) in persons and in community. The Holy Spirit came to us to restore the fullness of divine life through the recovery of holiness in human beings. God expands his salvation to the whole creation through the responsibility of the human beings. This is all about God's plan of salvation for the eschatological new creation, that is "the divine economy," which should be the central message of the *missio Dei* in Christian mission In the Wesleyan understanding of God's salvation, Christian mission is ultimately sharing the good news that God provides the new creation in Jesus Christ through the renewal of the *imago Dei* in humanity and also the cosmic redemption of the whole creation by the sanctifying power of the Holy Spirit. This definition of mission clarifies the meaning of the redemptive work of the Triune God for creation, extending the broader dimension of the holiness message.

Third, based upon the divine ecological paradigm, we finally explore three dimensions of the ecological dynamics of the holiness message from the Wesleyan perspective. There are three dynamics of holiness which are interrelated and interconnected ecologically, providing the comprehensive missiological horizon toward Wesleyan teleological redemption of God for the whole creation.

(1) The experience of biblical holiness by the individual as well as the group throughout the history of Christian mission has often been *the* spiritual dynamic for the missionary activities of the church. For the early church, the Pentecostal experience of the Holy Spirit was *the* spiritual source of their fervent mission as well as the life of holiness. Therefore, the Day of Pentecost when they were empowered by the Holy Spirit had a profound meaning in Christian mission history. It was not only the inauguration of the Christian church, but also the sign of a new age of the Spirit. In the historical life of the church, Pentecost is the anniversary of the coming of the Holy Spirit in His fullness and power upon the followers of Christ.[24] When the Apostles and other believers became the holy disciples of Christ, they were able to conquer the Roman Empire with the Gospel. According to Donald Metz, "Holiness appears to have been the outstanding quality of the primitive church."[25] The life of holiness, as the outstanding characteristic of the Primitive Church, was the dynamic of the early Christian missionary activity that brought about the expansion of the church.

The experience of holiness in Christian life, however, never occurs without experiencing the holiness of God, the very nature and character of the triune God. God alone is holy in himself. All other holiness is derived from a relationship with him. Therefore, "to understand the full scope of holiness in Scripture, we must recognize that its essential meaning is derived from the nature and character of God."[26] At the same time, the holy God is a missionary God. His mission is to redeem his people in this world and make them his missionaries to expand his kingdom, revealing his holiness as the major dynamic power for the missionary activities. Gerald H. Anderson defines mission as "participation in the promise and purpose of God between the coming of Christ and the fulfilled kingdom of God."[27] To experience the holiness of God and become God's holy people are God's promises and purpose for all redeemed Christians and certainly for those who have a Wesleyan holiness heritage. In this sense, Christian holiness and Christian mission have a common ground in God's very nature and essence. In a word, the holiness of God and the mission of God (*missio Dei*) are two inseparable realities in the history of Christian mission.

(2) If God's salvation is to be holistic, then holiness of life cannot involve just the individual dimension, but must be extended to all aspects of society. Genuine holiness generates a social concern which seeks to

transform society. The outpouring of the Holy Spirit at Pentecost, a deeply corporate experience, was the sign of a new age. Two immediate consequences of the Pentecostal experience in Acts are noteworthy: "oneness in the Spirit," and "sharing all with others" (Acts 2:44-47; 4:32-37). According to Schilling, "such was the transforming effect of a direct encounter with the holy God."[28] These two biblical pictures show the real transforming dynamic in Christian mission, which is a Christian life embracing the social dimension of holiness.

As Schilling points out, social holiness was for Wesley not the transformation of social structures but "holiness experienced by persons who found mutual strengthening in Christian fellowship, and who practiced their faith in all their relations with other people."[29] Nevertheless, through his ministry, we see the transforming dynamic of social holiness. Recently, many Wesley scholars have rediscovered and reaffirmed the holistic nature of biblical holiness, the integration of personal and social holiness. Theodore Runyon, dealing with John Wesley's theology of sanctification, concludes that, "Salvation consists, therefore, not only in reconciliation but in service, not only in an experienced sense of God's reality and presence but in a life lived out of that reality, extending divine transforming power into every aspect of both individual and social existence."[30]

(3) Wesley's eschatological vision for the new creation offers us an extended view of the Christian message of holiness. Wesley saw holiness as the very character of God and, therefore, as the calling and potential experience of all Christians. However, the message of holiness also needs to be understood in light of Wesley's cosmic vision of the new heaven and new earth which would eventually be exhibited by the whole creation. One might call this "cosmic holiness," which might be an appropriate and relevant term for articulating the holiness message today consistent with scripture and Wesley's own theology. By cosmic holiness, therefore, we mean God's redemption of the whole creation or cosmos through the renewing power of the Spirit in his sanctifying grace.

In the eschatological sense, this implies God's new creation of the whole universe in the future, restoring and perfecting the original harmony of creation. This original harmony can be understood in terms of what today is termed "ecological balance." Yet it also signifies human beings' present participation in the new creation through their response to God's cosmic grace by environmental stewardship. Although Wesley never used the word "cosmic holiness," the term reveals Wesley's peculiar concern for God's cosmic redemption seen in his later sermons. In his sermon, "The General Spread of the Gospel," John Wesley used the word "universal holiness," which might be replaced with what may be called "cosmic holiness." He wrote that:

> [God] is already renewing the face of the earth. And we have strong reason to hope that the work he hath begun he will carry on unto the day of the Lord Jesus; that he will never intermit this blessed work of his Spirit until he has fulfilled all his promises . . . and re-established *universal holiness* and happiness, and caused all the inhabitants of the earth to sing together, "Hallelujah! The Lord God omnipotent reigneth!" "Blessing, and glory, and wisdom, and honor, and power, and might be unto our God for ever and ever!"[31]

Recent studies of Wesleyan theology by such Wesleyan scholars as Randy L. Maddox and Theodore Runyon support the validity of this cosmic dimension of holiness doctrine for God's new creation. They see that a Wesleyan understanding of God's redemption includes God's whole creation. Maddox interprets Wesley's practical theology in the framework of the "responsible grace" of God, which "focuses Wesley's distinctive concern on the nature of God and God's actions, rather than on humanity."[32] He concludes that the triumphant goal of God's responsible grace in Wesley's later thought (his mature eschatology) was the new creation which emphasizes the cosmic redemption of God both in individual lives and in creation as a whole. He remarks that, "Indeed, the new creation became one of the most prominent themes of his late sermons. These sermons leave no doubt that the new creation will be a physical place, though each of its basic elements will be dramatically improved over present conditions."[33]

In the more recent study of Wesleyan theology by Theodore Runyon, the "New Creation" is seen as the central theme of Wesley's thought. Runyon argues, "The renewal of the creation and the creatures through the renewal in humanity of the *image of God* is what Wesley identifies as the very heart of Christianity." He continues, "The cosmic drama of the renewing of creation begins, therefore, with the renewal of the *imago Dei* in humankind. This is the indispensable key to Wesley's whole soteriology."[34]

Colin Williams once stated, "There is a real sense in which Wesley stressed realized eschatology more than any other leading western theologian."[35] Robert V. Rakestraw interprets the remark this way:

> By "realized eschatology" in Wesley's thought Williams means that the "now" and the "not yet" are so closely related that the "not yet," rather than being only a distant goal to which the Christian looks forward, can and must become "now" through obedience of God. The major physical

changes that Wesley sees ushering in the new heaven and new earth cannot be obtained now, of course, but the Christian can seek, find, and promote in this life many qualities of the coming kingdom in regard to both individual piety and social righteousness.[36]

When we see Wesley's vision of the new creation in this way, we can broaden our theological horizon for discussing the holiness message of mission for the Korean context today.

Notes

1. Charles Van Engen, *Mission On the Way: Issues in Mission Theology* (Grand Rapids, Mich.: Baker Books, 1996), 17.

2. David J. Bosch, *Witness to the World: The Christian Mission in Theological Perspectives* (Atlanta: John Knox, 1980), 10.

3. Note Theo Sundermeier, "Theology of Mission," *Dictionary of Mission: Theology, History, Perspectives,* hereafter *Dictionary of Mission,* 429-37, ed. Karl Müller, S. V. D., et al. (Maryknoll, N.Y.: Orbis, 1997).

4. Sundermeier, 436-37.

5. Wilbert R. Shenk, "The Role of Theory in Mission Studies," *Missiology: An International Review,* hereafter *Missiology,* 24, no. 1 (1996): 31-45.

6. Heidi Hadsell, "Ecology and Mission," *Dictionary of Mission,* 114.

7. Theodore Runyon, *The New Creation: John Wesley's Theology Today* (Nashville, Tenn.: Abingdon Press, 1998), 22.

8. Jürgen Moltmann, *God in Creation: A New Theology of Creation and the Spirit of God,* trans. Margaret Kohl (New York: Harper and Row, 1985), xii.

9. Howard A. Snyder, *Liberating The Church: The Ecology of Church and Kingdom,* (Eugene, Oreg.: WIPF and Stock Publishers, 1996), 69-70.

10. John Wesley, *Works,* 11: 106.

11. Leon O. Hynson, "World Evangelization: A Wesleyan Proposal," *The Asbury Seminarian: The Wesleyan Message in the Life and Thought of Today* 37 (1982): 32.

12. K. J. Kim, "Personality of the Korean and Spirituality of Christianity," *Culture and Theology of Korea,* ed. Editorial Department of Christian Thought, (Seoul: CLSK): 40-41.

13. Jung Young Lee, *Marginality: The Key to Multicultural Theology* (Minneapolis, Minn.: Fortress Press, 1995), 8

14. K. J. Kim, 37.

15. Wilbert R. Shenk, "The Role of Theory in Mission Studies," *Missiology* 24 (1996): 40.

16. There are three works of John Wesley on the natural world and human health. In 1747 he published his well-known *Primitive Physic, or an Easy and Natural Way of Curing Most Diseases.* Later he published *The Desideratum; or Electricity Made Plain and Useful* in 1760. His third scientific work, published in

1763, was a two-volume set entitled *A Survey of the Wisdom of God in the Creation: or a Compendium of Natural Philosophy.*
   17. *Works*, 2: 396-97.
   18. Howard Snyder, *Coherence in Christ: The Larger Meaning of Ecology*, Mission Evangelism Series, no. 4, (New York: General Board of Global Ministries, The United Methodist Church, 2000), 7.
   19. *Works*, 2: 539.
   20. *Works*, 2: 538-39. See his sermon 111, "God's Omnipresence," for further suggestions of Wesley's view of the sustaining God.
   21. Albert Outler and Richard P. Heitzenrater, eds., *John Wesley's Sermons: An Anthology* (Nashville, Tenn.: Abingdon Press, 1991), 493.
   22. *Works*, 2: 508
   23. Snyder, 18.
   24. Donald S. Metz, *Studies in Biblical Holiness* (Kansas City, Mo.: Beacon Hill, 1971), 199.
   25. Metz, 200.
   26. W. T. Purkiser, *Exploring Christian Holiness* (Kansas City, Mo.: Beacon Hill, 1983), 19.
   27. Gerald H. Anderson, "Theology of Mission," *Concise Dictionary of the Christian World Mission,* ed. Stephen Neill, et al. (Nashville, Tenn.: Abingdon Press, 1971) 594-95.
   28. S. Paul Schilling, *Methodism and Society in Theological Perspective* (Nashville, Tenn.: Abingdon Press, 1960), 233.
   29. Schilling, 61.
   30. Theodore Runyon, *The New Creation: John Wesley's Theology Today* (Nashville, Tenn.: Abingdon Press, 1998), 223.
   31. *Works*, 2: 499 [emphasis added].
   32. Randy L. Maddox, *Responsible Grace: John Wesley's Practical Theology* (Nashville, Tenn.: Kingswood, 1994), 19.
   33. Maddox, 253.
   34. Runyon, 8-12.
   35. Colin W. Williams, *John Wesley's Theology Today* (London: Epworth, 1960), 194.
   36. Robert V. Rakestraw, "The Contribution of John Wesley Toward An Ethic of Nature," *The Drew Gateway* 56 (1986): 22.

14

"The Korea Pentecost": A Study of the Great Revival of 1903-1910 in Relationship to Contemporary Worldwide Holiness Revival Movements

Myung Soo Park

Many people have considered the Great Revival of 1907 as one of the great events in Korean church history. It was the climax of a series of revival meetings rooted in the revival of 1903 initiated by Dr. R. A. Hardie, a southern Methodist missionary. In 1903 revival meetings in Won San continued in Ham Heung, Song Do, Chemulpo, and Seoul. Its climax occurred under a Korean Presbyterian elder, Sunjoo Keel, in Pyengyang in 1907. As a result of the revival, the Korean church grew dramatically and became a self-supporting and self-governing church. Many missionaries have cited the Revival as one of the most successful stories in modern missions.[1]

The thesis of this paper is that the Revival of 1907 was the result of worldwide holiness revival movements of the late nineteenth and early twentieth centuries. There were many revival movements in the late nineteenth century such as the Wesleyan holiness movement and the Keswick Convention in America and England. These revival movements were basically of a holiness type. The main concern was confession of sin, holy living, and evangelism, which could be only done by the power of the Holy Spirit. Early missionaries in Korea were deeply influenced by these movements and wanted to bring this kind of revival to Korea. Many international revivalists visited Korea and the Revival of 1907 was the result of missionaries trying to reproduce these events in Korea. To describe the international roots of the Revival, we will trace the background of early missionaries, the story of international revivalists who visited Korea, and the revival work of missionaries and native leaders in Korea. Then, we will analyze some characteristics of the Revival in the context of the worldwide revival movement.

I

Korean Christianity was rooted in the late nineteenth-century revival movement. The most famous revivalist in late nineteenth-century America was Dwight L. Moody, who emphasized the power of the Holy Spirit for service, especially in foreign mission. Naturally, Moody's revival produced mission activity, the so-called Student Volunteer Movement. The last period of Moody's activity was closely related to the Keswick holiness movement. Moody introduced the Keswick meeting to America. Early missionaries to Korea were influenced by this revival missionary movement.

To understand the twentieth-century revival we must look beyond Moody's campaign and examine the even greater influence of two holiness movements of the late nineteenth century: the Wesleyan holiness movement and the Calvinistic Keswick Convention. Originating in the National Campmeeting Association for the Promotion of Holiness, founded in 1867, the Wesleyan holiness movement emphasized the teaching of holiness as the cleansed heart which could happen by the baptism of the Holy Spirit. This movement rapidly spread throughout Methodist churches and other denominations and finally led to the Pentecostal movement.

Rooted in the English ministry of the holiness teacher Hannah W. Smith in the 1870s, the Keswick Convention taught the triumphant Christian life by the power of the Holy Spirit. It represented a Calvinistic type of holiness teaching and became the center of British evangelicalism. Moody introduced the Keswick movement to America. America has had Keswick meetings regularly since 1913. Hudson Taylor of the China Inland Mission had a close relationship with the Keswick Convention.

The pioneers of mission to Korea were the Presbyterian Horace G. Underwood and the Methodist Henry G. Appenzeller, both of whom arrived at Chemulpo on the same day in April 1885. Underwood was influenced by the Salvation Army, a holiness group, while studying at seminary, and was called "the roaring Methodist." Originally Presbyterian, Appenzeller experienced new birth in a Methodist class meeting and became a Methodist. To the question, "Why did you transfer to the Methodist church?" Appenzeller answered, "I could not shout 'Hallelujah' in the Presbyterian church."[2] Therefore, we can conclude that the pioneers of Korean mission were from the revivalistic-holiness camp.

The first great revival of the twentieth century was the Welsh Revival of 1904-1905. The main figure of the revival was Evan Roberts, a young theological student of the Calvinistic Methodist Church, who prayed for revival for about ten years. In the spring of 1904, he underwent a series of unusual spiritual experiences after which he had a vision of 100,000 to be won for Christ and told his story wherever he could.

Roberts preached in numerous meetings. He was an early advocate of modern Pentecostalism as well as a leader in the Great Revival of 1907 in Korea. He proposed a four-point plan for personal blessing: "1. If there is past sin hitherto unconfessed, we cannot receive the Spirit—2. If there is anything doubtful in our lives, it *must* be removed.—3. An entire giving up of ourselves to the Spirit. We *must speak* and *do* all He requires of us. 4. Public confession of Christ."[3]

In nineteenth-century America, Methodism was as revivalistic as any other church. The early stage of the Revival in Korea was initiated by Methodist missionaries such as Hardie, Gerdine, and Cram. We should also point out that most Methodist bishops in charge of Korea were the revivalistic and holiness type. These bishops included H. W. Warren (1887), D. A. Goodsell (1891), W. F. Mallalieu (1892), R. S. Foster (1893), W. X. Ninde (1895), I. W. Joyce (1896-97), Earl Cranston (1899), D. H. Moore (1901-1904), and M. C. Harris (1905-1916).[4] Among these bishops, Goodsell, Mallalieu, Joyce, and Moore were endorsed by the General Holiness Association in 1901 which gathered a fellowship of holiness revivalists and made the doctrine and practice of the Wesleyan holiness movement clear.[5]

The President of Drew Theological School, R. S. Foster (1820-1893) was one of the most important holiness theologians. He tried to maintain the holiness movement in the Methodist Episcopal Church. Foster wrote numerous holiness books among which was *Christian Purity,* a volume considered a classic of holiness doctrine. Mallalieu wrote several holiness books such as *Salvation; or The Conditions of Regeneration and Sanctification,* a revival handbook titled, *The Why and How of Revivals,* and numerous prefaces for holiness books.[6] Joyce also had a close relationship with holiness people and influenced C. E. Cowman, the founder of the Oriental Missionary Society (OMS), to be a missionary.[7]

The Korea Evangelical Holiness Church (KEHC) is a result of OMS mission work. Harris, who worked as the first missionary to Hakodate from 1874, was appointed Superintendent of the Japanese mission on the Pacific coast of America where he continued until elected in 1904 as missionary bishop for Japan and Korea. Harris led a great revival from 1888 to 1889 for the Japanese people of the Pacific coast where Tetususaboro Sasao and other Japanese experienced "heart cleansing." These Japanese became leaders of the holiness movement in Japan and also influenced the Korean Holiness Church.[8] Harris was a Methodist bishop during most of the Great Revival in Korea.

II

Some direct causes of the Great Revival in Korea involved the visits of foreign missionaries and evangelists to Korea. The Great Revival began in the summer of 1903. It began in Wonsan, on the northeast coast of Korea, by a suggestion for a week's Bible study and prayer meeting by a woman missionary from the southern Methodist mission in China, Miss Mary Cutler White. In this meeting, Dr. Robert A. Hardie (whose work we will examine below) and other missionaries felt the lack of the power of the Holy Spirit in which lay the reason for their failure in the mission work.[9] They prayed for the fullness of the Spirit. God answered their prayer.

Another visitation to Wonsan was soon made by Rev. F. Franson, an evangelist in worldwide service and Director of the Scandinavian Missionary Alliance (later the Evangelical Alliance Mission). Franson was deeply influenced by D. L. Moody, whose methods of evangelism he adopted. He also had a close relationship with Hudson Taylor and A. B. Simpson who emphasized holiness teaching.[10] In Shanghai, Franson met a missionary from Korea, Mr. H. O. T. Burkwall, who wrote to Dr. Hardie asking for Franson to hold a revival meeting in Korea. In October 1903, Franson reached Wonsan where missionaries were already anxious to get a deeper knowledge and experience of God's grace and had confessed their sins before a public congregation. In the midst of these meetings, Franson arrived and ignited a fire. He remained in Wonsan for a week during which there were united revival meetings of Presbyterians, Methodists, and Baptists held in a Presbyterian church.

Hardie said that Franson showed him how to conduct evangelistic meetings. Franson did not have any special rules. He told Hardie that he should provide for the Holy Spirit to work freely. Hardie said that Franson in his closing prayer would cry out, "Father, Thou canst do it, Thou wilt do it, Thou shalt do it." He said that Franson came to them as a real messenger of God at an opportune time. After this meeting, Hardie continued to have revival meetings in his church. Hardie became a revivalist following the style of Franson. He was the main figure of the early Great Revival in Korea.[11]

From May to July 1904, a small group of Japanese revivalists visited Korea and conducted revival meetings throughout the country. The group was sent by the Japan Christian Alliance for cooperation between Korean and Japanese Christians during the Japan-Russia War. This team consisted of Honda, later a Methodist bishop, Nakada, one of the founders of the OMS, and Kihara, the first Methodist missionary for the Japanese in Korea. All of these leaders held Wesleyan holiness views. Nakada was often called "the Moody of Japan" since he was a holiness type revivalist. He preached in Presbyterian and Methodist churches in Seoul, Songdo, Pyengyang, Syenchun, Suwon, Kongjoo, and elsewhere. Nakada found that "the second coming of the Lord is clearly preached among them, but holiness is not, so I preached to them holiness which they were glad to hear."[12] As a result of Nakada's revival meetings, several Koreans went to Tokyo Bible Training Institute and studied holiness doctrine and established the KEHC.

Another visit was made by Dr. Howard Agnew Johnston of New York. Johnston visited Wales and Khasia, India, and witnessed great revivals. Then, he went to China and Korea and told about these revivals. Johnston arrived at Seoul in September 1906, when an annual meeting of the Presbyterian mission was held. Johnston spoke of the revivals in Wales and India and asked for missionaries to lead the same type of revival. Seoul missionaries received a great blessing from him. Johnston came to Pyengyang and while there spoke to Korean Presbyterians, telling of the wonderful manifestation of the Spirit in other countries. His preaching gave some Korean people a great desire to have the same blessing. In the meeting, Johnston asked, "Who will be the main person for bringing the great revival to Korea?" Elder Sunjoo Keel, later an important leader of the Great Revival, answered, "Yes, I will." From that time until the blessing of 1907, Koreans and missionaries in Pyengyang prayed that it might come.[13]

The Year of 1907 was the climax of the Great Revival in Korea. In January 1907, there was the Great Revival in Pyengyang. From this beginning, numerous revivals occurred throughout the country. At the same time, Dr. R. P. Mackay of the Foreign Mission Committee of the

Canadian Presbyterian Church planned to have mission tours to Asia, Jonathan Gorforth in Manchuria was asked to escort Dr. Mackay. A Presbyterian missionary, Gorforth had a close relationship with Hudson Taylor's China Inland Mission and was deeply influenced by the teachings of holiness and divine healing of A. B. Simpson and A. J. Gordon.[14] In the spring of 1907, they visited eight important mission stations for three weeks and saw major revivals there. Gorforth returned to Manchuria and told what they had seen of the Holy Spirit's working in Korea. This was the origin of other great revivals in Manchuria, Shansi, and other centers.[15]

Gorforth, one of the propagandists of the Great Korean Revivals throughout the world, wrote a pamphlet, "When the Spirit's Fire Swept Korea." In Canada, Gorforth tried to revive his home church using the same methods. He urged the General Assembly to confess their sins publicly. Many delegates must have been in shock, but Dr. Mackay said, "I do not remember another man who came home with such an asset."[16] Gorforth found good friends in the Keswick movement in America. Dr. Charles Trumbull, the Keswick holiness leader, invited him to his own Victorious Life Conference held at Princeton to speak about the revivals in Korea and Manchuria.[17]

In May 1907, another holiness group arrived in Seoul. Three foreign missionaries, Mr. and Mrs. C. E. Cowman, and E. A. Kilbourne, the founders of the OMS, and two Koreans, Sang-Joon Kim and Bin Chung, recent graduates of the Tokyo Bible Training Institute, conducted holiness revivals in Korea. They saw that the Korean people were hungry for "the deepening of the spiritual life and the outpouring of the Spirit." However, "'deepening of spiritual life' is not sufficient, except . . . where the Holy Ghost has first had opportunity to 'throughly purge His floor,' (Matt 3: 12) and 'burn up the chaff' (not pile it up and keep it down) but radically eliminate root and branch the feathering his own nest for an abode in the heart. Thus and only thus will the spiritual life be permanently deepened."[18]

Another visit to Korea in September 1907 was made by Gregory Mantle of London, who was an important leader of the Wesleyan Holiness movement in England. Mantle had a strong relationship with the Star Hall Mission from which came John Thomas, the first resident missionary for the KEHC.[19] He had been making an extended tour of China, Japan, and Korea in the interest of missions. Mantle held special revival meetings throughout the country with the interpretation of Heber Jones, senior Methodist missionary.[20] He also conducted the half-hour devotional services in the morning and afternoon sessions of the third annual session of the General Council of Evangelical Missions in Korea. "His utterances were deeply spiritual and they called all to a higher life and a deeper consecration in the Master's service. Surely, as Mantle said, "our view of Christ and His redeeming power must not be a low one, for God will not propagate a low standard or low ideals. Much good was done by these heart talks."[21]

The General Council of Evangelical Missions in Korea invited Barclay F. Buxton as the main speaker of Bible study for the fourth session held in September 1908.[22] Buxton, officially a missionary of the Church Missionary Society to Japan, and the most important holiness proponent in Japan, had good friends in both the Wesleyan holiness and Keswick meetings. Early holiness leaders such as Sasao in Japan studied under Buxton who organized the Japan Evangelistic Band, a Wesleyan holiness mission, with Paget Wilkes, an associate of Buxton. Buxton saw that the Korean people had earnestly sought heart purity and the fullness of the Holy Spirit. For such a higher spiritual life, the missionaries in Korea invited him.[23]

III

The person who was primarily responsible for the Great Revival in Korea was an independent Canadian missionary, Robert A. Hardie. He wanted to establish medical work and required much financial support. The southern Methodist mission offered him the post of medical missionary and Hardie transferred to the southern Methodists in 1898.

The Great Revival in Korea was begun in 1903 by Hardie after experiencing failure in his mission work. The cause of the failure was a lack of the power of the Holy Spirit. In the summer 1903, Hardie led a missionary Bible conference in Wonsan. At this meeting, Hardie experienced the fullness of the Holy Spirit and had peace and joy.

For years, Hardie had been yearning to see Koreans convicted of sin and led to repentance and faith evidencing its fruit. Up to that time he had not seen in his work any examples of plain, unmistakable, and lasting conversions. He had seen many led to an intellectual knowledge and acceptance of the faith, but he knew only a few who gave any adequate evidence of knowing it as an actual and living experience. As Hardie stood before his own Wonsan congregation the first Sunday morning after his experience of the fullness of the Spirit, they saw for the first time what conviction and repentance meant in actual experience. Hardie told them, "how by simple faith in God's promise [he] had claimed the gift of the Holy Ghost, and during the next three weeks they saw that there was unmistakable change in [his] experience and life, they learned a new lesson of faith, and of the power of God 'to save His people from their sins.'" Hardie called his experience, "the baptism of the Holy Spirit."[24]

Hardie became a great revivalist especially during 1903-1907 and continued revival meetings in his church:

> Through the whole series of meetings the people followed the lead of those who had first been convicted, and confessed their sin in public. On two or three occasions the pressure of conviction was so strong that it was impossible to preach. . . . The testimony of all was that they had never before known anything of religion as a personal and living religion. . . . As under the initial convicting power of the Holy Spirit, they had felt constrained to confess their sins in public, so they determined henceforth to do, whenever they should realize that Satan had gained an advantage over them. . . . This commendable method of dealing with sin has not been, so far as I have been able to see, abused. . . . And this is surely the course that ought to be followed where the Holy Spirit really dwells.[25]

Another southern Methodist missionary, J. L. Gerdine, had been a co-worker with Hardie in these revival meetings. Gerdine had worked with Hardie in Wonsan during 1902-1906 and experienced the fullness of the Holy Spirit.[26] Gerdine had given:

> his message in the quietest, gentle style, and much was a direct quotation from the Word. It was the Miracle of the Spirit convicting of sin. But there is a brighter picture, more wonderful and harder still to paint: the consciousness of . . . sin forgiven, the happiness of complete surrender, and praise God, the Baptism of the Holy Spirit.

When he conducted revival meetings in Ham Heung in January 1906, a Presbyterian missionary was surprised by the results of the revival led by a Methodist, ". . . today we rejoice in pointing to our church full of Presbyterian faith and Methodist joy, and say with Brother Hugh Miller of Seoul, 'you need not be afraid of a Methodist.'"[27] Gerdine was invited to Mokpo by southern Presbyterian missionary J. F. Preston, gave the same message, and got wonderful results.[28]

Gerdine was not only a revivalist, but also an observer of revival meetings. He explained the revival in Korea as part of the worldwide revival movement begun in Wales by Anglo-Saxon people. Gerdine, in April 1905, wrote, "The present manifestation of Divine grace and power, beginning in Wales, is already felt in England, Australia and in many of the great centers in America. It is as though the Anglo-Saxon people had a common spiritual nerve center and, along these nerves, heavenly power felt in one part causes a thrill and response throughout the whole body of the people."[29] Gerdine also insisted that the revivals in Korea could influence other oriental nations. He wrote, "China and Japan will need a demonstration of the suitability of revival movements to Oriental conditions and we should furnish it. Who can doubt that a national revival in Korea would inspire the workers in these neighboring empires as few things could?"[30] In addition to Wonsan, Songdo was also one of the most important centers of the revival meetings. The Songdo revival was begun by Hardie in February and March 1904.[31]

After these meetings, W. G. Cram, in charge of the Songdo Mission of southern Methodism continued to hold revivals in this area. Cram graduated in 1898 from Asbury College, a Wesleyan holiness institution. In his sermons:

> special stress was put upon the fact that salvation from sins was a matter of personal consciousness, bringing out prominently the doctrine of the New Birth and the witness of the Spirit. From the very first of the meeting, . . . an old time revival was upon us. The altar was crowded day and night with men and women seeking the light of a new heart.[32]

Cram maintained that one of the most effective ways for obtaining God's grace of saving and cleansing power is the revival.[33] "I thank God that His mighty transforming power is realized by the Korean heart in the definite experience. We are pushing the revival on these lines. God has given us gracious results. We know He will continue to manifest His saving and cleansing power among this needy people."[34]

In March 1904, Hardie conducted a revival meeting in Chat-Coal church, in which J. R. Moose took part. Most southern Methodist people and some others attended this meeting in which,

> conviction for sin was so deep that it led to many most disgraceful confessions and restitution of stolen goods. Many of the Korean people were brought to know for the first time what sin and forgiveness really mean. . . . These meetings have proved to us all that the Holy Spirit does move on the hearts of Koreans, resulting in conviction and the witness to present salvation. Too often it has been the case that our converts to Christianity in this country have had only a conversion of head while the heart remained ignorant of the cleansing power of the Holy Spirit.[35]

Rev. and Mrs. J. R. Moose were holiness people. Moose said that he excelled Mrs. Moose in professing holiness, but she excelled him in living it.[36] Moose knew the efficiency of revival very well. For him, the most important task in the mission field is, "to deepen the spiritual life of the Church. Once this is done we shall see the heathen coming by hundreds and thousands." The best means for this is the word "Revival." "It is bound up in the one word REVIVAL!" Moose wrote in the *Korea Mission Field* of January 1906: "But I do believe that what the Church needs now more that any thing else is a REVIVAL. Let every worker in Korea pray as never before that the coming Korean New Year may be the time when this revival shall come and this be the real beginning of Korea's Pentecost."[37] The Korea Pentecost of 1907 was the answer to this prayer.

IV

In the Great Revival in Korea there were not only missionary revivalists, but also native revivalists. Perhaps the first indigenous revivalist was Chun-Su Chung. Chung was of noble class from Seoul. His life had been wicked. Running away from his uncle's home to Wonsan, he had taken lodging in a Christian's home. There he began to hear the Gospel of Christ. He was persuaded to read the Bible and attend church. In Hardie's revival he was convicted and confessed his sins.[38] From the time of his public confession, his life showed the fruits of the Spirit and he continued to grow in power and usefulness.

Chung became a local preacher in 1906. J. L. Gerdine considered Chung and other native workers very effective revival leaders. In the annual report of 1907 Gerdine wrote:

> Most of the pastors have been unable to give the usual time to holding revival services in the churches, but it is encouraging to note the increasing efficiency of the native brethren in this most important line of the work. These brethren, having passed through revivals held by the missionaries, have learned much of revival methods; but more than this, their spiritual lives have been so deepened that, through prayer and consecrated labor, they are the instruments for the ministry of divine blessing to many.[39]

Sunjoo Keel can be considered one of the most important native revivalists. He became a main figure in the Korean church in 1907. Hardie and Johnston visited Pyengyang in 1906 and told about revivals. Missionaries in Pyengyang decided to hold prayer meetings for revivals such as those in Wonsan, Wales, and Khasia. However, they did not receive the direction for which they prayed. The Spirit was not yet with them in power. At Christmas a strong desire to have a special week of prayer moved in the hearts of those missionaries. With the close of the prayer meeting the Winter Bible Class began on 6 January 1907. In the evening all the Presbyterians in Pyengyang gathered for special worship in the Central Church which held 1,500 people.[40] The meetings seemed dead, however, and God's Spirit seemed to have departed from the meetings. The heavens over them seemed as brass.

> They were all startled as Elder Keel, the leading man in the church, stood up and said, "I am an Achan. God can't bless because of me. About a year ago a friend of mine, when dying, called to his home and said, 'Elder, I am about to pass away; I want you to manage my affairs; my wife is unable.' I said, 'Rest your heart; I will do it.' I did manage that widow's estate, but I managed to put one hundred dollars of her money into my own pocket. I have hindered God. I am going to give that one hundred dollars back to that widow tomorrow morning." Instantly it was realized that the barriers had fallen and the Holy Spirit had come.[41]

After his confession, Elder Keel rose to his feet asking all to join in singing, "Praise God from whom all blessings flow," and asked all to confess their own sins. After confessing their sins they felt God's peace in their hearts, made restitution for them, and received the power of the Holy Spirit.

Christians in Seoul as well as in Pyengyang prayed for revival for several years. "A real heart-hunger and soul-thirst has characterized many of God's children. Heart-cleaning and Spirit-filling has been the burden of their prayers." In the meantime, revival stories of Pyengyang had gone to all parts of Korea. Here and there similar manifestations occurred. A delegation went from the old city of Seoul asking that Keel should come and speak to them. Keel came to Seoul to conduct revival meetings.

> His preaching is in power and demonstration of the Spirit. In his mouth the word of God is quick and powerful, sharper than a two edged sword. . . . People broke down and wept under a burden of sin. . . . Even the leaders in the church confessed that they were guilty of horrible sins. Stolen money and other stolen articles were returned. . . . Similar incidents could be related in connection with the meetings held in other churches by Mr. Keel.[42]

The KEHC began in May 1907. Sang-Jun Kim, Bin Chung, and Jang-Ha Lee were enthusiastic holiness revivalists. They conducted street evangelism with beating drums and presented powerful messages about the Holy Spirit. Their revival meetings drew remarkable attention from churches in Seoul. Many pastors and missionaries attended these holiness revival meetings, repented of their sins, and experienced regeneration and holiness.⁴³

The news of these holiness preachers spread, and they were called to hold Bible conferences and revival meetings. In *Electric Messages* Mrs. Cowman said:

> Recently they were called to one of the largest churches in Seoul to conduct special meetings, and the missionary in charge has just written as follow: "The Gospel Mission here has been the means of great blessing. God has richly owned and honoured His servants in their life of prayer and testimony, and last week at the close of a week's consecration services many experienced God's mighty power as they did on the day of Pentecost." At present writing they are having special meetings in another large Church of the city. Night by night they are preaching straight Bible Holiness with no uncertain sound, and God is mightily witnessing to it.⁴⁴

Wesleyan holiness preachers continued to conduct revival meetings with other missionaries. John Thomas, the first superintendent of Korea mission of OMS, traveled with Underwood and Gerdine for evangelistic meetings.⁴⁵ In November 1912, Joseph H. Smith, an important Wesleyan holiness proponent, visited Korea and conducted many revival meetings throughout the country. Smith preached in Underwood's church for five nights and Gerdine's church three nights. In each church God gave remarkable results. Smith explained the doctrine of holiness to them by using Hill's book on holiness. "Even some of the staid Presbyterians are now rejoicing in this blessed experience."⁴⁶ At this time John Thomas conducted a week's meeting with Underwood and Gerdine at the YMCA in Seoul. At this meeting Thomas preached, "on such subjects as Repentance, Restitution, Faith, New Birth, etc., offering an uttermost salvation [holiness] to whosoever will, and over 200 responded to the invitation."⁴⁷ It is natural to conclude that Wesleyan holiness teaching was acceptable in early Korean Christianity.

V

There were numerous revivals in the first decade of the twentieth century throughout the world: Welsh revival (1904), Khasia revival (1905), Azusa Street revival (1906), Pyengyang (1907), and Honan (1908). Rooted in the late nineteenth-century holiness movements, early twentieth-century traveling revivalists ignited revivals around the world. Many revivalists visited Korea, told of worldwide revival movements, and encouraged such revivals in Korea. Thus, missionaries and native leaders of Korea were influenced by these international revivalists and consequently sparked the Great Revival.

The Great Revival movement in Korea was rooted in late nineteenth- and early twentieth-century holiness revival movements. Underwood and Appenzeller had been under the influence of holiness revival movements. Most Methodist bishops in charge of the Korea mission field maintained a Wesleyan holiness position. Many Wesleyan holiness revivalists such as Nakada and Cowman conducted revival meetings from 1904 to 1907. Mantle and Buxton, guest lecturers of the General Council of Evangelical Missions in Korea during annual meetings of 1907 and 1908, were definitely Wesleyan holiness revivalists. Most Presbyterian missionaries went to the mission field under the influence of D. L. Moody, A. T. Pierson, A. J. Gordon, and others, who had a strong relationship with the Keswick holiness convention. Franson, who visited Wonsan in 1903, and Gorforth, who visited Pyengyang in 1907, worked with Keswick holiness preachers.

The main characteristics of the Great Revival were typically holiness-revivalistic: conviction of sin, repentance, restitution, the blood of Christ, the cleansing of the heart, the power or fullness or baptism of the Holy Spirit, peace and joy as the result of surrender to Christ, and evangelism. We can summarize these characteristics in two categories: holiness of heart and the power of the Holy Spirit. The revivals emphasized conviction of sin, repentance, restitution, and the cleansing of the heart, all of which can be categorized as holiness messages. The revivalists also stressed the power of the Holy Spirit for evangelism and ministry.

It could be said that the Great Revival was conducted by holiness revivalists of both Wesleyan and Keswick types. Those at the beginning of the Great Revival were southern Methodists such as Hardie, Gerdine, and Cram, from the Wesleyan holiness tradition. The Wesleyan revivalists considered the revival Wesleyan and emphasized heart cleansing, a typical Wesleyan teaching.[48] With the exception of the OMS preachers' revivals, we cannot find radical Wesleyan holiness terms such as the second blessing after regeneration, or the eradication of depravity as holiness, in these revivals. The power of the Holy Spirit for evangelism was the typical message of the Keswick meetings as well as Wesleyan groups.

In late nineteenth- and early twentieth-century evangelicalism, there were great controversies over the baptism of the Holy Spirit. For Wesleyans the baptism of the Holy Spirit is a holiness experience after regeneration, while for Keswick, this experience is mainly receiving the power of the Holy Spirit. For Pentecostals, the initial evidence of the Holy Spirit is speaking in tongues. The revivalists often used the term, "the baptism of the Holy Spirit," as distinguished from water baptism or infant baptism. However, the revivalists did not have a definite concept about the baptism of the Holy Spirit. They used the term as including holiness and power.

The Azusa Street revival and the Great Revival in Korea occurred in the same period. However, we cannot find any mention in Korea of the Azusa Street revival where modern Pentecostalism began. Generally speaking, early twentieth-century evangelicals did not regard tongue-speaking as proper or genuine evidence of true revival. Therefore, there is no direct relationship between the two movements. However, there is a very interesting fact which might be related to tongues. Gale reported that during the revival Keel, Korean leaders, and Chinese who visited Pyengyang to see what happened in the revival prayed, "the Chinese in their unintelligible monosyllables, and the Koreans in their world-forgotten language of antiquity."[49] We are not sure whether it was a tongue-phenomenon or not. However, if it was tongues, it was the first instance. If so, the Great Revival might also be related to the Pentecostal movement.

Notes

1. Numerous reports of missionaries about the Revival appeared in the *Korean Mission Field* (*KMF*) (1905-1910), the official monthly magazine of the General Council of Evangelical Missions in Korea, and several official minutes or annual reports of Korea mission of the M. E. Church, M. E. Church, South, PCUSA, etc. Besides these, there are several pamphlets such as William N. Blair, *The Korea Pentecost: And Other Experiences on the Mission Field* (New York: Board of Foreign Missions of the Presbyterian Church in the U.S.A., ca. 1910); George H. Jones and W. Arthur Noble, *The Korea Revival: An Account of the Revival in the Korean Churches in 1907* (New York: Board of Foreign Missions of the Methodist Episcopal Church, 1910); and Jonathan Gorforth, *When the Spirit's Fire Swept Korea*, Korean trans. Young Yun Kim (Seoul: Life Line, 1977).

2. James S. Gale, *The Vanguard: A Tale of Korea*, Korean Translation (Seoul: The Christian Literature Society in Korea, 1993), 97.

3. Eifion Evans, *The Welsh Revival of 1904* (Port Talbot, Glamorgan, Wales: The Evangelical Movement of Wales, 1969), 70, 84.

4. *Official Minutes of the Korea Mission of the Methodist Episcopal Church*, hereafter *OMKMEC*, 1893-1910.

5. S. B. Shaw, ed., *Echoes of the General Holiness Assembly Held in*

Chicago, May 3-13, 1901 (Chicago: S. B. Shaw, 1901).

6. For information about these bishops in relationship to the holiness movement, see Charles E. Jones, *A Guide to the Study of the Holiness Movement*, ATLA Bibliography Series, no. I (Metuchen, N.J.: Scarecrow Press, 1974).

7. Mrs. C. E. Cowman, *Missionary Warrior: Charles E. Cowman* (Greenwood, Ind.: OMS International, 1928), 79.

8. Tetususaboro Sasao, "Out of Darkness into His Marvelous Gift," *Way of Holiness*, III: 3 (July 1911): 3.

9. "R. D. Hardie's Report," *Minutes of the Seventh Annual Meeting, Korea Mission, Methodist Episcopal Church, South* (hereafter *OMKMEC(S)*), 1903, 25-28; "Report of Miss Hounshell," *OMKMEC(S)*, 57.

10. O. C. Grauer, *Frederik Franson* (Chicago: Scandinavian Alliance Mission, 1939), 160.

11. Grauer,161; *OMKMEC(S)*, 1904, 24-25.

12. "Brother Nakada's Trip in Korea," *Electric Messages*, hereafter *EM*, (October 1904); "Nakada's Trip in Korea," *EM* (September 1904).

13. G[raham] Lee, *How the Spirit Came to Pyeng Yang* (New York: The Board of Foreign Missions of the Presbyterian Church U.S.A.: n.d.), 32.

14. Alvyn J. Austin, "Blessed Adversity: Henry W. Frost and the China Inland Mission," *Earthen Vessels: American Evangelicals and Foreign Missions, 1880-1980*, eds. Joel A. Carpenter and Wilbert R. Shenk (Grand Rapids, Mich.: Wm. B. Eerdmans, 1990), 50; Alvyn J. Austin, *Saving China: Canadian Missionaries in the Middle Kingdom 1888-1959* (Toronto: University of Toronto Press, 1986), 116-17.

15. For more information see James S. Gale, *Korea In Transition* (New York: Eaton & Mains, 1909), 215-21.

16. Austin, *Saving China*, 117.

17. Jonathan Gorforth, "The Spirit's Fire in Korea," and "God's Overflow in Korea," *The Victorious Life* (Philadelphia, Pa.: The Board of Managers of Victorious Life Conference, 1917), 183-200.

18. "Korea and Full Gospel," *EM* (June 1907).

19. Leslie D. Wilcox, *Be Ye Holy* (Cincinnati, Ohio: Revivalist Press, 1965), 182.

20. J. Gregory Mantle, "A Wonderful Work in Korea," *EM* (March 1908): 11-13.

21. "Editorial," *KMF* III: 10 (October 1907): 156; 158-59.

22. *KMF*, IV: 6 (June 1908): 88.

23. B. Godfrey Buxton, *The Reward of the Faith in the Life of Barclay Fowell Buxton 1860-1946* (London: Lutterworth Press, 1949).

24. "R. A. Hardie's Report," *OMKMEC(S)* (1904), 23-24; 27.

25. "R. A. Hardie's Report," *OMKMEC(S)* (1904), 25.

26. "Report of Wonsan Circuit," *OMKMEC(S)* (1904), 29-33.

27. Edith F. Mcrae, "For Thine is the Power," *KMF*, II: 4 (February 1906): 73-75.

28. J. F. Preston, "A Notable Meeting," *KMF*, II: 12 (October 1906): 227-28.

29. J. L. Gerdine, "National Revivals," *The Korea Methodist*, hereafter *KM*,

I: 6 (April, 10 1905): 84.

30. J. L. Gerdine, "National Revivals," *KMF*, I-6 (10 April 1905): 84-86; J. L. Gerdine, "Korea—A Great Religious Awakening," *KMF*, IV: 8 (August 1908): 127-28.

31. "Report of Songdo Circuit," *OMKMEC(S)* (1940), 37-38.

32. W. G. Cram, "A New Year's Revival in Songdo," *KM*, I: 5 (10 March 1905): 54.

33. W. G. Cram, "Revival Fires," *KMF*, II: 2 (December 1906): 33.

34. W. G. Cram, "A Genuine Change," *KMF*, III: 5 (May 1907): 67-68.

35. "Report of the Seoul Circuit," *OMKMEC(S)* (1904), 41.

36. J. L. Gerdine, "More Pioneers of Korea," 53.

37. J. R. Moose, "A Great Awakening," *KMF*, II: 3 (January 1906): 52.

38. "Report of Wonsan Circuit," *OMKMEC(S)* (1904), 31-32.

39. "Report of the District," *OMKMEC(S)* (1907), 16.

40. Lee, 33.

41. Jonathan Goforth, "The Spirit's Fire in Korea," 185. Cf. W. B. Hunt, "Impressions of an Eye Witness," *KMF*, III: 3 (March 1907): 37.

42. "Recent Work of the Holy Spirit in Seoul," *KMF*, III: 3 (March 1907): 41.

43. Myung Chik Lee, *A Brief History of the Oriental Missionary Society Holiness Church* (Seoul: OMS Publication, 1929), 52.

44. Mrs. Cowman, "How the Korean Work Began," *EM* (April 1909).

45. Mrs. John Thomas, "Christmas at the Seoul Mission," *EM* (February 1912): 11; Mrs. John Thomas, "Gospel Carriers in Korea," *EM* (March 1912): 8.

46. Mrs. John Thomas, "Christmas in Seoul," *EM* (February 1913): 1.

47. John Thomas, "A Week's Special Effort to Reach the Heathen Men of Seoul," *EM* (December 1912): 11.

48. Jones and Noble, *The Korean Revival*, 36.

49. Gale, *Korea in Transition*, 216.

15

An Interpretation of the Korean Church in the Wesleyan Perspective

Hong-ki Kim

I want to interpret Korean church history from a Wesleyan theological perspective because the mainline theological orientation of the Korean church is Wesleyan pietism. This discussion will begin with an historical assumption for my interpretation of Korean church history: a Wesleyan style pietism. Hence, we will show how historical facts support this historical understanding. Then our discussion will consider in what sense Korean Wesleyan pietism has some weaknesses and lacks the ideal feature of authentic Wesleyan theology. Real Wesleyan pietism will be interpreted as a harmonization of both dimensions of personal and social sanctification. Korean church history will be interpreted with chronological characteristics: the initial age of gospel, the healthy evangelical age, the unhealthy evangelical age, the dark age, and the age of bipolarization of the Gospel between evangelicals and ecumenists. The conclusion for the twenty-first century of the Korean church will be discussed with reference to an ideal indigenization of Wesleyan pietism in the Korean historical context for the reunification of North and South Korea.

I

While the most important point of Luther's theology is justification, the main point of Wesley's theology is sanctification. However, Wesley criticized the Roman Catholic concept of sanctification which disregarded justification by faith. For Wesley, justification by faith is the door of religion and sanctification is religion itself.[1] Thus, Wesley had theological debates with both Lutheran Moravians and Roman Catholics. In his sermon, "On God's Vineyard," Wesley criticized these two theological positions: "But it has pleased God to give the Methodists a full and clear knowledge of each, and the wide difference between them [i.e., justification and sanctification]."[2]

Most Korean Christians have a Lutheran Moravian style of pietistic faith rather than one that reflects Wesleyan pietism. Wesley had reservations about the former after his visit to Herrnhut, the Moravian center. He pointed out that the Moravians had a doctrine of stillness, quietism, and imputed grace, and an antinomian tendency. In the debate between Wesley and Zinzendorf there are clear theological differences. German-speaking Zinzendorf and English-speaking Wesley chose a way of better communication. They debated in Latin. They had their historic debate on 3 September 1741 at Gray's Inn Walks. It can be summarized in four main points.

First, Zinzendorf insisted that only Christ is our perfection and our perfection is in him (*in Christus*), whereas for Wesley perfection is in believers (*in se*) as well as in Christ (*in Christus*). Zinzendorf accepted Luther's "*simul justus et peccator*" with no perfection of inherent or imparted righteousness. So he said, "Christ is our only perfection" (*Christus est sola perfectio nostra*) and "All our perfection is in Christ" (*Omnis nostra perfectio est in Christo*).[3] For him all Christian perfection is simply faith in Christ's blood (*Omnis Christiana perfectio est fides in sanguine Christi*).[4] Wesley believed in our perfection in this life with the optimism of grace. He said, "Truly I believe that it is the Spirit of Christ that works in true Christians to achieve their perfection" (*Ego vero credo, Spiritum Christi operari perfectionem in vere Christianis*).[5] For Wesley the Christian believer should live a holy life and he or she is holy in himself or herself (*in se*) as well as holy in Christ (*in Christus*).[6]

Second, while Zinzendorf emphasized objective, passive, and imputed perfection (*imputata perfectio*), Wesley insisted on subjective, inherent, and imparted perfection (*inhaerens perfectio*). Zinzendorf said,

"I know of no such thing as inherent perfection in this life" (*Nullam inhaerentem perfectionem in hac vita agnosco*).⁷ For him Christian perfection is totally imputed and not imparted (*Est tota Christiana perfectio, imputata, non inhaerens*).⁸ However, for Wesley, Christian perfection is imparted and inherent. So there was no agreement between them.

Third, for Zinzendorf faith alone is the foundation of sanctification and perfection, whereas for Wesley love as well as faith is the foundation of sanctification and perfection. Zinzendorf claimed the Lutheran tradition again, "Faith is evangelical sanctification" (*Sanctitas evangelica est fides*).⁹ Therefore, Zinzendorf showed a tendency of solafideism, quietism, or antinomianism. However, Wesley understood that the growth and maturity of sanctification develops with the growth and maturity of love. Wesley asked whether sanctification grows through love, "Don't you believe that while he or she is growing in love, he or she is growing in holiness" (*Nonne credens, dum crescit in amore, crescit pariter in sanctate*)?¹⁰

Fourth, while Zinzendorf focused on momentary sanctification, Wesley insisted on gradual sanctification. For Zinzendorf the moment of justification is the moment of sanctification and love. Thus, he said, "In the moment of justification, sanctification is entire" *(Eo momento quo justificatur, sanctificatur penitus)*.¹¹ He said as well, "He or she loves totally in the moment, such as totally sanctified" (*Totaliter amat eo momento, sicut totaliter sanctificatur*).¹² He believed that both justification and sanctification do not increase or decrease because both justification and sanctification are realized in the same moment. However, Wesley held that we grow in grace gradually (*crescendum esse in gratia*) and are renewed day-by-day (*renovaamur de die in diem*).¹³ We can understand that Zinzendorf followed Luther's instantaneous imputation of justification and sanctification by faith through grace. Wesley affirmed the instantaneous imputation of justification by faith and the gradual impartation of sanctification by love through the influence of the Eastern Orthodox tradition with Gregory of Nyssa, John Chrysostom, and Macarius the Egyptian, and the western Catholic and Anglican mystical tradition of Jeremy Taylor, William Law, and Thomas à Kempis.

On the one hand, sanctification for Wesley is holiness, separation and detachment from the power of sin and evil nature. On the other hand, for Wesley sanctification is love. What is sanctification? Wesley said, "It is the loving God with all our heart, mind, soul and strength."¹⁴ It is love excluding sin, love filling the heart, taking up the whole capacity of the soul. Therefore, for Wesley sanctification needs both faith and good works in terms of faith working by love. To do good works means to grow in faith. Wesley insisted that initial salvation, justification, and regeneration, needs faith only, but final salvation, sanctification and entire sanctification, needs both faith and good works. For Wesley faith is the condition for salvation and love, or good work, and is the condition of the fullness for salvation. For Wesley, good works need the assurance of salvation and the fullness of salvation or final salvation.[15] Wesley observed that St. Paul and St. James spoke about justification.[16] For Wesley, St. Paul's justification by faith is imputed righteousness and St. James' justification by good works is imparted righteousness in terms of sanctification. Wesley understood that St. James spoke of good works after justification by faith.

For Wesley, love expressed as good works is identified as a social activity, social holiness, or social sanctification because we can and must practice love or good works in society.[17] Social sanctification is revealed in the social holiness of life with works of mercy, whereas individual sanctification is revealed in holiness of heart with works of piety.

Wesley preached, "Christianity is essentially a social religion."[18] For him, to turn Christianity into a solitary religion would be to destroy it. Wesley mentioned the concept of social holiness or sanctification in the preface of the Methodist hymnal:

> Solitary religion is not to be found there. "Holy solitaries" is a phrase no more consistent with the gospel than holy adulterers. The gospel of Christ knows of no religion, but social; no holiness but *social holiness*. "Faith working by love" is the length and breadth and depth and height of Christian perfection.[19]

Wesley's allusion to light and salt in his sermon, "On the Sermon on the Mount, IV," was strongly related to the issue of social religion as well:

> First, I shall endeavor to show that Christianity is essentially a social religion, and that to turn it into a solitary religion is indeed to destroy it. . . . When I say this is essentially a social religion, I mean not only that it cannot subsist so well, but that it cannot subsist at all without society, without living and conversing with other men.[20]

For Wesley, while we need separation or detachment from the world for personal sanctification, we need incarnation in the world for social sanctification to be light and salt in the world.

As Outler argued, Wesley's evangelicalism was healthy because faith expressed external social action. For Wesley, the essence of faith is inward and internal but the evidence of faith is outward and external in terms of social sanctification. As described in Outler's book, *Evangelism in Wesleyan Spirit*, there is harmony and a combination of internal and external sanctification, personal and social sanctification.[21] Outler believed that Wesley gathered his converts into society to reform the nation and to realize the Kingdom of God in history.

Wesley and early Methodists attempted social transformation as well as social service. When Wesley presided at the first annual conference in 1744 he insisted that God called Methodist preachers not to make a denomination but *to reform the nation*.[22] "To reform the nation" is as much a slogan for Methodists as "The world is my parish!" Methodist enthusiasm was a transforming influence. It was with this new self-awareness emanating in large part from the classes and class leadership that Methodism contributed to radical political movements in the nineteenth century. The early labor movement among farmers, miners, and workers consisted of twelve members and one leader just like the Methodist class system. Methodism was indirectly responsible for growth in self-confidence and the capacity for organizing working people. The new Methodist revival provided the dream of a millennium of ideal cooperation between the ruling class and the working class during a time of profound alienation between classes in Britain.[23] Sanctification is necessary to accept the challenge and risk the struggle for the fullness of life to make visible the kingdom of God, a kingdom of love and justice.

II

1885-1906: The Early Korean Church

The mainline theology of the Korean church is pietistic evangelicalism.[24] The first missionaries, Henry G. Appenzeller, a graduate of the Drew Theological School of the Methodist Episcopal Church in America, and Horace G. Underwood, a graduate of the New Brunswick Theological Seminary of the Dutch Reformed Church in America, came to Korea on the same day, Easter morning, 5 April 1885.[25] The previous year, in 1884, the first resident medical missionary, Horace Allen, arrived in Korea to do medical missionary work.

These early missionaries were Wesleyan style evangelicals. Even Underwood, the Presbyterian, was a type of Methodist. His nickname was "the roaring Methodist" and "the Methodist preacher of the Presbyterian mission."[26] Appenzeller was a pietistic evangelist as well. Appenzeller was concerned with cultural reformation and social sanctification. He was trained in Wesleyan social sanctification in theology and practice at Drew. His decision to become a missionary was influenced by nineteenth-century American revival movements. He was exceptional because most missionaries were concerned only with individual salvation and personal sanctification. It was a major tragedy when he drowned after saving a girl in the ocean along the shore of Korea. He laid down his life for a dying neighbor just as Jesus did. If he could have lived longer, he might have contributed to the Korean church having a harmonized balance of personal and social sanctification, individual and social salvation.

The early mission style was Wesleyan. Sir William Cecil, a British journalist, reported the 1907 Korean Great Revival Movement in *The Times* of London, "The Holy Spirit coming in Pyung Yang is very similar to Wesley's revival movement. If we look into Wesley's journal, we find out that the two movements are the same. . . ."[27] The missionaries emphasized Wesley's dimension of individual sanctification rather than social sanctification. The seeds of pietistic faith grew well and fast in Korean soil. The theological background of these missionaries was a kind of pietistic evangelicalism which included revivalism, individualism, and dualism.[28]

In keeping with the early Korean church tradition, most present-day Korean churches have revival meetings more than once annually. Every Korean Protestant church has Wesleyan style class meetings every Friday night. This has even taken place in Presbyterian, Baptist, and Pentecostal churches.

Korean pietistic evangelicalism is based on a form of dualism. Most American missionaries and Korean evangelists have separated secular matters and religious matters in terms of a radical separation of church and state. They have only been concerned with otherworldly spiritual salvation in order to maintain political quietism.[29] Most missionaries sustained an ambiguous political neutralism. When Korean Christians were persecuted by Japanese policemen, missionaries maintained neutrality. Moreover, missionaries believed that Korean Christians would obey the Japanese colonial power rather than protest against it.[30] The missionaries criticized the Korean Christians' independence movement as political involvement.

From 1885 to the beginning of Japanese rule in 1910, however, the number of Korean Christians rose rapidly because of the emotional shock resulting from Japanese annexation. Numbers of Koreans hoped that in Christianity they would find the answer to national weakness and their own personal insecurity and sanctification.[31] For Koreans, Christianity was not imperialism or colonialism as in Latin America or Africa, but a kind of benevolent gospel for their political and spiritual crisis under Japanese imperial and colonial power. Therefore, the mission to Korea has been much more successful than in other countries.

So, Koreans were actuated by a desire for protection and power, the desire for relief from political oppression.[32] Methodist young men participated in military training to fight against Japanese colonial power at the Sang Dong Methodist Church. At that church a secret mission to the Hague was planned.[33] Thus, evidence of social sanctification is noted during the earliest years of the Korean church. Korean Christians were interested in social sanctification, whereas American missionaries were concerned with personal sanctification.

The missionaries believed that the essence of the Christian spirit is based in mission and that a lack of missionary spirit represented a lack of Christian belief.[34] The nonpolitical concern of the missionaries, on one hand, and the political concern of Korean Christians, on the other, the Wesleyan evangelical factor and the Wesleyan factor of social justice, provided grounds for tension. The situation of the Korean church was serious.

III

1907-1919: The Age of Healthy Evangelicalism

From 1907 to 1919, the Korean church demonstrated a healthy evangelicalism in terms of personal and social sanctification. Politically, the Japanese protectorate which was established in 1905, resulted in annexation in 1910, and the political independence of the country was terminated.[35] The people were in dire need of sympathetic friends and encouragement.

In this situation a revival movement began in 1903 when a group of missionaries of the Methodist mission met for a week of prayer and the Bible study at Wonsan. Among them, Dr. Robert Alexander Hardie, a

Canadian Methodist missionary, made a confession of his missionary failure. From this meeting a Wesleyan revival emerged, prompted by Hardie's testimony. The members of both the Methodist and the Presbyterian missions invited Hardie to lead them in August 1906. They made conscious efforts to bring about a deepening spiritual experience[36]

The missionaries worked to bring their hopes to fruition during the time of the annual meeting of the Bible Teaching Class, which met at P'youngyang at the beginning of January 1907. These evenings were entirely devoted to special evangelistic preaching. At one of the evening meetings, a church officer arose and confessed a grudge which he had against a missionary and implored the latter's forgiveness. As the missionary stood and began to pray, a strange emotion overtook the congregation. They began to pray aloud in unison. This great spiritual awakening marked the spiritual rebirth of the Korean church.

The Wesleyan evangelical revival movement has developed more strongly in the Korean church since 1907. William Cecil wrote about the 1907 Korean revival movement as a Wesleyan revival movement in *The Times* of London, "The pentecostal fact which was in P'yung Yang is very similar to the pentecostal event which pre-existed in the Wesleyan great revival movement."[37]

Following the revival, the new religious experience was severely tested but has survived as a moral and spiritual force. The close contact between missionaries and Korean Christians during the years of preparation for the revival afforded new opportunities for close cooperation and correlation. The power of evangelization helped to develop strong social activity which in turn helped to realize the liberation and humanization of the Korean people.

One of the channels of the Independence Movement of 1919 was the Korean church in which the affirmation of eternal life brought about the appearance of active social participation in the liberation movement. Evangelical faith was linked with social action, the power of personal sanctification evolved into social sanctification through revival movements. Consequently, sixteen Christian leaders out of thirty-three national leaders signed the statement of the declaration of independence which Choi Nam-Sun wrote.[38] Among those sixteen Christian leaders, seven leaders graduated from the Methodist Theological Seminary. This was an interfaith movement in which Buddhist leaders and Ch'ondo Kyo leaders joined together. Most Korean people who participated in this movement experienced much suffering.

The most tragic event of persecution was the fire at the Jae Am

Methodist Church. Japanese policemen set fire to the chapel when twenty-seven young Methodists and Ch'ondo Kyo members were inside.[39] With rifles and knives, the Japanese policemen killed them all. Such courage, even to meet death for the cause of Korean independence, resulted from the deep personal experience of faith. Kwan Soon Ryu, a famous female leader of this movement, who was a student of Ewha Methodist mission high school and sixteen years old at that time, prayed in the mountains, "God, give me a spiritual power to cry out liberation just like Joan of Arc. . . ."[40]

Among them there was no gap between faith and social action. They thought that evangelical faith involved social action to realize social justice and to reform the nation. During that period, the Korean church was admired and respected in Korean society. It was "the light and salt" of the earth. This period was the most healthy missionary period in the history of the Korean Church and the number of Korean Churches rose rapidly. In 1900 the number of Roman Catholics totaled 42,000, and in 1911, 77,000.[41] In 1914 the number of Protestants was approximately 96,000.[42]

IV

1920-1944: The Age of Unhealthy Evangelicalism

After the Independence Movement of 1919, many Korean people crowded into the churches. Korean Christians were not trained theologically and they basically enjoyed emotional mystical experiences. Under the Japanese military rule the Korean church was afraid to participate in social action. Therefore, it became more mystical. Inner sanctification was emphasized whereas social sanctification was not.

The most typical mysticism of Korea was encouraged by a Korean Methodist minister, Rev. Yong Do Lee. It was a mysticism of the suffering Christ which imitated the crucified Christ on the cross.[43] He emphasized mystical union with God through the love of suffering. This concept of theology of the cross is very similar to Martin Luther's theology of the cross.[44] Lee confirmed that love is more important than faith. Justification by faith is the door of Christianity and sanctification by love is the center of Christianity. This seems to be a reinterpretation of John Wesley.[45] Lee was condemned by the Korean Methodist Church and the

Korean Presbyterian Church. He died at thirty-three. His ordination was restored the Seoul Annual Conference of the Korean Methodist Church in March 1999.

Kwang-Soo Lee, a prominent Korean writer, criticized the mysticism of the Korean church which had an emotional tendency. He suggested that true Christianity is not emotional, but rather an intellectual faith which should confess Christian faith theologically. However, Korean Christians related to emotional ecstasy and mystical experiences rather than a biblical, theological, and rational expression of faith. Lee rejected the dualistic thinking of the Korean church which divided sacred society and profane society completely and separated the physical tasks from the spiritual tasks.

The Korean church in this period resembled medieval mysticism's dualistic thought of spirit and flesh and its emotional ecstasy. Many Korean Christians, during this period, were not at all concerned with social participation and social welfare. Their ultimate concerns were individual salvation from an evil world and belief in the apocalyptic Kingdom of God which would take over this secular world including the Japanese colonial government.

The mystical Korean church was the target of criticism by the Korean intellectual class. Many intelligent young men left the church. The intellectual youth criticized the church as an otherworldly, emotional, and individualistic community. Radical evangelization and personal sanctification were transferred to mysticism. Radical enthusiastic revival movements were connected with Shamanistic ecstasy.

V

1945-1959: The Dark Age

Liberation from Japan came from God's providence like a thief in the night.[46] With the division of North and South Korea, however, the Korean church also experienced divisions. The Presbyterian Church has been divided into several denominations. During the Korean War, Korean Presbyterian churches were divided into three denominations—the Goshin Presbyterian Church, the Kidokkyo Presbyterian Church, and the Yesukyo Presbyterian Church. The causes of division were rooted, in part, in theological methodologies. The Goshin Presbyterian Church was concerned with conservative fundamentalism; the Kodokkyo Presbyterian Church emphasized liberal theological methodology; and the Yesukyo Presbyterian Church stood for orthodoxy. Rev. Jae-Joon Kim, a leader of the Kidokkyo Presbyterian Church said, "Even though we are very similar to the orthodox in the contents of theology, we are very different from them in the dimension of theological methodology."[47] In 1982, there were thirty-two denominations of Presbyterians.[48]

After the division of the Korean church and the Korean War the secularization of the Korean church made it powerless. Korean churches were blinded by their drive to gather money and to obey the unjust government. Korean Christians were asked to be loyal to the existing government by the missionaries in the early years of the development of Christian communities. Therefore, the Korean Protestant church never has spoken out against the unjust government of Sung-Man Lee. It aligned itself with the government because Sung-Man Lee was a Methodist lay elder. The missionaries often advised the people to avoid political involvement that opposed Chung-Hee Park's military government as well.[49] Furthermore, just like the medieval church, the Korean church of this era was very corrupt. It enjoyed its bureaucratic and financial security. Secular politics utilized the church and the church took advantage of the government.

VI

1960-1990: The Age of Polarization

With the Student Revolution of 19 April 1960 against Sung-Man Lee's reelection to a third presidential term, the modern Korean church was awakened from its passivity and lack of social concern. The mission of Christianity was reinterpreted in a new social content. Korean Christians were to be concerned with political, economic, and social development (social sanctification). An industrial ministry began to restore the rights of poor workers. The women's liberation movement attempted to realize the social equality of Korean women.

Political revolutionary movements have been developed in the modern church to realize a free democratic society. Some Christians accused the government of President General Chung-Hee Park and his

Democratic Republican Party of injustice, oppression, and cruelty.[50] At last, the Methodist missionary George Ogle and Catholic missionary James Sinnot joined together in criticizing the oppressive government. They were eventually expelled from the country.[51] Therefore, this movement was an ecumenical movement. The ecumenical movement has arisen naturally as a result of the sufferings of injustice. Their ultimate concern is not a utopian political victory, but the liberation in Christ of the Korean people from injustice, oppression, and suffering.

These individuals also have been persecuted by elements of conservative Christians who have not agreed with their actions. Korean conservative churches emphasize extreme separation between politics and church. The situation of the modern Korean church is very serious because most modern Korean churches concern themselves generally with evangelization and inner sanctification. The social sanctification or humanization-oriented churches are the minority. The majority are conservative evangelical churches and the polarization of the two opinions has been prominent. There is a serious conflict and split between traditional pietistic churches which are concerned about inner sanctification and the ecumenical churches which are interested in social sanctification.

The contemporary conservative group emphasizes the construction of beautiful and rich church buildings. They strive for large memberships. They have early morning prayer meetings at four or five o'clock every day and three worship services during the week: Sunday morning, Sunday evening, and Wednesday evening. Every Friday they have class meetings and all-night prayer meetings. Many young people have been enrolling in the theological seminaries and each seminary has more than 1,000 students.

VII

In this paper we rediscovered that the mainline of the Korean church has been developed through Wesleyan pietistic evangelicalism. Therefore, the Korean church is very experimental, otherworldly, spiritual, dualistic, antipolitical, antisocial, and missionary. The Korean church has had a strong *eccelsiola in ecclesia* movement such as class meetings and small cell group Bible study meetings. Korean laypeople have been training

An Interpretation of the Korean Church 213

wonderful missionary minds. But we have recognized that we must grow and make the Korean church more mature through Wesleyan theology. I have shown that inclusive, social, and ecumenical Wesleyan theology can contribute to the growth and maturity of the Korean church in order to make it more personal and social, evangelical, and ecumenical.

There are good signs for the harmonization between ecumenical and evangelical Christians since 1990. The Korean National Council of the Churches (KNCC) revised its constitution stating individual salvation as well as social salvation as its goal. KNCC accepted the Assemblies of God in Korea and the Greek Orthodox Church in Korea as members. For the realization of reunification of North and South Korea we need strong solidarity through a strong combination of Wesleyan theology of personal and social sanctification. For the Korean church in the twenty-first century the writer can suggest some points in the Wesleyan perspective as follows.

First, for both ecumenical and evangelical Christians, the power and presence of the Holy Spirit is strongly required. The Holy Spirit exists and works in both personal sanctification and social sanctification just as the Spirit existed and worked in the age of Wesley. While evangelicals must accept social sanctification as the work of the Holy Spirit, ecumenical Christians ought to accept personal sanctification as the work of the Holy Spirit. Wesley's pietistic strength can contribute to the ecumenical dialogue between the mainline Korean Protestant churches and the liberal ecumenical churches. In this Wesleyan theological understanding we can embrace even Korean minjung theology (ultraradicals) and Korean fundamentalists (ultraconservatives).

Second, we have to rediscover Wesley's concept of sanctification for both ecumenical and evangelical Christians. On the one hand, Korean evangelicals need spiritual exercise to imitate Jesus Christ in terms of the growth of personality and spirituality. Most Korean evangelists have preached repentance, instantaneous justification, and instantaneous new birth. However, they have never preached sanctification as a gradual process toward maturity. On the other hand, Korean ecumenical Christians also need spiritual discipline in terms of sanctification with meditation because the real and true power of social action comes from spiritual discipline.

Third, for the harmonious realization of personal and social sanctification, Korean Christians must have "faith working by love." For Wesley, faith is for initial salvation in terms of justification and regeneration, whereas love or good works are for final salvation in terms of sanctification and perfection. Most Korean Christians have enjoyed solafideism and antinomianism. Therefore, Korean Christians have to learn and practice Jesus's Sermon on the Mount and the Epistle of James, as well as Paul's Epistle to Romans.

Fourth, for the reunification of Korea, Korean Christians have to practice Wesleyan economic stewardship. Wesley's economic ethic points out the weakness of capitalism and highlights the sharing and redistributing of wealth, whereas it rejects forced and violent distribution through Marxist revolution. It is the third alternative to overcome the weakness of the capitalism of South Korea and the weakness of the socialism of North Korea.

Fifth, we can learn how to reform the nation of Korea from the Wesleyan social transformation movement. For political and economic democratization, and the reunification of Korea, Korean Christians ought to participate in a civil movement of social organization to reform evil social structures. Our inner, personal, and spiritual impartation must develop to external, social, and historical impartation. Individual perfection ought to link with social perfection in terms of the biblical Jubilee and the kingdom of God.

Notes

1. John Wesley, *Works* (Jackson), VIII, 472.
2. John Wesley, *Works*, vol. 3, 505-6.
3. Albert Outler, ed., *John Wesley* (New York: Oxford University, 1964), 369; W. Stephen Gunter, *The Limits of Love Divine* (Nashville, Tenn.: Kingswood Books, 1989), 102.
4. Outler, 369; Gunter, 102.
5. Outler, 369; Gunter, 102.
6. Outler, 369.
7. Outler, 369.
8. Outler, 369.
9. Outler, 370.
10. Outler, 370.
11. Outler, 371.
12. Outler, 371.
13. Outler, 371.
14. *Works* (Jackson), VI, 413-15.
15. *The Doctrine of Salvation, Faith and Good Works, Extracted from the Homilies of the Church of England*, ed. Albert C. Outler (New York: Abingdon

Press, 1956), 129-33.
16. *Works* (Jackson), VIII, 277.
17. Hong-ki Kim, "The Theology of Social Sanctification Examined in the Thought of John Wesley and in Minjung Theology" (Ph.D. diss., Drew University, 1991), 35.
18. *Works* (Jackson), V, 296.
19. Wesley, "Social Holiness," *A History of the Methodist Church in Great Britain*, ed. Rupert Davies, A Raymond George, and Gordon Rupp. vol. 4, 33.
20. *Works*, vol. 1, 529-30.
21. Albert Outler, *Evangelism in Wesleyan Spirit* (Nashville, Tenn.: Tidings, 1971), 26.
22. Minutes of the Methodist Conference, vol. I, (London: The Conference Office, 1812), 9-10. (Tuesday, 28 June 1744).
23. See Robert F. Wearmouth, *Methodism and Working Class Movement* (London: The Epworth Press, 1948), 95-96, and David L. Watson, *The Early Methodist Class Meeting* (Nashville, Tenn.: Discipleship Resources, 1987), 140.
24. Dr. Ryu Dong-shik describes three main theological streams in the Korean church history. They are Fundamentalism, Liberalism (Religious Theology) and Radicalism (Political Theology) (*A History of Korean Theological Thought*) (Han Kuk Shin Hak Eo Gwang Mack), (Seoul: Chung Mang Sa, 1983). However, I added one more, Pietism, when I wrote my Ph.D. dissertation at Drew University in 1991: "The Theology of Social Sanctification Examined in the Thought of John Wesley and in Minjung Theology." In my view, Pietism is the most mainstream theology in the Korean church history.
25. Kyung-Bae Min, *The Church History of Korea* (Seoul: The Christian Literature Society of Korea, 1972), 126-27.
26. Min, 164.
27. L. George Paik, *The History of Protestant Missions in Korea 1832-1910* (Seoul: Yonsei University, 1973), 390-91.
28. Kenneth Scott Latourette, *A History of the Expansion of Christianity*, IV, (New York: Harper and Brothers), 336.
29. Min, 127
30. Paik, 437.
31. Kenneth Scott Latourette, *Christianity in a Revolutionary Age*, vol. IV, (London: Eye and Spottiswoode, 1961), 449.
32. Paik, 102.
33. Paik, 129.
34. Paik, 356.
35. Paik, 357.
36. Paik, 370.
37. Paik, 390.
38. Paik, 380.
39. Min, 257.
40. Choon-Bae Kim, *Persecution Stories of the Korean Churches* (Seoul:

Sung Moon Hak Sa, 1969), 73.

41. *The Catholic Church in Korea* (Hong Kong: Nazareth Printing Press, Paris Foreign Mission Society, 1924), 68.

42. Kenneth Scott Latourette, *Christianity in a Revolutionary Age*, IV, (New York: Harper, 1962), 449.

43. Min, 312.

44. See Hong-ki Kim, "A Reinterpretation of the Spirituality of Rev. Yong-Do Lee in Historical Theological Perspective," Shin Hak Gwa Se Gye (Theology and the World), Methodist Theological Seminary, Seoul, Korea in the Spring of 1999.

45. See Hong-ki Kim, "A Reinterpretation of the Spirituality of Rev. Yong-Do Lee in Historical Theological Perspective."

46. Suk-Hon Ham, *A Korean History in Meaning* (Seoul: Je-il Publishing House, 1966), 332-34.

47. Min, 375.

48. *Han Kook Il Bo*, 13 April 1982, 6.

49. Wi-Jo Kang, "The Relationship between Christian Communities and Chung Hee Park's Government in Korea," *Missiology* vol. IX (July 1981), 345.

50. Kang, 346.

51. Kang, 352.

16

"A Spreading Fire": The Influence of Thomas Collins on the Formation of the Methodist Church of Australia

Daryl H. Lightfoot

Thomas Collins (1810-1864) never visited Australia, yet profoundly influenced Wesleyan Methodist expansion in New South Wales (NSW) through his three-year Sandhurst circuit term. Wesleyan missions in Samoa, Tonga, and Fiji also testify to his remarkable ministry. Born in 1810 in Warwickshire, England, Collins began attending class meeting aged seven, responding to the claims of Christ under the preaching of Irish evangelist Gideon Ouseley at Redditch in 1818. Falling away spiritually while at boarding school, Collins found renewed faith at Redditch under William Davies in 1826.[1] Davies organized bands to evangelize neighboring villages, placing Thomas Collins in charge of one of them. Educational groups for the Redditch Wesleyan Society members were organized, Collins becoming a group leader and lay preacher. An address on "Human Will" reveals his Arminian views.

Thomas Collins fully consecrated himself to Christ under Henry Breeden's ministry in 1830. His preaching and conversation style changed dramatically and, thereafter, his only business became the salvation of souls.[2] He immediately became a candidate for the Wesleyan ministry, offering himself for overseas mission service. Accepted by the Conference and placed on the President's reserve, he obtained permission to oversee a Wesleyan mission in Wark, Northumberland. Rules for his ministry

217

were settled and noted in his diary for his first day in Wark.³ During a revival which swept Wark almost immediately, Collins was called to enter the regular ministry, but permitted to continue at Wark until the 1832 Conference, which to Collins's surprise appointed him to Sandhurst circuit, comprising the Kent/East Sussex parishes along the river Rother.⁴

John Wesley made ten visits to the East Sussex-Kent areas, first in 1758 and finally to Winchelsea in 1790, where, he wrote, "I stood under a large tree . . . and called to most of the inhabitants of the town: The kingdom of heaven is at hand—repent and believe the gospel!"⁵ Established in 1795, the Rye circuit reported four ministers and 365 members that year, with 37 preaching places; 29 preachers, and 937 members in 33 Societies by 1815. The circuit was divided into Rye and Sandhurst (also known as Staplecross) circuits in 1816.⁶ The ties binding the former Rye circuit Wesleyans endured and were reinforced by class meetings and other traditional Methodist structures. The Wesleyans being a minority group, persistent opposition further strengthened these bonds. Traveling and local preachers ministered across home and neighboring circuits. Local Preachers', Leaders', and Quarterly Meetings ensured fellowship among the "people called Methodists," and intermarriage between Wesleyan Society members was commonplace. Constraints on mobility under the Settlement Laws, increasing unemployment, and the introduction of machinery into various industries contributed to increasing social unrest in Kent/East Sussex in 1830.⁷

Thomas Collins's first three Sundays at Sandhurst brought direct spiritual results everywhere except at Ticehurst. James Harris attended Collins's first service at Northiam, the text being, "No man cared for my soul." Harris followed Collins to Brede and noted several conversions the same evening.⁸ Collins's early Sandhurst converts included Silas Gill of Beckley, the "Giant for Jesus" later described as "perhaps the greatest lay evangelist of the Methodist Church in Australia."⁹ Collins's Sunday services and weekday meetings were followed by prayer meetings, often supplemented with old-fashioned revival meetings early the next morning, enabling agricultural laborers to attend before work. Methodism's genius lay in the connectional system, itinerancy, class meeting, prayer meeting, lovefeast, and seasonal celebrations including the watchnight service and renewal of one's covenant with God. Collins made full use of these and refined the art of "conversation evangelism" during his pastoral visits at Sandhurst. He utilized contemporary issues, such as a local man being sentenced to death for arson, for evangelistic purposes. Showing sensitivity to the pastoral needs of the circuit's women prior to his marriage during his Sandhurst term, Collins requested his sister Annette to assist him as a deaconess.[10]

Collins found his Sandhurst people prepared "to take fire, hold fire, and spread fire." About them he wrote, "There are some rare jewels in this circuit . . . fine fellows; they know how to lift when I flag. Many, both of the leaders and the Local Preachers, are men of flame."[11] Circuit membership dramatically increased by 184 under Collins's ministry in his first year, 162 in the second, and 200 in his final year, totaling 912 when he left the circuit in 1835.

Attempts were made to entice Collins from Wesleyan Methodism following the "Derby Secession" during his Sandhurst term. He was also called to honor his earlier commitment to overseas mission service. This was opposed by his Superintendent on account of Collins's poor health, supported by medical evidence, but the Missionary Secretaries uncharitably accused Collins of "declining to go abroad." Jabez Bunting unjustifiably declared Collins "defective in zeal," bringing a strong protest from Collins's colleague in the nearby Hastings circuit.[12] Another attempt was made to press Collins into overseas missions at the 1835 Conference, but following continuing opposition by Collins's Superintendent this call was ungraciously withdrawn and Collins was assigned to Orkney in the Shetland Islands, remaining in circuit work until retirement following a stroke while stationed in the South Bristol circuit.[13] Thomas Collins died in December 1864 aged fifty-four years, the memorial Minute to this outstanding "circuit evangelist" affirming that "the secret of his power throughout life was prayer."[14]

I

Pressures for immigration to NSW from the early 1830s were matched by pressures for emigration of the indigent poor from England, supported by legislation permitting parishes to raise money for emigration.[15] Increasing hardship and unrest prompted many parishes to implement these provisions and also accept loans offered by the Poor Law Commissioners to outfit departing emigrants, further easing pressures on parish funds. The colonial government also introduced the "bounty" emigration scheme, whereby a "bounty" was paid to private persons bringing mechanics and agricultural laborers and their families to NSW. Many groups from parishes comprising the Rye/Sandhurst Wesleyan Circuits emigrated under these programs, one consequence being a reduction in population over the period to 1851.[16] Wesleyan Methodists influenced by Thomas Collins's 1832 to 1835 Sandhurst circuit ministry themselves exercised a powerful ministry for God on immigrants, wherever they settled in NSW, and on generations of their descendants down to the present day.

Beckley parish lies on the Sussex/Kent county border, its northern boundary the river Rother. It was a typical rural parish in southeast England during the mid-nineteenth century. The parish church-wardens' and vestry meetings were responsible for providing relief for the poor and indigent. The "work-house" and other relief came from parish funds, entitlements to assistance deriving from the Settlement Laws which required each parish to provide for its indigent poor.

The Beckley Wesleyan Society membership in 1801 totaled eight, including John and Sarah Gill, parents of William and Silas Gill. Society membership in 1815 was 24, including John and Mary Gilbert, John being a farmer, a member of the parish vestry, and later a Wesleyan local preacher who also departed for NSW.[17]

Social changes and growing unemployment increased the burden on the parish in meeting the needs of the poor and Beckley Wesleyans were not exempt from hardship. In 1812, George and William, sons of John Gill, were employed under special parish arrangements, and by 1819, Silas and Daniel Gill had joined their brothers "on the parish," other Wesleyans experiencing identical hardships. Some Wesleyans, including the heads of the Gilbert and Playford families, assisted their poorer neighbors with clothing and/or parish-subsidized employment and in the administration of the Poor Laws.[18] When these relief measures were clearly inadequate, the vestry voted to enlarge the poor house, and later to restrict employment and relief to those parish residents having lawful "settlement" in Beckley. Problems persisting, the rate-payers met in April 1838 and voted to implement the 1834 Poor Law Amendment Act, and to raise 500 pounds sterling to assist eligible persons to emigrate.[19] Many accepted this offer, others emigrating under the "bounty" and "government" assisted emigration programs. Those who had means departed for NSW or other colonies. Beckley recorded population reductions from 1477 (1831) to 1412 (1841) and 1342 (1851).[20]

From 1837 to 1842, over 220 vessels conveyed assisted, bounty, and paying passengers to NSW. A few experienced an uneventful voyage, but for the majority there was hardship, illness, death of a partner or child, and some experienced shipwreck. Emigrating Wesleyans from the Rye/Sandhurst circuits were not exempt from these perils, and those following Henry Breeden's charge to Collins to "confess what they receive" were often ridiculed by crew and other passengers alike.[21] Departing Portsmouth in June 1837, the first immigrant vessel under these programs was the "Augusta Jessie" which carried 234 immigrants.

Surgeon-Superintendent Galloway directed education and worship, and utilized "natural leaders" among the immigrants to maintain authority. The immigrants included two Wesleyan local preachers, James Rootes and Silas Gill, who undoubtedly assisted Galloway in these matters. Arriving in October 1837, many "Augusta Jessie" immigrant families moved initially to rural areas southwest of Sydney, pioneering Wesleyan Methodism there prior to moving elsewhere in the colony.[22]

The Playford (from Beckley) and William Gill (from Icklesham) families, emigrating on "Juliana" in October 1838, had a very difficult time. The ship ran into storms, water poured into the berths, and many passengers contracted fever and cholera. Rations were short and the crew threatened mutiny. The passengers' morale was low and some, refusing to implement the Surgeon-Superintendent's instructions regarding health measures, were forced on deck with fumes of burning sulphur and cayenne pepper to permit cleaning the berths. When the "Juliana" was eventually wrecked entering Cape Town, the immigrants proceeded to NSW on other vessels.

William Gill of Icklesham was converted around the time of Thomas Collins's Sandhurst ministry. His obituary records his faithfulness throughout the "Juliana" troubles and that, "On board ship he reproved sin and sinners."[23] Other groups of East Sussex and Kent immigrants to NSW embarked aboard the "Maitland" in mid-1838. Scarlet fever and other illnesses broke out two days after sailing, progressively claiming the lives of five adult immigrants, one crew member, and 29 children. Many parents resisted their children's transfer to the ship's hospital and disputed dietary changes. Morale was low. Depression and hysteria appeared among some of the immigrants.[24]

On arrival in Sydney, "Maitland" was immediately placed in quarantine and the immigrants housed in makeshift accommodation due to overcrowding. Two bright lights shone through the misery of this voyage. Surgeon Smith reported that, "Schools were established under... one very able and Christian teacher John Vidler...."[25] Vidler was another who had been greatly influenced by the ministry of Thomas Collins at Sandhurst. Susannah, wife of William Gill of Beckley, lost an infant daughter and was pregnant throughout the voyage. Although free of disease, she obtained approval to remain in quarantine to care for her daughter Miriam who had sustained a fracture. Susannah herself finally fell ill and was among the last released from quarantine.[26]

The "Lady Nugent" followed "Maitland" and carried many Rye/Sandhurst Wesleyans, including Edward and Harriet (Gill) King, daughter of William Gill of Beckley, whose second child was born on the voyage, and the Southwell and Richard Baker families from Salehurst. In contrast to "Maitland," this voyage was relatively uneventful. Some months later, other East Sussex and Kent Wesleyans boarded "Roxburgh Castle" for the long voyage to NSW, including two local preachers, John Wheatley and John Gilbert, who had sold his farm prior to departure. William Clarke, an Anglican clergyman, kept a diary throughout the voyage, describing the journey aboard the "Roxburgh Castle." Clarke's diary reveals personal discontent, and an unjustifiable cynicism about some migrants, and is informative concerning social relations on board. Clarke recorded a Wesleyan prayer meeting being interrupted by "some idle fellows in the cabin." A few days later he noted that:

> This evening a party of Wesleyans came upon deck, and seating themselves under the main mast commenced singing hymns and psalms accompanied by a bass viol. On the starboard side of the deck at the same time, another party—chiefly sailors—were dancing jigs to the tune of a violin. . . . There was a stir among the passengers. Sundry oaths were uttered and many people who ought to have known better joined in. . . . I took the part of the Wesleyans because whether judicious or not, their conduct was Christian.

Clarke also recorded the death of the only child of John Gilbert, Jr. of Beckley, describing preparations for the burial at sea, the mother's distress, and his own pastoral efforts. Ignorant of the standing of John Gilbert, Sr. both in Beckley parish and as a Wesleyan local preacher, Clarke later recorded Gilbert's death from "jail fever, the effect of bad living and crowded air" and his burial at sea.[27]

Many Wesleyan families migrated in 1839, including large numbers from Robertsbridge, Salehurst, and Mountfield parishes. Some of these families went to Canada and evidence is emerging of similar pioneering Wesleyan work in Canada to that described here. Other ships bringing substantial numbers of assisted migrants to NSW from these places included "Neptune" and "Prince Regent."[28] Dr. Galloway was Surgeon-Superintendent on the latter and his journal provides considerable information about the migrants' circumstances on board. Many "Prince Regent" passengers had received parish relief for some time prior to departure, but appeared to be in good health at embarkation. Scarlet fever, diarrhea, and other illnesses emerged shortly afterwards. Galloway concluded that some illnesses resulted from the migrants "indulging in fresh butter and cheese from the shore," delicacies to which they were unaccustomed. Migrant ships had additional hazards for their human cargo, especially the children. Samuel Baker, aged four, fell fourteen feet into the hold of "Prince Regent," but miraculously recovered.[29]

Arriving in Sydney, most new arrivals were housed in the Immigration Barracks until they obtained employment or other accommodation. Living at close quarters, incipient disease continued to claim lives. Many "died in quarters," others dying later from infections contracted in the Barracks.

The William Baker family of Salehurst on "Prince Regent" mourned the deaths of Sarah Baker and her daughter-in-law, Charlotte Baker, shortly after arrival. Sarah's younger children and the only surviving child of Charlotte Baker could not remain with their fathers who needed to find work. William Baker's four youngest children went to Orphan Schools, while his grandson Alfred, later a Wesleyan local preacher, was placed with his uncle Richard Baker who arrived earlier on "Lady Nugent."[30]

Ships' logs, surgeons' journals, diaries, correspondence of migrants, passengers, and crew, obituaries, and personal testimonies, reveal a people whose faith held strong in the face of disease, death, deprivation, and disaster over the months at sea and immediately afterwards. They went forward in that same faith to work, worship, and witness to the truths they had earlier received from Thomas Collins and his coworkers in the Rye/Sandhurst Wesleyan circuits.

II

New South Wales in 1835-1840 comprised what are now three states and a territory of Australia—NSW, Queensland, Victoria, and the Australian Capital Territory—and had been established less than fifty years when the first Rye/Sandhurst Wesleyan migrants arrived. The colony was established initially for the reception and management of convicts. Transportation to NSW still operated, but ceased around 1846. Sydney's population was about 25,000. Geographically, NSW is bounded on the east by the Pacific Ocean. The Great Dividing Range runs approximately north to south, separating the coastal fringe from the western pastoral slopes and plains which were settled less than 25 years prior to the first assisted and bounty immigrants' arrival. The only transport was coastal and river shipping, or horse or bullock-drawn vehicle. Many early immigrants, therefore, first found employment in rural areas around Sydney, the Illawarra area to the south, or the Hunter Valley in the north. Freedom of movement was limited and small close-knit communities similar to those in England were typical. A major difference was the limited social contact between these communities due to the distances and natural barriers involved. Wesleyan Methodism was in its infancy and in 1837 had just two chapels in the inner Sydney area. The Superintendent was John McKenny.[31]

The arrival of an immigrant ship was announced in the press with a summary of the immigrants' background, skills, and other information. A date was set for prospective employers to visit the Immigration Barracks to hire the newcomers. Most new arrivals were hired within the month allowed in the Barracks, but men with large families often had to accept lower wages or take their chances "on their own account."[32] Widows and widowers with children were similarly disadvantaged, or relinquished their children to the Orphan Schools, unless alternatives existed, as with the Baker families of Salehurst on "Prince Regent." New immigrants thus moved out into the rural areas of NSW where the former Rye/Sandhurst Wesleyans played leading roles in extending Wesleyan Methodism over succeeding years.

Through those converted or otherwise influenced during his Sandhurst term, Thomas Collins thus exercised a vicarious ministry in NSW extending long beyond his lifetime. Collins's influence was clearly far-reaching beyond anything which could conceivably have been achieved had the Missionary Secretaries successfully diverted Collins from Sandhurst to the overseas missions before completing his term in that circuit. However, who could foreknow the outcome had Collins himself been appointed to the Australian Wesleyan Mission District?

Australian evangelist W. G. Taylor was inspired by reading Collins's biography and later compared Silas Gill, converted under Collins, to Billy Bray. It has been suggested that Gill was perhaps the greatest lay evangelist of Australian Methodism.[33] A theme of this paper is timing, the timing of Collins's appointment to Sandhurst and the agricultural revolution in southeastern England, the timing of changes in immigration policy affecting NSW and the Poor Law Amendment legislation, and the timing of selecting officers' visits to the parishes comprising the Rye/Sandhurst Wesleyan circuits and the provision of new lands for settlement on the southern highlands, the Hunter and the NSW Northern rivers. On these, and numerous other counts, it is reasonable to affirm that God works "in the fulness of time."

The measure of Thomas Collins's vicarious work in NSW is known to God alone and continues even today. Case studies from ongoing research illustrate that Collins's people continued to "take fire, hold fire, and spread fire" for God in NSW.[34]

Many "Augusta Jessie" immigrants and those who followed settled in a rural area on the Nepean River southwest of Parramatta called

"Cowpastures." They included Silas Gill, former parish apprentice in Beckley, of whom Thomas Collins had prophesied, "Here comes a giant for Jesus." Gill committed himself to Christ in a Sussex chapel early in Collins's Sandhurst ministry. Silas Gill was known to walk sixteen miles to meetings at Quarry Grove, carrying his child in his arms, and arriving home around 2:00AM.[35] A "hired local preacher," Francis Glass, and an assistant missionary, William Lightbody, were appointed to the Cowpastures in 1842 and 1843. Silas Gill, the Roots brothers, Tom Brown, John Wheatley, and John Vidler had already been "Methodizing" the area for five years and a Wesleyan chapel was established in Thomas Foster's home.[36]

Of these pioneer Wesleyans James Colwell wrote, ". . . attracted to other parts of the colony, many of these men carried their zeal and piety with them and became the pioneers and afterwards the mainstays of Methodism. Their piety was boisterous, but it was robust. . . ."[37] Many moved from this area in the late 1840s, some moving south, others proceeding to the Hunter, joining family and friends undertaking similar ministries since their arrival around 1838. Later migrations to the NSW north coast and New England areas saw further Wesleyan expansion through those influenced by Collins during his Sandhurst term. John Vidler and his family returned to the NSW south coast. The sons of Joseph Nash moved to the Macquarie and Lachlan rivers and the Wheatley and Brown families moved to the southern highlands, maintaining long-standing family associations. "Old Tom" Brown was born in 1805 in Burwash in Sussex. Organizing a group to disrupt John Wheatley's preaching in Sussex, the preaching touched him and he joined the Wesleyans, but later became a slave to alcohol. Arriving in NSW in April 1838, he found peace with God during a violent thunderstorm.[38] Tom Brown joined Silas Gill in preaching, often leading services at Stoney Range. Camp meetings were held in William Brown's paddock. It was disputed who was the louder, Silas Gill in hymn-singing, or Tom Brown in prayer. Tom Brown in later years undertook Wesleyan pioneering work south of Goulburn around Gunning.[39] Churches which sprang up throughout the Riverina district in later years were strengthened by the presence and witness of the Rye/Sandhurst Wesleyans and their descendants.[40]

An Irish Wesleyan lay preacher with credentials from Gideon Ouseley settled at Maitland in the late 1830s. A chapel was opened in 1839, and Jonathan Innes was appointed to preach in 1840, having oversight north to the present Queensland border.[41] Below Maitland were Morpeth (Greenhills) above the Hunter and Paterson River junction, and further downstream at the Hunter and Williams junction, the town of Raymond Terrace. Wesleyan pioneers at Raymond Terrace were William Gill, brother of Silas, and his daughter and son-in-law, Harriet and Edward King from Beckley, arriving in late 1838. Harriet King had been converted at an early age under the ministry of her uncle Silas Gill.[42]

Other Wesleyan families from Kent and East Sussex followed, including the Boots and Waters (Wattus) families and the family of Mary Gilbert of Beckley, whose local preacher husband John Gilbert had died on "Roxburgh Castle." Mary Gilbert immediately opened her home for the first Wesleyan services in 1840, the Wesleyan Society at Raymond Terrace consisting of members of eight families.[43] Members of the Gilbert family moved north into Bulahdelah and Stroud. Others moved to Newcastle and made a substantial contribution to the Wesleyan Methodist cause. Several descendants of John and Mary Gilbert later became Salvation Army officers.[44]

The influence of Thomas Collins and the Rye/Sandhurst Wesleyan pioneers in Raymond Terrace went even further. A young man was converted to Christ in the Raymond Terrace Wesleyan church in 1891. That man was George Carpenter, later General George Carpenter, world leader of the Salvation Army.[45]

William Gill later moved upriver to Woodville on the Paterson River, continuing his pioneer Wesleyan work, remaining a local preacher and class leader until his death in 1869. He was followed by Edward King who settled on "Wallalong" below Woodville.[46] William Gill encouraged his brother Silas to join him. Silas and his family arrived from the Cowpastures in 1845/1846. Other Kent/Sussex Wesleyans were already ministering at Cooley Camp (Bolwarra) and elsewhere in the Maitland district, including William Burgess who came on "Augusta Jessie," Levi Lambert, John Delves, and the Eggins families from Ewhurst. Another Ewhurst family, the Unicombs, came from the Cowpastures around this time.[47]

In 1846/1847, class meetings, prayer meetings and preaching were commenced in William Gill's Woodville home. The Plan for February 1847 scheduled services for both Sunday mornings and evenings. The class leaders were William and Silas Gill. Nine months later, the Society reported 24 members. William Gill's home was often "crowded to excess." Monthly services led by the Maitland minister were transferred to the barn of William Gill's son-in-law, Henry Lee.[48] A chapel seating 100 was opened at Cooley Camp in 1847 and a slab church built by voluntary labor at Woodville was opened in 1850.[49]

In 1849, Silas Gill moved again, residing some fifteen miles south of Maitland near Sugarloaf. He stayed briefly, following the gold rush on the

Turon River west of the Great Divide. He returned briefly to the Hunter, moved north to the Hastings, and finally further north to Kempsey on the Macleay River on the NSW north coast where he continued his pioneering ministry until his death in 1875.[50]

While on the Hunter, Silas rejoiced in the conversion of two of William Gill's younger children and Edward King through his faithful ministry.[51] King became a much loved leader, Conference delegate, and lay preacher. His preaching followed the simple style of Silas Gill and Thomas Collins, one illustration being, "The grace of God be like a butt of beef—you can cut and come again!" King was a successful farmer and shipbuilder and much given to good works. One of his sons, Edward King, Jr., entered the Wesleyan ministry and his daughter, Louisa, married Wesleyan minister Wesley Stocks.

Churches and preaching places around Maitland were in every sense "Thomas Collins churches." They were established and sustained for generations primarily by Wesleyans from the Rye/Sandhurst circuits in England and their descendants.

Silas Gill was one of many Wesleyans who moved further north after successive floods and droughts on the lower Hunter during the 1850s. The rich Manning River flats became home and mission field to many descendants of William and Susannah Gill, some of whom married descendants of other Rye/Sandhurst Wesleyans after their arrival in NSW. The Hastings district north of the Manning was in a low state when Silas Gill and his coworker, John Boltwood, arrived and successfully revived the work there. They moved on to Kempsey where Gill became known as the "Apostle of Methodism on the Macleay."[52] Further north on the Clarence River, the Rye/Sandhurst Wesleyan influence was evident through the Starr and Doust families among many others.

III

Thomas Collins and his biographer Samuel Coley believed strongly that "conversational evangelism" with everyday unsophisticated people was far superior to mass evangelism and public preaching to win people for Christ. Coley provides the following quote from Baxter, of whom Thomas Collins strongly approved, "If you would fill narrow bottles, you must take them separately; you must pour the wine into them one by one—not throw it over them in a crowd."[53] This clearly begs the question of the best approach to evangelism in ministry today, whether this be of ordained ministers or the laity. The influence of Thomas Collins on the Uniting

Church in Australia, formed in 1977 by a union of the Methodist, Congregational, and a majority of Presbyterian Churches, continues today through the lives of Collins's spiritual descendants, especially in NSW.

Notes

1. Charles H. Crookshank, *History of Methodism in Ireland*, vol. 2 (Belfast, Ireland: R. S. Allen, 1886), 434-35: "Perhaps the most precious fruit of [Ouseley's] labours was the conversion of the youthful Thomas Collins." Samuel Coley, *The Life of Rev. Thomas Collins* (London: E. Stock, 1869), 1-14.
2. Coley, 19-24.
3. Coley, 26-28; 33-34.
4. Coley, 45-49.
5. *John Wesley's Journal* (London: Dent and Sons, 1906) vol.2: 429-30; vol.3: 308; vol.4: 116, 144, 302, 453, 458, 512-13.
6. British Conference Minutes, 1744-1792; Rye Wesleyan Circuit Rolls, 1801-1815, Plan Oct. 1814 - Jan. 1815 in East Sussex County Records Office, files NMA4/1/2; NMA4/8/1.
7. Home Office 42 (1815) 142-43; Home Office 40 (1829) 23; B. Hammond and J. L. Hammond, *The Village Labourer* (New York: Harper, 1970), 220-25.
8. Coley, 61-62.
9. E. G. Clancy, *A Giant for Jesus* (Waitara, NSW: n.p., 1971), 1.
10. Coley, 68-72, 77-80.
11. Coley, 83; Simpson Johnson, *Thomas Collins—A Typical Evangelist* (London: Charles E. Kelly, 1906), 10-12.
12. Benjamin Gregory, *Sidelights on the Conflicts of Methodism during the Second Quarter of the Nineteenth Century 1827-1852* (London: Cassell and Company, 1899), 145-46.
13. Coley, 478-79, 488.
14. British Conference Minutes, 1865, 220-21.
15. Acts of the British Parliament 4 & 5 under William IV, c.761, 1834.
16. A. B. M. James, "Poor Law Emigration to Australia" *Descent*, December 1989, 158-65.
17. Beckley Wesleyan Class Rolls 1801-1815; Beckley Vestry Minutes 1813-1819 in East Sussex County Records Office.
18. Beckley Vestry Minutes in East Sussex County Records Office.
19. Beckley Vestry Minutes, 29 March 1817; 19 January 1820; Beckley Vestry Minutes, PAR237/12/3 in East Sussex County Records Office.
20. Census statistics, Beckley.
21. Coley, 56-58; W. B. Clarke, Roxburgh Castle ms. diary, Mitchell Library, Sydney, NSW, 139/7.
22. Clancy, 10-12.
23. Margaret and Rosemary Playford, *We Came From Beckley: A Playford Family Story* (Alstonville, NSW, 1995), 6-7; *Christian Advocate*, 20 (1865): 6.

24. *Historical Records of Australia*, vol. XIX (1) 684, 787; *Historical Records of Australia*, vol. XX (1) 24.
25. Report of Surgeon-Superintendent Smith, 21.11.1838, Archives Office (New South Wales) 4/1126.
26. Archives Office (New South Wales) 4/2426; Immigration papers 38/12124, 38/12341.
27. W. B. Clarke, Roxburgh Castle ms. diary, Mitchell Library 139/7.
28. M. J. Burchall,"Sussex Emigrants" Passenger lists photocopy, publication details unknown, private paper in author's possession.
29. Medical Journal of "Prince Regent" Public Records Office, 3214; Galloway's report, Archives Office (New South Wales) 4/2473.1.
30. Orphan Schools Correspondence, Archives Office (New South Wales) 46/3209; death certificates of Sarah and Charlotte Baker; New South Wales Census return 1841-Richard Baker; obituary of Alfred Baker,"Maitland Mercury" 15 July 1919.
31. James Colwell, *Illustrated History of Methodism. Australia: 1812-1855. New South Wales and Polynesia: 1856-1902* (Sydney: William Brookes, 1904), 228.
32. William Gill had this experience. It was further complicated by Susannah's delayed discharge from quarantine. William went to the Hunter "on his own account." The Hicks family on "Maitland" were "expelled from the buildings for refusal to engage" and also went to the Hunter.
33. W. G. Taylor, *Taylor of "Down Under": The Life-story of an Australian Evangelist with an Account of the origin and Growth of the Sydney Central Methodist Mission* (London: Epworth Press, 1920), 35; William George Taylor, *Pathfinders of the Great South Land* (London: Epworth Press, n.d.), 9; Clancy, *A Giant for Jesus*, 1.
34. Coley, 83.
35. Colwell, 282; article on Silas Gill, *The Methodist*, 2 September 1911.
36. Clancy, 19-23.
37. Colwell, *The Methodist*, 21 October 1911.
38. Obituary for Silas Gill, *The Christian Advocate*, 4 January 1876. W. J. M. Campbell, Old Tom Brown of Wesley Vale Dalton (Canberra: Federal Capital Press, 1938), 6-7.
39. Campbell, 6-7 Clancy, *A Giant for Jesus*, 25.
40. Margaret Reeson, *Certain Lives. The Compelling Story of the Hope and Tragedy of Three Generations of Women* (Sutherland, NSW: Albatross, 1989).
41. Clancy, 30; Colwell, *The Methodist*, 257-65.
42. Clancy, 37.
43. Colwell, *The Methodist*, 261, 265.
44. D. H. Lightfoot, "A Hunter Heritage," unpublished mss, 1986.
45. L. Raymond Clipsham, *Terrace Historical Society Bulletin* 4(3) 1981, 97; P. Harris, *It All Began . . . The History of the Wesleyan Church and the Uniting Church in Australia at Raymond Terrace from 1838 to the Present* (Raymond Terrace, 1986).
46. D. H. Lightfoot, *A Cow and a Haypress* (privately published, 1988), 71-

80.
    47. Clancy, 30-31
    48. Obituary of Henry Lee, *Christian Advocate*, 21 January 1888; New South Wales District Minutes, 1846-1847.
    49. New South Wales District Minutes, 1846-1847; *The Methodist*, 2 February 1907.
    50. Clancy, 3-5.
    51. Obituaries of Naomi (Gill) Lambert and Andrew Gill, *The Methodist*, 21 January; 26 September 1896; Clancy, 31-32.
    52. Clancy, chs. 4, 5.
    53. Coley, 472, 479.

17

The Early Impact of Wesleyanism on Continental Europe: The Case of the Germans

Michel Weyer

Our task is to treat the German aspect of the "global impact of Wesleyanism." Since we are sufficiently familiar with the history of the emergence and development of the several churches in the Wesleyan tradition in which present-day German-speaking European United Methodism is rooted, we will adopt another way of retelling the story.[1]

It is easy to observe the constant apologetic dimension that characterizes the German literature published by the different sorts of Methodists from 1830 onwards in the context of their early missionary efforts in countries like Germany, Switzerland, and Austria. Since many people in these German-speaking parts of Europe considered Methodism an exotic and odd kind of Christianity, many prejudices had to be overcome. It was necessary to show what the Wesleyan vision of Christianity really was.

This raises the question of how Wesleyanism was perceived from its beginning. Prior to the Methodist mission, what was the image of Methodism already present in that part of the world? John Wesley himself seems to have been much concerned with the question. In his sermon, "On Laying the Foundation of the New Chapel" (1777), he expressed his astonishment that German people had not taken more notice of the revival under his direction.² J. A. Bengel had ignored the Methodist revival in his *Ordo temporum*, published in 1741, so that Wesley could ask with a touch of frustration: "How could so great a man be ignorant of what was transacted no farther off than England?" Having heard of early German reports on him and his Methodism, he added, ". . . especially considering the accounts then published in Germany, some of which were tolerably impartial." Wesley also mentioned an account sent by him in 1742 to J. A. Steinmetz in order to make Methodism better known in that part of the world. This account seems not to have survived. Could the Germans have overlooked the Methodist revival?

I

Historians have disclaimed any serious awareness of Methodism in Germany prior to the nineteenth century. Wilfried Eisenblaetter, who studied the influence of English Christianity on continental Europe, claimed that the attention of European Protestants had been drawn to Methodism no earlier than the end of Wesley's century.³ Having demonstrated that no serious encounter ever occurred between Methodism and Halle's Pietism, Karl Zehrer also suggested that German Pietists did not really become aware of the importance of early Methodism.⁴ What seems to have become an unquestioned assumption in German historiography should be received with some caution. There is still great ignorance as to what was really known of Methodism in Wolfgang Goethe's country prior to the Methodist mission. Neither Eisenblaetter's assumption nor Wesley's own pessimistic view on the question should lead us to conclude too quickly that Germans remained uninterested in, or even aware of, the contemporary Methodist revival.

Some signs, indeed, should make us more circumspect. At the moment when Wesley complained that the Germans had not taken enough notice of him, Gottfried Achenwall, professor of political science at the University of Goettingen, was publishing a translation of the *Calm Address,* drawing the attention of Germans to the political ideas of the Methodist leader in regard to what was happening in the American colonies.⁵ Another sign that should make us wary is the mention of Methodism in a poem of Germany's greatest author, just three years prior to Wesley's expression of consternation. In J. W. Goethe's *Eternal Jew* (1774), reference is made to a religious man, "half an Essenian, half a Methodist, a Moravian, even more: a separatist, since he was agreeing so much with cross and pain." Goethe's relationship to religion has been well investigated,[6] but nobody knows exactly what he could have heard about Methodism. Obviously, Methodism was not unknown to him. His acquaintance with some of his mother's Moravian friends in Frankfurt has likely been the means for his becoming aware of the existence of Methodists as the representatives of a special blend of Christianity. He seems to have heard the name Methodist in close connection with German Pietism in its radical form and there was no difference in his mind between an Essenian, a Moravian, and a Methodist, all odd people with ascetic views and separatist tendencies, people not akin to the hedonistic mood of the times, but in full harmony with cross and pain!

II

One of the first printed references to the Wesleys is found as early as 1737 in the *Acta historico-ecclesiastica,* an ecclesiastical review with the greatest circulation in the Empire.[7] Readers were told that Governor Oglethorpe had arrived in Georgia in company with the two Wesleys as missionaries of the Church of England. The event was understood as a mission effort of the Society for the Propagation of the Gospel to non-believers in Savannah.[8] After Wesley's return from Georgia and the outburst of the revival, the periodical published, "About the Methodists in England,"[9] three long reports that were interestingly placed just after news about Count Zinzendorf's people. Given the close kinship he supposed to exist between the English Methodists and the German Moravians, the Lutheran editor estimated that news about the two religious movements should appear together. In all our sources, Methodism is associated with German Pietism, mainly with its Moravian blend.

The first major published account[10] made readers familiar with the "Origins of the society in Oxford." It was the German translation of the well-known article "The Oxford Methodists," published in London in 1733.

The following account was the reprint of a letter written in September 1738 from London by F. M. Ziegenhagen, the celebrated German Pietist closely tied with Halle,[11] who had been an observer of Methodism from the beginning. The pastor of the German congregation of St. James Chapel wrote how glad he was to see a renewal of the Gospel within the Church of England. People accustomed to hearing sermons on "virtue" and "rational arguments" for the existence of God and the truth of Christian religion were now thinking they were listening to completely new things when being told of "reconciliation" and "new birth," but what Methodists were preaching was, instead of "Socinianism," nothing other than the old "word of Jesus Christ crucified." Therefore, the violence directed against Wesley and Whitefield had to be considered "humiliation for Christ's sake."

The third report[12] depended on several articles published in a secular newspaper in Hamburg. Methodist field-preaching and its new style of religion would generate more trouble in England than the Moravians in Germany and the Netherlands. Sarcastic commentaries were made on the anti-intellectual character of Methodist sermons with reference to Whitefield who, although educated at Oxford, relied only on Holy Scripture and personal experience of the Holy Spirit, claiming that this alone is true Christianity. As evidence of the intolerable behavior of the new enthusiasts, the newspaper reproduced Whitefield's letter to Tucker in Bristol in which he had asserted that the celebrated writers of the Church of England had no true Christian theology but at best "a good system of Ethics." Whitefield's verdict also reported that John Tillotson, the former Archbishop of Canterbury, "knew no more of true Christianity than Mahomet." Several anti-Methodist publications like Dr. Joseph Trapp's sermons against those who wanted to be "too righteous," or the Bishop of London's "Pastoral Letter," were also published for the readers. The conclusion was that the resistance to the Methodist preachers was absolutely appropriate.

Since Methodism had not stopped making trouble, the *Acta* published by the end of 1740 four additional texts on the nature and intention of Methodism.[13] The editorial introduction presented new information as most important for a correct interpretation of Methodism by German readers. Despite the initial good intention aiming for "the renewal of the doctrine of new birth and salvation through faith," Methodism would now reveal its true character, the editor wrote. He saw in Whitefield's "enthusiasm," "vanity," "arrogance," and "selfishness," the indication that the movement was now "going astray." Methodists, a "new blend of mystics," "assume they have discovered a special method for reaching salvation." What followed drew largely on a most critical French report, earlier published in the *Bibliothèque Britannique*. The French periodical drew on extracts of Whitefield's *Journal* as well as on English writings like, *The true Character of Mr. Whitefield*, or the even more critical, *Life and particular Proceedings of the Reverend Mr. George Whitefield*, a pamphlet containing a severe censure of the Methodist practice of public confession of sin. Whitefield's insistence on the special action of the Spirit was interpreted as totally against "sound reason." Methodists and Quakers were presented as similar in theology. The arguments the Bishop of

London had developed against Methodists were extensively cited. Whitefield's close friendship with all kinds of sectarians like Anabaptists, Independents, Quakers, and Moravians, confirmed the heretical nature of the movement, the author wrote. The nervous convulsions that frequently happened as the dramatic response of the hearers to the Methodist message was interpreted as further evidence of the enthusiasm of the movement. Much blame was also attributed to Wesley for his indulgence of extraordinary phenomena.

In the 1850s, Methodism seems to have lost favor with the kind of periodical press represented by the *Acta*. News about Methodism gradually decreased, disappearing nearly completely during the 1860s. This can be partly explained by the emergence of another category of sources of information concerning our subject, namely books with much more than the isolated and haphazardly arranged news found in newspapers and periodicals. The time seemed to have arrived for a more complete, analytical, and coherent presentation of Methodism.

The first formidable attempt to assess Methodism is found at the beginning of the 1850s in G. W. Alberti's, *Letters concerning the newest state of religion and sciences in Great Britain*.[14] The author, a Lutheran pastor, studied philosophy and theology in Goettingen. He was influenced by Joachim Oporin, an orthodox theologian receptive to the vital piety of Pietism and well known for his resistance to the early Enlightenment that had already emerged in Germany. Alberti went to London where he resided from 1745 to 1747. He was shocked by what he considered a tendency to apostasy within English Christianity. He disapproved most of the "enlightened" ideas he confronted in England. He wrote down his whole British experience in open letters dedicated to Oporin, his former teacher. Nine of these letters contributed to make German public opinion acquainted with a much more detailed and complete image of Methodism than was the case up to then. Alberti knew the offensive picture of Methodism given by the printed material mentioned above. He wished to defend Wesley's movement against the charges formulated there, warning his German readers against an uncritical reception of such negative reports on Methodism. Their authors, he claimed, were people with prejudices and private purposes that colored their judgments. German Lutherans living in the British capital, Alberti wrote, would generally consider Methodists as "true christians, who God is now bringing into play in order to restore in England the pure doctrine of the savior of the world." In so doing, he referred explicitly to Ziegenhagen's opinion as expressed in the letter already mentioned. Claiming to be "impartial," Alberti wrote that his own portrait of Methodism mixed appreciation with criticism. Actually, his presentation is nothing but a defense of a movement he was anxious to defend against the charge of "religious delusion" as expressed in Henry Stebbing's famous sermon against the Methodist preaching of the new birth. This sharp anti-Methodist writing had already been translated into German and Alberti apprehended that it could compromise the opinion German readers had not only of Methodism but German Pietism as well.

Alberti was, to be sure, sympathetic to Pietism, especially its Hallesian variety, not the Moravian variety that was considered in Goettingen as dangerous to church unity. Accordingly, Alberti underlined strongly that Wesley was by no means a separatist. The controversy between Wesley and Zinzendorf was sketched in a way that showed that the author was not sympathetic to the Count. Alberti also refuted Bishop Smallbrook's attack against the enthusiasm of the Methodists, pointing explicitly to the pneumatological insufficiency of the contemporary Church of England. This church, he wrote, has a dramatic need of a sound "doctrine of the Holy Spirit and his operations," which English orthodox theologians themselves frequently deplored. So Bishop Smallbrook's satirical writing against Methodism was in Alberti's opinion a contemptuous and mocking attack, not only against the faith of the Methodists, but also against what true Lutherans have to confess, that is the "godly faith" itself.

For the vigilant reader it is hard to escape the impression that Methodism was becoming a helpful instrument for Alberti's own theological combat against the emerging Enlightenment in Germany. Like his teacher, Oporin, he tried to resist the ideas that were going to become dominant in German Protestantism where the power of orthodoxy and Pietism was already declining. It is not accidental that German readers who did not share his theological presuppositions immediately challenged Alberti's view of Methodism. The author was labeled "a friend of Methodist enthusiasm." Preferring to be on the side of "people who preach the pure doctrine of justification" than on the side of what he considered Deism, or Socinianism, in his own Lutheran church in Germany, he accepted the charge.

III

Lorenz von Mosheim's famous church history handbook, which was first published just two years after Alberti's *Letters*,[15] and which was to become the best known Protestant exposition of church history of the century, offered a negative portrait of Methodism without esteem for reason and learning. From 1755 onwards the Germans had to face this almost official image of a successful, but dangerously enthusiastic, religious movement under the leadership of men for whom the only rule was to follow blindly the urging of their imaginations and whose aim was the gathering of a "better church" in which only emotions and feelings had place.[16]

Despite the harsh and quite ultimate judgment contained in such a celebrated handbook, some German theologians tried to meet Methodists while sojourning in England. The example of Johann Ludwig Fricker, theologian and scientist in Tübingen, who visited Wesley in 1757 and became a bridge between Methodism and his Swabian Pietism, should become the object of research. Wesley's *Character of a Methodist*, and *Life of Mrs. Richardson*, published in German in 1753, raised interest in many pietistic circles,[17] but could not become the successful counterpart to the negative image of Methodism that would now be dominant for many years.

The next noteworthy German depiction of Methodism was G. F. A. Wendeborn's clear attempt to counterbalance Alberti. It is found in his renowned book on England, originally written in German, then translated into several languages.[18] Interestingly, the author gave in the German original a far more extended treatment of Methodism than in his own English translation. On thirty-four pages, plenty of mud was thrown at a Methodism which became, for Wendeborn, an instrument for combat against a form of Christianity he wanted to see expelled from his ecclesiastical tradition. Son of a pietistic Lutheran pastor, Wendeborn had wished to become a medical doctor but had been compelled to study theology in Halle.[19] He was ordained and in 1766 went to London where he dramatically failed in his two attempts to become the pastor of one of the German congregations of the capital. These congregations had such a strong pietistic orientation and were so preponderantly on a line with Ziegenhagen and Alberti, that Wendeborn had no chance. The small liberal party in the German congregation of the *Hamburgerkirche* seceded and appointed the unsuccessful candidate as their pastor, founding a new congregation in Ludgatehill especially for him. Wendeborn served there from 1770 to 1790. His fame grew rapidly. However, he was embarrassed by most of the Christian beliefs he had to preach officially, so he left the ministry in order to recapture his "philosophical freedom." His interest had moved from theology to philosophy and politics. He became a freelance author and a distinguished correspondent for several continental periodicals.

Given his deistic conception of religion, Wendeborn found nothing in Methodism that he appreciated. He disapproved theologically of missions at home as well as abroad. Since the practice of virtue was in his opinion sufficient to be a Christian, the traditional missionary message, grounded on the "mysteries of Christian theology," did not make sense to him. He considered the missionaries of the Anglican SPCK weak-minded enthusiasts and had nothing but disdain for the numerous Germans who were interested in becoming such "apostles sent to the heathens." Like many "enlightened" men of his day, Wendeborn was sympathetic to Indian culture and not at all disposed to compare it unfavorably with Christianity. To be sure, he was aware of the strong ethical aspect of Methodist preaching, but he could not appreciate its emphasis on Christian life because it was related to too many traditional dogmatic beliefs like original sin, the merits of Jesus Christ as savior, justification of the sinner, and the existence of hell. Wendeborn also strongly opposed the self-qualification of Wesleyans as Arminians, since true Arminians would not preach original sin as Wesley did, nor would they be trinitarians as Methodists were. Commenting on the reference of Methodists to the German Reformer Luther as the great man who had rediscovered the doctrine of justification by faith through grace, Wendeborn held that Luther was to be considered chiefly as an example of a religiously "free thinking" person. If Luther were still living he would surely not accept the reason for which he was appreciated by the Methodists. According to Wendeborn, the fact that Lutherans like Ziegenhagen or Alberti had underlined the doctrinal affinity between Luther and Wesleyanism was not at all appreciated as an argument in favor of Methodism, but was to be considered a simple consequence of the unfortunate similarity between Pietism and Methodism!

IV

What has been observed in Alberti's and Wendeborn's description of Methodism was to become archetypal for all subsequent important German publications on the issue. Two examples may suffice to show how the making of the early German image of Methodism occurred in the tension between the pietistic appreciation of the one and the enlightened criticism of other observers.

Johann Gottlieb Burckhardt studied philosophy and theology at the University of Leipzig. He served there as a lecturer in philosophy until he came to London where in 1781 he became the new pastor of the German Lutheran congregation of St. Mary-in-the-Savoy. By the end of his pastoral career Burckhardt became an important bridge between the young London Missionary Society and the German pietistic circles that were going to play a significant role in the emerging German Protestant missions.

As soon as he discovered John Wesley's writings and met Methodist people, Burckhardt was convinced that Wesleyanism was the right mix of sound doctrinal foundation, pietistic concern for vital religion of the heart, and openness to reason. Common sense, sanity of judgment, and reasonableness were much more important to Burckhardt than to Alberti. He was, to be sure, a Pietist, but of another breed than former pietistic generations. As most of the so-called "late Pietists," although resisting the "new theology," he was influenced by the general mood of the Enlightenment. Burckhardt was one of those Pietists who declared themselves supporters of "true" Enlightenment, which was not against biblical revelation. This was exactly Wesley's position. Burckhardt liked the Wesleyan appeal to "men of reason and religion." He met Wesley several times and informed him of his purpose to write a book to correct the problematic image of Methodism that had been given to the Germans by authors like Mosheim and Wendeborn. He also asked him for documentation. With the 368 pages of his sensitive and perceptive, *Complete History of the Methodists in England,* Burckhardt in 1795 gave the Germans their very first monograph on Methodism.[20] Since Burckhardt was also a member of the *Deutsche Christentumsgesellschaft,* an association of Protestants who resisted the Enlightenment's radicalization, it is not accidental that he published his remarkable apology of Methodism in a publishing house totally at the service of the goals of that society. Thus, Burckhardt also made Methodism an instrument in his own struggle for biblical doctrine and vital piety in the German church. In so doing, he contributed to the emergence of the wave of evangelical revivals that was to become the hallmark of German Protestantism in the first decades of the next century.

Before his manuscript was published, Burckhardt was asked by August Hermann Niemeyer for permission to read and use his manuscript for his own publication on Wesley. This descendant of August Hermann Francke kept his distance in respect to his great pietistic family tradition. As professor of theology in Halle, where "enlightened" ideas were now well-established, Niemeyer was concerned about the first symptoms of the approaching reaction of the Prussian government against the spirit of Enlightenment in the church. In order to draw attention to the danger of a possible return to the kind of religion which was dominant before the emergence of the "new theology," Niemeyer decided to publish something that would illustrate what he considered to be the weakness and danger of Pietism. The case of Methodism functioned as his demonstration. Niemeyer simply translated into German the book that John Hampson, one of the preachers who had left Wesley over their exclusion from the "Legal Hundred," had published just after Wesley's death.[21] Hampson had mixed sharp criticism with appreciation. In many additional annotations and commentaries to Hampson, Niemeyer could take into account what Alberti, Wendeborn, and Burckhardt had already written on the subject. Although Niemeyer was a more conciliatory figure than Wendeborn and had no bad opinion of some aspects of the Wesleyan religious and social achievement, he shared most of Wendeborn's negative judgments. Niemeyer acknowledged that Burckhardt had not been totally blind to some weak aspects in Methodism, but he found that he was on the whole too much an admirer of Wesley, while Hampson was a much more "objective" judge.

Beginning with Burckhardt and Niemeyer, Methodism was interpreted in the light of its important position on the ecclesiastical scene. It always became an argument for, or against, the type of religion the authors wished to see represented, or not, in their own church. As Jung-Stilling, the future "father of the German revival," decided to undertake something "against the frightful progression of Enlightenment,"[22] he also chose Methodism as an instrument for his undertaking. In 1799, he gave a description of the Wesleyan revival in his periodical, *Der Graue Mann*, recommending on the same occasion Burckhardt's book for more details.

V

Methodism was for many pietistic oriented Germans the inspiring example of a successful and blessed foreign revival. These people wished for their native land a Wesleyan renewal. However, this did not mean that German Pietists were ready to accept a Methodist mission in their own country. The contrary is true.

In 1832, Johann Christian Fr. Burk, editor of the periodical *Der Christenbote*, published an essay, *Methodism and Pietism*.[23] Burk was well acquainted with what he called, "the English variety of our German Pietism." As an admirer of what Methodists had achieved in England, he praised their victory over "speculative theology," "rationalism," "Neology," all trends that Pietists also combated in their own country. Despite this community of goals, Burk did not see any need for Methodism in Germany in its organized ecclesiastical form since Methodism had separated from the Church of England, which, in his opinion, had led to "a great loss" of quality. A Wesleyan mission had already begun in Swabia about 1830. Burk exhorted his pietistic readers to be cautious. Imported Methodism would cause separatist troubles in German Protestantism! Certainly, Methodism was to be appreciated as "a divine benediction," but for England, not for Germany!

Six years later, Johann Wilhelm Baum, a liberal Alsatian Reformed theologian, published a study on Methodism that represented a particularly hard assault on Wesleyanism.[24] Since in many circles it now had the reputation of being a good model for church renewal, there was obviously a want of an authoritative theological statement on Methodism. At variance with Burk, Baum considered Methodism by no means a divine benediction, neither for England nor for any other place in the world. Methodism embodied what Baum hated. According to Baum, church and state had the sacred duty of "watching over true Protestantism." They had to protect people against Methodism as well as against Pietism, these dreadful "twin-forms of Christianity" that had nothing to do with "true Protestantism." True Protestantism was for Baum nothing other than "the spirit of freedom . . . born in the Enlightenment," the religious power that liberates reason from all imprisonment.

VI

Despite the difficult situation Methodist missionaries had to face in German-speaking countries, after only a few decades of missionary labor there were already three expanding Wesleyan (or Methodist-related Evangelical) church bodies in that part of the world. Methodism, however, could never establish itself there as a really strong ecclesiastical body. Thus, if one has to consider with Henry Rack that, "Wesley's most obvious and measurable achievement and legacy must necessarily be the Methodist churches worldwide," one must conclude that the "impact of Wesleyanism" among the Germans has been a limited one. The question remains, however, whether the impact can be evaluated in the light of this sole criterion. Even where Methodism was resisted, and finally rejected, even in the last third of the nineteenth century, when the holiness movement led to a new wave of Methodist expansion in German-speaking Europe, not a few of the Wesleyan accentuations and methods were adopted by the established churches, becoming sometimes a part of their strategy for a more efficient resistance to Methodism.[25]

Notes

1. See the occasional ongoing publications of the German United Methodist Historical Society (*Mitteilungen der Studiengemeinschaft für die Geschichte der Evangelisch-methodistischen Kirche*) begun in 1980 by the UMC Publishing House in Stuttgart, Germany. See also *Geschichte der Evangelisch-methodistischen Kirche . . . unter besonderer Berücksichtigung der deutschsprachigen Länder Europas*, ed. Karl Steckel and C. Ernst Sommer (Stuttgart: Christliches Verlagshaus, 1982).
2. John Wesley, *Works*, vol. 3: 579-80.
3. Wilfried Eisenblaetter, *Carl Friedrich Adolph Steinkopf (1773-1853). Vom englischen Einfluß auf kontinentales Christentum zur Zeit der Erweckungsbewegung.* (Ph.D. diss., Zürich, 1974), 80.
4. Karl Zehrer, "The Relationship between Pietism in Halle and Early Methodism," *Methodist History* 17 (1979): 211-24.
5. *Einige Anmerkungen über Nord-Amerika . . . verfaßt von Hrn. D. Gottfried Achenwall. Nebst Herrn John Wesleys Schrift von den Streitigkeiten mit den Colonien in Amerika* (Helmstedt: Johann Heinrich Kuehnlin, 1777). Pages 55-72 contain Wesley's *Calm Address*.
6. See the bibliography given by Paul Raabe in his edition of *Johann Wolfgang von Goethe, Träume und Legenden meiner Jugend . . .* (Leipzig: Evangelische Verlagsanstalt, 2000).
7. *Acta historico-ecclesiastica oder Gesamelte Nachrichten von den neuesten Kirchen-Geschichten*, published in Weimar (Heinrich Hoffmann) from 1736 onwards by Wilhelm Ernst Bartholomaeus, preacher of the court and librarian of the Prince of Saxony-Weimar; henceforth quoted as *Acta*.
8. *Acta*, 1737, 407-8.
9. *Acta*, 1740, 287-303.
10. *Acta*, 1740, 288-93.
11. See Daniel L. Brunner, *Halle Pietists in England: Anthony William Boehm and the Society for Promoting Christian Knowledge* (Goettingen: Vandenhoeck and Ruprecht, 1992), 57-59, 67-69.
12. *Acta*, 1740, 295-303.
13. *Acta*, 1740, 727-84.
14. Georg Wilhelm Alberti, *Briefe betreffende den allerneuesten Zustand der Religion und der Wissenschaften in Gross-Brittanien*, vol. I (Hannover: Johann Christoph Richter, 1752).
15. Lorenz von Mosheim, *Institutiones historiae ecclesiasticae antiquae et recentioris* (Goettingen,1755, second ed. Helmtedt, 1764). What became the most read book of church history was in fact the German translation and update by von Eimen (1769-1778). Von Eimen had avoided choosing clearly between Pietism and Enlightenment, but this was no longer the case for Johann Rudolph Schlegel who also translated and updated, with additional commentaries, Mosheim's work, *Vollständige Kirchengeschichte des Neuen Testaments*, vols. 1-7 (Heilbronn and Rottenburg: Friedrich Ludwig Wilhelm Hemling, 1770-1796), taking clearly the side of the Enlightenment.

16. See Schlegel's translation, vol. 4 (Heilbronn: Friedrich Ludwig Wilhelm Hemling, 1780), 602.

17. *Das Muster eines wahren Christen in der Beschreibung eines Methodisten, von Johann Wesley . . . Und Christliches Beyspiel einer sogenannten Methodistin an der Frau Hanna Richardson, von Carl Wesley . . .* (Frankfurt and Leipzig: Johann August Raspe, 1753).

18. G. F. A. Wendeborn, *Der Zustand des Staats, der Religion, der Gelehrsamkeit und der Kunst in Grosbritannien gegen das Ende des achtzehnten Jahrhunderts, Dritter Theil* (Berlin: C. Spener, 1785), 138-72; Fred. Aug. Wendeborn, *A View of England Towards the Close of the Eighteenth Century* (London: G. G. J. and J. Robinson, 1791).

19. Michael Maurer, "Gebhard Friedrich August Wendeborn (1742-1811). Ein Aufklaerer von kulturgeschichtlicher Bedeutung," *Euphorion* 82 (1988) : 393-423.

20. *Vollständige Geschichte der Methodisten in England . . . Von D. Johann Gottlieb Burkhard* (Nürnberg: Verlag der Raw'schen Buchhandlung, 1795).

21. John Hampson, *Memoirs of the Late Rev. John Wesley, A.M.; with a Review of His Life and Writings, and a History of Methodism*, 3 vols. (Sunderland, printed for Author by James Graham, 1791). Niemeyer's German translation: *Leben Johann Wesleys Stifters der Methodisten nebst einer Geschichte des Methodismus . . . Aus dem Englischen. Mit Anmerkungen, Zusätzen und Abhandlungen . . .* (Halle: Buchhandlung des Waisenhauses, 1793).

22. Gerhard Schwinge, *Jung-Stilling als Erbauungsschriftsteller der Erweckung* (Goettingen: Vandenhoeck and Ruprecht, 1994).

23. *Der Christenbote* (Stuttgart: Verlag Steinkopf, 1832), 150-52.

24. Johann Wilhelm Baum, *Der Methodismus* (Zürich: Orell, Fuessli and Co., 1838).

25. See Theodore Christlieb, *Zur methodistischen Frage in Deutschland* (Bonn and Gernsbach, 1882).

18

John Fletcher: Paradigm for the Global Impact of Wesleyanism

Timothy M. Salo

In spite of his position and prominence in Methodism, John Fletcher remains understudied. However, he is unparalleled as a paradigm for Wesleyan globalization because of his unique character and role in the English Methodist Revival. It seems Fletcher simultaneously exists as enigma and exemplar.

This essay will seek to portray Fletcher as a paradigm while remembering his humanity as well. It is not another attempt at biography or Methodist history, although these elements provide suitable material.[1] It will be an organization of data to support a structural apology for Wesleyanism and its spread. Thus, this will not be new material as much as it will be a new look at the old.

John Fletcher characterizes Wesleyanism dynamically in three ways: 1) as imprinted with Methodism through his conversion; 2) as an influence on Methodism through his ministry; 3) and as an impact for Methodism through his mission efforts. By his own admission, nothing so struck Fletcher as the religion of the Methodists, nor so forcefully drove him to influence others by it. If the metaphorical style of the Vicar of Madeley be allowed, no metal shone more brightly or less full of dross than that of John Fletcher in the forge of the divine work of the Methodist Revival.

John Fletcher was supposedly introduced to Methodism in the year 1754 by an old woman who questioned him about his faith. His employer and hostess, Mrs. Hill, remarked that this encounter might turn him into a Methodist, whereupon Fletcher replied: "Methodist, madam! pray what is that?"[2] Fortunately, Fletcher was delivered from that early oblivion—Methodism was almost a generation old—and went on to become one of its leading figures. Since the meeting with the old woman is not well documented and may be apocryphal, it is hard to tell who sought whom first. However, after the conversation with Mrs. Hill, Fletcher decided to locate the Methodists because of their reputation for prayer. He sought out Methodist societies, was converted under Methodist preaching in 1755, and received Wesley's counsel and writings. His connection with the Methodists made him seriously reconsider preparation for ministry which he had abandoned in Switzerland. During this time he maintained close Methodist contacts and had opportunities for service with them.

It is difficult to describe when Fletcher turned from being imprinted with Methodism to that of influencing it because of his responsibilities for ministry at Madeley. Logically, we could suppose this happened after Fletcher became vicar, subscribed to the Church of England's Articles and conformed to its liturgy, appointed his own curates, and began to initiate uncustomary Anglican practices with Methodist motives.[3] His Sunday evening vespers and catechetical exercises were not as extraordinary as his societies, but were unusually pietistic. When he formed societies, however, they had the appearance of conventicles for which he was accused as a Dissenter. This happened around 1761. The first rules for his Religious Society were formed in 1762.[4] During this six-year stretch of his life, Fletcher was influenced by all the major figures and friends he found among the Methodists. His English religious experience was a formative one. What remains both a mystery and strength of Methodism in this period is why it would reach out to a foreigner like Fletcher.

From all accounts Fletcher was very Swiss in character, very French in accent, and very Reformed in doctrine (despite his aversion to absolute predestination).[5] When he first came to England he had no working knowledge of English, no employment, no personal acquaintances, and no place to live. His letters of recommendation were seized at customs, he risked exchange of his money to a stranger, and he had no immediate plans but to learn English. Depending on how we view English Methodism, he was either a most unlikely prospect for the revival of religion, or as a newly arrived immigrant, a highly desirable one. Fletcher certainly was open to spiritual growth because of his unsettled religious experience in those days of wanderlust.

Incidents throughout Fletcher's life draw attention to his particular character and heritage. John and Charles Wesley disapproved of his stark and strange habits of eating, study, sleeping, and charity. Fletcher often ate little or not at all (long fasts for Bible study), not regularly, often of a peculiar and repetitive diet, and sometimes as fast as he could to save time for more worthy pursuits. He was given to intense periods of study of up to sixteen hours a day with few breaks.[6] The Wesleys were not totally in favor of this behavior and thought it might have contributed to later illness in life.[7] Fletcher also slept little at times, and certainly fitfully later in life when he suffered from consumption (tuberculosis). He had a peculiar habit sometimes of staying up as late as he could to read a book in bed by candlelight until he fell asleep. This resulted at least once in his bed, curtains, nightcap, and book catching on fire. He dreamed that they had been extinguished, but was chagrined to find evidence of a fire miraculously extinguished the next day. In contrast however, he could be up on a Sunday morning in outlying villages at 5:00, ringing a bell and awaking dog-tired miner families for worship services in Madeley.[8] In keeping with his ascetic ways he often gave his own personal and parsonage items away to those in need, almost like a parish food and clothing pantry. He saw nothing unusual with using only what he needed at the moment, as long as it worked, and despite its condition. This itself was strange in view of his noble birth and moderate family wealth.[9]

He evidenced the learning of a scholar without the standard degrees. He had considerable training in linguistics and was a wordsmith in speech and with pen. He had considerable personal bearing, although he was reserved and had a sickly appearance when ill. He was taken to making spiritual analogies about everything and everyone at any moment in conversation. This was annoying to some degree, but often spiritually powerful. As Wesley observed, what fit Fletcher's manner would have looked totally ridiculous in any other.[10] Literally, it was eccentric behavior, but in Fletcher it was an acceptable exception. His Swiss bluntness and honesty contrasted sharply with genteel English ways.[11] Although Fletcher was not as much an enthusiast as some Methodists, he was enthusiastic and thus broke the mold of the common curate or vicar.

Fletcher's French culture and Swiss humanistic training would not have been readily accepted in England. There had been constant English/French tension for decades with hardly a fair interlude between episodes of hostility and a French accent would not be readily welcomed. The type of training Fletcher probably received was of a high Calvinism moderated by the Helvetic Confession and a type of humanist scholasticism that had crept into the Genevan academies. Fletcher would have found a much different theological agenda in England due to Catholic devotion, Anglican spirituality, and Puritan pietism. Presumably he would not have joined an English group without some amount of scrutiny or even suspicion.

That Fletcher did join the Methodists and had a meteoric rise to prominent leadership says good things about the early Methodists. Far from being desperate for recruits, isolated as fanatics, or tagged as English Nonconformists, Methodists were open-hearted in an inclusive and accepting way. Kindred spirits found each other in serious passion for holy spirituality and zeal for evangelical ministry. That more than anything else describes Fletcher's demeanor the night he ran to Wesley's aid to serve the Eucharist, after receiving holy orders. This vividly portrays a genuine aspect of Methodist spirituality found in the text of Wesley's sermon, "Catholic Spirit": "Is thine heart right, as my heart is with thy heart? . . . If it be, give me thine hand" (II Kings 10:15).

It seems Fletcher's serious religious inquiry, humility, zeal, and desire for holy living made him a prime and glad convert for the Methodists. Despite his idiosyncracies, he had a warm heart and a cool head. Here was someone the Methodists could not only assimilate, but use for their work. They met him halfway. As Fletcher sought to fit into his adopted home and faith, he found Methodists eager to help him, first to find his own peace with God, and then to help others.

It is true that Fletcher became a Methodist by society membership, but remained an Anglican, subscribing to its faith and doctrine. It is true he never became an itinerant or regular preacher for Wesley, but became an Anglican curate and vicar. He could be a parish priest, Methodist educator, and Wesleyan-Arminian apologist, all in one, and see no conflict. Even in this unique position though, he would go on to influence Methodism as few ever did, especially as a second generation leader, or as he liked to say, "an unworthy servant" to Wesley.[12]

John Fletcher was an influence on Methodism itself. From the very beginning of his vicarage at Madeley he introduced methods in religious practice that gave the group its reputation and name. Although these were always framed as good evangelical practice within the Anglican tradition, they nonetheless resembled Methodism from the start. Although accused of Nonconformity, Fletcher's methods were never officially investigated, he was never brought to trial, and Fletcher's bishop never broached the subject. The opposition Fletcher faced in his parish ministry from Anglican and Dissenter alike shows his unique Methodist character. However, Madeley was one of the few English parishes where Methodists held sway well into the nineteenth century. From Fletcher's appointment as vicar to his wife's last catechetical and preaching efforts in the 1810s, Methodism influenced Madeley as perhaps no other parish in all of England.[13]

Every dynamic movement needs dynamic leaders and Fletcher's work gave testimony to his skills. He was priest, evangelist, pastor, preacher, prayer-warrior, writer, educator, poet, apologist, ecumenist, organizer of societies and clergy associations, liturgist, scholar, linguist, mystic, theologian, interlocutor, pietist, Prayer-book man, catechist, mentor, chaplain, correspondent, philosopher—and some might say—prophet, saint, and apostle.[14] Fletcher seemed to have a rare combination of judiciousness, holiness, humility, reason, zeal, and the "otherworldly" quality of a mystic, which qualify him for this nomenclature.[15] It was recognized by Wesleyan and Calvinist Methodists alike, much to the awe of the former and the slight postcontroversy annoyance of the latter. Enemies, opponents, critics, rivals, and the jealous were similarly disarmed at times by his noble visage, gracious manner, and gentle spirit.[16] Most everyone who spoke or wrote of him deemed him unusual, if not fair and provocative.

Fletcher blossomed as a Methodist in his transition from follower to leader. From the start he was in close contact with the Wesley brothers, Whitefield, and the Countess of Huntingdon, as well as other Methodist leaders such as Walsh and Berridge.[17] He was probably closest in friendship and character to Charles Wesley. The tendency to run in leadership circles made Fletcher a leader. With his natural and endowed gifts he began to have an influence on Methodism itself soon after his appointment to Madeley.

At Madeley the principles of the Methodists were tried and tested in an established Anglican parish. There he welcomed a Methodist presence and work. There a pulpit was open to all who preached the Wesleyan message of real justification and sanctification. There Anglican parishioners were gently prodded to Methodist circles of influence. In the years following Fletcher's death Madeley became an unofficial "Mecca" of Methodism, or in the French, a *rendezvous* for Methodists serious about the spirit and message of the movement.[18] Bishop Nuelson said, "For Wesley the world was his parish, for Fletcher his parish was his world."[19]

He adequately proved that by continually practicing reconciliation with all persons, his congregation and opponents alike. All the countless and selfless acts of ministry which surrounded him showed his love for both God and man.

From Madeley, Fletcher also connected with Methodist education efforts at Trevecca College, where he acted as teacher, advisor, spiritual director, and president. While he enjoyed his time there, the Methodist Conference of 1770 and the dismissal of Joseph Benson prompted Fletcher to sever his ties with Trevecca over the doctrine of justification and works, as well as the preaching of Christian perfection. This incident led to the greater part of Fletcher's writings which in turn had a great influence on Methodism. It should be pointed out, however, that most of Fletcher's literary efforts were occasional. Fletcher had a polemical flourish, but, except for the 1770 controversy, he did not set out to write against opponents as a personal goal.[20] This task fell to him almost by default when John Wesley could or would not take the time to do the same and when no one better qualified was found. It might be apropos to suggest a certain irony involved in engaging a former Reformed student to answer the very doctrinal issues he objected to since his youth. A young Thomas Coke wrote to Fletcher in August 1775 saying he had been both impressed and influenced by reading the *Checks to Antinomianism*.[21]

Second to his writings, but not less effective, Fletcher influenced Methodism with his saintly life and ministry. Wesley attested to this in his famous letter of 1773 in which he asked Fletcher to succeed him. Despite his personal reservations, Wesley told him there was no one else more qualified as a leader than he,[22] and most other Methodists would seem to concur. Some believe if there had been anything like canonization in Methodism Fletcher probably would have been first.[23] The reputation he built in life and the legacy he left in death were almost, without exception, as holy as anyone thought a Methodist could or dared to be.

John Wesley realized Fletcher's potential as a Methodist leader when he expressed his disappointment at Fletcher's decision for parish ministry. Wesley realized he would not have Fletcher's sanctity and skills at his immediate disposal, but as events happened it probably did work out for the best. Fletcher could never have kept pace with Wesley due to his many bouts of consumption and Wesley would have kept Fletcher from his deep desire for pastoral ministry. It is well known that at various times Wesley expressed his wish that Fletcher follow him as leader of the

Methodist Conference, the prospect of which Fletcher himself postponed and even expressed reticence. His reluctance was probably due in part to his deference to Wesley's reputation. Fletcher may not have viewed himself as *the* leader of Methodism, despite Wesley's desire, but he was a leader in his own right, successor or not. In any case, as early as 1764 Wesley had viewed Fletcher as "a Methodist of the *old* type."[24]

Fletcher's influence shows Methodism's expressive and aggressive nature even from its origin. These cues may not be popular adjectives today, but they describe how early Methodists felt about their faith. One did not join the Methodists to keep their faith quietly a private matter. Rather, a Methodist was expected to testify to his spiritual life and growth and actively recruit others for evangelical conversion and a holy life. John Fletcher was a model of the idea that as soon as society members were brought to evangelical faith, discipled, and trained they should be immediately put to work in spreading Christian faith and Methodist principles. All members were expected to be contributors as soon as possible. This not only added to the creative genius of early Methodism, not to mention a diversity that rivals our postmodern times, but created a tremendous pool of talent and resources which leaders could draw on to increase the scope of Methodist work. Without this expressive and aggressive approach to faith, life, and ministry, all the organizational efforts of the Wesley brothers would have proved of no use. This outlook was as much caught as taught and was encouraged by the Methodist leaders themselves. Fletcher modeled this paradigm and began to influence the growth and development of Methodism. He inspired Methodists to live and work with zeal for the Kingdom of God.

Finally, we view John Fletcher as an impact for Methodism on others outside the societies. By necessity this coincides with Fletcher's influential role on Methodism, but chronologically it happened in later stages, venues, and periods of his life. Fletcher's work with Wesley and his work as curate represented an early and somewhat halting effort. Fletcher recounted that he was still experiencing his own spiritual growth, tentatively preparing for ministry, and still learning the English language and customs. However, two incidents mark this early period, indicative of future things. The first was preaching to French prisoners of war at Tonbridge (Kent) at the request of Lady Huntingdon. There he won immediate popularity with the prisoners, but not the Anglican hierarchy. The second was an invitation by Nathaniel Gilbert, speaker of the House of Assembly in Antigua, who had in 1758 become a Methodist on a visit to England, to go to the West Indies as a missionary. Although this would have been a triumphant first for Methodism, Fletcher declined because he did not feel providentially led to go.[25]

In Madeley his parish ministry effected a change in that community that turned "a Sodom of wickedness into a Shiloh of privilege and grace."[26] As both an industrial center (coal and iron) and river trading town, Madeley had a cross-section of some of the roughest, immoral, and faithless people in England.[27] Although it was a low paying position without prominence, Fletcher took his parish as a challenge and a litmus test of Methodist religion. With time Fletcher did succeed and evangelical faith flourished.

In subsequent years of ministry Fletcher had opportunities to speak to French refugees in England, conduct a few preaching tours (Wales and Ireland), and continue to minister to those ill, dying, destitute, and in prison, all with considerable success. His writings certainly impacted those outside Methodism and invited exchange between not a few Anglicans, Dissenters, and Roman Catholics. What probably stands in greatest testimony to Fletcher's influence, though shrouded in history, are his two trips to his home in Switzerland.

The initial visit of January 1770 came nearly eighteen years after Fletcher first went to England, and the second followed in December 1777. The first was for five months (presumably Fletcher was back just before Wesley's early August Conference of 1770), and the second for three and a half years. Fletcher had a purpose and a motivation for each trip. The first trip was to visit family and relatives after a long absence, and was suggested (and funded in part) by James Ireland, who had business in France and desired Fletcher's company. The second trip was to recover Fletcher's health at his family home (again accompanied by Ireland) and also to help William Perronet recover a Swiss family estate. Several factors about these trips, however, unmask other purposes, the results of which superceded personal matters and became missionary instead.

One factor involved a pattern of visiting the same French towns and churches on his way to and from England. This was done on the way to Switzerland in 1770, and both ways in 1778 and 1781 respectively. The return trip of 1770 is not recorded. There might have been several reasons for this pattern. Fletcher said of his first trip in Ireland's company that he had a desire to visit the Huguenots of southern France and to recover his fluency in French before proceeding to his home.[28] However, his interest in the heart of Roman Catholicism seems to be an unstated purpose. His journey south would have brought him right through the papal enclave of Avignon. Records show he proceeded to Rome and Naples with their accompanying Romanist shrines. No doubt Fletcher was gathering material to counter the new Catholic chapel in Madeley which opened before his departure. In Montpellier, James Ireland convinced Fletcher to speak in a French Protestant church, as he did later in Marseilles. On this trip Fletcher also engaged a young man in spiritual conversation and another gentleman in Christian debate.[29] In Nyon he found that pulpits there and in surrounding areas were open to him and he was received with great reverence and gratitude. It is recorded that one young man entered the ministry as a result of a sermon by Fletcher and at this native son's departure weeping multitudes crowded around him with final farewells. Fletcher proved you can "go home again," but as yet he was not the prophet he would be on his next visit.

On the second trip Fletcher took the same route again to the south of France, pausing for three months to winter there. He seemed to have a much more leisurely pace, which afforded more preaching and visitation possibilities, especially in Aix and Montpellier. Again in Switzerland Fletcher filled pulpits, but with increasing resistance by some to his doctrine. He held catechetical sessions, first in the woods, and then in an approved place after being accused of irregularities. He had opportunity to traverse the western French-speaking section of the country as well as Savoy and Jura in France. His return to England was delayed at the request of a little pietist society that had formed after his preaching in Nyon. On his way back he went the same way he had come, preaching again at Montpellier, and making stops at Lausanne, Geneva, and Paris.[30]

While on his trips Fletcher continued to write letters to friends in England, many of which have the tone of a Pauline epistle. This was especially true of the second trip where his extended stay required communication with his curate Mr. Greaves and his Methodist acquaintances. This trip was also the occasion of his published works, *Of Grace and Nature* and *The Portrait of St. Paul*. Both were written in French, the latter to pastors and ministers, and according to Joshua Gilpin they were meant for publication in his own country.[31] The Genevan civil war and Fletcher's own departure prevented this. A straightforward assessment of *The Portrait of St. Paul* shows the missionary concern of an Anglicized Methodist among Reformed humanists.

Finally, on at least two different occasions, once in ministry and another in his will, Fletcher sent money from his estate income back to Nyon to be distributed among the poor. In life he was concerned about the falling rate of currency exchange which affected his native town, and in death his provision for the poor of Nyon was his only request outside of a widow's income for his wife Mary.[32]

Fletcher's two trips to the Continent, far from the mere pacification of familial relations or the needed recovery of health, became apostolic journeys filled with preaching, teaching, visiting, writing, counseling, and evangelizing. In spite of his very ill health on the second journey, Fletcher refused to be idle and seized opportunities for ministry that his travels afforded him. Some might question if this Methodist could really have helped himself and do no other, despite his own condition. However, the record stands with enough evidence to name Fletcher the first Methodist missionary outside the English world, the first to the Continent, and the first to the cradle of the Swiss Reformers. What Providence forbade him do in the West Indies, it allowed him opportunity in Europe.[33]

John Fletcher holds a unique place in Methodist history. He is the first and foremost figure to be imprinted by Methodism, in turn to influence it, and then impact others on behalf of the Wesleyan message of full and free salvation. The first generation Methodist leaders, of course, could not be imprinted themselves. Few leaders after the Wesleys and Whitefield were ever acknowledged as influencing Methodism as Fletcher did. For the myriads of Methodists who won the hearts and minds of new disciples in the Wesleyan revival, Fletcher stands as a premier model of Methodist ministry and the holy life of Christian perfection.

Almost 250 years have passed since Fletcher first had his evangelical experience with the Methodists and began his ministry. Today he remains a paradigm for the globalization of Wesleyanism by his providential encounter with Methodism and his shining witness to its divine favor. From his rather strange beginning as an unconverted foreigner, to his English parochial ministry, and his continual contacts with the Continent and his own Swiss French culture, he led a remarkable life that provides a glimpse of the spirit of early Methodists.

The Fletcher paradigm is the preeminent one for the global impact of Wesleyanism because it applies to every culture and people. His writings may need translation, but the dynamic movement of the Wesleys lives on in his model. Over the centuries countless others have done the same, but with less than Fletcher's saintly accolades. Yet this is the real power and genius of the Wesleyan message—caught, thought, and taught. Whatever successes Methodism has achieved in human terms has followed this paradigm. Wherever Methodism has missed the mark it have failed due to its absence. The more we study Fletcher and expand the field of scholarship concerning his writings, the stronger and clearer this paradigm will become. Methodism has had great days in English and American history and around the world, but it also shows signs of its age. The crystallization of all human religious structures has meant, at times, a choice between institution and movement. However, institutions are sustained by infrastructure, not paradigms! Methodism has again a choice to sound the call for a movement of earnest Christianity, Wesleyan Christians daring to reflect how they have been impacted by their faith through holy evangelical ministry and zealous personal evangelism. Methodism can again be inclusive, expressive, and expansive—the envy of the religious world, but friends to all. John Fletcher shows us how it might be done. The Great Commission shows us where it must be done.

Notes

1. There are histories of Methodism, biographies of Fletcher, and dissertations that do this. One of the best examples of what I attempt to do here is George Lawton's *Shropshire Saint: A Study in the Ministry and Spirituality of Fletcher of Madeley* (London: Epworth Press, 1960). Lawton opens with a survey of Fletcher's biographers and is unique in his presentation of Fletcher as parish minister, author, theologian and spiritual director. Lawton was a former assistant curate of Madeley. Another helpful model is James Wiggins's *The Embattled Saint: Aspects of the Life and Work of John Fletcher*, Wesleyan Studies no. 2 (Macon, Ga.: Wesleyan College, 1966), which is a theological biography of sorts. It is a well-documented focus on the key themes of Fletcher's life and work. The most recent and definitive work on Fletcher is by Patrick Philipp Streiff published in German by Peter Lang. The recently published English version by Streiff is entitled *Reluctant Saint? A Theological Biography of Fletcher of Madeley*, trans. G. W. S. Knowles (Peterborough, England: Epworth Press, 2001).

2. Luke Tyerman, *Wesley's Designated Successor: The Life, Letters and Literary Labors of the Rev. John William Fletcher, Vicar of Madeley, Shropshire* (New York: Phillips and Hunt, 1883), 14.

3. See Frederick W. McDonald's, *Fletcher of Madeley* (New York: A. C. Armstrong & Son, 1886), 58-59, fn. 1, for a chronology of Fletcher's Anglican orders, license, induction and subscription. See also Brigadier Margaret Allen's *Fletcher of Madeley* (London: The Salvation Army Publishing Department,

1905), 26, for Fletcher's letter to Lady Huntingdon describing his amazement that hurdles to appointment at Madeley were swept away, when even his opponents signed testimonials for his ministry, as did the Bishop of Lichfield without objection. That Fletcher clearly had opponents before his appointment shows the strong effect he had on people, considering he had only been engaged in preparation for Anglican ministry for three years!

4. Tyerman, 86-87.
5. Lawton, 8.
6. Tyerman, 354.
7. Allen, 37-38.
8. Joseph Benson, *The Life of the Rev. John W. de la Flechere* (New York: Carlton and Phillips, 1854), 31, 62.
9. Lawton, 11.
10. MacDonald, 80-81, fn. 1.
11. Lawton, 8.
12. Tyerman, 264.
13. One other exception might be the parish of Vincent Perronet at Shoreham, known as the "Archbishop of Methodism," a Swiss by origin as well (John Fletcher Hurst, *The History of Methodism* (New York: Eaton and Mains, 1902), 664 and Tyerman, 385. See Hurst, 907, for the story of Mary Bosenquet Fletcher, who in 1815 just before her death objected to the newly appointed curate at Madeley, who in turn demanded that Methodists and Anglicans be separate.
14. Tyerman, v. Cf. Lawton's categories. This is not to mention his roles as student, soldier, mathematician, tutor, nobleman, etc.
15. His intense desire for purity and holy character made him lay for hours on the floor in fits of repentance and pools of tears, seeking a release from an unholy temper. See Allen, 32.
16. See Wilfred C. Lockhart, *John Fletcher: Evangelist* (London, Epworth Press, 1939), 26.
17. See Tyerman, 180, for a timeline of Fletcher's acquaintances with Methodist leaders.
18. Lawton, 3
19. Wiggins, 7.
20. Wiggins, 9ff.
21. Tyerman, 331.
22. Tyerman, 1-2.
23. Lawton, 131.
24. Tyerman, 96-97. John Wesley's journal entry from a July 21 visit to Madeley.
25. J. Marrat, *The Vicar of Madeley: John Fletcher* (London: Charles Kelly, 1902), 29-31. Fletcher had two curates who were involved in missions to Africa, the younger Mr. Nathaniel Gilbert and Melville Horne, the latter of which served as founder of the London Missionary Society. See Abel Stevens, *The History of*

the Religious Movement of the Eighteenth Century Called Methodism, vol. 2 (New York: Eaton and Mains, 1895), 17.

26. T. Alexander Seed, *John and Mary Fletcher: Typical Methodist Saints* (New York: Eaton and Mains, n.d.), 39.

27. Allen, 27-28.

28. Robert Cox, *The Life of the Rev. John William Fletcher, Vicar of Madeley* (Philadelphia, Pa.: George and Byington, 1836), 63.

29. Cox, 70.

30. Cox, 103-32.

31. Tyerman, 455-56.

32. Tyerman, 498.

33. See Benson's account, *The Life of the Rev. John W. de la Flechere*, 125f., and 199f., for his stylistic comparison to St. Paul and his missionary journeys.

19

Wilhelm Nast (1807-1899): Founder of German-speaking Methodism in America and Architect of the Methodist Episcopal Church Mission in Europe

William Harrison Daniel

During the time of Methodism's great early expansion under the leadership of Francis Asbury, Methodist itinerant preachers ranged across the American landscape. The efforts of Asbury's preachers not only created a connected church on the frontiers of America, but the piety, the preaching, and the organization of the Methodist Episcopal Church helped to tame the wilderness and shape the American nation. The missionary beginnings of the Methodist movement and the role of Asbury's band of preaching circuit riders has been the subject of much historiography. But that historiography has often underplayed the role and contribution of the German-speaking immigrants to the Methodist mission in North America and their subsequent impact on the foundations of Methodism in Europe. Our purpose here is to narrate the story of Wilhelm Nast, the founder of Methodism among German-speakers in North America and the architect of the German-American mission back to the European continent. By examining the life and thought of Nast, fully accessible only through German sources, we will recover a greater appreciation of this "Asbury among the German Peoples." Moreover, such a study promises to remind us anew how Methodism, even in its earliest development, displayed a stunning ability to translate itself into new linguistic and cultural forms, and thereby function with a global missionary impulse and reach.

The story of German Methodism and Nast's role in it, begins in the earliest period of American Methodist history. During Asbury's tireless preaching tours, he encountered many German-speaking immigrants, but at the time there were only a few German preachers and translators available to mount a sustained mission among these German-speakers.[1] A number of Germans were converted by itinerant Methodist preachers before 1800. Some of these Germans preached to other immigrants in both German and English. Jacob Albrecht (Albright), a Methodist local preacher, itinerated among some of the Germans in 1790. He would have set up German-speaking Methodist Churches, but Asbury resisted the idea.[2] Ultimately, Albrecht seceded from the Methodists in 1807 to serve better the German immigrant population in their native tongue, founding his own popular movement that became known as the Evangelical Association. Asbury continued, however, to resist sanctioning separate work among the German immigrants. He hoped in vain that they would simply join the English-speaking Methodists, thereby avoiding the need for separate services and churches.[3] In 1808 Asbury grudgingly conceded that German-speakers needed ministry in German; he therefore allowed Henry Böhm to translate parts of the Methodist *Discipline* into German and encouraged the German immigrants awakened under Methodist preaching to be served by Albrecht's Evangelical Association.[4] Yet these events demonstrate how Asbury underestimated the desire of German immigrants to retain their language and culture in worship styles.[5]

Over a decade after Asbury's death, the Methodist Episcopal Church nevertheless came to see the need to work formally among the continuing stream of German-speaking immigrants. Bishop John Emory issued the first call for German preachers (and French preachers for their respective community) in the 1833 edition of the periodical, *Western Christian Advocate*.[6] It was noted at the time how difficult it was to find men as qualified in their spiritual life as in their knowledge of the German language.[7] Nevertheless, Wilhelm Nast responded in 1835 to one of the calls published in the *Western Christian Advocate*, thus starting a remarkable missionary career.

Nast was born in Stuttgart, Germany, in 1807 and confirmed in the Lutheran Church at fourteen as was customary. Through a combination of strong family Christian influence and exposure to Lutheran pietistic prayer meetings, Nast felt an early and strong call to missionary service. He even talked seriously about attending a missionary training institute until his family convinced him of the advantages of a more traditional theological education and his gifts for pastoral service.[8] He subsequently entered a

Lower Seminary as preparation for his entry to Tübingen University where he was educated on a government scholarship. After some struggle with his pastoral call, Nast declined to take a pastoral appointment in the state-supported Lutheran Church (thereby having to repay the state for his theological education). Launched on a search for employment, Nast's desire to become a teacher of classics led him to emigrate to America, where the dearth of available persons to teach classics became Nast's opportunity.[9] After teaching for a number of years, most notably as German teacher at the U.S. Military Academy at West Point, Nast was attracted to the same pietistic elements in Methodism which had also so impressed Wesley in Savannah: the German protest against ecclesiastical formalism, the stress on inner regeneration, and an emphasis on the "priesthood of all believers."[10] With an outstanding theological education already in hand, Nast was ready to answer Bishop John Emory's call for German-speaking Methodist preachers. Nast, thereby, became the formal founder of the German-speaking Methodist movement in 1835, when he was sent by the Ohio Annual Conference to be a German missionary on probation in Cincinnati.[11]

Nast quickly synthesized in a vigorous way his teenage ambition to be a missionary, along with realizing the promise of his pastoral and theological gifts. Through his long ministry many German immigrants were gathered around him in Methodist classes which formed the basis of the German Districts of the Methodist Episcopal Church in America. Some of the first contacts who met with Nast in these class meetings were K. H. Doering and L. S. Jacoby, who later became District Superintendents for the Pittsburgh German District and the St. Louis German District, respectively.[12] Even more significantly, Jacoby later returned to Germany to take up a post as Superintendent of the fledgling Methodist Episcopal Church in Bremen, Germany, a key center from which Methodism spread wider into Germany.[13]

Nast's commitment to a theologically grounded group of itinerant German preachers can be seen in his drawing up of an "Authorized Study plan for the German Traveling and Local Preachers," which appeared in 1856 in the *Church Order (Kirchenordnung)* of the German Conferences.[14] A further step towards pastoral and theological education for German-speaking Methodism was taken when Nast accepted responsibility for the training of German preachers at German-Wallace College, Berea, Ohio, beginning with forty students in 1864.[15]

Apart from the individuals who were influenced by Nast to enter the ministry to German immigrants in America, Nast engaged in other activities which had the effect of consolidating the German Districts in their mission in America. His work at the General Conference of 1848 gave the German Districts their vision and legal standing to become integrated, but separate Conferences within American Methodism, charged with the task of reaching the 5,000,000 German immigrants that would arrive.[16] This move demonstrated that for Nast and the other first generation German immigrant Methodists, "connectionalism" was more than a Methodist administrative approach or theological principle. It was a way of life that nourished their lives together as German-speakers and as Christians, and was critical to their survival in America. With this goal of promoting the German-speaking Methodist connection, Nast subsequently provided the first translations of foundational Methodist documents to sustain the German-speaking movement. He was the first translator into German of complete parts of the Methodist *Book of Discipline*, such as the "Teaching and Church Order," "Articles of Religion," and "The General Rules." In addition, he translated a collection of Wesley's Forty-Four Standard Sermons, as well as a forty-part collection of German hymns (1839), not to mention various other administrative documents which nourished connectionalism among the German Districts within the wider American Methodist body.[17] That such documents were published in portable, pocket formats of 8cm x13cm, for the convenient use of Methodist preachers itinerating on horseback, indicates the practical seriousness of Nast's theological vision of Methodism as essentially a mission movement.

Also significant for creating a shared sense of mission and connectionalism was Nast's work as editor of regular theological publications. Most importantly, Nast published and edited the influential German language Methodist weekly periodical *Der Christliche Apologete*, first published in January 1839 and continuing under his editorship until his son took it over in 1889.[18] This weekly periodical, along with Nast's multiple series of German catechisms, was widely read and influential. The tone and theology of *Der Apologete* was thoroughly missional with Nast's primary concern always to "save souls among all German immigrants."[19] That is not to say Nast's writings were merely devotional or evangelistic propaganda. On the contrary, *Der Apologete* contained many long, well-notated articles by Nast that reportedly taxed his German readers who often complained about their length![20] Nevertheless, through *Der Apologete* and his many other publications, Nast nourished and unified the German-speaking Methodist communities. A remarkable range and depth of learning, based in his Tübingen education, was exhibited in his published works.[21]

A significant strand of thought in all Nast's publishing was the connection of Methodism to the amalgam of Reformed and Lutheran theology so dominant in the state church in Germany, and thereby known to his German Methodist readership.[22] The German-speaking immigrants of North America received a solid theological education drawing largely on the strengths of the Tübingen school of Lutheranism through Nast's many publications.[23] As for the relationship of Methodism to Lutheranism, Nast saw no problem. He often quoted the statement of one Professor Lezius: "Methodism is nothing other than the right understanding of Luther."[24] With regard to Lutheran theology, Nast was clear in his editorial and theological policies when he took on the editorship of *Der Apologete:* "In the issues of *The Apologete*, all those biblical teachings will be represented and defended, which by Martin Luther and his honored co-workers and disciples in the Reformation have been performed and proved as essential to salvation."[25] Here was the principle that Nast and, subsequently, the other early German missionaries in North America and the Continent stressed: commonality on the essentials pertaining to salvation. Such a principle was crucial, for in this way the relationship to the Reformation tradition was treated as a valued strength for the first generation of German Methodists to draw upon. Nast's publications influenced countless Germans on the North American continent who hailed from such diverse traditions as Lutheran, Reformed, and Mennonite (even in some cases Catholic). His work convinced many that they could find a home in Methodism without throwing away their valued theological tradition. Even those German-speakers who did not join the Methodist Episcopal Church, finding their home instead in churches started by German-speakers under the influence of Wesleyan preaching, found Nast's publications helpful to reconcile their past with the new Christian reality of living in North America. Many ecumenical links were established among this first generation of German-speakers in Methodism with the "Albright People" who later became the Methodist-influenced Evangelical Association (started by Jacob Albright in the late eighteenth century) and also with the loosely Methodistic United Brethren Church (founded by Philip Otterbein and Martin Böhm in 1800).[26] These groups were highly instrumental in the establishment of churches in Germany which would later unite with the Methodist Church to form the United Methodist Church.

Although Nast's writings were widely influential with Germans beyond Methodism, his relationship with other Christian traditions could at times be complex. Indeed, he offered biting critiques in *Der Apologete* of any who published against Methodism or its theological tenets, most often pointing his attacks towards Catholicism. Nast was also not above engaging in heated debate with Germans from the Lutheran or Reformed churches in North America. In particular, Nast drew heavy criticism on his Methodist theology and leadership from none other than Philip Schaff, the leading church historian of the German Reformed Church in North America.[27]

Nast's strong self-awareness concerning Methodism's similarities and differences with Lutheranism would greatly assist later missionaries to Germany in relations with state church Lutherans. In particular Nast was at great pains to encourage all the German-speaking Methodist preachers to focus entirely upon the mercy and saving grace of God in Christ.[28] Like the Lutherans, Nast affirmed justification by faith and a covenant of grace, through which God stands ready at all times to engage with humanity, and because of which we may receive forgiveness of sins "in and for the merits of the Lord Jesus."[29] Nast clearly framed his soteriology with expressions drawn directly from his Lutheran background.

Yet if Nast found commonalities with the Lutherans, he also stressed the nurturing contribution that Methodist connectionalism could make within the German community as it sought to be a faithful minority in North America. In Nast's German-American Methodism, the Lutheran heritage clearly predominated, but it was combined with Methodist structures that promoted piety and community, structures such as the class meeting and the American camp meeting.[30] These positive, group-building aspects of Methodist practice proved highly effective in solidifying the faith of the German minority in America as shown in the rapid rise of German-American Methodism. For Nast, the Methodists had reclaimed something lost in German-speaking Lutheranism, namely, Wesley's teaching emphasis on holiness and sanctification.[31] Sanctification formed one of the core themes of Nast's writings in *Der Apologete*. Nast held that conversion was the great central experience in a person's religious life and the key to salvation and life everlasting, but this Lutheran summary did not go far enough for classic Wesleyan theology. Accordingly, Nast emphasized in endless articles that conversion was but the first step to complete sanctification, where the heart was completely victorious over all sinful elements in a person's character, thereby setting himself apart on this point from the classic Lutheran theology.[32]

Nast propounded other distinctive Methodist views which he felt were great improvements upon tendencies within later Lutheran theological development. Most notable of these were Nast's views on the Bible. He was quite conversant with Lutheran Tübingen's emerging emphasis on higher criticism having studied there alongside David Strauss under F. C. Baur. Yet Nast never allowed higher critical views to cloud his convictions that the Bible was the inspired Word of God, never to be questioned, and accepted in all parts.[33] In this regard he felt Methodism should allow theologians to expound sharper meanings of the biblical text for which he was sometimes criticized as being too liberal. Yet Nast forcefully opposed all attempts by German "rationalists" to question the Bible as revelation. In his view, that had corrupted Lutheranism on the continent.[34]

Nast's clear articulation to his preachers and readers alike of both the similarities and the distinctions of Methodism in relation to continental Protestant theology clearly helped Methodist missionary activity among German-speakers in America. Moreover, his vision ultimately helped to guide the Methodist mission return to Germany. Nast believed that the Methodist structures which so promoted group cohesion and nourished the faith among diverse German-speaking communities in North America would prove equally effective in stimulating the faith in Germany among a Free Church minority community surrounded by state church Lutheranism. For these reasons, Nast developed concepts of mission, connectionalism, and ecumenism that proved decisive in the development of German and continental Methodism, as we shall see later. Indeed, Nast's publications stressed the connectional nature of Methodism as a strength for its mission task. Without Nast's efforts, the missionizing impulse for German-Americans both for their own community in America, and later abroad on the continent, would have certainly been lost.[35]

Nast's pioneer missions to German-Americans prospered so quickly, that as early as 1844 the Methodist Episcopal General Conference considered ways to explore mounting a mission back to Germany itself. Thus, Nast and the other German-American Methodists wasted no time organizing a mission to their homeland, although it began informally. Letters back home to family and friends had provided for many years the first Methodist preaching in Germany.[36] Among the leading German-American Methodists who had studied in German theological seminaries, such as Nast, awareness of theological developments on both sides of the Atlantic was easily obtained through contacts with school friends. Through such means Nast and others perceived parallels between Methodist and Lutheran revival movements in Germany, and many felt the conditions were ripe for a more formal mission attempt.[37] Toward that end, Nast sought to find avenues for a missionary re-immigration to Germany in order to found a Methodist Episcopal Church in Germany.[38] With such a goal in mind, Nast embarked on his tour of Germany in 1844 under commission of the General Conference of the Methodist Episcopal Church. On that tour he sought persons and families with whom he had some prior connections in order to scout the prospects of mounting a sustained Methodist mission in Germany supported by the German-American Conferences.[39]

Nast met with a number of contacts who were involved with the various awakening and revival movements in Germany, hoping to find common ground there for future Methodist work and with a prospect of distributing Methodist literature to those considering emigration to America.[40] It became increasingly clear to Nast on the trip that there were some fundamental differences of culture and historical conditions between these German revival movements and Methodist structures and forms of piety.[41] Thus, Nast saw no real prospect of channeling Methodist influences through these revival groups, but instead saw the clearer need for a permanent and formal Methodist mission in Germany. By the end of 1849, only fifteen years after Nast had experienced the beginnings of German-speaking Methodism, such formal mission activities were launched in Germany by the Methodist Episcopal Church in America, supported largely through both the personnel and financing of the German-speaking Conferences.[42]

Of course, Methodism had first entered Germany in 1830 through the British Wesleyan Methodist Mission Society work of Christoph Gottlob Müller, a refugee who came to England during the Napoleonic Wars, who was converted to Methodism in Britain, and ultimately returned to start Methodist lay classes in his home of Würtemberg.[43] He was a true lay evangelist, gathering many interested farmers to hear the witness of how he had experienced God's salvation. However, after twenty-five year's work, Müller died leaving only a loosely organized group without leadership or formal church structures.[44] The Wesleyan Mission Society continued to send workers, because up to that time no baptisms or even celebrations of communion had taken place in Müller's society. Yet the Wesleyan Methodist Mission Society would go many years until its first baptism in 1872, with its success largely in forming small groups in Baden, Bayern, Schlesien, Böhmen, and even the first society in Austria.[45]

In contrast to the difficulties of the Wesleyan Methodist Mission Society from Britain, Nast and his German-speaking American Methodist Episcopal Church followers entered Germany remarkably quickly and with a lasting mission contribution.[46] Superintendent L. S. Jacoby, early protege of Nast and the superintendent of the German District in St. Louis, was sent to Bremen in December 1849 at age thirty-six, against his wife's wishes and armed with only five dollars worth of tracts to found and oversee the work in that city. Due to Bremen's atmosphere of relative religious freedom, Jacoby was soon able to bring his gifts for organization to the mission and gather believers into a formal church. This church is known as the first effectively organized Methodist church in Germany.[47] Jacoby's successful work in Bremen soon spread.[48] Another German-American who had been trained by Nast, Ludwig Nippert, was sent to Berlin in 1858 as the first ordained Methodist pastor in that great capital. Nippert served the longest of all the German-American Methodist missionaries and became the outstanding leader of German work.[49] The success of the small, but growing band of German-American Methodist missionaries could be traced back to Nast's leadership training and his mission scouting tour of 1844.[50]

When the Methodist Episcopal Church entered Germany in 1849, directly after the Revolution of 1848-1849, it did so with high hopes. The Methodists, as a Protestant Free Church, hoped that with the momentum in the northern German states swinging away from Catholicism to Protestantism, mission there would be easier. The German-American immigrants were hopeful they could openly bring with them the thoroughly democratic means of administration that had developed in Methodism's historical spread across America. However, Methodism in Germany would still suffer for many years in the face of considerable opposition from both government and state church opponents. Despite this harsh political climate, German-American Methodist missionaries received occasional support and enhanced prestige due to connections with the new consuls from the United States, who were often Methodists themselves.[51]

The spread of Methodism through Germany, despite obstacles found in a political climate that was not yet fully familiar with the democratic principles within Methodism, occurred relatively quickly. Having only entered Germany in 1849, by 1850 Jacoby had gathered twenty-two adults into a community along with several hundred children. By 1860 a flourishing publishing house was established in Bremen and by the 1890s German Methodism had become so vigorous and self-supporting that it mounted further missions into Switzerland, Austro-Hungary, and Russia.[52] In 1891 Germany had 72 German Methodist preachers and 10,580 members, with Switzerland claiming 5,307 members.[53] The Methodist work so flourished throughout the Continent that by 1925, despite the ravages of World War I, a Methodist Central Conference was formed by Bishop John Nuelson, headquartered in Zürich, which comprised delegates from eight Conferences where German missionaries had labored: Northern Germany, Southern Germany, Switzerland, Austria, Hungary, Bulgaria, Yugoslavia, and Russia.[54] Nast's German mission in North America had spread with astounding reach to include most of Europe, even before he died in 1899 at 92 years of age.[55]

The international reach of the German-American Methodist mission was due to several key factors. Clearly, the German-speaking Conferences in America were committed to the work and sent their best German preachers, in some ways sacrificing the work of the Methodist Episcopal Church in America for the sake of the wider mission in Germany. These missionary preachers also had a cultural and linguistic familiarity with Germany that gave them great advantage. Through their considerable contacts with family and friends, these missionaries did not suffer from the same extreme sense of isolation as other missionaries in the late nineteenth-century missionary movement. Moreover, the German-American Conferences under the leadership of Nast not only provided much financial help for the mission, but also deployed to Germany the theological documents developed to missionize Germans in North America. Not only were tracts and copies of *Der Christliche Apologete* regularly sent to the mission posts in Germany, but all the translations of *The Discipline*, "The Articles of Religion," Wesley's sermons, as well as hymn books, that had effectively reached the Germans in Pittsburgh, Cincinnati, and St. Louis, were ready to be used quickly to form a Methodist church in Bremen, Berlin, Basel, and ultimately Vienna and the wider territories of Hapsburg Austro-Hungary.[56]

In light of this, the relatively quick spread of Methodism in Germany was clearly due in large part to Nast's leadership in the North American Methodist mission and his role as a bridge figure between English-speaking Methodism and continental worldviews. He was effective at theologically reconciling Tübingen Lutheranism with Methodism, thus providing a welcome point of contact in Methodism for incoming German immigrants to America. This was essential in effectively building up and unifying the German-American Methodist community from among the various German church traditions. The fact that German American Methodism hailed from such diverse denominations only made its mission back to Germany, vis-à-vis the German state Lutheran Church, more ecumenically sensitive. At the same time, Nast's exposure to previous continental theologies and his ability to expound to his preachers on points of continuity and discontinuity with Methodism made this group of German-American missionaries more aware of the real contributions Methodism could make in Germany to "reform the nation with scriptural holiness."

As far as Nast's own role in the Methodist mission back to Germany, we must not forget the significance of his three visits to Germany to support the work in 1844, 1857, and 1877 (at the age of 70). Yet Nast's most enduring contributions to German Methodism were his translation of the foundational documents used to sustain the mission movement in Germany and stirring Germans in America to use their transatlantic networks in order to promote mission in Europe. Nast built these transatlantic connections upon a shared German language and culture, reinforced by Methodist connectionalism and mission theology. This unique form of German connectionalism became decisive in supporting the spread of Methodism into the German-speaking parts of Europe and beyond. It was Nast's mission vision that guided these transatlantic links in the latter half of the nineteenth century and continued to bear fruit for mission in other European lands long after his death.

The trajectory of the Methodist Episcopal Church's mission in continental Europe was most clearly stamped by Wilhelm Nast in the latter half of the nineteenth century and his influence continues today. Consequently, Wilhelm Nast is appropriately known by German Methodists today as "The First German Methodist Missionary" as well as the founder and organizer of the German branch of the Methodist Episcopal Church.[57] Yet the truly international nature of Nast's legacy also endures, as Bishop Wunderlich of Germany wrote in a 1963 biography of Nast, *Brückenbauer Gottes* (Bridgebuilder of God): "It is impossible to completely measure his (Nast's) influence on this side of the Ocean or on that side (America).[58] Such an assessment of Nast's international impact reminds us again of Methodism's early and remarkable ability to translate itself with great vitality into a global and connected Christian missionary movement.

Notes

1. Karl H. Voigt, in *Geschichte der Evangelisch Methodistischen Kirche*, eds. K. Steckel and C. E. Sommer (Stuttgart: Christliches Verlagshaus GmbH, 1982), 40. Heinreich (Henry) Böhm and a certain Dr. Romer were counted among Asbury's translators; other preachers who could address the German immigrants were named in the German language sources as Jacob Gruber, John Swartswelder, William Folks and Simon Müller.
2. Carl Wittke, *Wilhelm Nast: Patriarch of German Methodism* (Fort Wayne, Ind.: Wayne State University Press, 1960), 35-36.
3. Wittke, 35-36.
4. Wittke, 35-36; see also Voigt, 40.
5. On some of the difficulties encountered by the German immigrants of the early eighteenth century with Methodist worship styles, it is instructive to note the following: German immigrants found particularly difficult those parts of Methodism so stamped by American culture, namely the open air revival meetings, and the preacher's incessant itinerant moving on horseback from

settlement to settlement. The Germans were, on the contrary, used to a highly ordered, stable parish church tended to by one pastor, and were generally opposed to such aimless wandering across the land by traveling preachers or *Reisepredigern*; see Voigt, 40.
    6. Voigt, 41.
    7. Voigt, 41.
    8. Wittke, 56.
    9. Wittke, 56.
    10. Wittke, 28.
    11. Voigt, 41.
    12. Voigt, 45, 47.
    13. Voigt, 87.
    14. Voigt, 51.
    15. Voigt, 51.
    16. Voigt, 48; statistic from the Methodist Episcopal Church, *Journal of General Conference 1864*, 196, 428.
    17. Voigt, 46-50; Henry Böhm translated earlier, less complete sections of the Discipline at Asbury's request.
    18. Voigt, 50.
    19. Wittke, 84-86.
    20. Wittke, 91.
    21. The range and depth of his learning is shown in a selection of Nast's published titles. These include translations of Wesley's biography, a revision/translation of Christian Keller's *Kurze Seelenlehre, gegründet auf Schrift und Erfahrung, für Eltern, Prediger und Lehrer* (Brief Instructions for the Soul, Based on Scripture and Experience, for Parents, Preachers and Teachers*)*, *Philosophie des Erlösungsplans* (Philosophy of the Plan of Redemption), *Christologische Betrachtungen nach Dr. van Oosterzees Bild Christi* (Christological Observations according to Dr. van Oosterzee's Picture of Christ), *Das biblische Christenthum und seine Gegensätze* (Biblical Christianity and Its Opposition*)*, *Was ist und will der Methodismus* (What is Methodism and What Does It Want?), and *What is a Spirit?* Perhaps his most penetrating studies were on the New Testament including *The Gospel Records: Their Genuiness, Authenticity, Historic Variety, and Inspiration, with some preliminary Remarks on the Gospel History*, and what Nast considered as his *magnum opus*, his *Commentary on the New Testament*, published in both German and English, officially authorized by the Methodist General Conference in 1852, appearing in the first German edition in 1860, and still unfinished in 1894; see Wittke, 162-71. Interesting also were Nast's excursions into books on physiology and psychology.
    22. Voigt, 51.
    23. Voigt, 51.
    24. Voigt, 52, quoted from Berhnard Kiep, *Urteile über den Methodismus*, (München: 1948), 15.
    25. *Der Christliche Apologete*, 1839: 3, author's translation.
    26. Arthur C. Core in *Geschichte der Evangelisch Methodistischen Kirche*, ed. K. Steckel and C. E. Sommer (Stuttgart: Christliches Verlagshaus GmbH, 1982),

60-62.

27. For a complete discussion of Schaff's critique and debate with Nast, see Charles Yrigoyen, Jr., "Mercersburg's Quarrel with Methodism," *Methodist History* 22 (1983): 16-17. In summary, Schaff criticized the lack of depth in Methodism, and thought it particularly shameful in German Methodism, because Nast should have known better with his education. To such charges, Nast's response was fairly mild, namely that Schaff had little firsthand knowledge of Methodism by his own admission. Nast lamented that despite Schaff's great learning, he was greatly misinformed in his distorted judgements. See William Nast, "Dr. Schaff on Methodism," *The Methodist Quarterly Review*, XVII (July 1857): 434-36.

28. Wittke, 158.
29. Wittke, 158.
30. Voigt, 52.
31. Voigt, 52.
32. Wittke, 157; for a treatment in German of Nast's period studying under F.C. Bauer and other Tübingen professors, see Voigt, 42.
33. Wittke, 155.
34. Wittke, 155.
35. Voigt, 49.
36. Voigt, 56.
37. Voigt, 56.
38. The Evangelical Association and the United Brethren also sought to bring their types of revivalist, Methodist influenced churches back to Germany. See Core, *Geschichte der Evangelisch Methodistischen Kirche*, 59-84. Due to space limitations we will limit our discussion to the Methodist Episcopal Church mission on the continent.
39. Voigt, 56.
40. Voigt, 56.
41. Voigt, 56.
42. Voigt, 56.
43. Voigt, 85.
44. Voigt, 85.
45. Voigt, 86-87.
46. Voigt, 89.
47. Voigt, 87.
48. Voigt, 87; The strategic value of entering Bremen first was clear; there was hardly a city in Germany with more connections to the German-American immigrants than Bremen.
49. Voigt, 87; see also Wittke, *Wilhelm Nast*, 180.
50. The spread of Methodism in Germany, which has been treated in other German and English studies, will not be pursued in further detail here. See Paul F. Douglass, *The Story of German Methodism: Biography of an Immigrant Soul* (New York: The Methodist Book Concern, 1939) and K. H. Voigt, *Warum kamen die Methodisten nach Deutschland?* (Stuttgart: BGEMK Bh 4, 1975) and *Die Anfänge der Evangelisch Methodistichen Kirche in Hessen.* (Stuttgart: BGEMK

12, 1982).
51. Voigt, *Geschichte der Evangelisch Methodistischen Kirche*, 56-57.
52. Wittke, 184-85.
53. Wittke, 185.
54. Wittke, 185.
55. Wittke, 185, 188-89; see also Voigt, *Geschichte der Evangelisch Methodistischen Kirche*, 53.
56. Voigt, *Geschichte der Evangelisch Methodistischen Kirche*, 57-58.
57. Voigt, *Geschichte der Evangelisch Methodistischen Kirche*, 50.
58. F. Wünderlich, *Brückenbauer Gottes* (Frankfurt/Main: BGM 7,1963), 43.

Part III

20

The Impact of *Obras de Wesley* in the Hispanic World

L. Elbert Wethington

The global impact of Wesley is a very broad subject. We have selected a piece of the globe by looking at the Hispanic world and the availability of the published Works of John Wesley. Treatment of that smaller scope still requires vulnerable generalizations. An academic colleague used to say: "he who generalizes, generally lies." Moreover, since the Works of John Wesley have existed in Spanish less than two years, we can only conjecture what might be the future impact of *Obras de Wesley* in the Hispanic world. Fortunately, hopes and prognostications cannot be held to the same standards of scholarly accuracy as reviewing and evaluating past history!

A first thesis: In the twentieth century the impact of Wesley in Latin America has been very significant, but largely incognito. In retrospect, some causes for that kind of influence are fairly clear.

Christianity arrived in South America under the banners of Spanish and Portuguese conquest. The Latin expression of Roman Catholicism was both the beneficiary of and the apologist for that military, political, religious, economic, and social imperialism. Under Spanish and Portuguese colonial rule, indigenous religious rites were partially obliterated, grudgingly tolerated, and sometimes allowed to be practiced before or after the Latin mass, but always under the hegemony of the

Catholic hierarchy. Evangelical mission work in the Spanish language began in Latin America in the last four decades of the nineteenth century, but Protestant denominations did not show much growth until the twentieth century. Latin America never experienced the Protestant Reformation or the Wesleyan revival which impacted England and the United States of America in the first century of its existence. Evangelical missionaries from North America faced a new challenge in Latin America which they had not experienced in non-Christian countries. The new evangelical churches which were planted are still struggling with their own identity, although some, e.g., Pentecostal churches, have experienced phenomenal growth in numbers. Even those converted to evangelical Christianity tended to experience their new faith through an apperceptive mass formed predominantly by Roman Catholicism. In Latin America there were no spiritual "great awakenings" in the nineteenth century, and the "industrial revolution" didn't arrive until the twentieth century There were only occasional and minor expressions of significant theological/ethical change in Catholic leadership until Vatican II (1961-1963) "opened the windows" to Christian ecumenism and authorized ecclesiastical engagement with the urgent human issues of the world community. According to Dr. John Mackay, in the early decades of the twentieth century many missionary statesmen alleged that Protestantism, "is utterly foreign to the Latin spirit, and for that reason can never become a natural expression of the religious life nor a creative element in the cultural development of a Latin people."[1] Of course, that assessment has been largely refuted by several generations of evangelical experience and the impact of secular cultures.

The new churches which split off from "traditional" or mainstream Methodism in the United States perpetuated through each of their missions the distinctive emphasis or issue which had been the source of their existence, e.g., holiness, clergy-dominated authority, social ministries, and varieties of Pentecostalism, some of them without a strong sense of obligation to represent the "whole Wesley" in dialogue with indigenous and Latin cultures. Traditional Methodism established itself as a major force in the USA and acculturated itself *without* a strong emphasis upon the distinctive heritage, doctrines, and disciplines of Wesley. Early nineteenth-century Methodists suffered divisions over doctrines and polity which gave birth to many new Wesleyan denominations. Mainline Methodism was finding its identity by minimizing doctrinal and organizational issues and by its role increasingly in the twentieth century in promoting faith at work in the world and cultivating ecumenical relations. Certainly these are biblical and Wesleyan emphases. But for a century (1850 to 1950) Wesley's own theology and spirituality were slighted. Therefore, as one might expect, "mainstream" Methodist missions in Latin America tended to follow the "home" pattern. Their missions appealed to the small middle class in Latin America through effective ministries of high quality education, social service, and formal worship. Dr. Justo Gonzalez wrote, "in many of our countries schools were founded for commercial courses, but not an equal impact on evangelism of the country or in the beliefs of Methodism."[2] When the mission churches became autonomous they were often without the stewardship base for continued financing of expensive institutions, buildings, and land. But more important for this thesis, the mission churches were largely without an acquaintance with John Wesley himself and without a clear identity as Methodists, and therefore had a strong tendency toward division.

The Latin American direct descendants of the "mainstream" North American churches are a minority in the Wesleyan family of churches. If one-half of the 75,000,000 evangelicals in Latin America have roots in Wesley, the majority of those are in the Holiness and Pentecostal churches.[3] While the relatively small middle class responded to traditional Methodism, the marginal and poorer class were more attracted to the Holiness and Pentecostal expressions of Wesleyanism. Thus, Professor Gonzalez writes that today "there are millions of persons who, many without knowing it, are spiritual heirs of Wesley and the Methodist movement of the eighteenth century."[4] Their inspired spiritual leaders emphasized the Wesleyan doctrine of the work of the Holy Spirit to sanctify those who are willing to receive the transforming power of God and the gifts of the Holy Spirit. Holiness and Pentecostal churches differ from each other in the relative emphasis they put upon the gifts and fruits of the Holy Spirit, such as sanctification, speaking in tongues, interpreting tongues, and divine healing. A common element is their minimal emphasis upon formal education and "uniting the two so long divided, knowledge and vital piety." Clearly, the whole Wesley is not being faithfully taught by either "mainline Methodists" or the Holiness and Pentecostal churches. The question: Will *Obras de Wesley* help restore the missing link and become a major resource and common authority for Wesleyan doctrine and practice among the Hispanic churches of the expanding Wesleyan family?

I

Why Wesley in Spanish? We find no evidence that John Wesley ever considered having his Works translated and published in Spanish. According to entries in his Journals and Diaries, he had a strong personal desire to learn Spanish for two special reasons: 1) to communicate the Gospel to Sephardic Jews, Spanish traders, and mestizos when he was a missionary in the colony of Georgia; and 2) to read the Spanish mystics, especially Miguel de Molinos and Gregorio Lopez, who were highly commended by Wesley, along with the French Archbishop Fenelon, as spiritual mentors in the pure love/perfect holiness which can be experienced as a gift through uninterrupted contemplation of God (holy love). But such interests of Wesley were generally not known by members of the Wesleyan family of churches in Latin America. Neither should we be surprised there are no widely recognized scholars in Wesley's theology and spirituality among the Hispanic evangelical churches. Some highly esteemed, evangelical, Latino (Hispanic and Portuguese) educators and ecumenical leaders have distinguished themselves in the twentieth century. However, none have been recognized as prominent Wesley scholars and promoters of Wesley studies among Latinos. This condition among the Latin American evangelical churches obviously reflects the lukewarm interest in Wesley in the western hemisphere, at least until about 1960 when the academic discipline of Wesley studies and "The Bicentennial Edition of The Works of John Wesley" were given birth at Duke University by Divinity School Dean Robert E. Cushman and Dr. Frank Baker, the English Methodist bibliographer of Wesley's Works. English readers have had no excuse for not knowing Wesley. But Hispanics have been virtually deprived of the Works of Wesley for the past 200 years. Yet, the Spanish language, we are told, is spoken by more people in the western hemisphere than English.

A century ago there was an effort to make some of Wesley's sermons available in Spanish. The fifty-two Standard Sermons of Wesley were translated by the Rev. Primitivo Rodriquez, of Mexico, and published, 1891-1892, in two small volumes by the Publishing House of the Methodist Episcopal Church, South, in Nashville, Tennessee. Only a few rare copies of these have been identified in Latin America in recent years. Those sermons of Wesley in Spanish were not reprinted until the

Nazarene Publishing House requested permission and was given the copyright. That reprint in 1983-1984 was distributed largely among Hispanic pastors and students of the Church of the Nazarene in the United States and Latin America and are now out of print.

Enter *Obras de Wesley*. The project to produce the major Works of Wesley in Spanish began in 1989 with a simple request for assistance in building the resources of a theological seminary library in Peru, response to which exposed the appalling absence of Wesley's writings in Spanish. Further inquiry disclosed that many evangelical church leaders had long been aware of this vacuum. Increasingly, this was considered an urgent need because they were suffering badly from the lack of Wesleyan identity and increasing divisions in their churches. Yet, nothing was being done to correct the situation because translating and publishing *Las Obras de Wesley* was not commercially profitable. Repeatedly, the cry was heard from Hispanic evangelical leadership: "What we need is Wesley himself preaching the Gospel and teaching the Methodist discipline."

As a modest effort to consider that neglected need, the Wesley Heritage Foundation, Inc. was chartered in August 1990. An international design team of Hispanic and Anglo scholars and church administrators met in October 1990. They designed a project to produce a Spanish text and publish in fourteen volumes the major Works of Wesley in just the same scholarly form Wesley had published them. Non-scholarly options, topical selections, and other halfway measures were rejected. The design team strongly affirmed that the best way for persons in Latin America to know John Wesley is to let Wesley speak for himself. The intention was both scholarly and missionary, a rejection of the premise that those two are mutually exclusive. *Obras de Wesley* was proposed not only as a means of helping Methodists to know their own identity, but as an instrument of the Holy Spirit for the renewal and unity of the whole Body of Christ, as Wesley himself would have wanted it. The Wesley Heritage Foundation adopted that design. Thus began a ten-year antiphonal liturgy of woes and joys. After attempting several options which were dead ends, the Wesley Heritage Foundation made an awesome decision whether to drop the whole project or assume full responsibility for its completion. Some of us were convinced it was truly providential when a contract for General Editor was signed with Dr. Justo L. Gonzalez, the preeminent Hispanic church historian, theologian, and prolific author, along with seventeen other translators. By August 1996, volumes 1-4 were published, and all fourteen volumes of *Obras de*

Wesley were published by October 1998 by the grace of God.

What were the initial responses? On 9 August 1996 the first four volumes of *Obras de Wesley* were introduced to the World Methodist Council, meeting in Rio de Janeiro, Brazil, at the seminar on "Wesley, Our Heritage, and the Global Holiness/Pentecostal Movement." Dr. Mortimer Arias, Bishop Emeritus of the Methodist Church in Bolivia, made this statement:

> The publishing in Spanish of The Works of Wesley in 14 volumes is a major undertaking without parallel in the history of Methodist publishing around the non-English speaking world. We can be sure that the availability in Spanish of the Wesley Works will respond to the growing demand for identity and renewal of life and mission of the churches of "The people called Methodist" in the whole hemisphere.
>
> And we can hope that for the next century Wesley may become a fertile source of inspiration, doctrinal formation, and pastoral orientation for pastors, lay leaders, students, teachers and academic researchers of the always expanding Wesleyan family, including forms of Methodism as well as Holiness and Pentecostal churches, especially in Latin America.
>
> We needed a visionary venture like this. We are grateful for it and we should commit ourselves to make these works accessible for reading and study all over the hemisphere and the Spanish speaking world.

In his cycle of six lectures in San Juan, Puerto Rico in October 1997, Gonzalez asked the question, "Por que Wesley en espanol?" His reply, "The answer is clear! Because today in Latin America, and among the Spanish-speaking people in the United States, there are millions of spiritual sons and daughters of John Wesley. And because the impact of Wesley among us has been such that we do not understand him nor do we understand our own selves."[5] In April 1999 a third-generation Methodist and lay pastor in Peru said to us with uncontrollable joy, "At last I have found my own identity in Juan Wesley." A District Superintendent said, "They *(Obras)* are the best gift of the century for us." And Bishop Emeritus in Chile, Dr. Raimundo Valenzuela, wrote, "So many persons are saying they *(Obras)* have helped us find our true identity as Methodists." The initial impact indicates that these resources of the Gospel in Spanish are meeting at least one of the urgent needs, identity. In February 2000 an oral report came that Bishop Pereira had given Cuba's President Fidel Castro a volume of *Obras* and a few weeks later he was asked how he liked reading Wesley. His reply was, "Now I understand why Methodists care so much about the poor. I'm going to read some more." We can safely predict that the reasons for attraction to *Obras de Wesley* will vary.

II

Will *Obras* be a catalyst for encounter, dialogue, and/or an agent of the continuing work of the Holy Spirit for the renewal and unity of the Church as the Body of Christ in the world? What will be the impact? In truth, we have some foreboding mixed with a deeper confidence. Many of these diverse Wesleyan churches have become aware they are heirs of Wesley. But what will happen when they begin to recognize that their denominational founders/leaders have been selective in their espousal of John Wesley, the Oxford don, Fellow of Lincoln College, the great revivalist? Even with the amazing signs of the presence and power of the Holy Spirit, Wesleyan spiritual leaders have brought forth new denominations giving special emphasis to different aspects of John Wesley's Methodism. Certain other emphases are neglected. Will the study of *Obras* help to restore the whole Wesley or will it prompt more controversy and new denominations?

Dr. Mortimer Arias cites the report of the Methodist Bishop of Sao Paulo, Brazil who named fifteen separate denominations in Brazil which acknowledge their major roots in Wesley.[6] The largest denominations with major evangelical influence, of course, are the Pentecostals. Bishop Arias also quotes the Bishop of the very large Iglesia Metodista Pentecostal de Chile, who affirms, "Our standards are the Sermons of Wesley." Another Pentecostal bishop on the same occasion affirmed: "Wesley is our beloved grandfather, and we are his grandchildren, and we are able to acknowledge with gratitude to our fathers and sons that we will be their mediators." Dr. Arias reviews the impact of Pentecostalism on the traditional formality of Methodist worship and the demands for a more spontaneous, celebrating worship, with "more corporal and emotional liberty."[7] Added to that were some Latino and Caribbean rites and a major emphasis upon holiness, prayers for the sick, etc. Some Methodists began to speak about "the pentecostalization of Methodism." There has been an increasing recognition that Wesleyan "roots" have become entangled with other traditions. Without acquaintance with objective norms of doctrine and tradition, the third or fourth generation begins to be confused about its own identity. Speaking in Chile to the leadership of the large Wesleyan family of churches, Mortimer Arias extended an irenic appeal to their unity, "together we are able to rediscover Wesley."

If renewal and unity among the Wesleyan family of churches involves "rediscovering" the essential or "whole Wesley," should we begin to identify and address the agenda or simply wait for the interactions to confront us with the issues? Could we surmise that one of the greatest challenges of introducing Wesley himself is how "the essential Wesley" will be lifted out of his eighteenth century context, pruned and replanted in twenty-first-century Latin America? Some Methodists have rejected Wesley because he did not project in his own eighteenth-century model of social ethics for the twenty-first century. Dare we suggest that no Wesley scholar is likely to develop a Wesleyan social ethics for the twenty-first century unless it is deeply rooted in John Wesley's essential theology? We cannot forget how the Spirit-filled dynamics of the Methodist revival kept Wesley's theology geared to the practical level of guiding, nurturing, and transmitting its mission, a lively reality which should be appealing to Latin America. We who are working "double-time" to distribute *Obras de Wesley* may be forced to acknowledge that a widespread, intensive study, research, writing, seminars, and publishing in Wesley studies may occur only as a result of a revival of the Christian faith rather than a contributing cause of the revival. Certainly any claim to find in *Obras* a "user friendly" theology and liturgy will be a misreading of Wesley. On the other hand, allowing Wesley to focus our hearts and minds upon the essentials of the Gospel may open our spirits to the illuminating power of the Holy Spirit.

Will Latinos find in Wesley the essentials of the Gospel needed for revival? Will personal and congregational acquaintance with Juan Wesley attract persons to the Gospel of Jesus Christ, open hearts and minds to the real presence of the Holy Spirit, prepare them for repentance and receiving Divine reconciliation and the gift of holiness with its perfect love of God and neighbor? What model of social ethics vital to Latin America can grow out of Wesley's doctrine of holiness and responsible discipleship? How may *Obras de Wesley* serve to familiarize the Wesleyan family of churches with its roots and wholeness, and accept the Christ-given unity for the Wesleyan Hispanic denominations and embrace the other evangelical denominations as well? In continuing obedience to the Holy Spirit would they not find themselves harmonizing also with the Roman Catholic fellowship? Wesley's conviction was that it was for this purpose, preaching holiness, that God raised up the people called Methodists. Holiness is a biblical and catholic doctrine. Does Latino culture tend to reject the doctrine of sanctification any more than North American capitalist society? Did not Wesley despise dissimulation in human relations as blatant disregard for the presence of God who knows every heart? Is not original sin a universal condition which requires radical healing, "a new birth from above," as Wesley insisted? Can Wesley's doctrines and spiritual discipline contribute to a new era for the wholeness of the Gospel and the church, and invite a united affirmation of evangelical grace and catholic holiness, the means and the substance of salvation? What a challenge!

Some may reply: What more do people need for revival than the Bible and the presence of the Holy Spirit? We quickly agree those are essential. Yet, can we forget that most of the great watershed type of revivals and reformations in the history of the Christian church have been associated with Christ-called persons who had personally experienced new enlightenment in God's Word through the writings of some other disciple of Christ? Martin Luther's study of St. Paul, or John Wesley's hearing one read from Luther's Preface to his Commentary on the Epistle to the Romans? Reading Wesley was my own personal Aldersgate. Might reading the Works of Wesley become an Aldersgate experience for the new Hispanic leaders of a surprisingly new pattern of Christian reformation radically affecting all Latin America, an event which cannot be predesigned by human ingenuity? Such an early twenty-first-century awakening in Latin America may even spread northward to awaken Anglo America to the power of the Gospel to transform lives inwardly and outwardly according to the Gospel/catholic doctrine of the divine gift of holiness as John Wesley preached and taught it. The crucial and most important question is: With, or in spite of, the Wesleyan, the Reformed, the Lutheran, or the Roman Catholic traditions, will the living Christ be rediscovered in Latin America so as to produce "a new creation" of the whole Body of Christ, *al la gloria de Dios*?

While the Resurrection Event assures us that God has defeated the powers of evil and the Kingdom of God is most surely established, yet we must contend with the threatening forces of evil which have not yet surrendered. What chance does the Wesleyan renewal of the doctrine of "the fullness of faith," holiness, have against the overpowering, increasingly worldwide, secular confidence that we humans are able to "get along okay without God, thank you"? Are Wesleyans able, against the odds, to continue our witness that with God all things are possible?

Might *Las Obras de Wesley*, in particular his teachings of "accountable discipleship," serve to sharpen the issue between the Gospel and the world, especially the economy of material lust, which both Karl Marx (socialism) and Adam Smith (capitalism) agreed controls everything else? If, as John Wesley taught, authentic holiness is "inward and outward," is always a "faith working by love," and cannot be solitary, how will disciples of Christ, living in the Reign of God, help to shape the future agenda of the world? John Wesley does not allow us to capitulate to the powers of darkness while we simply pray and piously wait for the end of the world.

Finally, in our anticipation of the future impact of Wesleyanism we must not allow our hopes, apprehensions, and forecasts to leave the impression that we can set limits upon the surprising work of the Holy Spirit. "The wind blows where it will," and we are not able to understand it or preview its course. Wesleyans believe above all else in the primacy of grace: it is God whose grace initiates, sustains, and fulfills. Salvation is "the entire work of God." Ours is a faith judgment. Therefore, we trust God who produces whatever fruit God wills. Yet God works sometimes through humble, faithful servants, if we are willing; and sometimes God works in spite of human rebellion.

Notes

1. John A. Mackay, *The Other Spanish Christ* (New York: Macmillan, 1933), 259.
2. Justo L. Gonzalez, *Juan Wesley: Herencia y Promesa* (San Juan, Puerto Rico: Publicaciones Puertorequenas, 1998), 6.
3. Mortimer Arias, "El Rostro Wesleyano de Americana Latina Y El Caribe," (Montevideo: unpublished paper, 1999), 7-9.
4. Gonzalez, 10.
5. Gonzalez, 11.
6. Arias, 3.
7. Arias, 3.

21

The Methodist Archives and Research Centre at the John Rylands University Library of Manchester

Gareth Lloyd

The John Rylands University Library of Manchester, England, is home to one of the world's finest collections of early printed books and manuscripts. It is particularly rich in material for the study of English Protestant Nonconformity. Among its holdings in this field are archives relating to the Moravians, Baptists, Congregationalists, and Christian Brethren. However, the largest single collection in the library is that relating to the British Methodist Church and associated evangelical movements. It is this resource and its accessibility to researchers that will form the subject of this article. However, before considering the Methodist archives in detail, it is important to describe briefly the physical and research environment of the John Rylands Library.

I

The library was founded one hundred years ago by Mrs. Enriquetta Rylands as a memorial to her husband. John Rylands was a textile merchant who built up his family's company from small beginnings until it was the largest cotton concern in the British Empire. When he died in

1888, he left an estate worth £2,750,000, a huge amount of money for the time.

His widow Enriquetta was born in Cuba to an English father and a Spanish mother. She was John's third wife and was considerably younger. Despite the age difference, the couple shared a love of books and were devout Congregationalists. Enriquetta, therefore, decided that a fitting memorial to her husband would be a theological library built in the heart of the city of Manchester, the center of world trade in cotton.

The library took almost ten years to build and no expense was spared in its construction. Regarded as an architectural masterpiece, it is one of the most striking buildings in the city and is considered one of the finest examples of modern Gothic architecture in Europe. Many of its fittings are original and all were executed to the highest standards of craftsmanship from the finest materials available.

II

Mrs. Rylands originally intended that the institution would be public reference and lending, with a strong theological, specifically Protestant nonconformist bias. The collecting policy however quickly widened when she was able to purchase the book collection compiled by Lord Spencer, one of Princess Diana's forebears. The Spencer collection of 43,000 early printed volumes was then the richest in private hands. Its acquisition immediately established the Rylands as a library of international significance. She went on to acquire the Crawford manuscript collection before her death in 1910, comprising 6,000 items, chiefly from the medieval period.

A trust fund was created for the library's endowment and by 1956, holdings had reached almost 500,000 books and 17,000 manuscripts. Originally founded as an independent institution, the library merged with the Manchester University Library in 1972 to form the John Rylands University Library of Manchester. The original library building now houses the university special collections which essentially comprise the collections acquired before the merger together with a great many others transferred by the University.

The Rylands is the third largest university library in Britain and its early printed and manuscript collections are regarded as among the world's finest. With regard to printed books, the library has 4,000 incunabula, representing over 500 European presses including the largest collection of Aldines in the world. There are approximately 12,500 books printed between 1475 and 1640 and some 45,000 between 1641 and 1700; eighteenth- and nineteenth-century holdings comprise 160,000 and 400,000 volumes respectively. The manuscript collections cover more than fifty languages and span five millennia. They include cuneiform tablets, estate papers, medieval title deeds, a particularly rich church collection, and twentieth-century business archives. The most famous single item at the library is the St. John fragment, which dates from the early second century A.D. and is the earliest known extant piece of New Testament writing.

III

The library began collecting Methodist material in 1903 with the purchase of a printed collection of 818 works in 858 separate volumes. The publication dates ranged from 1735 to 1898, with almost half of the titles appearing in John Wesley's lifetime. The subject matter was varied, ranging from anti-Methodist works to local histories and hymnals as well as several hundred publications by John and Charles Wesley.

During the years that followed, the collection received additions on a casual but regular basis as part of the traditional policy of acquiring Protestant nonconformist material. Among the serial publications to which the library subscribed during these years were the connexional magazines of the several British Methodist denominations, the Minutes of the Annual Conferences from 1744, and the *Proceedings of the Wesley Historical Society*.

The major manuscript accessions consisted of sixteen bound volumes of the personal papers of Presidents of the Wesleyan Conference and other ministers and laymen. Among other significant acquisitions were three manuscript notebooks of Old Testament criticism compiled by the well-known Primitive Methodist theologian Professor Arthur Samuel Peake.

In 1973 the Rylands Methodist collection received a major boost with the deposit of Manchester's Hartley Victoria College library. Hartley Victoria trained Methodist ministers for nearly a century and was active in collecting books and manuscripts connected with the early history of Methodism for much of that time. The most important part of this acquisition was the Hobill collection comprising over 3,000 pamphlets, 191 books published between 1655 to 1798, 687 later monographs, and 475 volumes of periodicals including such scarce journals as the radical *Wesleyan Times*. The collection as a whole relates to all aspects of the Methodist tradition but is particularly strong on Primitive Methodism and the Methodist New Connexion. Other subcollections of the wider Hartley Victoria deposit included the private libraries of Arthur Samuel Peake, John Atkinson, and the Manchester, Salford, and District Council of Churches.

IV

In 1977, the British Methodist Church transferred its official printed and manuscript collection to the library on permanent loan. This deposit was so huge that it immediately transformed the Rylands from being merely a significant collector in the field to the status of possessing the world's finest collection of research material connected with Methodism and related evangelical movements in Britain and to a lesser extent North America.

When the collection arrived in Manchester it consisted of over 26,000 printed items and about 600 feet of manuscript shelving. In the years since 1977, new deposits of material have been added on a regular basis. These have come principally from the Methodist Church, but some items have also been acquired by purchase or on loan, or as a gift from other institutions and individuals.

Much of the manuscript collection predates 1800 and includes the world's largest archive connected with the Wesley family. There are over seven hundred letters by John Wesley, accounting for about one third of the extant correspondence anywhere in the world. Other John Wesley manuscripts include diaries, sermons, and personal accounts. As for Charles Wesley, approximately six hundred of his letters can be found in the archives together with sermons, a journal, and approximately six thousand manuscript hymns. There are also several thousand items connected with other members of the family including Samuel Wesley of Epworth (1662-1735) and his wife Susanna (1670-1742), the famous "Mother of Methodism."

The largest single manuscript resource in the Methodist archive is the Fletcher-Tooth collection, which consists of 44 boxes of letters, journals, legal documents, class papers, scripture notes, sermons, theological treatises, and pocket books. The collection covers the years 1759 to 1843 and was created by the famous Vicar of Madeley, John Fletcher (1729-85), his wife Mary Bosanquet (1739-1815), and her long-term companion Mary Tooth (1777-1843).

John Fletcher was one of the great theologians of the Revival and his works on holiness have had a marked and lasting influence on that tradition, particularly in the United States. Bosanquet and Tooth were both preachers and were at the center of a network of female evangelists and their male sympathizers. Despite the significance of the Fletchers and the astonishing size of the archive they left, much of the collection remains unpublished and very much underused.

Prominent eighteenth-century evangelicals, other than the Wesleys and John Fletcher, whose personal papers are represented in the collections include George Whitefield (1714-1770), the Countess of Huntingdon (1707-1791), Howell Harris (1714-1773), and Benjamin Ingham (1712-1772).

The Archives also include extensive smaller collections of personal papers of approximately 4,000 ministers and lay Methodists from the eighteenth century to the present. These include Thomas Coke (1747-1814), Adam Clarke (1760-1832), Hugh Bourne (1772-1852), Jabez Bunting (1779-1858), John Ernest Rattenbury (1870-1963), and Rupert Davies (1909-1994). Such collections range in size from one or two items to the 4,000 letters written to or from Jabez Bunting.

The institutional records of Methodism are well represented. These include the papers of the Methodist Conference from 1744 to the present, including manuscript minutes, journals, accounts, ministerial candidates' records, disciplinary papers, and the records of the various administrative committees that evolved in the early nineteenth century. There is material relating to all the major pre-union Methodist denominations.

The archives also contain records from three ministerial training colleges, namely Richmond, Hartley Victoria, and Ranmoor. Of these collections, that of the Wesleyan college at Richmond is by far the most extensive covering the years from 1843 until the college closed in 1972. It includes the papers of the House Committee, the tutors' meetings, financial accounts, student registers, and college magazines.

While the Wesleyan Connexion is by far the best represented of all the pre-union denominations, there are substantial collections for the others. The Methodist New Connexion archive, for example, includes the personal papers of its founder Alexander Kilham (1762-1798), consisting of over 400 letters and a box of sermons.

The records of the Methodist Church of Great Britain, which was formed by the union in 1932 of the several independent denominations, provide a detailed picture of the activities of the British church in modern times. There are large collections appertaining to Conference and the several administrative divisions such as Social Responsibility, Education, and Property. Such archives typically include correspondence files, policy documents, accounts, minutes, and annual reports. These are continually augmented by new accessions of material.

Turning to printed works, the Archives contain over 5,000 serial volumes. Of the 142 titles of British Methodist periodicals listed by the historian Allan Rose, 93 are available at the Rylands and 60 of these exist as a complete run. Some of the titles are not, as far as is known, held by any other British library. They include the connexional magazines of all the major Methodist churches as well as publications relating to such specific areas as Sunday Schools and the Wesley Deaconess Order.

The archives have the world's finest collection of publications of John and Charles Wesley, together with works published in opposition to them. To summarize, there are nearly 3,000 copies of approximately 1,800 works by the Wesleys and about 400 copies of 348 anti-Methodist items.

Of particular note in any description of early Methodist printed material are the personal libraries of Charles Wesley and John Fletcher, consisting of 429 and 134 volumes respectively. These came into the library as a result of the closure of Richmond College in 1972. From the same source came 2,500 volumes of theology and church history, which once comprised the library of the Methodist minister and historian Thomas Jackson (1783-1873). These books also include over 500 bound volumes of tracts, containing about 5,400 separate titles.

The pamphlet section of the Methodist collections is exceptionally rich. There are two main sequences, one of which is chronological, the other arranged by subject. The chronological sequence is largely Wesleyan in origin and subject matter and contains nearly 5,000 titles published between 1562 and 1965. The subject sequence is more diverse and includes sub-collections relating to the controversies from the 1790s, the Leeds Organ dispute of the late 1820s, several break-away Methodist groups from the first quarter of the nineteenth century, the Warrenite controversy of 1834-1836, the birth and early growth of the Wesleyan Reform movement of 1849-1856, publications of the Wesleyan Tract Society, and material concerned with the Anglican-Methodist conversations of the late twentieth century. In total, the subject sequence contains well over 4,000 titles.

The archives also contain three major collections of hymnbooks and related works. The largest is known as the Percy collection, named for J. C. B. Percy who deposited it with the Manchester Mission in the 1920s. It consists of about 1,600 volumes published mainly in the nineteenth and twentieth centuries, but also containing material dating back to 1631. It is multidenominational but with a bias towards Nonconformity and Methodism. The second collection contains over 1,500 volumes from the eighteenth to the twentieth centuries, mainly consisting of hymnals, but also including orders of service and liturgies. It was acquired over many years in a piecemeal fashion. Again, it relates mainly to Methodism but also has a strong Moravian element. The third collection was given to the Archives by Arthur Holbrook in 1983 and comprises 365 volumes published between 1749 and 1969.

V

In January 2000 a catalogue of the Methodist printed collections was made available on the internet site <http://rylibweb.man.ac.uk/catalogue/>. This database lists all the published works including pamphlets and tracts with the exception of some local histories. It can be searched by keyword, author, and title.

A general printed guide to the manuscripts was prepared by the American researcher Homer Calkin in the early 1980s. This consists of summary descriptions of all the collections. The personal papers are arranged by name while institutional records are listed by parent connexion. Useful as this publication is as a straightforward way of accessing the collections, it is now nearly twenty years out of date and the references no longer have a bearing on location or arrangement.

Many of the individual manuscript letters are catalogued on index cards which are available in the main Reading Room. This includes all the Wesley material and an overwhelming proportion of other personal papers.

In addition, detailed calendars have been prepared for a small number of the collections. These include the personal papers of Charles Wesley and members of his family, John and Mary Fletcher, Joseph Benson (1748-1821), and Hugh Bourne (1772-1852). A full list is given on the Methodist internet site. The calendars consist of detailed descriptions of individual documents within the collection and they are also indexed by name, place, and subject. Printed catalogues of some of the institutional collections such as the Conference Archive are also available. The Methodist Archives internet site is to be found at:

http://rylibweb.man.ac.uk/data1/dg/text/method.html

The site contains general information concerning the collections as well as opening hours and other practical information. It also has several major online exhibitions including one on John Wesley and another on his preachers. There is also a Methodist biographical index containing information on over a thousand individuals and a virtual library of over 100 online texts. As part of the internet site, there are guides to using the

Methodist archives for the purposes of family history, researching chapels, and a very popular guide to sources for women's studies.

The original constitution of the John Rylands Library specified that the building and its collections would be open to public use and this policy of open access was honored by Manchester University at the time of the merger. The Methodist Archives in common with the rest of the special collections can, therefore, be consulted by any researcher free of charge, which is unusual for a British university. For reasons of security, there is however a necessity to produce identification and a reference when applying for a reader's ticket. Readers are advised to contact the library in advance of an initial visit.

VI

The John Rylands University Library of Manchester is without question one of the great libraries of the world. Its collections document many areas of human activity and relate to a wide variety of cultures and time periods. Within this wider picture, the Methodist archives occupy a very important place illustrated by the fact that users of the Archive represent the largest single category of readers in the Rylands Special collections.

Even allowing for this popularity, there remain enormous areas of the Methodist Archives that are underused. It would be no exaggeration to say that some areas of early Methodist history could be substantially revised or even rewritten by a detailed examination of collections such as the Fletcher-Tooth or the Conference Archive. This is an exciting time in the story of the Methodist Archives as the internet makes possible wider use and certainly a greater appreciation of the collection. Close links have also been developed in recent years with overseas institutions that have related collections, particularly in the United States. It is hoped that such interaction will result in a deeper understanding of what we can learn from the past and individuals like the Wesleys who have proved to be a constant source of inspiration.

Index

Abrams, Anna, 20
Achenwall, Gottfried, 232
Africa, 17, 81-90, 91-104, 105-18
Africa Gospel Church, 95, 98
Africa Inland Mission, 95
African Methodist Episcopal
    Church, 107, 112
Ahlstrom, Sydney, 7
AIDS, 85
Alberti, G. W., 235-40
Albright, Jacob, xix
Allen, Richard, 15, 107
Allison, James, 113
Andersen, Andew M., 95
Angola, 83
Appenzeller, Henry G., 186, 187,
    197
Argentina, 18
Arias, Mortimer, 281, 282
Asbury, Francis, xviii, 13, 259,
    260
Asbury Theological Seminary, 4
Ashcraft, Henry, 95
Australia, 17, 217-30

Baker, Frank, 50, 51, 278
Bangs, Nathan, 16
Baptism, 73
Baum, J. W., 241
Benedictine, 3
Benin, 83
Bishop, James R., 96

Bishop, Mary, 70
Bissonette, W. S., 133
Boehm, Henry, 260
Boehm, Martin, xix
Bolivia, 18
Bosch, David, 171, 173
Bourne, Hugh, 289
Boxer Rebellion, 121
Buddhist, 144, 153
Bunting, Jabez, 219
Burckhardt, J. G., xxiii, 238-40
Burk, J. C. F., 240
Burkwall, H. O. T., 188
Burundi, 83
Buxton, Barclay F., 191, 197

Calvinism, 153
Carey, William, 15
Caribbean, 17
Carroll, Ewing, 60
Ceylon, 15, 17
Chile, 18
China, 52-4, 119-30, 131-42
Choi, Nam-Sun, 208
Chubb, Theophilus, 110
Chung, Chun-Su
Clarke, Adam, 289
Cobb, John, 88
Coke, Thomas, xix, 13
Coley, Samuel, 227
Collins, Thomas, xxiii, 217-30
Congo, 81, 83

Couch, Beatrix Melano, 4
Countess of Huntingdon, 289
Cowman, C. E., 187, 190, 196, 197
Cram, W. G., 193, 197
Crowther, Samuel Ajayi, 28
Cushman, Robert, 278

da Silva, Jose Antunes, 60
Dake, Vivian, 21, 22
Davies, Rupert, 289
Davies, William, 217
Dickson, Kwesi, 99
Doering, K. H., 261
Donkey Church, 114
Dow, Lorenzo, 13
Dubs, C. Newton, 122
Durnbaugh, Donald, 10
Dutch Reformed Church, 93, 94
Dwane, James, 111, 112, 116

East Africa Holiness Association, 97
Edwards, Maldwyn, 164
Eisenblaetter, Wilfred, 232
Embury, Philip, xviii
England, 17
Eucharist. *See* Lord's Supper.
Evangelical Association. *See* Evangelical Church
Evangelical Church, xix, 119, 120, 122-126
Evangelical United Brethren Church, xxi, 119-28

Ferguson, Theodore Pollock, 94, 95
Fiedler, Klaus, 99, 100
Fiji, 28, 29
Finney, Charles G., xx
Fish, Gerald, 95
Fish, Burnette, 95
Fishburn, Janet, 134
Fletcher, John William, xxiii, 245-58, 288, 289, 291
Ford, Clara, 97
Foster, R. S., 187
Frankl, P. J. L., 92
Franson, F., 188, 189, 197
Free Methodist Church, 20, 22
Freeman, Thomas Birch, 28
Friends Africa Industrial Mission, 95
Fuller, Lucius B., 94

Gerdine, J. L. 192, 193, 194, 196, 197
German-American Methodism, 259-72
Germany, 231-44
Ghana, 28
Giddy, James, 113
Gill, Silas, 220, 221, 224, 225, 226, 227
Gill, William, 223
Goforth, Jonathan, 190
Gonzalez, Justo, 279, 280
Gordon, A. J., 190
Gow, Francis, 112
Graham, Billy, 8
Graham, Gael Norma, 133, 134, 138
Groves, C. P., 30

Halmhuber, Karl, 123
Halverson, Sarah, 121
Hamm, Thomas D., 96
Hardie, R. A. 185, 187, 188, 189, 191, 192, 193, 194
Harris, James, 218
Harris, Howell, 289
Hartzler, Jacob, 123
Hatch, Nathan, 7
Heck, Barabara, xviii
Hole, Arthur Chilson, 95
Hole, Edgar, 95
Holiness, 13-26, 91-104, 143-56, 171-84, 185-200

Index

Holy Communion. *See* Lord's Supper.
Honda, Koji, 146
Hopkey, Sophia Christiana, xvii
Hotchkiss, Willis R., 95
Howard, Arthur T., 124
Hudson, Winthrop, 6
Hwa Nan College, xxii, 131-42

Immanuel General Mission, xxii, 10, 143-56
India, 17
Ingham, Benjamin, 289
Innes, Jonathan, 225
Ishigura, Takejira, 125
Islam, 84

Jacoby, L. S., 261, 266, 267
Jager, Johannes, 108
Japan, 119-30, 143-56
Johns, Griffith, 122
Johnston, Howard Agnew, 189, 194
Jones, E. Stanley, 23

Keel, Sunjoo, 194, 195, 198
Kendrick, John, 108
Keswick, 93, 94, 185, 186, 190, 191, 197
Kilner, John, 113
Kim Jae-Joon, 211
Kim, Kyung Jae, 176
Kirkpatrick, Faye, 98
Kirkpatrick, Virgil, 97
Knipp, J. Edgar, 124
Kramer, Lois, 124
Krecker, Frederick, 123
Kyodan, 125, 126

Lamplough, Robert, 111
Latin America, 69-80, 275-84
Law, William, 161
Lea, Allen, 109
Lee, Jesse, 15

Lee, Jung Young, 175
Lee, Kwang-Soo, 210
Lee, Sung-Man, 211
Lee, Yong Do, 209
Leonard, Orville, 98
Liberia, 83
Ling, Moy, 121
Links, Jacob, 108
London Missionary Society, 29
Lord's Supper, 49-66
Love Feast, 50-4, 61, 63, 64
Luther, Martin, 157, 162
Lutz, Jessie, 136, 137

MacGowan, Andrew, 51
Mackay, R. P., 189, 190
Maddox, Randy, 182
Mantle, Gregory, 190, 191, 197
Manye, Charlotte, 112
Martin, John, 99
Mashaba, Robert, 114
Mauk, Laura, 125
Mayer, Paul S., 124
Mbiti, John S., 92
Methodist Episcopal Church, 13-7, 259-72
Metz, Donald, 180
Mexico, 52
Middlemiss, George, 108
Missiology, 13-26, 27-48
Mokone, Mangena, 110-15
Moody, D. L., 8, 186, 188, 197
Moose, J. R., 193, 194
Moravians, xviii, 202
Mozambique, 83
Msimang, Daniel, 114
Msimang, Joel, 114
Muller, C. G., 266
Murray, Andrew, 93, 94
Mushete, Alphonse Ngindu, 88
Muslims, 30

Nakada, Juji, 145, 146, 149
Nast, Wilhelm, xxiii, 259-72

National Association for the Promotion of Holiness, 93
National Holiness Missionary Society, 93, 97, 100
New Zealand, 28
Niebuhr, H. Richard, 10
Niemeyer, A. H., xxiii, 239-40
Nigeria, 83
Noyes, John Humphrey, xx
Nuelson, John, 267

Oberlin Perfectionism, xx, 8
Obras de Wesley, 275-84
Ogle, George, 212
Omar, Yahya Ali, 92
Oriental Missionary Society, 145, 146, 147, 172
Otterbein, Philip William, xix
Outler, Albert, 5

Pamla, Charles, 17, 18
Panama, 18, 74, 75
Park, Chung-Hee, 211
Patterson, Austia, 121
Payne, Manie, 94
Pelagianism, 160
Peniel Mission, 94, 95
Pentecostal, 18
Peru, 18
Pickett, J. W., 20, 23
Pietism, 4, 119, 120
Pollard, Samuel, 54
Power, David, 58
Presbyterian, 54, 95, 186
Primitive Methodist Church, 30
Pui-Lan, Kwok, 139

Rack, Henry, 241
Rakestraw, Robert V., 182
Ramashu, Malakia, 115
Rasmussen, Ann Marie Bak, 96, 100
Rattenbury, J. E., 289
Ratzinger, Cardinal Joseph, 57

Reber, Calvin, 123
Reformation, 77, 78
Richey, Russell E., 93
Ricoeur, Paul, 4
Robert, Dana, 131, 132
Roberts, B. T., 22
Roberts, Evan, 187
Rodriquez, Primitivo, 278
Roman Catholic Church, 69, 70, 71, 74, 75, 77
Runyon, Theodore, 182
Rwanda, 99
Rylands, John, 285, 286
Rylands Library, 285-92

Samoa, 29
Sanctification. *See* Holiness.
Schaefer, John, 127
Schaff, Philip, 6
Schilling, S. Paul, 181
Scott, Peter C., 95
Seamands, E. A., 23
Semmel, Bernard, 74
Senegal, 81
Seventh-day Adventism, 8
Shaw, Barnabas, 108
Shaw, William, 108
Sherman, Bessie, 20
Sherman, Charles W., 20, 22
Shinto, 144, 145
Shively, A. B., 124
Shoop, Charles, 121
Shoop, Kathryn, 121, 122
Shorter, Aylward, 60
Sickafoose, Ellen, 121
Sickafoose, George, 121
Sierra Leone, 83, 108
Simpson, Albert B., 95, 190
Smith, Amanda Berry, 93, 94
Smith, Edwin W., 30
Smith, Robert K., 98
Song, C. S., 58, 60
Soothill, W. E., 30
South Africa, 105-18

Steere, Dorothy, 96
Steere, Douglas, 96
Strawbridge, Robert, xviii
Sundermeier, Theo, 172
Swahili, 92, 97
Swaziland, 111, 113, 114, 115
Sweetman, J. Windrow, 30
Synan, Vinson, 9

Tahiti, 29
Takenaka, Masao, 55
Taylor, J. Hudson, 122
Taylor, William, xx, 13, 14, 16, 21, 22, 93, 94
Taylor, Woodford, 97
Thirty-nine Articles, 70
Thoburn, James, 20, 23
Thomas, John, 196
Threlfall, William, 108
Tile, Nehemiah, 110
Tonga, 28, 29
Torrey, R. A., 145, 148
Trimble, Lydia, 132, 137, 138
Troeltsch, Ernst, 10
Troxel, Cecil, 97
Tsutada, Tsugio David, 143, 147, 148, 149
Turner, Henry, 112
Tutu, Desmond, 82

Underwood, Horace G., 186, 196, 197, 205, 206
United Brethren in Christ, xix, 119-26

Van Engen, Charles, 171
Vanguard Mission, 20, 21
Vasey, Thomas, xviii
von Mosheim, Lorenz, 236

Wallace, Harden, 95
Wang, Lucy C., 135, 136, 139, 140

Watkins, Owen, 108
Watson, Richard, xx, 31-42
Wendeborn, G. F. A., xxiii, 241-4
Wesley, Charles, xix, 249, 287, 288, 290, 291
Wesley, John, xvii, xviii, xix, 8, 13, 14, 50, 69-74, 86, 87, 89, 92, 93, 105, 106, 149-51, 157-67, 174, 176-83, 202-6, 213, 231, 232-41, 246-52, 254, 261, 275-84, 287, 288
Wesley, Samuel, xvii, 288
Wesley, Susanna, xvii, 288
Wesleyan Methodist Church, 147, 148
Whatcoat, Richard, xviii
White, Mary Cutler, 188
White, Ellen G., 8
Whitefield, George, xviii, 234
Wilberforce University, 108
Williams, Colin, 182
Woman's Foreign Missionary Society, xxii, 131, 132, 135, 138, 139, 140
Woman's Missionary Association, 121
Wong, Peter, 122
World Council of Churches, 57
World Gospel Mission, 95, 96, 100
World Methodist Council, 69

Xhosa, 30

Zaire, 81
Zambia, 30
Zehrer, Karl, 232
Ziegenhagen, F. M., 232, 235, 237, 238
Zinzendorf, Nicholas Ludwig, 202, 203, 236

About the Contributors

Laura A. Bartels is a Ph.D. candidate in Wesleyan and Methodist Studies, Caspersen School of Graduate Studies, Drew University, Madison, New Jersey.

Jose Míguez Bonino is professor emeritus of Systematic Theology and Ethics, Instituto Superior de Estudios Teologicos, Buenos Aires, Argentina, and co-president of the Permanent Assembly for Human Rights in Argentina.

David Bundy is librarian and associate professor of Church History, Christian Theological Seminary, Indianapolis, Indiana.

Chongnahm (John) Cho is president of the Wesley Society of Korea and former president of Seoul Theological College and Seminary, Seoul, Korea.

William Harrison Daniel is visiting assistant professor of History and Mission, Candler School of Theology, Atlanta, Georgia.

Robert Danielson is assistant librarian, Florida campus, Asbury Theological Seminary, Orlando, Florida.

Donald W. Dayton is visiting professor of Historical Theology, The Theological and Graduate Schools, Drew University, Madison, New Jersey.

Hong-ki Kim is associate professor of Church History, Methodist Theological Seminary, Seoul, Korea.

About the Contributors

Hyun Seok (Joseph) Kim is a Ph.D. candidate at the E. Stanley Jones School of World Mission and Evangelism, Asbury Theological Seminary, Wilmore, Kentucky.

Kiyoshi Nathanael Kunishige is a Ph.D. candidate in Theology and Religion, Caspersen School of Graduate Studies, Drew University, Madison, New Jersey.

Robert Kipkemoi Lang'at is a Ph.D. candidate in Wesleyan and Methodist Studies, Caspersen School of Graduate Studies, Drew University, Madison, New Jersey.

Daryl H. Lightfoot is archivist/librarian, New South Wales Synod, Uniting Church in Australia, and a member of the editorial board of *Church Heritage*.

Gareth Lloyd is Methodist Church Archivist, John Rylands University Library, Manchester, England.

Joan A. Millard is professor of History, the University of South Africa, Pretoria, South Africa.

J. Steven O'Malley is John T. Seamands Professor of Methodist Holiness History at Asbury Theological Seminary, Wilmore, Kentucky.

Myung Soo Park is professor of Church History, Seoul Theological Seminary, Seoul, Korea.

Timothy M. Salo is a Ph.D. candidate in historical theology, Caspersen School of Graduate Studies, Drew University, Madison, New Jersey.

Andrew Walls is curator of collections, Centre for the Study of Christianity in the Non-Western World and an honorary professor, University of Edinburgh, Edinburgh, Scotland.

L. Elbert Wethington is professor emeritus, Lebanon Valley College, Annville, Pennsylvania and president of Wesley Heritage Foundation, Inc., publisher and distributor of *Obras de Wesley*

About the Contributors

Michel Weyer is professor of Church History and Methodist Studies at the United Methodist Theological Seminary, Reutlingen, Germany

David K. Yemba is professor of Systematic Theology and Ecumenical Studies and dean of the faculty of Theology, Africa University, Mutare, Zimbabwe, and the moderator of the Faith and Order Commission of the World Council of Churches.

Charles Yrigoyen, Jr. is general secretary, General Commission on Archives and History, The United Methodist Church, and editor of *Methodist History*, Madison, New Jersey.